Origins of the *Dred Scott* Case

Studies in the Legal History of the South

EDITED BY PAUL FINKELMAN, TIMOTHY S. HUEBNER,
AND KERMIT L. HALL

This series explores the ways in which law has affected the
development of the southern United States and in turn the
ways the history of the South has affected the development of
American law. Volumes in the series focus on a specific aspect
of the law, such as slave law or civil rights legislation, or on a
broader topic of historical significance to the development of
the legal system in the region, such as issues of constitutional
history and of law and society, comparative analyses with other
legal systems, and biographical studies of influential southern
jurists and lawyers.

AUSTIN ALLEN

Origins of the *Dred Scott* Case

Jacksonian Jurisprudence

and the Supreme Court

1837–1857

The University of Georgia Press
Athens & London

© 2006 by the University of Georgia Press

Athens, Georgia 30602

All rights reserved

Set in Minion by Bookcomp, Inc.

Printed and bound by Maple-Vail

The paper in this book meets the guidelines for
permanence and durability of the Committee on
Production Guidelines for Book Longevity of the
Council on Library Resources.

Printed in the United States of America

10 09 08 07 06 C 5 4 3 2 1

10 09 08 07   P 5 4 3 2

Library of Congress Cataloging-in-Publication Data

Allen, Austin, 1970–

   Origins of the Dred Scott case : Jacksonian jurisprudence
and the Supreme Court, 1837–1857 / Austin Allen.

     p. cm. — (Studies in the legal history of the South)

Includes bibliographical references and index.

   ISBN-13: 978-0-8203-2653-5 (hardcover : alk. paper)

   ISBN-10: 0-8203-2653-4 (hardcover : alk. paper)

   ISBN-13: 978-0-8203-2842-3 (pbk. : alk. paper)

   ISBN-10: 0-8203-2842-1 (pbk. : alk. paper)

   1. Constitutional history—United States—Sources.

2. United States. Supreme Court—History—Sources.

3. Slavery—Law and legislation—United States—History—
Sources. 4. Scott, Dred, 1809–1858—Trials, litigation, etc.

5. Sanford, John F. A., 1806 or 7–1857—Trials, litigation, etc.

I. Title. II. Series.

   KF4545.S5A948   2006

   342.7308'7—dc22   2005024354

British Library Cataloging-in-Publication Data available

Much of chapter 8 and portions of chapters 4, 6, and 7, the
epilogue, and the note on method appeared in "The Political
Economy of Blackness: Citizenship, Corporations, and Race in
Dred Scott," *Civil War History* 50, no. 3 (2004): 229–60. They are
reprinted with permission of Kent State University Press.

For my dad

Contents

Acknowledgments

I HAVE INCURRED DEBTS to numerous persons and institutions while working on this book. I can now attempt to repay them. Of the institutions, the University of Houston's History Department tops the list for providing me with the training and financial support that made this project possible. The Department of Social Sciences at the University of Houston–Downtown later provided a fine academic home that allowed me to finish this book. Along the way, the staffs of the National Archives (in Washington, D.C., and College Park, Maryland), the Manuscript Division at the Library of Congress, the Missouri Historical Society in St. Louis, the Virginia Historical Society in Richmond, and the Southern Historical Collection at the University of North Carolina, Chapel Hill, helped me locate evidence crucial to this study.

A number of individuals aided me by listening to my ideas, reading drafts, or offering other forms of support. I absolve all those persons listed here of responsibility for any errors in this work and apologize to anyone I neglect to mention. Jo Bailey, Richard Blackett, Amy Blackwell, Bill Blair, John Boles, Bill Brigman, Bob Buzzanco, Mark Carroll, Mike Dressman, Paul Finkelman, Ellen D. Goldlust-Gingrich, Joe Glatthaar, Nancy Grayson, Tom Green, Brett Hulett, Doug Irwin, Ben Kler, Derek Krissoff, Nelson Lankford, Ken Lipartito, Don Lutz, Jim Martin, Steve Mintz, Bob Palmer (to whom I owe my greatest intellectual debt), Kristina Robert, Christopher Waldrep, and Eric Walther all deserve high praise for the help that they have given me.

I am most indebted to my family: my three parents, two in-laws, and an ever-growing community of others. Gail, Dottie, Sue, Charles, Charlie, Alison, Todd, Tammy, Kristin, Kerri, Sharon, Lin, Krystal, Misty, Christian, Travis, Kyle, Kaelin, and Ethan have stood by me for years, although I am sure they wondered if I would ever finish. Karmen, my wife, has no particular interest in *Dred Scott*—or in history, for that matter—but she has lived with this book as much as I have and has been supportive throughout. I do not think Karmen ever doubted that I would finish, but I know she would have liked me to do so sooner. During the time I worked on this book, in fact, we brought two kids into the world. Emily and Aidan contribute very little to scholarly productivity, but I could not imagine life without them. When I look at Karmen, I know that what I have produced here pales in comparison to what we are building together.

I dedicate this book to my father, who beat a brain tumor shortly before this book went to press. He always said I would make a good historian, even when he doubted that I would finish high school. Words cannot express how happy I am to give him this book.

Origins of the *Dred Scott* Case

Introduction

Beyond the Sectional Crisis

ON MARCH 6, 1857, Chief Justice Roger B. Taney secured his claim to infamy when he delivered the Supreme Court's ruling in *Dred Scott v. Sandford*. Speaking for a fragmented majority composed of all five of the court's southerners and two of their northern colleagues, Taney held that no African American had ever been or ever could be a citizen of the United States. He then declared that Congress possessed no authority to limit slavery's expansion into the federal territories.[1] With that ruling, the Supreme Court inserted itself into the central political debates of the 1850s and helped push the United States toward civil war. Commentary on *Dred Scott* has invariably linked the decision to the sectional crisis that dominated American politics on the eve of the Civil War. Some critics have considered *Dred Scott* a legally correct ruling issued by a court that failed to understand the limits of its own authority, while others have viewed the decision as a hopelessly partisan ruling that was, in the words of Republican editor Horace Greeley, "entitled to just so much moral weight as would be the judgment of those congregated in any Washington bar-room." Either way, these observers have assumed that sectional politics constituted the primary motivation behind the decision.[2]

Contemporary understanding of *Dred Scott* owes much to the criticism developed by Republicans such as Greeley in response to the Supreme Court's ruling, which in effect declared unconstitutional their stance against slavery's expansion. As David Potter has noted, Republicans circumvented charges that they stood for "Revolution and anarchy," in the words of one paper, by shifting their criticism away from the decision's merits and focusing instead on the court's failure to confine itself to the issues necessary to resolve the case.[3] Republicans therefore contended that Taney and his asso-

1

ciates bypassed an opportunity to dismiss *Dred Scott* on a narrow, relatively uncontroversial, point and instead rendered a sweeping ruling that favored the proslavery positions of the court's southern justices, all of whom had connections to the Democratic Party. The circumstances surrounding the case raised other questions as well. Why did the Democrats insist in the early 1850s that slavery's status in the territories was a "judicial question"? Why did the justices delay rendering their decision until after a presidential election in which the Republican Party had emerged as a serious contender? Why did the newly inaugurated president, James Buchanan, shortly after exchanging whispers with his fellow Democrat, Taney, preach adherence to the decision two days before the court handed it down? "These things," future president Abraham Lincoln said in 1858, "look like the cautious patting and petting of a spirited horse . . . when it is dreaded that he might give the rider a fall."[4]

For Lincoln and other Republicans, the answer to these questions was obvious: the Supreme Court had become an instrument of a "slave power" conspiracy. Taney and his associates overreached because they planned to open all federal territory to slavery and to set the stage for the institution's expansion into the North. Lincoln outlined this scenario in his famous 1858 "House Divided" speech: "I believe this government cannot endure permanently half slave and half free. . . . It will become all one thing, or all the other. Either the opponents of slavery will arrest the further spread of it . . . or its advocates will push it forward, till it shall become alike lawful in all the States, old as well as new—North as well as South." Lincoln then discussed an elaborate conspiracy in which Senator Stephen Douglas of Illinois, Presidents Franklin Pierce and James Buchanan, and Chief Justice Taney followed a plan in which they simultaneously barraged the public with amoral arguments to "care not whether slavery be voted down or voted up" outside of their own states and pursued a legislative and judicial strategy designed to impose slavery in both the western territories and the North. "We shall lie down pleasantly dreaming that the people of Missouri are on the verge of making their State free, and we shall awake to the reality instead, that the Supreme Court has made Illinois a slave State."[5]

Most historians would now reject the particulars of Lincoln's conspiracy theory, which he admitted he could not prove. Yet few scholars would deny the Republicans' larger premise that *Dred Scott* was the product of judicial overreaching and sectional partisanship among the court's members. From the beginning, students of the *Dred Scott* case have assumed a direct connection between the decision and the sectional crisis of the 1850s. They have differed mainly regarding which set of partisans should bear responsibility for the consequences of the court's ruling. The first generation of Civil War historians, who generally adhered to the Republicans' interpretation of events, blamed the court's southern members, whose actions helped bring about the bloodshed of the 1860s for which the South was responsible.[6] Revisionist historians writing in the early twentieth century typically lacked sympathy for African Americans and greeted antislavery motives with skepticism but never questioned *Dred Scott*'s connection to the sectional crisis. They merely inverted the Republicans' argument. For them, *Dred Scott* was a badly timed decision forced on the court by a minority of overly zealous antislavery justices whose actions contributed to the outbreak of an unnecessary civil war.[7] In the 1960s and 1970s, a new generation of historians, writing in the wake of the civil rights movement, revived the Republicans' argument, although their accounts rejected or downplayed the role of conspiracy. These scholars emphasized *Dred Scott* as an abuse of the court's power of judicial review and as a failure of partisan justices to steer their court away from contentious political and social issues that it was not equipped to solve.[8] Although their studies addressed valid concerns about the proper role of judicial power within the United States, these scholars never questioned *Dred Scott*'s link to the sectional crisis of the 1850s.

Don Fehrenbacher's Pulitzer Prize–winning book, *The Dred Scott Case: Its Significance in American Law and Politics* (1978), represents the culmination of these late-twentieth-century accounts and stands as the most important study of the decision ever produced. Fehrenbacher placed *Dred Scott* in the context of the political struggles over slavery's place within the Union from 1787 to the Civil War, portraying the decision as "essentially a vain effort to turn back the clock of civilization." Taney's opinion was "a sectional credo," expressing "the southern mood—fearful, angry, and defiant—in the late stages of a national crisis." Fehrenbacher's close reading of the opinion found the chief justice to be egregiously wrong on almost every count. The decision was morally flawed by both late-twentieth- and mid-nineteenth-century standards. Its substantive arguments were logically distorted, historically inaccurate, and constitutionally specious. Its failures could be traced directly to the partisan motivations of the Supreme Court's southern majority. These men, who united loosely behind Taney, used their positions to strike against the growing strength of the antislavery movement. Like many late-twentieth-century critics, Fehrenbacher also used his analysis to warn of judicial review's potential dangers. *Dred Scott* revealed the dark side of judicial activism—"democracy's non-democratic alternative to representative government when the latter bogs down in failure or inaction"—and provided a reminder that "judicial sovereignty" entailed great risks even as it promised potential benefits.[9] Historians have received Fehrenbacher's study as the final word on *Dred Scott*.[10] The book is indeed a fine piece of scholarship, and it demonstrates conclusively that the Union's sectional politics played an important role in shaping the court's decision.

Even so, *The Dred Scott Case* remains a flawed work. It is too indebted to twentieth-century assumptions concerning judicial review and too dependent on the Republicans' powerful but partisan criticism of the decision. *Dred Scott v. Sandford*, in fact, offers no simple lessons concerning the contemporary use of judicial review, despite what seems to be a reflexive tendency to invoke the decision as an example of a Supreme Court gone awry.[11] Members of the Taney Court and their contemporaries agonized over the proper scope of judicial authority, but they did so in terms that were alien to the debates over the "countermajoritarian difficulty," judicial self-restraint, and original intent that have dominated academic and political discussions of constitutional law for the past half century.[12] Antebellum Supreme Court justices worked in an intellectual and institutional context that differed significantly from that of modern justices. Earlier justices' understandings of which issues required confrontation and which might be evaded depended on a set of political, professional, ideological, and institutional assumptions that ought not be dismissed as mere partisanship or judicial activism.

Fehrenbacher's reliance on the Republicans' criticism of *Dred Scott*, however, makes viewing the case as anything but partisan exceedingly difficult. Republican politicians not only found the decision to be morally outrageous but also followed a political strategy that hinged on achieving an electoral victory by unifying northern voters against what they perceived to be a southern threat. Very little strategic advantage would result from dwelling on issues that did not fit their interpretation of sectional politics. Following the Republicans' lead, Fehrenbacher never seriously considered the possibility that factors other than the politics of slavery might have exerted a decisive influence on the justices. He simply assumed the primacy of sectional politics and researched accordingly. From such a perspective, *Dred Scott* could only be a story about the politics of slavery—one that overstated the influence of sectional politics and obscured other factors that may have influenced the Supreme Court's decision.

This book breaks with the Republican interpretation of *Dred Scott* by placing the decision in its judicial context. The argument emphasizes the ways in which the members of the Taney Court—rather than their Republican critics—understood the issues before them. Reconstructing this understanding requires the use of evidence that is either new or not usually considered relevant to the study of *Dred Scott*. This study rests on a careful tracking of the arguments made by individual justices as they worked through more than sixteen hundred reported cases between 1837 and 1861. (Readers interested in the method employed in this study will find a discussion at the end of the book.) By examining the Taney Court's entire body of work during this period, this account highlights relationships among legal doctrines that scholars usually perceive as separate areas of inquiry, such as the laws relating to corporations and slavery. This approach also provides extended attention to the written opinions of dissenting and concurring members of the court, which permits an analysis of factionalism and coalition building on the court by allowing one to follow the rhetorical and doctrinal movements of individual justices over time. Moreover, keeping track of those movements highlights the competing assumptions, agendas, and commitments that were at play on the court and helps explain the formation of decisions such as *Dred Scott*. The argument that follows also draws on the justices' personal papers and the court's working records, especially the National Archives' collection of extant manuscript and galley versions of the justices' opinions. These documents, which scholars have not yet used systematically, contain revisions that sometimes reveal information about the justices' assumptions or about the concessions a particular justice may have made to pull a majority of justices to his side. Such evidence provides insight into the internal dynamics of the Taney Court and reveals the origins of *Dred Scott* to be far more complex than historians have thus far recognized.

Dred Scott involved far more than furthering southern interests or defending slavery. Questions about Dred Scott's status—whether he was a citizen or whether he was free at all—were entangled with other concerns. Scott and his wife, Harriet, wanted only freedom for themselves and their two daughters, but the unpretentious litigation they initiated in Missouri during the 1840s went badly and dragged on for a decade.[13] By the time the case reached the U.S. Supreme Court, the lawyers and judges involved had packed it with meanings that none of the original litigants had anticipated. Some of the implications that legal professionals discovered in or injected into the case had unambiguously sectional dimensions, yet the Taney

Court's interest had little to do with sectionalism in any direct sense. Rather, the court's members confronted the issues *Dred Scott* raised according to the terms of a conceptual framework that they had spent two decades developing. Over the course of hundreds of reported decisions, the justices had created a body of jurisprudence that balanced partisan goals with institutional and professional obligations, that defined the differences among individual justices, and that gave expression to their shared sensibilities and anxieties concerning antebellum American culture. During the 1850s, the questions that took on critical importance within this framework did not merely involve the protection of slavery. Instead, they centered on the best way in which the court could protect slavery, preserve both federal power and state sovereignty, promote economic development, and secure the legal foundations of an emerging corporate order—all at the same time. The issues beneath *Dred Scott* ranged across numerous doctrinal areas, from choice of law, to fugitive slaves, to the scope of federal power over commerce, to the limits of state police power, to slave transit, to the regulation of corporations and state taxation under the Obligation of Contracts Clause, and ultimately to the standing of both corporations and free blacks in the federal courts. Developments in any one of those areas sometimes had ramifications that extended across the others. By 1857, in fact, a number of these ramifications had converged in such a way that a sweeping decision such as *Dred Scott* appeared not only unavoidable but absolutely necessary.

This book explains why the members of the Supreme Court found the ruling to be inescapable. The thesis is straightforward. *Dred Scott* developed as an unintended consequence of the Taney Court's balancing of its members' desires to protect slavery, to preserve federal and state power, and to promote economic development while containing factionalism and maintaining both doctrinal consistency and fidelity to a particular vision of judicial authority in a democratic republic. This book divides the argument into three parts. Part 1 describes the Taney Court's vision of judicial authority, which this study terms "Jacksonian jurisprudence." In the years following his appointment, Taney and his colleagues developed a jurisprudential framework that they believed promoted popular sovereignty through a combination of deference to legislatures and coercion of individuals. Their approach allowed the court to provide legislatures with maximum leeway to formulate policy and ensured that individuals stood by the obligations they incurred in the market. Balancing that combination of coercion and deference while maintaining the Taney Court's self-image as a facilitator of self-rule led to a series of procedural rulings that created the jurisdictional arena in which *Dred Scott* would emerge. Part 2 examines the court's application of its Jacksonian jurisprudence in the areas of corporate and slave law. During the 1840s, the justices elaborated a framework for handling slavery cases, but their solution generated a number of unintended consequences in corporate law, especially on matters of jurisdiction and citizenship. By 1855, the justices' failure adequately to address these issues produced a faction of three southern members who sought to protect slavery by destroying the Supreme Court's corporate law doctrine. Part 3 provides a sustained analysis of the *Dred Scott* case. The section begins by explaining why the justices found the case so difficult to avoid and then discusses the ways in which Taney's *Dred Scott* opinion constituted both a response to the challenge presented by the southern faction and an effort to incorporate the territories into the jurisprudential framework that the court had spent years developing.

This book does not deny that sectional concerns shaped the court's rulings but refuses to accept the primacy of sectional partisanship and rejects contentions that sectional pressures directly manifested themselves in judicial outcomes. In the pages that follow, the analysis offers a conceptual framework that views the court's stance toward slavery as part of a larger, coherent strategy of judicial governance that perceived intimate connections between human bondage and other areas of legal development. Readers will find no effort to defend Taney, his colleagues, or the body of Jacksonian jurisprudence that they created. Readers will encounter, however, an effort to convey an understanding of the antebellum concerns and sensibilities that infused *Dred Scott* and made its rulings appear unavoidable and indispensable to a majority of the Supreme Court's members.

PART ONE

Beneath *Dred Scott*

Jacksonian Jurisprudence and the Dimensions of Self-Rule

IN 1837, PRESIDENT ANDREW JACKSON delivered his final address to the American people. "In your hands is rightfully placed the sovereignty of the country, and to you everyone placed in authority is ultimately responsible." "The great body of the people" held the power to ensure that its "wishes . . . are carried into faithful execution," and its will "must sooner or later be obeyed." Jackson did not engage in mere flattery; he gave his address at a time of considerable popular involvement in politics. For decades, state after state had lowered or abolished restrictions on white male suffrage. Although three-quarters of the states had imposed property requirements for voting in 1790, only one in three states continued to do so in 1830, and by 1855 the ratio was less than one in ten. Voter participation—stimulated by rapid social and economic change as well as by the organizational efforts of Jackson's allies and enemies—increased from around 25 percent in 1824 to 78 percent in 1840, remaining at that level for decades. Jackson claimed to speak for this burgeoning electorate and portrayed himself as the representative of all the people. By exploiting this stance, Jackson expanded the power of the presidency, removing federal officers appointed by previous administrations and vetoing laws simply because he disliked them. He also used his immense popularity to pursue several controversial policies, notably the removal of Native Americans from the Old Southwest, the authorization of military force against South Carolina's opposition to the federal tariff, and the destruction of the Second Bank of the United States. When he retired in 1837, Jackson left a legacy that dominated American political life until the 1850s, and his judicial appointments ensured that his legacy dominated the Supreme Court as well.[1]

Jackson's presidency divided American political culture into two highly competitive and increasingly well-organized parties that offered distinctly different visions for the future development of the United States. By 1840, Jackson's opponents, disturbed by what they considered irresponsible and abusive governance, had established the Whig Party. Whigs sought a disciplined, orderly plan of national development that emphasized social progress through the market's civilizing influence and individual betterment through self-improvement. They advocated protective tariffs, a national banking system, and federally sponsored internal improvements as a way to harmonize the Union's diverse interests and to provide opportunities for advancement to people at all levels of society. Members of the Democratic Party considered such proposals little more than, in Jackson's words, "an engine to undermine . . . free institutions, and . . . to engross all powers in the hands of the few and to govern by corruption or force." Jackson's supporters lowered tariffs, stifled federal support for internal improvements, and destroyed the Second Bank of the United States because they believed these programs placed special privileges in the hands of a small elite who would benefit at the community's expense. Democrats countered with calls for equal rights so that no citizen could claim rights not held by others and demanded limited government because active governments generally created artificial divisions in society by rewarding some and punishing many others.[2]

On the Supreme Court, Jackson's legacy lived through his appointees, who dominated the institution by 1837. Many of his justices spent the rest of their lives standing against persons Jackson identified as "those amongst us who wish to enlarge the powers of the general government." Over the years, they articulated Jackson's vision of constitutional governance, which maintained "unimpaired and in full vigor the rights and sovereignty of the states and [confined] the action of the general government strictly to the sphere of its appropriate duties."[3] Arguments calling for the limitation of federal power were old as the republic itself, but under Roger B. Taney, whom Jackson elevated to chief justice in 1836, they received a new vigor. Although Taney and his colleagues fiercely upheld federal authority when they believed its exercise to be appropriate, they aggressively rolled back, as much as institutional constraints permitted, limitations on state authority they considered to be illegitimate. Support for popular sovereignty drove this agenda. Most if not all members of the Taney Court believed that their predecessors under John Marshall had unjustly used their authority to limit legislatures to prevent the people from truly ruling themselves and to establish the court as a guiding elite within the Union. Under Taney, the Supreme Court became reluctant to second-guess legislatures, and the court developed an antielitist understanding of judicial authority that refused inquiry into the morality or justice of state policy. Such questions belonged to legislatures alone, and the court would not strike down legislation because its members found it disagreeable. By resorting to such tactics, the Supreme Court enabled the people to rule themselves through their state legislatures with little fear that nine elite judges would thwart their wishes, a position that underpinned a federal stance of laissez-faire toward economic development and essentially gave the states free rein to treat their nonwhite inhabitants as they saw fit.

The Taney Court's vision of popular sovereignty extended beyond collective self-rule, as its members confronted the internal pressures "from cupidity, from corruption, from disappointed ambition and inordinate thirst for power" that Jackson considered the Union's chief threats when he left office. Taney Court justices insisted that individuals act as sovereigns in the conduct of their daily affairs and, in contrast to the court's often deferential stance toward legislatures, regularly coerced litigants into tightly governing themselves and their subordinates. Two elements contributed to the justices' behavior. Despite a partisan appointment process, court members identified themselves primarily as lawyers and judges, and their sense of professionalism produced a rule-oriented jurisprudence that they applied rigidly against individuals. Anxiety over social disorder also factored into the court's rigidity. The United States experienced tremendous growth between 1790 and 1860. The country's population increased at a rate between 33 and 36 percent every decade, and the rate of growth in the cities often nearly doubled that (and occasionally surpassed it by even more). Indeed, the number of cities (places with populations greater than twenty-five hundred) increased by a factor of more than sixteen between 1790 and 1860. Population growth and rapid mobility combined with increasing levels of alcohol consumption and violence (the number of reported riots increased nearly sixfold between the 1820s and 1830s) underscored a sense of social breakdown among the Union's elite. Also in the early 1830s, a host of new egalitarian political demands burst onto the scene—including movements for immediate abolition, labor rights, and free land—taking Jacksonian Era demands for equal rights to extremes that most justices would not accept. Through their rulings, Taney Court justices encouraged social cohesion and contained the intensifying egalitarian impulses by forcing individuals to

stand by the obligations they incurred in the market; the justices thus coerced potential litigants to conduct their affairs in a manner befitting a
member of the sovereignty.[4]

This value-laden shaping of individual behavior ran counter to the Taney
Court's fundamentally amoral stance toward collective behavior. The justices reconciled these two elements by drawing a sharp distinction between
their decisions and the law. On the Taney Court, *law* denoted the will of the
people as expressed in either legislative enactments or constitutional provisions, and the justices proved reluctant to go beyond a strict interpretation
of language in such documents because they feared assuming a legislative
authority that would usurp popular will. Judicial decisions represented, in
the words of Justice Joseph Story, "at most, only evidence of what the laws
are" and were consequently not subject to the same degree of deference.[5]
By maintaining this distinction, court members could remain deferential to
popular will in matters of statutory and constitutional law while pursuing
an agenda designed to promote social control and cohesion through the
numerous nonstatutory, common-law cases that came before the Supreme
Court. The reconciliation, however, carried unintended, long-term consequences and in effect created the conditions that made *Dred Scott* possible.
Over time, the justices' distinction quietly transformed their understanding
of federal jurisdiction as they became increasingly willing to ignore state judicial decisions. By the 1850s, in fact, all of the procedural mechanisms that
would have enabled an evasion of the sweeping and divisive ruling rendered
by the court in 1857 had eroded as a result of the justices' effort to manage
their commitments to both a collective and an individuated vision of popular sovereignty.

CHAPTER ONE

Realizing Popular Sovereignty

Partisan Sentiment and Constitutional Constraint in Jacksonian Jurisprudence

OVER THE PREVIOUS TWO DECADES, complained the *Southern Quarterly Review* in 1850, the Supreme Court of the United States had suffered a "great and lasting change of the confidence, respect and veneration" it had once held among the public. "We have no doubt, the decay is . . . a necessary consequence of that great era and change in public sentiment of which General Jackson was the Great Pioneer." President Andrew Jackson and his successor, Martin Van Buren, the *Review* charged, made a position on the court "the reward of political jobbing," with "partisan zeal, and skill in political strategy" counting more "than long professional labour, experience, and study."[1] Although it overstated its case, the *Review* underscored the way in which the appointments by Democratic presidents had shaped the court. Jackson's appointees held a majority of the court's seven seats by 1837, and Van Buren had appointed other like-minded men when the number of seats expanded to nine.

Under the leadership of Chief Justice Roger B. Taney, these justices rejected the nationalist and elitist orientation that characterized the Supreme Court's jurisprudence under Taney's predecessor, John Marshall. Marshall and his associates had worked within the constraints established by the Constitution and Congress to restrain state legislatures from committing acts that the justices considered irresponsible or immoral. Taney and his associates shifted the court's jurisprudence toward an antielitist, amoral conception of judicial authority that sought to maximize legislative power. The justices strove to make their court a facilitator of self-rule that would help transform popular sovereignty from a theoretical abstraction to a believable, albeit decidedly fictional and exclusionary, description of the social order. With a few exceptions, this stance bore a strong relationship to a majority of justices' identification with the mainstream of the Democratic Party in the 1830s and 1840s. Partisan identity continually impinged on their legal reasoning. Yet justices' understanding of the duties of their office and their court's role within the Union mediated their politics. Members believed themselves bound to interpret the Constitution within the constraints limned out by Congress and their predecessors on the Supreme Court. Although three members consistently voiced their opposition to the Taney Court's jurisprudence, a majority of members serving between 1836 and 1861 pursued an agenda infused with Democratic sensibility but constrained by their perception of constitutional boundaries.

A strong partisan orientation characterized the Taney Court. Twelve of the fifteen justices serving between 1836 and 1861 supported the Democrats before coming to the court, and most continued, in one capacity or another, to do so thereafter. Justice Peter V. Daniel of Virginia illustrated the depth of this sentiment when he proudly reported to his daughter that he and Justice James M. Wayne of Georgia had attended a dinner party where no Whigs were present.[2] Such sentiments appeared in public as well. Currents of partisan ideology ran through Taney Court discourse, and justices self-consciously used their positions to further the perceived interest of middling white males against predatory elites and potentially competitive, largely dark-skinned, social subordinates. The court's rulings in commercial and corporate law as well as its decisions concerning slavery and race revealed that tendency clearly enough, but the justices' politics shaped their perception of duty and continually infused their decision making. Court members rejected contentions that social order required elite guidance and disciplined development imposed from above and refused to allow their institution to take on such responsibilities. Rather, the Taney Court developed an antielitist, fundamentally amoral conception of judicial authority that took deference to popular will as its foundation and both furthered the court's larger agenda and supported, not always consciously, the disparities of racial and class power within the Union.

Taney Court members, especially those appointed by Jackson and Van Buren, loyally served the Democratic Party in the critical period of its formation. Seven of the eight men elevated to the court by these two presidents actively campaigned for Jackson in 1828 against John Quincy Adams and his proposals for a nationally guided program of internal improvements. These seven men also supported Van Buren in his maneuvers to become Jackson's dominant adviser and eventual successor. Each of the seven, with varying degrees of commitment, participated in the political struggles of the 1830s that defined partisan alignment until the 1850s. They stood by Jackson as he vetoed internal improvement bills and as he refused to aid the Cherokee while Georgia stripped them of their land. These men supported him as he faced down the South Carolina Nullifiers and especially as he fought and killed the "monster" Second Bank of the United States. Future chief justice Roger B. Taney, while serving as Jackson's secretary of the treasury, took the actions against the bank that made Jackson's victory possible. None of the six justices appointed after 1841 boasted such partisan credentials, but they came to the court amid assurances of their loyalty and commitment to sustain, as one supporter said of future justice Robert C. Grier, "the cause of Democracy with unwavering firmness."[3]

The future justices' participation in the central events of Jackson's presidency underscored their desire to allow "the people"—an undifferentiated mass of white males generally lacking individual influence—opportunity to rule themselves. Resistant Cherokee and South Carolina Nullifiers, as Richard Ellis has argued, offended Jackson men in part because such groups offered illegitimate resistance to the will of the majority in the relevant polities (Georgia and the Union, respectively). Likewise, the Jacksonian resistance to internal improvements and to the Second Bank of the United States stemmed from a demand that federal policies not bend to the influence of wealth and power. Democrats envisioned their party as engaged in a struggle on behalf of common white folk against men of aristocratic pretension who meant to thwart the people's right to rule themselves for the sake of personal aggrandizement. The Democrats' opponents, of course, hardly constituted an actual aristocracy, but evangelical influence and nationalist sentiment among the Whig and later Republican leadership prompted proposals for an elite-guided program of ordered and disciplined social development that Democrats found positively alarming. Democratic members of the Taney Court participated in this partisan struggle through a conspicuous rejection of a judicial role as guiding elites, a role the Marshall Court had embraced.[4]

Taney Court justices considered their institution a facilitator of popular will, as expressed through constitutional provisions and statutory law. "Every constitutional act of Congress," one justice wrote in 1845, "is passed by the will of the people of the United States." As another stated in 1850, "The sovereign will is made known to us by legislative enactment. And to this we must look in our judicial action."[5] This equation of popular will with legislation, together with the justices' desire not to be a guiding elite, produced a rigid style of statutory interpretation. When they confronted a statute, the justices avoided imputing any legislative intention not expressed clearly in the document itself and accorded the document's language its literal meaning. So in 1850, the justices revealed their literalism when they unanimously upheld the conviction of one Ephraim Briggs for removing forty white oak and hickory trees from public land. Briggs's conviction rested on an 1831 federal statute that, according to its title and first clause, penalized persons who removed timber that Congress had reserved for naval use, specifically live oak and red cedar. None of the trees taken by Briggs fell into those categories, but a jury found him guilty anyway because the statute's enabling clause penalized anyone who removed "any live oak, or cedar tree or trees, or other timber" without naval authorization. Briggs's counsel argued that the term *other timber* applied only to trees reserved for the navy and that Briggs had thus committed no crime. Justice John Catron of Tennessee, speaking for the court, disagreed. He admitted that the title indicated that only the removal of certain timbers carried penalties, "but the enacting clause is general, and not restricted to live-oak or red-cedar, nor to timber specially reserved for naval purposes."[6] The cutting and removal of any sort of tree from public land constituted a crime, and Briggs would be punished.

Catron's choice of a more stringent reading over an interpretation that both favored Briggs and accorded with the probable intentions of the act underscored the justices' desire to carry out statutorily expressed popular will to the letter. The pattern repeated itself hundreds of times. When the court lacked clear statutory law to structure its rulings, however, the justices flatly refused to extrapolate and impose their own sense of legislative intention. *Bank of Augusta v. Earle* (1839) showed that reticence at work. Alabama's 1819 constitution, a document drafted in the midst of a financial panic, stringently restricted the legislature's ability to incorporate banks and required it to invest heavily in the few it could establish. The relevant question in *Bank of Augusta* concerned whether a constitutional limitation on the number of banks chartered within Alabama also excluded the out-of-state banks that hoped to fill the void. In an 1838 circuit court ruling, Justice John McKinley of Alabama held that the constitution forbade corporations chartered in other jurisdictions from conducting business in the state. The Supreme Court promptly overturned the ruling. Writing for the majority, Taney conceded the clarity of the state's policy toward its own banks but maintained that the implications for foreign (out-of-state) corporations remained indeterminate since neither the constitution nor the legislature had directly addressed the matter. Maybe the state desired to close itself completely to foreign banks, or maybe it wanted to limit only certain banking practices. Perhaps, Taney suggested, the legislature wished "to extend the utmost liberality" to foreign banks because such actions might encourage other states to welcome the business of those banks in which Alabama had invested so heavily.[7]

Such policy goals involved issues of political economy and fiscal management best left to legislative discretion. No state, said Taney, would consent to treat such questions "as a problem to be worked out by the Courts of the United States, from a few general principles, which might very naturally be misunderstood or misapplied."[8] Without clear statutory language stating otherwise, the court assumed that the common law, which recognized the legality of banking, controlled the court's action. This strategy reemerged two years later in *Groves v. Slaughter* (1841). Mississippi's 1832 constitution outlawed the introduction of slaves for market after May 1833. *Groves* centered on whether a contract made after that date bound the parties involved. Justice Smith Thompson of New York, speaking for a fragmented court, answered in the affirmative. The provision's language clearly stated Mississippi's policy, but the legislature neglected to specify the consequences of a violation. Mississippi may have wanted an absolute prohibition on the introduction of slaves for sale, or it may have planned merely to discourage the practice by taxing such transactions, and the provision was silent about when the penalties attached or which party suffered them. A five-member majority considered these issues matters of legislative discretion. They offered no opinion on how Mississippi should implement its policy and treated the case as if it were a normal commercial transaction at common law.[9] That Thompson's *Groves* opinion left the interstate slave trade intact should come as no surprise, since a majority of the court generally sympathized with slaveholders. An instrumentalist argument, however, cannot explain the reasoning behind the decision. Similar reasoning in *Bank of Augusta* expanded corporate power, even though the justices usually desired, especially in the Taney Court's earliest years, to limit such authority. A proper understanding of Taney Court jurisprudence requires looking beyond the beneficiaries of particular decisions. Historians must examine the underlying vision of judicial authority that provided a coherent defense of both corporations and slavery in a rapidly democratizing Union.

A rigid interpretive style and reluctance to extrapolate policy in fact went to the core of this vision of judicial authority. Members' reticence to expound state policy in the place of elected representatives developed from a belief that such action, as Taney noted in *Bank of Augusta*, "would savor more of legislation than of judicial interpretation." Certain matters, as the court's actions revealed in its handling of laws in Alabama and Mississippi as well as in Pennsylvania and Rhode Island, properly belonged only to legislatures. This behavior, known to scholars as the "political question doctrine," emerged neither as a mechanism to avoid potentially controversial issues nor as a means of concealing the justices' personal political agendas. Rather, the Taney Court's self-restraint issued from a larger effort to promote the people's self-rule through the legislatures and a refusal to make law in their stead. The justices' rigidity implied an amoral stance toward legislation out of respect for popular sovereignty. The law, the long-serving Catron wrote before he joined the court, embodied "not a system of ethical philosophy" but a body of rules "to maintain the ancient state of things regardless of the sanctions giving rise to it." As Taney once said, concerns over the "expediency and moral tendency" of statutory law properly belonged with the legislatures.[10]

While serving as Jackson's attorney general, Taney offered an elaborate discussion of the amoral vision of judicial authority that would dominate his court. In an unpublished 1832 opinion concerning South Carolina's Negro Seamen Act, Taney defended a state's right to pass a blatantly oppressive law. Following the discovery of an alleged slave revolt, the state's legislature mandated the immediate jailing of any free black sailors entering Charleston's harbor and authorized their sale into enslavement if their ships left without them. According to Taney, who would restate this position several times in the years before *Dred Scott*, southern states possessed a right to protect their population from an influx of free people of color. Their right to do so emerged from their status as sovereign states, which endowed them with a so-called right of self-preservation that they had never ceded to the federal government. Taney considered the law "more severe and oppressive than necessary," but the choice to exercise a legitimately held power, whether through a mild policy or a harsh one, was a matter of legislative discretion that lay beyond the federal courts' rightful scope of inquiry. Such discretion, he contended, represented a general attribute of legislative authority, whose abuse could not be remedied by judicial action.[11]

Taney cited the Second Bank of the United States, an institution he hated, as a case in point. Congress held a legitimate power to tax, and that implied both the authority to create fiscal agents and full discretion over whom it selected and the scope of their authority. If Congress desired to create "a vast monied monopoly" with "capital infinitely beyond" its needs and the power "to exercise a controlling influence . . . over . . . the Government and to bring ruin on any portion of the community which should venture to oppose its wishes," it was free to do so. Federal courts, Taney argued, had no power to restrain such legislation. A ruling stating that Congress had endowed its treasury agent with too much capital and power implied that the court could specify the appropriate amounts. These issues, like those Taney and his colleagues would later confront in *Bank of Augusta* and *Groves*, involved matters best suited for legislators. [12]

The Taney Court's amorality sanctioned a wide range of hierarchical social relationships within the Union. Taney's defense of the Negro Seamen Act supported the South's brutal mixture of racial and class subordination. And Catron's statement that judges should not moralize appeared in a letter criticizing the Marshall Court for holding unconstitutional Georgia's Indian removal policy. [13] Court rulings also exhibited this stance, but members by no means applied it only to people of color. Justices consistently sustained hierarchical relations among whites, although not as self-consciously as when dealing with racial regulations. Most justices considered the states' aggressive employment of their eminent domain power to reallocate property from private to public use an aspect of a sovereign right of self-rule and self-preservation. Just as South Carolina's exercise of this right in the Negro Seamen Act involved questions of discretion into which the court could not inquire, so did expropriations under the eminent domain power. The court therefore refused to address issues of adequate compensation, states' adherence to their takings regulations, and even obvious and admitted abuses of authority. "It rests with state legislatures and state courts," Catron wrote in one such case, "to protect their citizens from injustice and oppression of this description." [14]

Remedy for these abuses lay with the vote. An electorate faced with oppressive laws, Taney argued in his opinion on the Negro Seamen Act, could vote the oppressors from office and compel the successors to revise the offending legislation. His contention, although problematic, did not prove wholly unrealistic. Jackson's supporters considered themselves engaged in precisely such a struggle when Taney wrote this opinion in 1832. The institutionalized rivalry between Whigs and Democrats, despite a large amount of theatrics, hyperbole, and crass manipulation, assumed that the Union's frequent, participatory elections involved high stakes. Taney's argument contained some obvious limitations. A large number of people in the Union—some immigrants, most blacks, and all women—lacked the power to vote. Widespread disenfranchisement highlighted the flaw in Taney's remedy. Not only did such persons often become the targets of oppressive legislation, but access to the franchise rested on the same discretionary authority to which the Taney Court so consistently deferred.[15]

An 1849 decision, *Luther v. Borden*, underscored the limitations of the court's vision. *Luther*, in short, recognized a state's authority to exclude the majority of its white male population from the electorate without fear of judicial intervention. Until 1843, Rhode Island operated under its colonial charter, which contained heavy suffrage restrictions that excluded most of the state's white population. Discontent with the charter mounted through the first third of the nineteenth century, and in 1841 the charter government's opponents, under the leadership of Thomas Dorr, established a new government claiming to represent the people, which in all probability it did. The charter government forced a crisis, declared martial law, and crushed the Dorr Rebellion. Defeated in the field, Dorr's supporters sought to defend the legitimacy of their government at law. Writing for the unanimous justices, Taney closed the matter, arguing that the court could not adequately address such (political) questions because its deference to state law implied a bias toward the established government. "It is the province of a court to expound the law, not to make it." A federal court had no "right to determine what political privileges the citizens of a State are entitled to, unless there is an established constitution or law to govern its decision." Like *Bank of Augusta* and *Groves*, the questions in *Luther* involved matters of discretion in which the court refused to intervene, even if those issues centered on a fundamental remedy to governmental oppression.[16]

Despite the indiscriminate support it gave to relations of subordination, the Democratic members of the Taney Court considered their theory of judicial authority an instrument of self-rule. Their stance freed—or forced—the people to govern themselves as they saw fit through their legislatures. An amoral approach to statutory law also underscored the justices' rejection of a role in which they acted as a guiding elite. Their vision contained significant policy implications. It sustained the people's efforts to pursue the public good against those individuals who sought to use their vested rights to profit at the community's expense, and it enabled the people to treat nonwhites as brutally as perceptions of safety required. For Taney Court justices, the will of the legislature represented the will of the people, and the justices held tightly to that formulation even when cases such as *Luther v. Borden* opened it to question. The court's partisan vision of judicial authority produced a rigid and literal style of interpretation that emerged continually in the court's rulings. Partisanship constituted only one factor shaping the court's jurisprudence. In *Luther*, for example, Taney noted that congressional statutes and long-standing precedent imputed an institutionally imposed bias against Dorr's supporters, and as he did so the chief justice revealed an awareness that he and his colleagues faced certain restraints on their action.

Taney Court members faced limits on their ability to impose a Democratic regime on the Union. They inherited a matrix of institutional constraints that defined their court's role and shaped their rulings. Like all Supreme Court justices before and since, Taney and his associates worked within a tradition of constitutionalism, a complex and malleable body of interrelated discourses, values, and expectations concerning patterns of institutional behavior and governance. *Constitutionalism* here denotes a belief that a written document, purporting to be the highest expression of the people's sovereign will, limits and guides governmental power in the name of a higher end. Exactly what goals constitute that higher end and what interpretive strategies achieve fidelity to that document's letter or spirit—assuming fidelity is desirable—have been and remain a subject of heated debate among legal commentators. Taney Court members generally favored strict literalism as their mode of interpretation, and they defined the higher end as the preservation of a Union organized by what is now termed federalism, an institutional division of governing authority between the state and general governments. Despite its reputation as a defender of states' rights, the Taney Court envisioned a union of concurrently sovereign state and federal governments, each supreme within its sphere and possessing a maximum discretion within its jurisdiction. This vision owed much to the justices' partisan orientation, but it also had a strong foundation in the constitutional and statutory texts that court members routinely interpreted; by the 1820s, it even had a basis, although a rather ambiguous one, in the rulings of the Marshall Court.

The U.S. Constitution established a system in which the federal and state governments differed not only in their concerns (general or local) but also in their nature. Sovereignty—a supreme and unaccountable authority to do, in the words of the English legal commentator William Blackstone, "every thing that is not naturally impossible" within a particular jurisdiction—theoretically resided in the people of the United States. Yet under the Constitution, framer James Wilson explained in 1787, the people of the United States delegated a portion of their authority to each government, but the character of that power differed fundamentally at each level. The federal government, although sovereign, rightfully exercised power only over those areas enumerated in the Constitution. States, by contrast, exercised "every right and authority" their constitutions "did not in explicit terms reserve." State governments possessed what became known as the "police power," an inherent and amorphous ability to regulate on the behalf of health, safety, and morality. Very few aspects of social life, as William Novak has demonstrated, escaped the police power, which qualified property rights, oversaw market activity, and restrained behavior understood as immoral, all in the name of the people's welfare as perceived in particular localities. Within their borders, therefore, states were in every sense sovereign, and their internal governments faced no limitations beyond those they placed on themselves and the few contained in the Constitution. Beyond their borders, as Wilson later argued from the Supreme Court, the states had no sovereign character and stood in a strictly subordinate relationship to the federal government.[17]

The success of this system depended on the state and federal governments' adherence to the jurisdictional boundaries outlined in the Constitution, and the document invested the judiciary with the power to enforce those limits. Although it nowhere used the phrase "judicial review," the Constitution conferred on the federal courts a jurisdiction extending to "all Cases, in Law and Equity," arising under its provisions and then declared itself "the supreme Law of the Land." Members of the constitutional convention, participants in the ratification debates, and subsequent jurists under the federal system—men such as James Madison, James Wilson, Robert Yates, Patrick Henry, and John Marshall—understood the statements' combined effect as a grant for reviewing legislation, and, if the law in question conflicted with the Constitution, for striking it down. As Alexander Hamilton wrote in the *Federalist*, "The courts were designed to be an intermediate body between the people and the legislature in order, among other things, to keep the latter within the limits assigned to their authority." Judicial review of legislation became a routine practice of the federal courts in the nineteenth century, although decisions striking down federal laws, like

Dred Scott, remained rare. Even before 1800, federal judges assumed that their courts possessed the power of review.[18]

Taney Court justices approached federalism and judicial review through the doctrinal legacy of Chief Justice John Marshall. Under Marshall, the Supreme Court emerged as the final interpreter of the Constitution and a staunch defender of national power. His court conclusively, if not to everyone's satisfaction, established its authority to strike down both state and federal legislation on the grounds of its unconstitutionality and to review certain state court decisions. Marshall's court used this power mainly to assert the supremacy of the Constitution and federal law within the Union. In one of its most important rulings, for example, the court struck down a tax that Maryland had imposed on the controversial Second Bank of the United States. Such taxation impaired Congress's authority to manage the Union's financial needs through its chosen agent. Marshall and his associates pushed federal authority beyond the probable intentions of the framers, extending the Constitution's prohibition on state impairment of contractual obligations to include first grants of property and then corporate charters. As he presented these arguments, Marshall employed liberal constructions of constitutional language and sweeping statements of general principle that gave his rulings an air of inevitability.[19]

With its rulings, the Marshall Court set itself up as a guiding elite bent on protecting the Union's republican social order from irresponsible state legislatures. Most significantly, the court developed a vision of the Union's political structure that countered the arguments of compact theorists. Advocated by Thomas Jefferson, his Virginian followers, and John C. Calhoun, compact theory asserted that the Union developed out of an agreement among the states. This mutual, perhaps temporary, arrangement emerged out of convenience, placed no limits on the states' sovereignty, and conferred on the federal government no power to intervene in the states' internal affairs. The court responded in a succession of important cases that the Union represented a government of the people that placed the states, for certain purposes, in strict subordination to the federal government. By the 1820s, the court had effectively demolished compact theory as a basis for argumentation before the Supreme Court. Although the theory became increasingly influential in southern political circles, the Taney Court made no effort to revive it.[20]

Despite their sweeping assertions of national supremacy, the members of the Marshall Court as a whole never rejected the states' claims to sovereignty and ultimately remained faithful to the federal structure established by the Constitution. Most justices remained cognizant of the federal government's enumerated nature. In 1812, the court ruled that it possessed no inherent common-law authority to assume criminal jurisdiction: the enumerated character of federal power allowed the court to take such cases only when authorized by statute. The court's most assertive statements concerning federal supremacy likewise contained references to the enumerated character of federal power. Even during the 1819 term, when the court's nationalist sentiment ran at its highest, the court saw limits to federal authority. In one case, for example, Marshall backed away from a previous statement where he argued that the court should construe the language in the Constitution's Obligation of Contracts Clause in the broadest extent possible. Such a reading embraced contractual relationships such as marriage, which he believed properly belonged under the jurisdiction of the states' internal government. So Marshall opted for a narrower interpretation of the word *contracts* that embraced mainly agreements involving some sort of property. By the mid-1820s, the court increasingly recognized the presence of what Marshall called "that immense mass of legislation, which embraces every thing within the territory of a State, not surrendered to the general government: all which can be most advantageously exercised by the States themselves." The later Marshall Court thus envisioned, sometimes grudgingly and incoherently, a union of concurrent sovereign authorities, consisting of states with "immense" regulatory power held together and kept within proper limits by a general government, supreme within its sphere, that possessed a power flexible enough to meet its delegated ends.[21]

John Marshall and his associates left the Taney Court a complex legacy under which its members both bristled and flourished. They reacted strongly against the Marshall Court's elitist restraint of state legislatures, which they believed impeded the people's ability to rule themselves, but considered themselves bound by the rulings of their predecessors and struggled for ways to limit the scope of such precedents. Other aspects of the Marshall Court's legacy proved less problematic. Taney Court justices accepted without question their institution's power to review state and federal legislation and to strike down laws that conflicted with their understanding of the Constitution. They also ultimately accepted the later Marshall Court's recognition of the Union as a combination of concurrent sovereigns, although this acceptance did not come about without a great deal of debate that lasted until the early 1850s. Indeed, as the complaints of the *Southern*

Quarterly Review demonstrated, the Taney Court's broad areas of agreement with its predecessors were not immediately clear, but no member contemplated a complete rejection of Marshall's legacy.

Although it rejected the Marshall Court's elitist conception of judicial authority, the Taney Court worked comfortably within the structural parameters established by Marshall and his associates. The new justices, to be sure, possessed little desire to use their positions to protect the vested rights of established elites or the lives and property of nonwhites such as the Cherokee. The justices' sentiments effectively raised the threshold concerning what became perceived as unconstitutional, but the new members did not consider themselves at liberty to reject the Marshall Court's body of jurisprudence, even if they had wished to do so. They accepted that their predecessors' decisions bound their court and understood that they would need to explain any departures in the context of the concepts and categories set up by the Constitution but elaborated by the Marshall Court. Yet Taney Court justices embraced and developed more fully the concurrent nature of state and federal sovereignty that their predecessors had recognized in the final decade of Marshall's tenure and that had always been implicit in the Constitution. An amoral stance toward legislatures among the court's personnel, moreover, permitted both the state and federal governments to expand their authority to its perceived constitutional limits. For the Taney Court, judicial responsibility centered on allowing the Union's concurrent sovereigns maximum discretion within those bounds while ensuring that neither government moved beyond them.

Taney's court struggled to maintain a clear line of separation between federal and state authority without placing undue limits on either. Its resolution of potential conflicts arising out of the Constitution's Commerce Clause revealed that effort. In *Gibbons v. Ogden* (1824), Marshall claimed federal supremacy over all commercial intercourse not "exclusively internal" to a particular state, but he refused to concede, either then or later, that this jurisdiction provided grounds for striking down all state legislation touching foreign or interstate commerce. Marshall wavered largely because those laws regulated a wide range of activity, such as quarantine and inspection procedures, policies for public health and morality, and internal transportation, as well as protected southern slave regimes. (The year before Marshall issued his ruling, in fact, one of his associates had held the Negro Seamen Act unconstitutional on Commerce Clause grounds.) The

Commerce Clause, Marshall argued, certainly allowed Congress to pass laws that would trump any state statutes to the contrary, but he equivocated on the issue of whether the clause prevented the states from passing such legislation. The Taney Court initially brought little clarity to the issue. In the midst of the sectional tension emerging from the Mexican War, the Taney Court confronted two major Commerce Clause cases, but the justices fragmented so deeply that none of them, despite wide areas of agreement on the outcome, spoke for the court.[22]

In 1851, the newly appointed Benjamin Robbins Curtis of Massachusetts, the only Whig placed on the court during this period, resolved the impasse in *Cooley v. Board of Wardens of the Port of Philadelphia*. Curtis's ruling allowed the federal and state governments to maintain their concurrent sovereign authority, as represented by their respective possession of the Commerce Clause and the police power, but also provided the court with grounds to strike down state legislation when its members perceived a conflict with federal law. *Cooley* involved a protest against the constitutionality of a state law requiring all ships, with a few exceptions, to hire pilots to take them into Philadelphia or to pay an amount equal to half of the pilot's fee into a fund designed to support "distressed and decayed pilots" and their families. The challenge rested in part on an assertion that the Commerce Clause stripped from the states all powers touching interstate and foreign intercourse. A "mere grant of such a power to Congress," Curtis responded, "did not imply a prohibition on the states to exercise the same power." Only when Congress actually exercised a power did it provide grounds for striking down state legislation. Until then, the states could pass police regulations suited to local needs.[23]

Cooley provided a coherent statement of the Taney Court's policy to allow both governments maximum flexibility within their spheres. Although he recognized ultimate federal supremacy over commerce, Curtis maintained that Congress had opted to leave to the states the regulation of pilots, as it had many other matters. The justices, although deeply fragmented on occasion, thus allowed the states to push their police powers to the limits of their constitutional boundaries. States could compel shipmasters to post bonds to cover the cost of sick, widowed, or orphaned immigrants likely to become dependent on the state for relief but could not levy a tax on healthy immigrants.[24] States could impose restrictive licensing requirements on persons who sold liquor in quantities small enough for human consumption but not on persons dealing in large amounts who were likely to be engaged in interstate commerce.[25] States held no authority to punish the makers of counterfeit currency, which fell exclusively in federal jurisdiction, but could punish people who passed bogus money, for that activity involved matters of confidence and trust among parties falling within the purview of the police power.[26] Finally, the states possessed the right to pursue improvement schemes as long as they exerted no direct impact on major interstate transit routes, such as the Ohio River.[27]

States may have skirted the edge of their authority, but the Taney Court compelled them to remain within their constitutional bounds. Although they raised the threshold concerning what activities they considered unconstitutional, justices exhibited little hesitancy in striking down state laws. Like its predecessor, the Taney Court jealously protected the scope and supremacy of the federal sphere. Building on Marshall's recognition of Congress's power to create a national bank, the court rejected state attempts to tax the salaries of federal officers or to attach the money that indebted officers handled in the course of their duties. Such powers could impede the enforcement of federal law, which, as the Constitution stated, was the supreme law of the land.[28] The Taney Court also denied state attempts to control the scope of its jurisdiction. When Mississippi attempted to protect its citizens from out-of-state creditors by passing a law designed to prevent removal of cases involving negotiable instruments into the federal courts, the justices disregarded Mississippi's measure. They also overturned state court rulings that unjustly barred litigants from moving their cases into federal jurisdiction. Taney's court also rebuffed a few state efforts to expand its jurisdiction. The scope of the court's authority represented a matter of exclusive federal cognizance, and the states possessed no right to influence it in any way.[29]

This concern for nature of the Union's structural integrity revealed itself in the justices' rigid enforcement of their court's jurisdiction. Congress, in the Judiciary Act of 1789, disallowed the full scope of judicial power limned out in the Constitution. Marshall and his associates chafed under these restrictions, and, when possible, they broadly construed the act's language. Congress, for example, gave the court the authority to review state court decisions when their rulings, for various reasons, conflicted with the Constitution, a federal law, or a treaty but only when the conflict appeared "on the face of the record." The Marshall Court interpreted that restriction to mean that the issue in question must merely emerge from the substance of the record, although the point need not be stated explicitly. Such a reading allowed the court to inquire into potential constitutional conflicts even if the litigants did not directly argue the question in the lower court. Marshall's court also exploited the Judiciary Act of 1802's grant of appellate jurisdiction over cases where the two members of a federal circuit court divided on a legal point. The justices, who sat on the circuit courts as well as the Supreme Court, considered the division of opinion a good mechanism for shepherding potentially important cases before the full court. When an interesting question emerged on circuit, the two members routinely split as a matter of form without troubling to develop conflicting opinions on the matter.[30]

Tancy Court members reacted against this relatively loose handling of jurisdictional matters. They required that the "face of the record" actually reveal an effort to raise the constitutional issues in the lower court and in 1842, 1847, 1851, 1856, 1857, and 1861 unanimously dismissed cases that failed to do so.[31] Under Taney, the court also tightened up procedures on pro forma divisions. Although they also saw the utility of this avenue, the justices demanded that cases coming up for review under certificates of division demonstrate an attempted consideration of the issues involved by the circuit court.[32] Taney's court in fact rigidly enforced all sections of the Judiciary Act and routinely threw out cases for want of jurisdiction.[33] Some of that rigidity probably emerged as a response to the court's continual failure to keep pace with its expanding docket, but Taney provided another rationale, apparently added as an afterthought to an opinion dismissing an obscure case. Through its stringent adherence to the Judiciary Act, he argued, the court protected the "general government in the free and uninterrupted exercise" of its constitutional powers and prevented the states from throwing "any serious impediment" in its way. At the same time, the court's rigidity ensured that the federal government remained confined to its legitimate sphere, acting only when doing so was both legal and appropriate.[34]

A concern for maintaining the perceived boundaries between the Union's concurrent sovereigns continually impinged on the justices' behavior, occasionally impelling them to rule opposite of the way they would have if there had been no jurisdictional bar. Both the law and most of the justices, for example, carried a predisposition toward masters, but a unanimous court in 1838 refused to review a Missouri Supreme Court decision recognizing the free status of a black woman because her owner had failed to raise any constitutional issues in the lower court. Four years later, the court's unanimous dismissal of a case in effect protected the vested rights of an established corporation (a ferry franchise) over a newly chartered competitor, even though the court usually went the other way when it had jurisdiction.[35] No case revealed the powerful hold jurisdictional considerations had on the justices better than their unanimous dismissal of an 1852 case involving a Mississippi law that they had twice ruled unconstitutional. Speaking for his brethren, Taney stated frankly that they would "undoubtedly" strike it down again if the court could take the case; however, the litigants in the state courts had for some reason failed to raise the issue of the act's constitutionality, and the court therefore could not take cognizance under the Judiciary Act. Despite federal repudiation of the statute, this Mississippi ruling stood.[36]

Taney's statement that the court, if given the opportunity, would again rule Mississippi's statute unconstitutional also revealed the justices' comfort with their institution's power of review. The court's Jacksonian members styled themselves as antielitist, democratic-minded justices who believed their institution functioned as a facilitator of self-rule, but these same men gave no indication that they perceived a conflict between their commitment to democracy (for white males) and their responsibility to strike down unconstitutional laws passed by popular majorities. Modern theorists of constitutional law have made a central concern of judges' tendency to place their courts between the people and their democratically elected legislatures—a phenomenon Alexander Bickel memorably termed the "countermajoritarian difficulty."[37] For contemporary jurisprudence, such concerns are warranted, but reading those concerns back into the nineteenth century is a misplaced effort. Antebellum jurists simply did not think about judicial authority in the same way as do modern lawyers, who must contend with the complex institutional and doctrinal legacies left by the Civil War, Reconstruction, Progressivism, and the New Deal as well as realist and postrealist styles of legal reasoning.

Rather than perceive judicial review as an affront to democracy, the court's Democratic members may have considered it an affirmation of popular sovereignty. The Taney Court's understanding of its powers of review resembled a theory of federalism that Bruce Ackerman has labeled "dualist democracy." Taney Court justices recognized two forms of popular will: legislation (a transient version of the people's will) and constitutions (supreme expressions of the people's voice). Court members likely would have agreed with Hamilton, who wrote in *The Federalist* that the review of statutes did not set the judiciary above legislatures; rather, "it only supposes that the power of the people is superior to both." Combined with the Jacksonian justices' ideological attraction to strict construction, the Constitution's countermajoritarian affirmation of popular sovereignty produced a jurisprudence that was at times highly insensitive to changing popular opinion. Most court members accepted this feature of court doctrine without apology, although their positions courted controversy, invited criticism, and sometimes—as in *Dred Scott*—revealed the justices to be decidedly out of step with partisan currents in both the North and the South. The Supreme Court's role in administering the boundaries of Union thus introduced institutional considerations that tempered Taney's and his colleagues' effort to force the people to govern themselves through their legislatures.[38]

Taney Court jurisprudence emerged out of the interplay between the justices' political persuasions and the institutional constraints limned out in the Constitution and established by Congress and the Marshall Court. This interplay ensured not only that the court's interpretive strategies shaped the Union's governmental structure but also that the Union's structure shaped the court's interpretive strategy. The justices' amoral stance toward legislatures made the court far less likely than its predecessors to strike down statutes passed by either the federal or state governments, giving both, especially the states, greater flexibility to pursue their policy goals. Domination of the court by men so inclined probably encouraged states to become more assertive against their own populations, against each other, and against the federal government. The justices by no means gave the states free rein and worked to keep them within their constitutional boundaries. That effort in fact infused their entire jurisprudence, for the court's deep concern for jurisdictional issues embodied its members' desire to keep both state and federal governments within their perceived limits, although that desire often generated a great deal of controversy among the justices.

Despite a handful of revealing aberrations, the Taney Court's political and institutional visions reinforced each other, prompting a few justices to maintain a regular critique of court doctrine. Unlike the Marshall Court, which largely concealed its disagreements from the public, the Taney Court regularly experienced open differences of opinion among its members. The court fragmented in about 20 percent of its decisions—four times so badly that no justice spoke officially for the majority.[39] These divisions usually emerged from an individual justice's discomfort with a particular application of a generally compelling jurisprudential framework. Such splits embodied little disagreement with the court's larger agenda, which the consistent, amoral, and antielitist enforcement of sovereign popular will through its concurrent expression in state and federal legislation sustained. The promotion of self-rule in this fashion, as the justices well knew, carried significant implications for power relations in American society, and the directions in which the court moved deeply disturbed three members, although for different reasons. According to their separate critiques, Taney Court jurisprudence insufficiently restrained state legislatures, slighted individual liberties, and even trampled states' rights.

Joseph Story of Massachusetts became the first and most powerful critic of Taney's court. A Supreme Court justice since 1812, a professor of law at Harvard College, and a publisher of numerous legal treatises, Story was a leading intellectual of the American bar. Sitting alongside Marshall, to whom he was intensely devoted, Story helped develop the Supreme Court's nationalist and elitist jurisprudence. The 1837 term, when Jackson's appointees first asserted their dominance, left Story disillusioned. Although generally inclined to suppress his disagreements with the court's official opinion, Story wrote three dissents responding to the new justices' elevation of the constitutional threshold. At the close of the term, Story wrote to Justice John McLean of Ohio, who would later emerge as an internal critic, expressing fear that court would never again strike down a law, "for the old constitutional Doctrines are fast fading away." Story located the source of this declension in the Union's intensifying democratization, "a change . . . from which I auger little good." Demagogues had swept the Union, and the Supreme Court under Taney had abdicated its duty to resist the tide of the public opinion. "Is not the *theory* of our govt.," he asked McLean in 1844, "a whole failure?" Fighting back urges to resign and often dissenting in silence, Story served, with "a pained heart and a subdued confidence," until shortly before his death in 1845.[40]

For all of his talk of being "the last of an old race of Judges," however, Story remained quite influential on the court. His nationalist constitutionalism fell flat among his brethren, but in equity and admiralty cases as well as in other areas of private law, Story remained a dominant figure. He also possessed a formidable legal mind and the ability to craft opinions challenging Taney's jurisprudence but couched in language that a majority of the justices found appealing. The court, for example, readily embraced the analytical framework Story elaborated in his *Conflict of Laws* (1833), a treatise on the law of nations. Its assertion that every nation "possesses an exclusive sovereignty and jurisdiction within its territory" provided Taney and his associates a compelling way to conceptualize interstate relations in a union of concurrent sovereigns. Story exploited this appeal and gathered majorities around positions that complicated the court's ability to protect slavery, a major policy goal of Taney and most of his associates.[41]

Following Story's death, McLean continued the nationalist critique of the court's rulings, although he gave more emphasis to individual rights. He rejected the vision of concurrent sovereignty that Curtis limned out in *Cooley*. Congress's power over commerce, McLean contended, remained exclusive, and the states possessed no power to legislate on the matter (although they could apply to Congress to do it for them). With hyperbole, McLean argued that Curtis's ruling would allow the states along the Mississippi to tax ships at will and those along the Atlantic to tax healthy immigrants. Giving the states such free rein threatened to produce precisely the same problems that the framers expected the Constitution to squelch. Like Story, McLean believed the government had fallen into the hands of "wire workers," "designing men," and "demagogues." Unlike Story, who viewed this apparent declension through an erudite blend of elitist republicanism and liberal Christian morality, McLean grounded his perspective in a democratized, evangelical Christianity. "A free government cannot be sustained except on a moral basis," he wrote to a correspondent in 1857. "I mean that basis of morality which is only found in the Bible, and maintained by Christian instrumentalities."[42]

McLean brought this vision into public life. "We seem to have forgotten," he wrote in an open letter to the Young Men's Christian Association, "that a Christian morality is the only basis of rational liberty—that it is to a nation the same as to the character of an individual." The court's amoral stance toward public law aggravated McLean, and he responded with demands that governments reveal their adherence to correct principles by according respect to individual rights. These demands most frequently emerged in his dissenting and concurring opinions in public law cases involving slavery, an institution that McLean fervently opposed. With less consistency, he extended his moral vision beyond racial issues. In 1837, he assailed state legislatures on moral grounds for chartering competing corporations, although he concurred with his brethren that the court possessed no authority to stop them. He also rejected the court's ruling that the crimes associated with counterfeit money (making and passing it) split between federal and state jurisdictions because the formulation placed criminals in a situation resembling double jeopardy.[43] McLean's jurisprudence therefore offered a significantly less oppressive alternative to that promoted by Taney and his associates. Unfortunately, McLean lacked Story's talent for legal argument and possessed little ability to manipulate legal sources in a way his colleagues found convincing. "McLean writes the opin.," Catron once told a correspondent, "& a scattering thing he'll make of it."[44]

The court's final consistent critic suffered a similar problem, although his lack of influence emerged from a rigid defense of states' rights. Peter V. Daniel became the Taney Court's only advocate of compact theory. After Van Buren appointed him to the court in 1841, Daniel increasingly expressed fears that federal power represented a threat to the states. Like McLean, Daniel wrote a separate opinion in *Cooley* rejecting the theory of concurrent sovereignty. The regulation of pilots, he argued, remained exclusively within the state police power. These laws, necessarily tied to local needs, functioned to protect the lives and property of people within the states in the same manner as mooring regulations or quarantine policies. "This is a power," he wrote, "which is deemed indispensable to the safety and existence of every community," and the states certainly had not ceded it to the federal government.[45]

By the time of *Cooley*, Daniel had developed a strong sense of sectional identity. Thanking his daughter for some fruit, he remarked, "I wonder when *The north* . . . would ever produce anything like these oranges! or indeed anything else that is good or decent." "Oh! That vile north!" he wrote while complaining about some cold weather, "it infects and spoils even that atmosphere we breathe!" While on circuit in Arkansas, he told his daughter that the mosquitoes and the "Buffalo Gnats"—"an insect so fierce & so insatiate, that it kills the horses & mules by bleeding them to death"—made the area unlivable. Yet he underscored his disgust with northerners: "Yankees flock hither as numerously almost as the insects & flourish and fatten amongst them."[46] His letters to Van Buren, with whom Daniel maintained a running correspondence until the mid-1840s, revealed a concern that the North was plotting against the South. These specters haunted Daniel on the bench as he railed (usually alone) against the court's intrusion into state policy making by asserting jurisdiction over corporations and inland waterways.[47] Like McLean, Daniel possessed only average legal abilities and lacked the talent to shape doctrine into a persuasive alternative that would attract his brethren. Although his opinions indicated that he was uncomfortable with the drift of Taney Court rulings, Daniel never effectively distanced himself from the court's jurisprudence. The best he could do was ignore it.

Most members shared Taney's jurisprudential persuasion. This agreement emerged in part because the partisan appointment process generated like-minded justices and in part because Taney, like Story, possessed an ability to employ legal sources in a way his colleagues found persuasive. Justices, of course, did not move in lockstep with each other; each had his own ideas concerning what positions the court should take. Some tended to uphold federal power; others, state power. All tended to shift depending on the issues involved in a particular case. Taney and Wayne, for example, generally agreed with each other on most questions but split occasionally when the court confronted cases pitting federal exclusivity against states' ability to control their internal populations. Wayne, whom Curtis labeled "a high-toned federalist," supported federal exclusivity, while Taney took the other side, a position that cast him among the dissenters more than once.[48] Court majorities consisted of loose coalitions that changed in composition as new members joined and as the justices faced different issues.

The Taney Court, despite frequent division, experienced little factionalism. Because Jackson's appointees replaced most of the Marshall Court's members in a very short period, only two members of the older court confronted a fully constituted Taney Court. Story's reservations about dissenting opinions pushed him to follow despairingly the new majority and look for more subtle ways to prevent it from damaging the Union. McLean and Daniel staked out and held more extreme positions in opposition to the court, but they received only occasional support from their brethren, who from time to time joined them in dissent and then quickly rejoined the majority. Two exceptions to this trend occurred in the 1840s and 1850s in cases involving slavery. In the 1840s, the justices gathered into identifiable coalitions that split over the degree to which the federal government should extend its support to slavery. Partly because the court experienced a high level of turnover in the 1840s, these divisions never hardened into factionalism, and the court effectively settled the matters in the early 1850s. In the mid-1850s, however, a faction of justices did develop. Two southern justices, notably the newly appointed and very talented John A. Campbell of Alabama, joined with Daniel and crusaded to compel the court to face the implications its rulings in corporate law (mainly) held for slavery. The southerners' faction fell apart immediately after the court issued its ruling in *Dred Scott*, and Daniel again stood alone. Such a rapid collapse raises the possibility that Taney subtly responded to his colleagues' concerns in the course of his opinion. At any rate, the court then fell back into the pattern that generally characterized its division: a loose cohesion among a majority of justices flanked by individual dissenters unwilling or unable to articulate persuasive alternatives to the court's overall vision.

The members of the Taney Court approached the cases that came before them through a style of reasoning that expressed both their partisan identity and the place of their institution within a union of concurrent sovereigns. The justices' literalist readings of statutes and the Constitution revealed a belief that judges should enforce to the letter legislatively expressed popular will. Indeed, they transformed their court into a facilitator of popular sovereignty, although the justices' amoral and antielitist stance helped sustain inequities within the Union's social order. Members of the Taney Court, however, fully understood that legislatively expressed popular will remained subordinate to the ultimate expression of popular will embodied in the federal Constitution. This understanding continually mediated their partisanship, even as their politics shaped their perceptions of the state structure. The configuration of partisan sentiment and constitutional constraint that emerged on the court generated recurring divisions among the justices, but only three members persistently challenged the Taney Court's jurisprudence. The loose cohesion surely represented a consequence of the appointment process's ability to pack the court with like-minded Democratic partisans, yet the process also contributed to cohesion by ensuring that those partisans were professional men of elite standing.

CHAPTER TWO

Imposing Self-Rule

Professionalism, Commerce, Social Order, and the Sources of Taney Court Jurisprudence

"NOTHING BUT THE MOST STRINGENT enforcement of discipline, and the most exact and perfect obedience to every rule and order emanating from a superior," Justice Robert C. Grier wrote in 1853, "can insure safety to life and property." Grier wrote these words when he found a railroad company liable for the injuries suffered by Elias H. Derby, who had jumped from one of the company's locomotives before it collided with another company train headed in the opposite direction. Although the company's agents had given an order to keep the track clear and the conductor of the second train admittedly acted contrary to instructions, Grier declared the railroad negligent. Steam locomotion's immense and potentially dangerous power required "the greatest possible care and diligence."[1] "Any negligence, in such cases," he added in words heavily emphasized in his manuscript, "may well deserve the epithet of 'gross.'"[2] Grier applied the unforgiving common law rule of *respondeat superior* (literally "let the master respond") against the company. The rule held employers responsible for an employee's wrongful act "whether the act be one of omission or commission, whether negligent, fraudulent, or deceitful." It even considered employers liable for actions undertaken without their knowledge or against their express disapproval. Responsibility for Derby's injuries thus lay with the company, because allowing "one who will not submit to control, and render implicit obedience to orders" to operate a locomotive, Grier wrote, "is itself an act of negligence."[3] Only the tight regulation and close supervision of employees would ensure public safety.

Grier's ruling captured both the status anxiety and professional sensibility that ran through much of the Taney Court's discourse, especially in its common-law rulings. In contrast to their antielitist stance in constitutional law, Taney Court members used their decisions in private law to coerce individuals to stand by obligations incurred in the market. This attitude, like other aspects of Taney Court jurisprudence, was strongly related to the justices' effort to make popular sovereignty an approximately accurate description of the social order. Such coercion forced litigants to govern themselves properly for sake of social stability. Yet Grier's invocation of *respondeat superior* underscored the form this judicial coercion would take. Despite the partisan process that brought them to office, Taney Court justices identified themselves as legal professionals and therefore couched their concerns in the turgid language of the common law. This commitment to common-law reasoning predisposed the justices to a rule-oriented jurisprudence that brought them cohesion and shaped their perception of every issue that came before them. The justices' concern for popular sovereignty only intensified their dedication to this style of reasoning, for the strict application of legal rules imposed a genuine expectation of self-government on potential litigants. Such impositions also countered the perceived corrosive impact that the attempted realization of self-rule—and especially the intense egalitarian impulses that came with it—exerted on elite authority. Indeed, a desire to promote social and national cohesion, through the strict and professional application of common-law rules and the coercive enforcement of market obligations, lay at the core of Taney Court jurisprudence.

By the 1830s, many of the Union's elite feared, the sovereign people had created for themselves a violent democracy of cupidity and licentiousness.[4] Americans drank heavily. They tore themselves apart in vicious brawls. They rioted with disturbing frequency. They risked everything they owned in rampant speculation. They moved about frequently and increasingly rejected the authority of established political and religious leaders. These concerns were by no means imaginary: historians have documented notable increases in drinking, rioting, migration, and commercial activity as well as ever more democratic forms of politics and Protestant Christianity.[5] Like elites throughout the Union, Taney Court justices responded to the decline of deference and the apparent disorder it generated by emphasizing in their decisions the importance of self-control. Court members, many of whom saw themselves as facilitators of popular sovereignty, carried an ideological predisposition for this stance. An expectation that individuals attend closely to their personal affairs in fact represented one of the burdens of membership in the sovereignty, and it gave people firsthand experience with the responsibilities of self-government. This predisposition intermingled with the justices' anxiety over the state of the social order and produced an emphasis on an individuated popular sovereignty that expressed simultaneously the court's partisan and cultural concerns. Few decisions revealed this process more clearly than the superficially unremarkable case of *Bend v. Hoyt* (1839), a decision involving a paltry sum and raising no overt questions of political or legal consequence. Historians have given no attention to *Bend*, but its mundane consideration of tariff collection procedures revealed the justices' participation in a widespread ideological effort to reconceptualize social relations in the wake of the rise of popular sovereignty and the decline of deference.

The case involved a dispute between merchant William B. Bend and Jesse Hoyt, a duty collector, over $127. In March 1837, Bend swore an oath and signed an affidavit affirming the accuracy of an invoice for eight boxes he had imported, and he posted the bond for the estimated duties. When the bond became payable (more than a year later), Bend informed Hoyt that the invoice contained an error. The document stated that the boxes contained cotton gloves, on which the tariff law imposed a duty, when they allegedly contained silk hose, on which there was no duty. Hoyt refused to remit the money. Bend sued him, and Hoyt defended his actions by arguing that the merchant had waited too long because he habitually tended to his business affairs sloppily. Speaking through Justice Joseph Story, the court ruled for Hoyt, emphasizing the importance of standing to one's obligations and chiding Bend for not governing himself correctly. Tariff law entitled one to repayment for money wrongfully collected, but Bend's lax business practices rendered difficult any determination of whether the mistake was innocent or an effort to defraud the government. Story refused such an inquiry and instead focused on the implications of Bend's invoice. Bend swore to the accuracy of that document, which, when placed under the collector's seal, became the final statement concerning the value of the goods listed as well as "the nature, quality, and description of the goods." Tariff law allowed Bend the option not to rely on the invoice; he could have demanded that Hoyt inspect the contents of the packages before assessing the duty. Bend decided not to do so, and he had to live with the consequences. Story thus implied that taking the oath and affixing the collector's seal created a contractual obligation to pay the duty on the goods listed in the invoice—whether correct or not.[6]

Story effortlessly equated the invoice with a contract, and his decision to do so illustrated the way in which the Taney Court sought to promote social order and cohesion in an increasingly democratic Union. Speaking with obvious hyperbole, Story maintained that a court policy allowing merchants to recalculate their duty payments long after the initial transaction threatened disaster. There "would be no certainty whatsoever" in the collection of duties, and merchants might practice "the grossest frauds and evasions . . . with perfect impunity."[7] Story here touched on a theme that emerged recurrently in Taney Court rulings: the court must force litigants to adhere to the letter of their obligations to prevent disorder. As the French aristocrat Alexis de Tocqueville noted, the spread of equality divided "Americans into a multitude of small private circles." No aristocracy or hierarchy of permanent status barriers defined the social order, so people connected themselves to one another "by many small and almost invisible threads, which are constantly broken and moved from place to place."[8]

Cohesion among these groupings emerged out of the mutual consent of the members. People lived where they wished, joined whatever church they wished, voted for whichever candidate they favored, and worked for the employer of their choice for a term of their choosing.[9] Indeed, the link between workers and employers pointed toward the cohesive force that connected this multitude of private circles: self-interest and commercial exchange. Such relationships linked people in distant regions who might have never seen each other as they made agreements rooted in mutual calculations of self-interest to buy and sell goods of all sorts. In this context, acts as banal as the sale of chickens, the production of cotton linens, the shipment of nails, or the consumption of tobacco, sugar, and whisky contained immense social significance.[10] Bend's invoice, despite its paltry monetary value, likewise contained such significance, for the cohesive force that countered the centrifugal tendencies inherent in rapid commercial and territorial expansion and rejection of established authority depended on people's adherence to the obligations they incurred to one another.

Taney Court members believed that this cohesive force needed protection, and they placed fidelity to one's commercial obligations in a high position in the hierarchy of legally enforceable values. Story's treatment of Bend illustrated the importance the justices placed on the issue. Whether an overpayment had actually occurred did not matter: Bend would pay what he had agreed to pay. Justice Smith Thompson of New York dissented because he thought the court handled the issue too rigidly. Story's argument discounted the possibility of mutual error or a mistake by the collector, and Thompson apparently considered that a major weakness of the opinion. His manuscript revealed that he elaborated the point after he had constructed his larger argument. Thompson's differences with Story and the majority, however, centered on a question of a particular application of a general principle and went no further. Thompson usually stood with the rest of the court and demanded a rigid adherence to one's obligations.[11]

Taney Court justices, like lawyers throughout the Union, maintained repeatedly that the legitimacy of a contractual obligation emerged as a consequence of an agreement between the parties (or a convergence of their wills) rather than out of the fairness of the exchange. "The value of a thing is what it will produce, and it admits of no precise standard," said Justice Peter V. Daniel, repeating a common refrain in 1854. "One man, in the disposal of his property, may sell it for less than another would." By setting aside obligations merely because one party struck a bad deal, he continued, the courts "would throw every thing into confusion, and set afloat the contracts of mankind." Without evidence of fraud, even contracts that "shock[ed] the conscience" bound the parties.[12] On these grounds, the court upheld in 1852 and 1856 agreements in which parties essentially contracted away all of their possessions. Both cases involved instances in which individuals signed documents conveying all of their property to religious communities. Those contracts, ruled Justices John McLean and John A. Campbell (both writing for unanimous courts), barred any claim the signers might subsequently make after they or their heirs left in disillusion.[13]

Few litigants before the Taney Court desired to pass all their property to a religious community, but many looked to the court to save them from obligations that had ceased to work in their favor. And the court repeatedly refused. In 1849, the court rejected a railroad corporation's claim—based on a plan McLean considered "legal and perhaps wise"—to land needed to ensure its economic survival because its agents had neglected to secure the approval of all the creditors to which the railroad had incurred obligations.[14] Likewise, the court refused in 1836 to grant an injunction on the sale of a house, used to secure a loan with usurious interest, because the litigant requesting that action made no offer to pay the principal along with legal interest.[15] The debtor, in other words, showed no willingness to stand to the obligations incurred when the loan was accepted. Of the hundreds of cases the Taney Court heard between 1836 and 1861, only two strayed from the general pattern, and those cases did not pass without significant dissent.[16]

These rulings, although they carried obvious economic implications, expressed themes concerning proper behavior in an increasingly democratic society that permeated elite discourse. Parties' inability to meet their obligations raised questions about their ability to manage their affairs—or in other words, about their ability effectively to govern themselves. These themes manifested themselves in the discourses propagated by the two dominant classes represented on the court, the southern planter class and the emerging middle class. Although these differing backgrounds at times contributed to divisions on the court, their common concerns also pulled the justices together. In starkly different ways, elite discourses linked patterns of self-control and self-government to the stability of social order. The southern planter elite lived in what historians have labeled an honor culture, which attached great significance to the duel.[17] Although it could culminate in violence, the affair of honor surrounding potential armed conflict constituted an elaborate ritual of controlled passions and language. If the parties involved followed the code, the antagonists never came into direct contact until they met on the field of honor. All communication took place through carefully worded letters in which parties clarified their positions and determined whether an exchange of shots was indeed necessary. This ritual of self-control mitigated against widespread violent conflicts among and within powerful southern families by confining potentially destabilizing incidents to ritualized maneuvers between the two men directly involved.[18] Southern members of the Taney Court considered themselves men of honor. Daniel had killed a man named John Seddon in an 1808 duel, and Chief Justice Roger B. Taney, when confronted about his revisions of his *Dred Scott* opinion, responded to Justice Benjamin Robbins Curtis with demands for clarification characteristic of an affair of honor.[19] The southern justices thus understood that a failure to govern themselves correctly carried potentially deadly consequences and that social stability depended on their self-control and that of the people who came before the court.

Other justices, like Story and McLean, would certainly have believed that dueling constituted a lack of self-control, but they viewed that ritual through the emerging sensibilities of the northern middle class. Antebellum northerners witnessed a surge in moralistic advice literature stressing to middle-class parents and children the importance of individual discipline and self-control in one's day-to-day routine. As members of the sovereignty, wrote one such writer, a person needed "the same independence of mind, the same personal virtues, and sense of personal responsibility, as he would if he were clothed in purple, and wearing a diadem."[20] People exhibited those traits through an exercise of self-control as displayed through adherence to an increasingly elaborate code of etiquette governing how they ate, what they bought, where they spat, even the manner in which they blew their noses. The code advocated tight strictures on sexual activity, including denunciations of adultery and masturbation. Control of these "bestial" impulses, said the advice writers, would produce a more harmonious society.[21]

We need not draw too hard a distinction between planter and middle-class patterns of self-control, for they intermingled—as the Daniel family's experiences illustrated. Although he often defined himself as a farmer, the Virginian Daniel had absorbed the values of the planters' honor culture. No evidence suggests that he engaged in an affair of honor after 1808, but he accepted that younger members of his family sometimes needed to do so. In 1851, for example, Daniel reported to his family that an affair involving his "hot headed" nephew, John Mason Daniel, had "been terminated amicably and without bloodshed" and "that the adjustment is honorable and satisfactory."[22] A few years later, after John Mason had engaged in another altercation, Daniel advised him to "be very cautious in furnishing any pretext to others for assaulting" him lest his enemies set him up and use his temper to damage his reputation.[23]

An emphasis on self-control as the proper means to preserve an honorable reputation also ran through the Daniels' letters of advice to Richard Barnes Gooch, an idle and apparently alcoholic son of a prominent Virginia family. In late 1847, Daniel encountered Gooch "in a state of extreme intoxication" and walked away, "with a sensation amounting almost to horror." He later wrote a series of letters calling on the young man to give up liquor. The old justice's concern centered on the damage such displays caused to Gooch's reputation and on the willingness of "the virtuous and respectable in the community" to "promote you in business." "Let me beg of you," Daniel said in another letter, "that immediately you will resolutely and absolutely break off every habit and association . . . which is calculated to destroy your usefulness and respectability, and to blast forever your own peace of mind." Gooch vowed to give up drinking, but the vow apparently proved hollow. Within a few months, Daniel's son, Peter Jr., wrote a letter to Gooch pleading with him to stop drinking.[24]

Unlike his father, Peter Jr. sounded less like a man of honor than a middle-class moralist concerned with Gooch's capacity for self-control. The young Daniel offered Gooch an escape from his fate in "two words. *Self-Confidence* and avoiding temptation." He advised his friend to "resolve *at once* . . . that from *this* day *forever* no drop of *ardent spirit, wine,* or *fermented liquors* shall pass your lips, except by the direction of your *regular* physician." Even one taste, Daniel cautioned, threatened to undermine Gooch's ability to control his drinking and thus his actions. Complete abstinence provided the only solution: "Utterly banish from your own home what is to you more dangerous than a magazine of gunpowder beneath your feet." The younger Daniel realized that he asked a lot of his friend. Yet compared to the "suffering mental and physical" and the "hopeless ruin temporal and eternal" that he now risked in a life bound to move "thro' every stage of loathsome degradation to a drunkard's grave," Daniel's request offered nothing less than salvation. "Self-control," a phrase that appeared four times in young Daniel's letter, would liberate Gooch from an "enslaving and ruinous passion" and restore him "to that position in society and to those bright prospects of success and happiness which your talents education and character would ensure you." [25] In the end, however, neither Peter Jr.'s advice to end Gooch's suffering nor the older Daniel's concern for his young friend's reputation saved him: Richard Gooch died just a few years later. The letters illustrate the way in which a motif of self-control and self-government ran throughout antebellum culture, and the discourse of the Taney Court justices, both publicly and privately, was no exception.

One of the reasons Story treated the merchant so harshly in *Bend v. Hoyt* was that the overpayment of the duties emerged from Bend's lax business practices. Bend's affidavit, Story noted, revealed "a habitually loose manner" of transacting business at the customhouse. Bend admitted in that document that the mistake resulted from "the ignorance of his own clerk," who could not determine what the packages contained. Despite the clerk's difficulties, Bend swore to the contents of the packages and made no effort to examine them either at that time or when Hoyt delivered them. Bend finally notified Hoyt of the mistake nine or ten months later, a period long enough to make an investigation into the matter exceedingly difficult. Bend's loss, Story wrote, if there had been one, "accrued from his negligence and inattention to duty"; therefore, he could not recover. In another addition to his manuscript, Justice Thompson maintained that Story's opinion represented bad policy because it either forced a merchant to suffer silently from innocent mistakes or compelled him to "attend in person to make his entries," thereby "entirely changing the course of business." [26] That, perhaps, was precisely the point of Story's argument. A judicial demand requiring those engaged in business to govern themselves more closely and thus render themselves more likely to perform the obligations they incurred could only strengthen the promise of social cohesion that the justices believed commercial interaction offered.

An expectation that litigants tightly govern themselves and their affairs appeared frequently in the Taney Court's rulings, and the justices exhibited little sympathy for those who handled their affairs laxly. In 1836, the court refused even to inquire into potential mistakes in a lower court's order to sell some land to cover the debts of the owner. Not only had the parties requesting review waited too long to appeal their case, Justice Henry Baldwin of Pennsylvania argued, but they had not shown any interest in the land they had lost until it began increasing in value.[27] Likewise, McLean scolded a man named Henry Brush who had bought a tract of land without checking to see if anyone else held claim to it. "The question is not," McLean wrote, "whether the defendant in fact saw any of the muniments of title, but whether he was not bound to see them." A purchaser could not "close his eyes to the facts" and disregard "the exercise of that diligence which the law imposes."[28] A few years later, Daniel rejected a town's assertion of ferry rights in its charter because it had exhibited laziness in their defense. Jeffersonville, Indiana, had "slept, long slept" on its rights and allowed a group of individuals to operate a ferry under a different grant for around forty years, making no complaint until those individuals sold their rights to an out-of-state buyer. In the face of such "a want of reasonable diligence, . . . this court must remain passive, and can do nothing."[29] Finally, Taney rejected in 1850 an attempt to collect a debt on a judgment because the creditor, his administrator, and that administrator's successor had waited forty-six years to do so. Despite a general knowledge of the debtor's whereabouts during this period, the creditors made no effort to collect because they thought him too poor to pay, although they showed no "due diligence" in determining his actual financial status.[30] In all of these cases, the losing parties neglected their duties and attempted to assert their legal rights at their luxury. The justices in turn revealed little patience for people who managed their affairs badly, leaving them to suffer the consequences of their actions.

Through *Bend v. Hoyt* and other rulings expressing similar concerns, the members of the Taney Court participated in a larger debate concerning issues of self-control in an increasingly democratic society. Beneath the dry, technical language and through their hyperbolic explanations saying why the court *must* rule one way and not another, court members addressed deeper ideological concerns and cultural anxieties. The blunt, persistent repetition of Taney Court rulings pushed individuals toward sovereignty by setting high expectations concerning the meeting of obligations and attention to duty. People who failed properly to handle such matters suffered the consequences. The justices' demand that potential litigants stand to their obligations and accompanying lack of interest in the substance of such arrangements pointed toward the justices' vision of social control. Social order depended on "almost invisible threads," as Tocqueville called them, that in turn rested on, as one middle-class moralist phrased it, the "principle of *mutual confidence*," or consensual transactions rooted in self-interest.[31] The stability of the social order thus rested on people's willingness to incur and to maintain obligations to one another.

Despite their use of their positions to further their partisan agendas and combat their status anxieties, Taney Court members were first and foremost members of a judicial institution, and they identified themselves most readily as lawyers and judges. The appointment process may have placed staunch partisan elites on the bench, but it usually elevated partisan elites with long histories of experience in private practice or on state or federal benches. Such backgrounds left appointees prepared for judicial work, which on the Supreme Court only rarely presented questions of political importance. Most cases involved commonplace matters concerning the transmission of property or the collection of debts, issues of interest to few but lawyers and their clients. Taney Court justices handled these issues capably and with little dissension, and they did so because they viewed themselves as lawyers rather than as party functionaries. As Justice John Catron wrote in 1857, "the Bench has been filling up for some years past with *lawyers*, and that of the best the circuits afforded." Even the deeply partisan Daniel could admire the "great professional research & ability" of "distinguished . . . Yankee lawyers," including his political enemy, Daniel Webster.[32] Their self-recognition implied a belief in an external and binding yet malleable body of legal rules that constrained the justices' decision making. That belief in turn served as a cohesive agent among the members and contributed to the rule-oriented character of the court's jurisprudence.

Their partisan identities aside, most justices believed that their appointments ended their involvement in elective politics, and they cultivated an image of aloofness from partisan struggle. Upon receiving his position, Curtis promptly told Webster, his political patron, that he could make no repayment for his appointment except "to do my duty to our Country in this great office with entire fidelity." Other justices privately offered advice on strategy and legislation but crafted a public image of judicial propriety. Taney, who admittedly discussed politics "freely and without reserve" among his friends, refrained from public comment "under the firm conviction that any other course would destroy the usefulness of the Supreme Court, and create the belief that it was a mere party body, acting for the interests of a party." There were exceptions. Both McLean and Justice Levi Woodbury of New Hampshire hoped that their seats on the court would constitute stepping-stones to the presidency. Yet McLean and Woodbury were also the only members who came to the court after a decade or more of moving from one political office to another, and they had relatively little legal experience. By contrast, the court's most talented members—Story, Taney, Curtis, and Campbell—had spent the majority of their precourt careers in private practice. Among the court's members, in fact, legal ability served as a foundation for mutual respect and potential influence.[33]

Taney Court justices' proud self-identification as lawyers underscored their commitment to work within the interpretive constraints established by the emerging legal profession. Those constraints developed within an inherited framework that Roscoe Pound long ago termed the "taught legal tradition," a centuries-old pattern of thinking about rules hammered into practitioners' minds in the course of their training. The common law, a nonstatutory body of regulations originating in twelfth-century England and passed from generation to generation through judicial decisions, pleading forms, and the occasional treatise, comprised the substance of this tradition. As Peter Karsten has demonstrated, the taught legal tradition exerted a powerful hold on antebellum judges' thinking. English courts had enforced at least since the sixteenth century many of the same rules that nineteenth-century American courts did.[34] When the court refused in 1853 to set aside a contract on the grounds of inadequate consideration, for example, Daniel employed language strikingly similar to that used by the English justice Lord Baron Eyre nearly seventy years earlier. Daniel never indicated that he was quoting, and Eyre himself merely restated a centuries-old common-law doctrine.[35]

Taney Court justices worked as comfortably with these ancient and "unwritten" rules as with they did with statutes. Even so, the history of antebellum legal development hardly represented a story of continuity with medieval English law. Particular doctrines may have changed little, but the context in which judges applied them transformed significantly. Appellate courts, like the Supreme Court, were new creations of postrevolutionary governments, and these forums ensured that trial courts applied the law correctly, repeatedly setting aside jury verdicts because the lower court judge provided inaccurate instructions. Such procedures gave the law's application a harsher edge because juries frequently favored communal standards of fairness and equity over doctrinal fidelity, but the new system reined them in.[36]

The taught common-law tradition, moreover, underwent both a rediscovery and a reinvention during the antebellum period. Starting roughly around 1815, legal commentators worked diligently to make the common law more accessible to average practitioners by providing overviews of various doctrinal subjects in legal treatises and by promoting the publication of appellate court decisions. This project proved remarkably fruitful. By 1840, lawyers could learn about doctrine and precedent through more than 650 law books, far more than the mere handful of such works available three decades earlier. Treatise writers also advocated a new way of thinking about law. Commentators followed William Blackstone and presented the common law as a science, an organized body of rational knowledge whose coherent structures would reveal themselves under rigorous analysis. Freeing themselves from the procedural concerns that left practitioners mired in what seemed a mess of disaggregated technicalities, treatise writers discovered and expounded (or invented and shaped) the underlying principles on which the social order (or their vision of it) rested.[37]

The Supreme Court participated fully in these developments. Under Marshall and Story, the court established itself as a practitioner of the science of law. The Marshall Court announced its rulings with sweeping statements of principle designed to guide the future of the court in particular and of the republic in general. Its decisions took on a teaching function, and the justices used the perceived excesses of state legislatures as opportunities to educate the populace on the legal principles that sustained a republican union.[38] The Taney Court's participation in these developments proved more muted. Its members rejected the elitist role of educator and, like the profession generally, drew on the growing number of law books only to ground themselves in doctrine and precedent.[39] With the exception of Story, Taney and his associates acted like mere legal practitioners, not legal scientists. Instead of expounding underlying principles, the Taney Court focused on discovering the rules applicable in a particular case and rendering a decision. Their discussions often exhibited tedious and narrow investigations into obscure rules to which the justices considered themselves bound.

Taney Court members felt the weight of precedent and doctrine constantly impinging on them. In its entire history, the Taney Court overturned none of its own and only two Marshall Court rulings, doing so only after Congress passed statutes authorizing such action.[40] The court even unanimously followed Marshall's ruling that the federal government oversee the removal of Indians despite some Taney Court members' previous criticism of that decision.[41] With the exception of Story and possibly Daniel, no justice perceived these constraints arising out of some metaphysical force—the law—that compelled judges to rule in a particular fashion. A quite pedestrian reason lay behind their consistency. Their court's influence depended on its ability to attract and maintain a constituency of lawyers that would advise clients to pursue their interest in the federal courts instead of through a competing state forum (if available) or by forgoing litigation altogether. Achievement of that goal came through adherence to precedent so that its lawyer-constituents could predict potential outcomes of their clients' suits and advise them accordingly. Grier captured this dynamic as he explained why the court so regularly dismissed suits for want of jurisdiction. "Our decisions may fail to command respect, unless we carefully confine ourselves within the bounds prescribed for us by the constitution and laws."[42]

Precedent did not imprison the justices; they understood as well as anyone that courts needed to shape doctrine to meet perceived social needs. The Taney Court formed in the midst of an era that legal historians consider a period of transformation and Americanization. Antebellum judges openly shaped the law in ways that apparently furthered the interests of groups they favored over those they did not. Judges at times merely adopted already established doctrines to meet these ends, although some wrote in a grand style that created an impression of originality. Other cases required real innovation.[43] Legal change constituted an expected feature of the judicial landscape, as Justice Samuel Nelson of New York candidly admitted as he recognized Missouri's abrupt shift in its handling of slave law in *Dred Scott*. "What court has not changed its opinions? What judge has not changed his?"[44] When they could, Taney Court justices shaped their rulings to favor "the people" over subordinate racial groups and—before the 1850s at least—corporations but placed a high priority on maintaining an image of consistency. The court occasionally made decisive shifts in doctrine, but the opinion invariably demonstrated (to a majority's satisfaction) that any change represented a logical extension of settled principles.

A justice's ability to push a policy agenda through the court hinged on his capacity to embed innovative reasoning in interpretations that incorporated a majority of his colleagues' understandings of precedent and statutory law. Story, as later chapters will demonstrate, could push the court in nationalist and even antislavery directions precisely because he could dazzle enough of his brethren by couching his goals in language that played to their concerns for popular sovereignty and police power. Taney, although with far less elegance, employed the same strategies to provide a counterweight to Story during his life and to dominate the court thereafter. McLean and Daniel's relative lack of influence stemmed from their inability effectively to manipulate precedent. Both of these justices, especially Daniel, generally ignored or dismissed precedents with which they did not agree, and few of their colleagues attempted to respond to their running critiques. Taney, however, did respond when Campbell joined Daniel's states' rights crusade, for the new justice squarely confronted court rulings and found them wanting. Campbell's presence in a developing faction could have produced a shift in the court's decisions concerning corporations, but Taney apparently appeased Campbell in *Dred Scott*. Henry David Thoreau therefore did not stray far from the mark when he wrote that the "lawyer's truth is not Truth, but consistency or a consistent expediency."[45]

Despite precedent's relative flexibility, Taney Court justices believed themselves bound by the rules they discovered in the course of their duties. Members repeatedly found conventions that impelled them to rule in ways that they otherwise might not have. In *Luther v. Borden*, for example, the court turned away the proponents of the Dorr government in large part because, if the court held consistently to its interpretations of the relevant state and federal laws, Dorr would certainly lose. The court depended heavily on the rules its members discovered because these regulations provided a source of cohesion among the justices. The most bitterly fragmented decisions—the *License Cases*, the *Passenger Cases*, and to a lesser extent the territorial question in *Dred Scott*—occurred mainly because the cases presented very few or even no hard-and-fast rules to which the justices could lay hold. The justices' political biases—notably their deference to legislatures—not only made them reluctant to reason from general principles but rendered them manifestly inept at doing so. An assumption that a knowable law existed somewhere beyond the justices' personal agendas counteracted the politically influenced fragmentation and allowed the court to achieve consensus and frequently unanimity.

Taney Court members reached that consensus mainly in private, common-law cases arising through diversity jurisdiction. Diversity cases enabled citizens of different states to litigate in a federal court rather than in a state tribunal. In the *Federalist*, Alexander Hamilton stressed that such jurisdiction maintained interstate harmony because courts without "local attachments" would not favor citizens of one state over another. McLean echoed that sentiment more than fifty years later: "One great object in the establishment of the Courts of the United States and regulating their jurisdiction was, to have a tribunal in each state, presumed to be free from local influence; and to which all who were non-residents or aliens might resort for legal redress."[46] These cases contributed significantly to the court's workload and kept the docket populated with mundane litigation concerning property and indebtedness. Taney Court justices rigidly enforced the boundaries of the court's diversity jurisdiction, routinely dismissing cases where parties failed to state their citizenship or to sue for the minimum amount required by statute. Beyond these nominal thresholds, however, the court became rather lax, and the justices never seriously grappled with the question of which persons could claim citizenship until the 1850s. Such laxity made diversity jurisdiction highly accessible to litigants, and both Morton Horwitz and Tony Freyer have demonstrated that business interests frequently resorted to the federal courts to escape the uncertainty engendered by a plurality of state laws. Even so, the court's laxity may have been less about promoting economic interests than about the justices' effort to facilitate national cohesion and impose order on a union perceived to be increasingly chaotic. Indeed, the body of common-law doctrine to which diversity cases gave access enabled the justices to use their position to coerce individuals to act as sovereigns.[47]

The Taney Court's patterns of legal reasoning expressed both the justices' sense of themselves as legal professionals and their desire to constrain the intense egalitarian impulses that accompanied the shift toward popular sovereignty. Members of the court, united by the taught legal tradition and their anxiety over the erosion of elite authority and general social chaos, joined together and encouraged social and national cohesion by coercing individuals to stand by the obligations they incurred to one another in the market. Yet the court's support for commerce, through an imposition of a legal regime of individuated self-rule, extended beyond a desire to promote entrepreneurial interests. An insistence on the proper governance of oneself affirmed the justices' commitment to popular sovereignty's realization yet simultaneously contained the egalitarian impulses that the commitment stimulated. This convergence of the justices' professional identity, fidelity to self-rule, and elitism gave their jurisprudence an intensely rule-oriented character. Taney Court jurisprudence thus developed from a variety of sources, including an antielitist partisan identity and a manifestly elitist configuration of status and class sensibilities. These elements pulled the justices in different directions. One demanded the court take an amoral stance that gave legislatures free rein within the perceived bounds of the Union's state structure. The other impelled the court to use its authority to force individuals properly to govern themselves. Taney Court justices thus had potentially contradictory concerns but established procedural mechanisms that prevented conflict in the 1842 case of *Swift v. Tyson*. Their solution, however, would eventually undermine their efforts to evade the troublesome issues raised by *Dred Scott*.

CHAPTER THREE

Evidence of Law

Popular Sovereignty and Judicial Authority in Swift v. Tyson

IN 1856, MONTGOMERY BLAIR, an attorney for Dred Scott and his family, struck at a weakness that the Taney Court's aggressive pursuit of differing agendas in its common-law and constitutional cases had created. Although the Missouri Supreme Court had found the Scott family to be enslaved despite its members' travels in free territory, Blair contended that the U.S. Supreme Court worked under no obligation to follow the Missouri ruling. Missouri's decision, he wrote, "so far from being conclusive . . . is of no weight at all, beyond what is due to the research, reason and authority which the opinion . . . displays or which may be due to the court which pronounces it." Blair's argument took advantage of recent developments in the Taney Court's handling of diversity jurisdiction, the pathway through which *Dred Scott* proceeded. Section 34 of the Judiciary Act of 1789 governed such cases, and it required the federal courts to follow "the laws of the several states . . . as rules of decision in trials at common law" unless the Constitution, a federal law, or a treaty stated otherwise. Over the course of the 1840s and 1850s, however, the Taney Court repeatedly claimed a right to ignore state court decisions, and its members—against the probable intent of the first Congress—increasingly refused to define such rulings as "law" within the meaning of the act. By the time *Dred Scott* came before the justices, Blair could remind them that while they could "respectfully consider the decisions of the State court," they remained free to "decide such questions according to their own judgment of the law."[1]

Blair's argument built on *Swift v. Tyson* (1842), which Morton Horwitz has identified as "one of the most interesting and puzzling developments in all of American legal history."[2] *Swift* inaugurated a quiet but ultimately fundamental transformation in the justices' perception of diversity jurisdiction. After 1842, the Taney Court became far less deferential to state policy in diversity cases than it was in other jurisdictional areas, and those decisions would ultimately undermine the Taney Court's effort to evade the controversial issues raised in *Dred Scott*.[3] *Swift* embodied a nationalist vision of judicial authority that, by the mid-1850s, carried potential for antislavery litigation strategy—as the Scott family's lawyers made clear. Despite these implications, no member of the Taney Court ever attacked *Swift*. Instead, the justices innovated in other doctrinal areas to compensate for any weakness the decision created. Their esteem for *Swift* had complex origins, for the opinion's author, Joseph Story, found a way to argue for expanded judicial authority while playing to his colleagues' support for commerce and their vision of the Union as a collection of concurrent sovereigns. His contention that state court decisions did not constitute law also permitted his colleagues to impose their individuated vision of popular sovereignty without styling themselves as an elite that usurped the legislatures' lawmaking authority. Finally, Story delivered his opinion during a brief moment of judicial consensus about slavery's place within the Union, and this agreement may have muted *Swift*'s antislavery implications. All of these factors converged in 1842 to create a ruling with immense ideological and institutional resonance that proved so compelling that the justices apparently found it irresistible.

As he argued on behalf of Dred Scott, Blair took full advantage of Supreme Court doctrine that had developed in the wake of *Swift*. His strategy, which the dissenting justices adopted, undercut the majority's efforts to evade *Dred Scott*'s controversial issues and pushed it toward the ruling that made the Taney Court infamous. Yet the doctrines that Blair employed for antislavery purposes enjoyed a wide acceptance among the justices that contributed to their perception that *Dred Scott* could not be responsibly evaded. The stance toward state judicial decisions that shaped the court's behavior in 1857 began taking form as early as 1842, when the justices unanimously supported Story's invention of a federal common law of commerce in *Swift*. This case, which was a very important ruling in its own right, turned on a technical question of commercial law that was far removed from the issues in *Dred Scott*. Even so, the court's resolution of that question carried implications for the justices' perceptions of their court's authority in diversity jurisdiction that structured decisively the contours of their behavior.

Swift emerged out of the complex exchange of negotiable instruments that formed a large portion of interstate business transactions in the antebellum United States. A *negotiable instrument* was a written and unconditional promise to pay a certain sum to another person at some point in the future (exactly when and to whom were specified in the documents). In a Union suffering from a chronic shortage of hard money, these documents circulated like cash, and businesspeople regularly exchanged the instruments in the course of their dealings. A note created by party A and given to party B in one transaction would often pass, upon endorsement, to party C in the course of another transaction. Party C could then either demand that party A pay the sum specified in the note or sign it over to party D in yet another transaction. Moreover, if A refused payment (because of bankruptcy or for another reason) C could then demand that B satisfy the obligation. These documents, in theory at least, could circulate indefinitely as the equivalent of cash. In practice, courts differed starkly over precisely which documents were in fact negotiable and over the proper conditions under which a negotiable instrument could legitimately pass from one party to another.[4]

Swift involved the question of whether a preexisting debt was valid consideration to make one a bona fide holder of a negotiable instrument. John Swift sued on a promissory note created by Nathaniel Norton and endorsed by George Tyson. The note had originated as part of a speculative—and fraudulent—scheme in which Norton and his partner, Jairus Keith, sold land in a remote part of Maine to a New York corporation, of which Tyson was a member. Norton and Keith presented themselves as the owners of this property, but they were not. A representative of the land's actual owner, identified in court records only as "a European," had offered the two speculators a chance to purchase the land, but they could not afford it. Instead of passing on the deal, however, Norton and Keith went to New York, presented themselves as the owners of the property, and sold a portion of it to members of the corporation. They then funneled the money to the actual owner's representative to secure title to the land that they were already selling.[5] Norton and Keith's plan fell apart during the Panic of 1837. Nationally, the supply of money decreased by around one-third, constricting the access to credit vital to the speculators' venture and rendering them insolvent.[6] As the scheme collapsed, creditors harassed Norton, especially since he refused to pay most of them. He did pay Swift, the cashier of a Maine bank, who for some reason covered one of Norton's debts out of his own pocket. Swift had first tried to ignore the debt, which rested on a note drawing on Norton's (empty) account at Swift's bank, but paid when the creditor became insistent. Norton then gave Swift a note endorsed by Tyson in exchange for forgiveness of the debt. Tyson refused payment, claiming that Swift was not a bona fide holder of the note (whether a preexisting debt constituted a valuable consideration sufficient to make the exchange valid was at least questionable). So Swift sued Tyson in diversity.[7]

If the court had adhered to New York's case law, which, because the note was payable in that state, presumably governed the suit, Tyson might have had a case. Between 1820 and 1840, New York's highest courts had ruled six times on the question, although they had done so inconsistently, ruling three times in each direction.[8] The problem was that treating antecedent debts as consideration sufficient to create a bona fide holder of a negotiable instrument theoretically encouraged fraud. It allowed debtors to collude with their creditors and pass off their debts to a more solvent third party (quite possibly the arrangement between Swift and Norton).[9] Tyson might have won under New York law, but Story, with the unanimous support of the court, refused to follow those decisions. After noting the unsettled state of the case law, Story maintained that even if New York had settled the question, the federal courts worked under no obligation to follow the decisions. A court's decisions, Story wrote, "are, at most, only evidence of what the laws are, and are not, of themselves, laws." Although it would adhere to state statutes and certain local customs, the court in cases dealing with commercial questions sought the basis for its rulings "not in the decisions of the local tribunals, but in the general principles and doctrines of commercial jurisprudence." Federal courts, in other words, would follow a body of rules growing out of merchant custom. Under these principles, Story wrote, "we have no hesitation in saying, that a pre-existing debt does constitute a valuable consideration . . . as applicable to negotiable instruments."[10]

With *Swift*, the Supreme Court invented a federal common law of commerce that held sway in the federal courts for nearly a century, and the members of the Taney Court unanimously participated in its creation. When he overturned *Swift* in 1938, Justice Louis Brandeis regarded Story's ruling as an unconstitutional assertion of federal authority that "invaded" rights properly reserved to the states.[11] Brandeis misread *Swift* but accurately described rulings that followed in its wake. By the mid-1850s, Taney Court justices ignored not only state judicial rulings on *Swift*'s choice-of-law grounds but also the occasional state statute. Such a stance lacked sympathy for states' rights and carried implications for antislavery litigation strategy, as Blair's *Dred Scott* brief revealed. Taney Court members showed a surprising lack of concern about these aspects of the *Swift* doctrine. Individual justices, of course, differed at times over particular applications of the decision, but they all agreed that a resort to federal common law over state decisions and occasional statutes represented a legitimate exercise of the court's authority. Even Daniel, the justice most concerned about potential threats to states' rights, wrote opinions employing *Swift*'s principles, and he once instructed a lower federal court to ignore a state statute.[12] The relative placidity over the court's behavior in diversity jurisdiction contrasted sharply with the tense exchanges taking place almost simultaneously over the scope of the Commerce Clause, admiralty jurisdiction, and corporate law. In all of these areas, the justices remained sensitive to the implications of their rulings for both states' rights and slavery.[13] Yet the developing *Swift* doctrine generated no such conflict. Even in *Dred Scott*, when Blair and the dissenters pushed *Swift* in antislavery directions, no justice attacked it. Indeed, the justices followed the ruling and allowed other legal doctrines, notably those concerning citizenship, to contain *Swift*'s potentially dangerous implications. The court's relative cohesion, given the ramifications of federal common law that were certainly obvious to the justices by the time *Dred Scott* reached them, was unusual, and the lack of conflict came about because the *Swift* doctrine fused the disparate elements of Taney Court jurisprudence into a fundamental expression of their judicial identity.

Swift remains a difficult case to explain. Despite its unquestionable importance to post–Civil War legal development, the decision apparently ran counter to the general tenor of the Taney Court's jurisprudence. Even more puzzling was the absence of any challenge to the ruling's nationalist implications, especially since the justices were often intensely sensitive to matters of states' rights. Scholars have produced powerful arguments centering either on *Swift*'s implications for commerce or on its relation to antebellum jurisprudential assumptions. Most studies, however, offer little explanation as to why no justice attacked *Swift* for its nationalist and even potentially antislavery implications, and they neglect *Swift*'s relationship to *Dred Scott*. An answer to these questions rests in the manner by which *Swift* structured the justices' perception of the nature of their authority in diversity jurisdiction. *Swift*'s power and subsequent importance lay in its fusion of the central concerns of Taney Court jurisprudence. Story's ruling expressed simultaneously the amoral and antielitist stance toward collective self-rule and the commercially oriented effort to impose a regime of individuated popular sovereignty on the Union, and it did so in a manner that placed *Swift* beyond reproach among the justices.[14]

Much of *Swift*'s resonance surely stemmed, as both Horwitz and Tony Freyer have argued, from the court's desire to facilitate commerce. Story explicitly justified the policy of his negotiability ruling in those terms. The "benefit and convenience of the commercial world," he wrote, depended on giving "as wide an extent as practicable to the credit and circulation of negotiable paper." Recognizing bona fide purchaser status for creditors who forgave a preexisting debt as consideration allowed debtors to stand to their obligations by treating their commercial paper as the equivalent of cash. A contrary policy could force debtors to sell their notes to third parties, "often at a ruinous discount," and perhaps push them into insolvency or bankruptcy, where their obligations would never be satisfactorily met.[15] Members of the court may have felt additional pressure to follow Story's reading of section 34 of the Judiciary Act of 1789. Some businesses already worked on the assumption that preexisting debts constituted valuable consideration for bona fide purchaser status. Approximately half of all banking transactions, contended Story—who was a banker in addition to his other duties—involved the creation of new notes designed to provide security for old debts. Lower federal courts, especially in Story's circuit, had long favored expanded negotiability and drawn on general principles of commercial law. A Supreme Court decision that upset these practices could thus be very inconvenient. The potential consequences of such a ruling, especially in the midst of the severe depression that followed the Panic of 1837, must have weighed heavily in the justices' considerations. Indeed, the court's decision to follow the trend toward expanded negotiability may have contributed to the development of antebellum credit markets that, according to recent work in economic history, were well integrated relative to those that existed in the decades after the Civil War.[16]

Swift thus represented a judicial contribution toward greater economic development, but we need not read the decision as merely an effort to release entrepreneurial energy or to bolster bourgeois social relations. Taney Court justices understood the facilitation of commerce as a way to reinforce their commitment to democratic governance. Their insistence that people stand to obligations incurred in the market represented both a positive affirmation of the values members associated with popular sovereignty and a vision of individuated self-rule invoked to counter egalitarian challenges to the social order. Even this caveat, however, explains only a portion of *Swift*'s resonance, for the decision enabled the court to reconcile the commercially oriented, morally tinged aspects of the court's private law rulings with the fundamentally amoral and antielitist features of its public law jurisprudence. The fusion of these elements accounted for *Swift*'s uncontested standing among members of the Taney Court, and Story achieved that fusion even as he furthered his personal legal agenda.

In *Swift*, Story moved closer toward his ultimate goal of placing federal jurisprudence on a common-law foundation. Story had repeatedly asserted on circuit that the federal courts rightfully possessed a general common-law authority over both criminal and commercial matters.[17] His brethren on the Marshall Court, however, simply ignored his most powerful statements on the issue.[18] With the exception of certain commercial questions and areas specially provided for by statute, the Marshall Court adhered to state law, including judicial decisions.[19] "There can be no common law of the United States," John McLean argued as late as 1834. "There is no principle which pervades the union and has the authority of law, that is not embodied in the constitution or laws of the union."[20] Eight years later, McLean and his brethren recognized a federal common law of commerce, an innovation that constituted a subtle but radical shift in the court's thinking. Scholars have correctly noted that state and federal courts had long recognized the existence of extraterritorial rules governing commercial transactions. Commercial law involved obligations that transcended the boundaries of particular sovereignties and implicated questions of international law. For guidance on these matters, American courts turned to the law of nations, of which the commercial law was a part.[21] The Marshall Court often resorted without comment to the general commercial law.[22] Even so, no disembodied collection of rules pervaded the entire Union. A court's access to the law of nations often rested on whether the legislature of a relevant jurisdiction had incorporated those rules into its law.

An early federal case, *United States v. Henfield* (1793), provided a good example of this process. Gideon Henfield, an American citizen who had taken possession of a British ship while working as a prize master on a French vessel, stood trial for various offenses against treaties and the law of nations. (The jury would acquit him.) Although the case was argued in federal court, the rules of decision derived ultimately from Pennsylvania law. In their arguments concerning the law of nations, the prosecutors relied on a Pennsylvania case that held, rather unceremoniously, that the law of nations comprised part of state law. When Justice James Wilson of Pennsylvania invoked those extraterritorial laws, he did so through state law, as required by the Judiciary Act.[23] Half a century later, in *Smyth v. Strader* (1846), McLean explicitly followed the merchant law as it had been incorporated by Alabama's statutes and court decisions.[24] Wilson and McLean's use of extralocal law differed fundamentally from Story's. Whereas the former traced those principles back to state law, Story treated them as a coherent body of rules pervading the Union. He even went so far as to claim that the New York court's decision to ground its negotiability rulings in the commercial law, as opposed to statute or certain local customs, justified the federal courts' departure from their decisions. Such decisions, after all, were not law but "only evidence of what the laws are."[25] Juxtaposing *Henfield* and *Smyth* against *Swift* can prove misleading, since the distinction between the two positions was subtle and easily elided in practice. Few cases using the law of nations as rules of decision hinged on whether the court regarded them as free-floating regulations pervading the Union or a body of rules incorporated into a particular state's common law. In practical terms, the question mattered little, and both positions often yielded precisely the same results. A lack of rigorous thought about the distinction between these two positions may, among other things, account for the unanimous support Story enjoyed in *Swift*, but his colleagues undoubtedly saw the ideological appeal of his formulation as well.

Swift's interpretation of section 34 in fact reinforced the vision of judicial authority that ran throughout the court's jurisprudence. In the United States, law constituted the will of the people, but that will became knowable to the court only through its transcendent embodiment in constitutional law or its transient expression in statute form. Either way, judicial decisions, as Story said, were not law but were merely evidence of law. Treating court rulings as law in effect endowed courts with a legislative authority and conferred on judges the elite role of guiding and ruling the social order. The Taney Court's members consciously evaded that role in the realm of public law even as they pursued a commercially oriented, private law agenda designed to promote and control the spread of popular sovereignty at an individuated level. The court had fused these stances before. In *Bank of Augusta v. Earle* (1839), the court recognized an interstate law of nations that facilitated commercial activity in a manner allowing the justices to circumvent the need to extrapolate Alabama law from the state's ambiguous banking policies. If it had done otherwise, Taney implicitly argued, the court would have usurped the legislative function.[26] With *Swift*, the justices announced that they regarded the institutions of their state counterparts in the same manner as they perceived their own court: as antielitist forums that discovered but did not make law. Law emanated only from the will of the people, as embodied in constitutions and legislative enactments, and the decisions of no high court could claim a similar status, especially when none of the court members, with the exception of those in Mississippi, stood for popular election.[27] Story's invocation of a federal common law of commerce, which his Marshall Court brethren had flatly rejected, proved immensely appealing to the Taney Court justices despite its nationalist implications. A challenge to Story's interpretation of section 34 indeed required a challenge and perhaps a shattering of his colleagues' conception of judicial authority. *Swift* must have struck them as irresistible.

The logic of *Swift*, moreover, invited the Supreme Court's state counterparts to treat its rulings in the same way it treated theirs. According to Horwitz, the court's resort to the general law anticipated the legal formalism and desire for uniformity that became increasingly influential among legal intellectuals around midcentury. The general law represented a metaphysical body of rules standing above policy concerns, which, if correctly applied, would create a unified, national commercial law.[28] Horwitz's emphasis on uniformity is misplaced. *Swift* became a foundational case in the thinking of late-nineteenth-century legal intellectuals seeking a unified body of rules that stood above crass policy concerns, but a wide range of scholars concede that the case itself brought little uniformity.[29] Taney Court justices proved exceedingly reticent to strike down state laws that came before it in diversity jurisdiction; indeed, they generally used the *Swift* doctrine as grounds to ignore those state laws.[30] The court showed little desire to impose its will on state courts except by the force of persuasive reasoning or through the convergence of judicial interests. State courts thus reached their own conclusions concerning the correct interpretation of the general law. In 1843, for example, New York's high court flatly rejected *Swift*'s negotiability ruling.[31] The resulting cacophony among court decisions reinforced the Taney Court's antielitist vision of its authority. Treating commercial decisions as evidence of law meant that justices could rule as they saw fit without declaring state policy because their decisions, from the states' standpoint, likewise constituted mere evidence of law.

Even as it underscored the antielitist character of the court's jurisprudence, however, *Swift* bolstered the justices' imposition on the Union of a regime of individuated popular sovereignty. Although the decision brought little uniformity to the state courts, the doctrine did provide a foundation for uniformity within the federal courts. If federal judges worked under the assumption that state judicial decisions constituted law, which they were bound to apply, then federal law could differ starkly in every circuit. State laws, moreover, often favored local debtors over out-of-state creditors and thus offered protection that could potentially frustrate the Taney Court's private law agenda.[32] *Swift* circumvented these problems; its interpretation of section 34 gave the justices free rein to pursue their agenda of promoting popular sovereignty and social cohesion through the coercive enforcement of market obligations. They could now impose their vision uniformly throughout their jurisdiction and ensure that all those with whom the justices came in contact, either directly or indirectly, properly conducted themselves, their affairs, and their subordinates. The intensification of the court's demand for a more intense regimen of self-rule occasioned by *Swift* probably satisfied the justices on a professional level as well. Mark Tushnet has argued that in *Swift* the justices seized the functions inherent in a court when Story claimed for himself and his colleagues the ability to rule based on "general reasoning and legal analogies."[33] The phrase, however, did not refer to a power to "make law" in the sense assumed by modern lawyers such as Tushnet. Rather, resorting to "general reasoning and legal analogies" allowed the maintenance of a consistency among federal decisions that appealed to the justices because they believed that the influence of their forum depended on their lawyer-constituents' ability to predict potential outcomes.[34] Too much uncertainty might drive litigants into the state courts and undermine the Supreme Court's effort to promote and control the spread of popular sovereignty.

Swift v. Tyson thus embodied the themes resting at the core of the Taney Court's identity. Its promotion of expanded negotiability supported the justices' effort to impose an individuated self-rule on the Union and to extend the socially cohesive powers of commerce. Story's severing of the link between law and judicial decisions not only furthered his own agenda for a federal common-law jurisprudence but also reinforced his colleagues' vision of judicial authority. With *Swift*, the Taney Court reasserted its stance as a finder, not a maker, of law even as the ruling permitted the court to pursue aggressively its commercially oriented private law agenda with an increasing disregard for state court decisions. By 1900, in fact, the general law Story invented embraced not only negotiable instruments but also insurance contracts, torts, wills, and riparian property rights. Freyer contends that *Swift* covered roughly twenty-six areas of law.[35] A vast majority of that development took place following the Civil War and lies beyond the scope of this study. *Swift*, however, unleashed a pattern of reasoning that carried significant implications for *Dred Scott*, for in the years between 1842 and 1856 the doctrine quietly eroded the procedural mechanisms that would have enabled the justices to evade the decision's most controversial issues. Thus, when Blair and the dissenters attacked the court's evasive efforts on *Swift* grounds, no justice questioned the appropriateness of his position; the assumptions underlying his argument were simply so fundamental to the court's conception of itself that they were beyond question.

Swift's timing remains unexplored. The court issued its ruling in 1842, but the case initially came up for argument in 1840. Because the justices disagreed over the proper way to express the questions involved, the court delayed the decision.[36] Why it did so is not clear: its members may have hedged regarding the nationalist implications of dissociating state judicial decisions and state law. Despite its ideologically compelling formulation, it also carried strategic implications for antislavery litigants who could use *Swift* to circumvent adverse state rulings. Indeed, counsel for the Scott family ultimately attempted this approach before the Supreme Court and pushed the majority toward a wider ruling in *Dred Scott*.[37] The justices unanimously acquiesced in *Swift* and remained committed to it thereafter, but their complacence may have emerged from a parallel development that briefly soothed their concerns about slavery. Throughout their tenures, the members of the Taney Court repeatedly sought a balance between the federal government's claim to supremacy within its sphere and their support for states' rights and concern for the security of slavery. This effort produced a great deal of division on the court, even in cases where slavery was not involved, as well as a series of compromises in which the court refused to subordinate federal policy to the South's perceived needs. These compromises generally broke down over time and required reconfiguration, but while they lasted, they allowed the justices to get on with other business. *Swift v. Tyson* emerged in the wake of the court's first compromise effort, in which the justices made a feeble but briefly successful endeavor to excise the slavery question from the court's interstate commerce jurisprudence.

Debate on these issues took place largely within the theoretical framework outlined in Story's *Conflict of Laws* (1834). Story's treatise offered the

Taney Court a powerful vision of interstate relations in a union of concurrent sovereigns. Every state, Story argued, "possesses an exclusive sovereignty and jurisdiction within its territory." Each regulated the rules of property, the social standing of its inhabitants, "the validity of contracts," the obligations arising out of them, and the mechanisms under which justice would be administered. Such authority ended at a state's borders: "No state or nation can by its laws directly affect property out of its territory or bind persons not resident therein." Although Story (questionably) maintained that they worked under no obligation to do so, states routinely gave effect to foreign laws through comity, a practice by which courts enforced extrajurisdictional laws out of deference to and respect for the jurisdiction in which they originated. Comity had limits. Judges need only apply foreign laws to the extent that they were commensurate with the rights of the foreign states' citizens, and no state need recognize a foreign law that ran contrary to the state's policy (usually as expressed in constitutions and statutes). Taney Court justices embraced Story's theory in *Bank of Augusta*, when the chief justice ruled that the principles of comity allowed banks to conduct business outside of the state in which they were chartered. Courts could thus assume that even a state such as Alabama, which had a clear policy limiting the activities of its banks, extended comity to foreign banks because its constitution and laws said nothing about them. By their silence, Story argued and Taney implied, states gave "tacit consent" to the laws of other sovereigns.[38]

The theory elaborated in *Conflict of Laws* appealed to the justices in part because it provided them a common framework through which they could pursue differing policy agendas. For the court's Democratic members, the emphasis on an unaccountable sovereign authority within the states supported their commitment to self-rule. The doctrine of tacit consent likewise ensured that "the people" would need to be assertive about stating their will through constitutions and statutes. It also facilitated the justices' effort to maintain their amoral and antielitist stance toward legislative output even as they imposed a commercially oriented, individuated vision of popular sovereignty on the Union's citizenry. For Taney in particular, the stress on a sovereign's control over the status of its inhabitants supported his contentions that a state, through a discretionary power of self-preservation, could pass laws such as the Negro Seamen Act.[39] Story, not surprisingly, formulated his *Conflicts* theory for different reasons. As he presented his "general maxims," Story adopted in a crucially modified form the principles developed by seventeenth-century Dutch jurist Ulrich Huber. In his writings, Huber maintained that personal status ascribed in one's domicile (along with the authority to maintain such) followed people wherever they went. Story undercut this argument by drawing on Huber's principle that no state need recognize laws hostile to its policy. The implication here (although it also worked in the other direction) was that states that had abolished slavery need not recognize within their jurisdiction foreign laws sustaining that relationship. Story also made clear that judicial discretion and common-law reasoning played a leading role in the resolution of comity issues. Through this argument, Story worked toward his long-frustrated goal of providing the federal courts with a mechanism for assuming common-law authority.[40]

Despite its ideological appeal, the framework elaborated in *Conflict of Laws* presented serious difficulties, for the states did not stand completely independent of one another, as did the European nation-states that formed the basis of Story's conceptual model. Rather, states occupied a position within a union held together by a potentially powerful general government, which itself possessed sovereign authority within its jurisdiction and which remained supreme over the states within its sphere. Moreover, the Constitution imposed obligations, like those contained in the Fugitive Slave Clause, that trumped the states' ability to grant or withhold comity and endowed the federal government with powers that could penetrate deeply into local communities. Members of the Taney Court remained committed to both federal supremacy and the vision of state sovereignty limned out in *Conflict of Laws*. Efforts to reconcile these two positions produced a great deal of conflict and division among the justices, even when the especially sensitive question of slavery was not directly implicated. Indeed, the Marshall Court encountered these difficulties late in its tenure, as its members struggled to define the scope of the Commerce Clause. Their efforts produced a divided court and a series of ambiguous rulings, and their successors under Taney would maintain that pattern throughout the 1840s.[41]

During the 1837 term, the justices received a taste, albeit a relatively mild one, of the estrangement that Commerce Clause questions could produce when they queried whether a New York police regulation violated that provision. *New York City v. Miln* (1837) concerned a state law compelling shipmasters to report information about passengers assumed to be likely to be health hazards or burdens on city resources (because widowed, orphaned, pauperized, or perhaps dark-skinned). The mayor could then use these reports to remove such persons, or he could compel the shipmaster to post a bond defraying the city's expenses. Writing for four of the court's then seven members, Justice Phillip P. Barbour of Virginia maintained that New York "has the same undeniable and unlimited jurisdiction over all persons and things, within its territorial limits, as any foreign nation," except where constrained by the federal Constitution. Although the law admittedly affected commerce, Barbour considered it a police regulation designed "to advance the safety, happiness and prosperity of [New York's] people, and to provide for its general welfare." Reporting on and removing certain persons, Barbour concluded, represented "precautionary measures against the moral pestilence of paupers, vagabonds, and possibly convicts," just as quarantine regulations guarded against "physical pestilence" arising from "unsound and infectious articles." This authority fell outside federal commerce power. Story disagreed. In dissent, he argued that the law clearly burdened commerce and therefore violated the Constitution. Smith Thompson staked out a middle position that the court would eventually adopt, arguing that although Congress possessed exclusive authority over commerce, it had passed no legislation touching on New York's law; thus, the law could stand until Congress passed an act to the contrary.[42]

Commerce Clause questions retained an inherently divisive character among the Taney Court justices until the early 1850s, and the insertion of issues involving slavery exacerbated the problem. The tendency emerged clearly in *Groves v. Slaughter* (1841). Speaking through Thompson, the court maintained that Mississippi's constitutional provision prohibiting the importation of slaves for sale required enabling legislation before it could take effect, but the justices split over issues that Thompson's opinion failed to raise, and Thompson's solution itself generated two dissents. McLean argued that the provision violated the Constitution's Commerce Clause because the importation of slaves as merchandise infringed on a power "exclusively vested in congress." Such a conclusion implied that Congress, not the states, possessed the power to regulate the interstate slave trade, a controversial position generally held by abolitionists. McLean avoided the implication by noting that the Constitution everywhere regarded slaves as persons and not property, and that definition removed them from federal jurisdiction. Slaves became property only by the force of local law, and the power to guard against slavery and its related problems, McLean concluded, "rests upon the law of self-preservation; a law vital to every community and especially to a sovereign state."[43]

In a separate opinion that received the concurrence of Story, Thompson, James M. Wayne, and John McKinley, Roger B. Taney distanced himself from McLean's position. "The action of the several states on this subject," wrote the chief justice, "cannot be controlled by congress, either by virtue of its power to regulate commerce, or by virtue of any other power conferred by the constitution of the United States." Power over slavery remained "exclusively" within the states, and each determined for itself "the manner and mode" under which the institution would be introduced, if at all, as well as the enslaved population's "condition and treatment" within the state's borders.[44] Pennsylvanian Henry Baldwin went even further, giving what William M. Wiecek has termed "a Black Mass of abolitionist constitutionalism."[45] Like McLean, Baldwin considered Mississippi's provision a violation of the Commerce Clause, but he contended that the Constitution considered slaves property and asserted a number of protections that document extended to masters.[46] *Groves* constituted a unique occurrence in the reported decisions of the Taney Court. Every justice sitting in the case stated his position on the relationship between slavery and federal power over commerce, although each man considered the question extrinsic to the case at hand. Even Thompson, who wrote the court's official opinion, signaled his concurrence (along with Story, Wayne, and McKinley) with Taney's argument. Their action pointed toward a consensus of sorts that laws pertaining to slavery remained strictly local concerns and thus lay beyond the reach of federal commerce power. Baldwin and McLean basically agreed, but their reasoning differed starkly from that of Taney and of each other.[47]

The justices learned quickly that their rough consensus on the locality of slavery solved little, especially since their formulation neglected the Fugitive Slave Clause, which gave the peculiar institution an extralocal dimension. The court confronted that issue late in the 1842 term, and its resolution of that matter fragmented the *Groves* consensus. The justices' handling of that matter gave rise to some of the central issues implicated in *Dred Scott*. Part 2 of this study addresses those issues, but *Groves* possessed a more subtle connection to *Dred Scott*. The former decision provided a window that allowed for the emergence of *Swift*. The *Groves* consensus held from mid-1841 to February 1842, when the court heard and decided *Prigg v. Pennsylvania*, a major case dealing with the Fugitive Slave Clause. During that brief period, judicial anxieties over the security of slavery may have been quelled enough to prevent them from dampening *Swift's* appeal. In January 1842, when the court finally decided *Swift*, the justices faced an opportunity allowing them to render an ideologically compelling ruling in a context where the slavery issue had been set aside, however briefly. January 1842 thus constituted an ideal moment to issue a nationalist ruling with potential antislavery uses. Story's ability to present his common-law agenda in terms that played off his colleagues' ideological sensibilities combined with the opportunity *Groves* provided must have made *Swift*'s reading of section 34 appear unobjectionable.

Benefiting from the opening created by *Groves*, Story furthered his agenda of placing federal jurisprudence on a common-law foundation by couching his arguments in terms that his Democratic colleagues found irresistible. *Swift v. Tyson* constituted a fundamental expression of the Taney Court's identity because it fused the commitment to an amoral and antielitist stance toward legislatively expressed popular will with the imposition of a commercially oriented regime of individuated self-rule. *Swift* enabled the justices simultaneously to maintain those two stances, and the combination proved so powerful that neither the decision's nationalist implications nor its potential usefulness to antislavery litigants visibly disturbed the Taney Court's members. When counsel for the Scott family attempted a realization of *Swift*'s antislavery possibilities, a majority of the court's members checked this potential by closing diversity jurisdiction to blacks through a denial of federal citizenship. The effort left *Swift* unscathed; the justices probably left it alone because a challenge to *Swift* was a challenge to their conception of themselves as judges in a democratic polity. *Swift*'s connection to *Dred Scott* remains subtle, but its presence would eventually exert a decisive impact on the outcome of that decision. In the interim, the justices confronted the collapse of the *Groves* consensus, and their resolution of that problem generated another that, like *Swift*, would ultimately entice the Taney Court to issue its infamous *Dred Scott* ruling.

PART TWO

Toward *Dred Scott*

Slavery, Corporations, and Popular Sovereignty in the Web of Law

IN HIS LETTERS TO HIS DAUGHTER, Justice Peter V. Daniel complained routinely. He regularly grumbled about the "rheumatism and hard work" that he endured while in Washington, but he also often criticized political developments. In 1849, he described the beauty of Washington in the spring and then contrasted "the placidity and loveliness of these grounds" with "the selfish, angry stormy conflict going on within the building seated in the midst of them." The conflict centered on the debate over slavery's expansion into the western territories, which the recent U.S. conquest of northern Mexico had just renewed. Daniel could not anticipate the outcome of the struggle: "Nothing I fear that is good—for high disinterested patriotism or even common integrity appears to have little influence on the political hacks and venal men who compose the public councils." Whatever the result, he fully expected the South to be sacrificed to the "corrupt selfishness" he saw all around him. He denounced Henry Clay's compromise resolutions as "insidious and driveling" and remained dissatisfied when a workable if temporary compromise did emerge in 1850. Daniel also complained about political matters in his home state of Virginia, although these concerns centered not on the slavery controversy but rather on the activities of corporations and their political allies within the state. He was pleased to read that his local newspaper had come out against an effort by "rascally Banks" to increase the number of notes in circulation, "but as the number of issuers, speculators, bank borrowers & bank todes [*sic*] greatly outnumber the honest and independent everywhere I am very apprehensive the Legislature will yield."[1]

Daniel's complaints concerning the slavery question and the power of banks touched on two of antebellum America's most significant developments. Slavery as an institution, of course, took root in what became the United States in the late seventeenth and early eighteenth centuries, but in the nineteenth century cotton cultivation gave the institution a renewed vigor. Cotton production, which increased by a factor of more than twelve hundred between 1790 and 1860, transformed the southern United States. Desire for cotton land enticed planters to push beyond the eighteenth-century confines of the Chesapeake Bay and the South Carolina and Georgia Low Country and brought cotton plantations to Alabama, Mississippi, Louisiana, and Texas, among other states. Desire for cotton profits discouraged consideration of emancipation in any form, contributed to the continued enslavement of a population numbering nearly four million African Americans by 1860, and sustained a forced internal migration that Ira Berlin has termed a "Second Middle Passage."[2]

Yet the expansion of slavery represented only part of a larger surge of economic activity that had been taking place in the United States at least since the 1790s, if not before. Taking advantage of the fluid institutional context created by democratic revolution and rapid internal migration, Americans threw themselves into the market, although historians continue to debate whether that development constituted a benefit or a detriment.[3] After 1815, two changes would shape this activity in ways that transformed American life. First, entrepreneurs, especially in the North, instituted a new division of labor that increased productivity and lowered prices by employing an unskilled workforce that commanded low wages but was nonetheless nominally free to negotiate for better pay or to switch employers. The emergence of this "free labor" pattern of development fed into northerners' tendency to view their region as defined by the absence of slavery, which in turn explained to northerners why by 1860 their region outpaced the South—at times by far—in such areas as railroad mileage, factory production, and total wealth produced.[4]

The second—and for this study more significant—change involved the increasing use of corporate organization, particularly in banking and transportation, to sustain the antebellum economic acceleration. Between 1834 and 1860, the number of banks operating within the United States tripled, providing negotiable instruments for a cash-strapped economy as well as what Howard Bodenhorn has described as an integrated capital market that underwrote the Union's agricultural and manufacturing productivity.[5] Transportation corporations constructed bridges, canals, and railroads and brought access to new markets either by connecting cities to one another or by linking remote but productive agricultural areas to port cities. Both banking and transportation enterprises required large amounts of capital that could be raised only through taxation or the pooling of private resources. For reasons too complex to explain here, states increasingly opted to encourage the latter by granting corporate charters. Incorporation encouraged investment by offering a bundle of privileges ranging from limited liability to guaranteed markets to exemption from taxation in exchange for the service provided by the corporation. For most of the antebellum period, however, access to these privileges required a special act of a legislature, a feature that kept these organizations concentrated in the hands of a few wealthy and well-connected individuals.[6]

These developments provided some of the central issues of mid-nineteenth-century American politics. Opposition to banking corporations, the Second Bank of the United States in particular, was a staple of Jacksonian orthodoxy, and banking policy formed a central point of contention between Whigs and Democrats in the 1830s and 1840s. Hostility toward the construction of transportation networks, at least as they were envisioned by the Whigs, also informed Jacksonian sensibilities. Daniel expressed that concern in a letter to his daughter: "If the mad schemes of internal improvement as they are miscalled . . . are permitted; the taxes on the people must go up, or the state driven to repudiation and disgrace."[7] Indeed, incorporation was suspect in Jacksonian circles—including the one that had formed on the Supreme Court—because both the process of receiving a charter and the benefits that followed raised the specter of special privilege. It is thus ironic, as John Larson has noted, that Democratic opposition to publicly supported internal improvement projects and to similar banking arrangements actually encouraged private incorporation and handed the responsibility of overseeing the economy to a new breed of corporate capitalists.[8] Exactly how the U.S. political system would handle this abdication would be a major issue for decades to come.

In the short term, the explosive question of slavery, which after 1848 dominated American politics, often overshadowed everything else. Slavery had always been an issue of contention—James Madison had predicted as much at the Constitutional Convention of 1787—but the issue of its expansion had become nearly impossible to manage by the early 1850s. Under the strain created by a radical abolition movement that had emerged in the 1830s and the recent acquisition of northern Mexico, the previous arrangement for handling slavery's expansion (dividing the western territory at the 36°30' line) collapsed amid bitter sectional wrangling. Congress ultimately worked out a new arrangement, which, among other things, organized territorial governments without mention of slavery and referred any questions on the subject to the Supreme Court. Yet the Compromise of 1850 came only after serious discussions of secession among southern politicians, including future Supreme Court justice John A. Campbell of Alabama.[9] Even after the compromise passed, Campbell still spoke in favor of disunion: "We have seen that a party at the North . . . favours a dissolution of the Union," he said of radical abolitionists. "We take it for granted, therefore, that secession would involve no perils." In private, Justice Daniel echoed those sentiments, telling a friend in 1851 "that I had cut myself completely loose from everything north of the Delaware and hoped that the southern people would not cooperate with the northern states in the selection of any man for high office, nor in any political measure whatsoever." When told that such a strategy would result in an abolitionist president and southern secession, Daniel replied "that we should be sure of an abolitionist and an enemy to the South if we took any northern man, for they all partook of the same feelings, and as for the dissolution of the Union, the northern men, by their flagrant infractions of [the] constitution . . . dissolved the Union long ago." Daniel and Campbell's interaction on the Supreme Court and their colleagues' reaction to it ultimately led to *Dred Scott*.[10]

Indeed, *Dred Scott* cannot be fully understood apart from the debates that dominated the court in the 1830s and 1840s, as the justices struggled to define the federal government's relationship not only to slavery but also to corporations. Both of these issues contained immense complexities because they forced the court to articulate in detail the ways in which these institutions fit into the Union's constitutional structure, and any solution on one issue could carry unintended consequences for the other. After a period of bitter debate that lasted throughout the 1840s, for example, the court rejected contentions that the states held an inherent right of self-preservation that trumped federal authority on any question dealing with slavery or social status. A majority of justices, led by Chief Justice Roger B. Taney, instead recognized the states' supremacy over slavery and social status within their jurisdictions but declared the federal government's power to trump such authority on a case-by-case basis. This doctrine emerged in 1851, about the time Daniel and Campbell were expressing their disillusionment with the Compromise of 1850.

The Supreme Court did not assert that power over slavery in the 1850s, but its rulings in corporate law raised the possibility of such a scenario. On the eve of *Dred Scott*, a majority of justices were invoking the federal Constitution, although grudgingly, against state efforts to abrogate tax exemptions that they had previously granted to corporations. Daniel, joined by John Catron and the newly appointed Justice Campbell, dissented from these rulings because they stripped the states of their inherent right of self-preservation. These three justices, all southerners, in fact formed a faction committed to gutting the court's corporate law doctrine or, failing that, to driving corporate litigants out of federal diversity jurisdiction. This last goal touched directly on the slavery question—although no justice ever explicitly made the connection—for the court's understanding of citizenship law treated corporations and free blacks as conceptually identical. If corporations had access to the federal courts, then free blacks probably did as well. And if the court protected their rights as it did corporate rights, then the South's system of racial rule faced a grave threat. Consequently, the southern faction advocated the destruction of the Taney Court's entire body of corporate law. By the 1855 term, Daniel, Campbell, and Catron had developed their critique to a level that demanded a serious response from the majority, and Chief Justice Taney provided one in *Dred Scott*.

CHAPTER FOUR

Moderating Taney

Concurrent Sovereignty and Answering
the Slavery Question, 1842–1852

IN 1852, FUTURE JUSTICE JOHN A. CAMPBELL expressed fear that the U.S. Supreme Court had become less protective of slavery. Although the court had stated ten years before that Congress held no authority to regulate the interstate slave trade, recent opinions by some justices "raised very painful apprehensions on this subject." They hinted, Campbell maintained, that Congress could outlaw slave trading throughout the Union, just as it had recently done in the District of Columbia as part of the Compromise of 1850. Only secession could protect southern institutions from the court's actions. A year earlier, however, abolitionist James G. Birney had come to precisely the opposite conclusion about the court's rulings. In an address to the Union's free black population, he charted a decline in its legal status in the decades following the revolution. The court's most recent ruling on slavery, which "not only overthrows the Constitution, but greatly disparages it," placed the social status of free blacks wholly at the mercy of state governments. This decision, together with the court's previous rulings and the recently passed and very harsh Fugitive Slave Law (also part of the Compromise of 1850), placed free blacks in great jeopardy, for these laws would work together to permit the wholesale kidnapping of the North's black population. Only migration to Liberia could protect northern blacks from the court's actions.[1]

Numerous legal historians have followed Birney and characterized the Supreme Court as an unambiguously proslavery bench.[2] Campbell's concerns, however, suggest that the court's stance toward slavery may have been more complicated than previously thought. Recent work in political history contends that although the United States was a "slaveholding republic"— to use Don E. Fehrenbacher's phrase—the actual amount of protection extended to slavery by the federal government constantly remained open to debate and redefinition. Even within the Democratic Party, which historians often write off as unconditionally proslavery, support for the institution among many northerners was tactical, provisional, and, by the early 1850s, decidedly at its limits.[3] Regulating slavery proved to be a very complicated business throughout the American political system. On the Supreme Court, the justices struggled to balance what they considered a constitutional obligation to protect slavery with their equally compelling commitments to upholding federal authority and facilitating commercial obligations. Throughout the 1840s, the court remained split between a minority of justices, led by Chief Justice Roger B. Taney, who claimed that state police powers always trumped federal authority on issues dealing with slavery and racial subordination, and a majority, who maintained that the Constitution had placed some limits on state power in that respect. The debate took the court to the brink of incoherence and lasted until Taney broke with the minority justices, abandoned his extreme states'-rights position, and opened the way to a new conceptualization that emphasized the concurrent sovereignty of the federal and state governments. By the early 1850s, Taney's maneuvering had allowed the Supreme Court to develop an approach to slave law that protected slavery without subordinating federal power to the South's perceived needs. In so doing, the court gave both Campbell and Birney cause to complain and created the doctrinal context in which *Dred Scott* would both emerge and be confronted.

A network of partisan, institutional, and professional assumptions underpinned the Taney Court's approach to slavery. Throughout the period under study, slaveholders held four of the court's nine seats, and they sat alongside a group of sympathetic nonslaveholders, most notably Chief Justice Taney, that kept any antislavery justices in the minority. Taney Court members also believed that the Constitution—a document that was, as Paul Finkelman and others have argued, staunchly supportive of slavery—represented a transcendent expression of popular will that functioned as a barrier to shifts in public opinion. And the justices had sworn an oath, pledging their supposedly immortal souls, to uphold the laws of the United States, and their office charged them with both a responsibility and a moral obligation to interpose the law against those who attempted to circumvent or resist it. Although Justice Peter V. Daniel worried that a "rank abolitionist" might one day fill a seat, these assumptions converged in a manner that rendered Taney Court jurisprudence inhospitable to antislavery positions.[4]

This aspect of the court's thinking emerged clearly in the 1840s and 1850s, but Taney had developed it as early as 1832. In his manuscript on the Negro Seamen Act, Taney argued that the Constitution excluded blacks from its provisions. "The african race in the United States[,] even when free, are every where a degraded class." Any liberties they enjoyed came at the "mercy" and "sufferance of the white population." Taney stressed his adherence not to "a technical and literal interpretation" of constitutional language but rather to the meaning the Framers allegedly intended that language to have. Terms such as the "citizens of each State," Taney admitted, "would perhaps embrace" blacks if a court used its contemporary (antebellum) meaning, but only if a judge rejected the Framers' "plain object and intentions." Courts, however, eschewed popular understandings and instead determined the meaning of language in its historical context, which placed blacks outside the constitutional order. Similar reasoning came from the bench. When he upheld the Fugitive Slave Law of 1793, for example, Justice Joseph Story implied that the Constitution applied to whites only, ignoring objections that the law violated alleged runaways' constitutional rights to trial by jury and due process. Five years later, Levi Woodbury would reject a call to strike down the same statute by asserting the court's official responsibility to uphold federal law: "this court has no alternative, while they exist, but to stand by the constitution and laws with fidelity to their duties and their oaths."[5]

Antislavery litigants thus found an unsympathetic audience on the court. Abolitionist lawyers pushed for a broad antislavery ruling in *The Amistad* (1841), a case involving the freedom of fifty-four Africans who had mutinied and unintentionally sailed to Connecticut after their illegal kidnapping in Africa and sale in Cuba. How could the federal government, asked one lawyer, remain consistent with the principles of the Declaration of Independence and "become a party to . . . the enslavement of human beings cast upon our shores and found in the condition of freemen?" With the support of all but one of his colleagues, Story responded by ruling for the Africans on the narrowest possible grounds. Because the Africans' original capture had been illegal, no one owned them. Story refused to discuss whether federal law conflicted with general principles of freedom. In 1847, another lawyer informed the justices that "no unprejudiced student" could deny the Constitution's antislavery character. The Declaration of Independence and the Northwest Ordinance revealed the Framers' belief in "the inviolability and inalienability of personal liberty." The Constitution excluded "all recognition of the rightfulness of slaveholding, and all national sanction of the practice." Federal laws, like the Fugitive Slave Law of 1793, thus did not bind the court. "No court," he informed the justices, "is bound to enforce an unjust law; but . . . every court is bound, by prior and superior obligations from enforcing such law." Woodbury, speaking for a unanimous court, rejected the argument. Supreme Court justices, he lectured, followed "a strait and narrow" path going where the "constitution and the laws lead," and the court would not "break both, by travelling without or beyond them."[6]

Despite its antiabolitionism, the court's jurisprudence did not uniformly favor slaveholders or even whites. Its exclusionary conception of the body politic barred John Rogers, a white indicted for the murder of another white in Indian country, from escaping trial in the federal courts. Rogers claimed that the Cherokee Nation, of which he was a member, had jurisdiction over the offense. A unanimous court rejected the argument because Congress had passed no statute allowing whites in Indian country to "throw off all responsibility to the laws of the United States." Rogers, Taney wrote, "was still a white man": just as he enjoyed rights and privileges under federal law that no other racial group could claim, he also incurred obligations that he could not escape. Taney Court justices also unanimously recognized, with a single exception, the freedom of claims of persons illegally held as slaves in the District of Columbia, which, under the terms of its cession from Virginia and Maryland, possessed liberal manumission statutes. In 1844, the court ruled that Moses Bell, a slave held in Alexandria County (formerly part of Maryland), went free because his owner sold him to a master who moved him to Washington County (formerly part of Virginia) and sold him again a year later. Bell's Washington County masters, said John McLean, violated a 1792 Virginia statute that freed any slave imported into the state and held for one year. A year earlier, Taney upheld a freedom claim based on a condition in a master's will that set free any slave that her heirs might decide to sell (an action allowable under a Maryland statute). Two years later, however, Daniel rejected a petition because the master failed to register a manumission deed within the time allotted by law. Yet as late as 1861, Justice John Catron upheld freedom claims resting on a 1796 Maryland statute that still bound the Supreme Court when it adjudicated cases arising in the District.[7]

Whatever their outcome, these cases displayed the same rule-oriented jurisprudence that characterized Taney Court discourse. McLean's decision in favor of Bell stuck closely to the relevant statutes. He carefully discussed the substance of the Maryland and Virginia laws touching Bell's case, demonstrated that Congress had passed no laws covering such a situation, and stressed his opinion's consistency with a previous ruling. Taney's, James M. Wayne's, and Catron's opinions exhibited similar traits. Daniel's denial of manumission likewise came in the form of a tedious and unusually lengthy discussion of the way in which legal rights and equities were created. The same network of assumptions that perpetuated slavery could also work to set slaves free, indicating the justices' belief in a legal structure that constrained their actions.

Such constraints usually generated acquiescence toward slavery, whatever a justice's personal view regarding the institution. No justice exhibited any consistent difficulty conceptualizing human beings as property. Like their southern colleagues, northern justices pondered slaves' value for jurisdictional purposes, recognized slaves as collateral on mortgages, regarded them as valid consideration for contractual obligations, and dispassionately divided families in accordance with lines of descent or creditors' claims.[8] Even McLean acquiesced. In 1852, he held a trustee liable for money that slaves left in his care could have earned. The trustee "treated the slaves with unusual indulgence and humanity" through liberal provisions of housing, food, clothing, and medical care. A trustee's duties, however, required one "to exercise a reasonable diligence in keeping them engaged in useful employments, so not only to pay their necessary expenses, but also to obtain a reasonable compensation for their labor." Indulgence and humanity toward slaves, McLean concluded, amounted to "gross negligence" in this case. Adherence to the law concerning the trustee's fiduciary obligations led even this antislavery justice to insist on more oppressive conditions for slaves.[9]

A general acquiescence toward slave law—the ability of justices to put their personal feelings aside (if necessary) and to treat human beings as property—ensured that internal debates over slavery took place within a very narrow spectrum. Members were very much aware of antislavery legal arguments, but they made little headway among the justices. Several justices considered these arguments worthless, but even those justices receptive to antislavery usually rejected them. American constitutional law supported slavery, and the justices' sense of duty required them to work within the constraints imposed by that support. Sometimes those constraints favored freedom claimants. Far more often, they favored masters, and this reality represented a feature of the legal landscape that even the most sincerely antislavery justices accepted.

Acquiescence did not imply an unabashed proslavery stance, and the justices fought bitterly over how much support the federal government would extend to slavery. Differences emerged less over questions concerning the morality of human bondage than they did over independently contentious issues involving the balance of federal and state power. Sharp divisions characterized the justices' debate over the precise relationship between state police power and the Constitution's grant of exclusive powers to the federal government. These issues had troubled the court at least since *Gibbons* and continued to do so in cases such as *Miln* and *Groves*. A rough consensus to keep the slavery question separate from this debate had emerged in *Groves*, but that case offered no guidance on how the court could do so, and the consensus quickly fell apart.

Slavery's intersection with questions concerning the scope of federal power generated passions that highlighted the stakes of both issues, and slavery cases thus became forums well suited for debating the extent of federal power. These debates deeply fragmented the court. A minority of justices, centered on Taney, demanded a recognition of an inherent power of self-preservation within the states that always trumped federal authority in matters concerning slavery and social status. Another minority, centered on Story, countered that federal power, when exercised within its constituted sphere, always remained superior to state regulations. A handful of justices searching for a middle ground stood in between. In his 1842 ruling in *Prigg v. Pennsylvania*, Story ensured that Taney's position would forever remain in the minority. Story's opinion blended antislavery and antiabolitionist themes in a manner that enticed the middling justices to join a nationalist coalition committed to defeating Taney's extreme conception of federal-state relations. Story's success demonstrated that the Taney Court's majority, despite its antiabolitionist predisposition, possessed no desire to subordinate federal power to the perceived needs of the South.

Every state possessed, Taney insisted throughout the 1840s, an unlimited authority over nonwhites as incident to an inherent power of self-preservation. With an argument somewhat anticipating *Dred Scott*, Taney thoroughly developed this position in his 1832 opinion on the Negro Seamen Act. South Carolina's exclusion of blacks represented "a power absolutely necessary to [the slaveholding states'] safety." Southerners, he asserted, "would as soon have surrendered their own lives" as part with that power. No constitutional provision required a relinquishing of that authority, and the southern states' consistent exclusion of free blacks—who, Taney maintained, held no claim to federal citizenship—revealed that the states had retained this authority. The federal government possessed no warrant to act when its power could affect racial relations within the states. Taney later tried to incorporate his vision into court doctrine. He made his first attempt in *Groves*, where he insisted that the states' regulation of slavery "cannot be controlled by congress, either by virtue of its power to regulate commerce, or by virtue of any other power conferred by the constitution of the United States." Four of the seven justices then sitting explicitly concurred with Taney's general point—that Congress had no power over slavery—but his colleagues refused to allow him to speak officially for the court. Instead, Smith Thompson delivered a ruling that circumvented any discussion of slavery's relationship to federal power. The decision to concur with Taney while allowing Thompson to speak for the court pointed to a dynamic that shaped court discourse throughout the 1840s. Every justice agreed, at least in the abstract, that slavery should be a matter of local policy free from federal regulation, but a majority of justices continually rejected Taney's effort to subordinate federal power to the perceived needs of southern self-preservation.[10]

Prigg v. Pennsylvania (1842), which undermined the *Groves* compromise and ultimately forced Taney to abandon his position, embodied this tendency. *Prigg* centered on whether the states could supplement the Fugitive Slave Law of 1793. This legislation enabled masters and their agents to capture alleged fugitives through self-help and, after an essentially ministerial hearing, carry them away from any place within the Union. The law permitted serious abuses, including the intentional kidnapping of free blacks. Some northern states responded with personal liberty laws that generally required slave catchers to work through state officials, permitted hearings in which captives could assert claims to freedom, and levied heavy penalties for noncompliance. Writing a separate opinion on a deeply fragmented court, Taney declared Pennsylvania's law unconstitutional. "This right of the master being given by the constitution of the United States," he said of the slave owner's authority to capture alleged fugitives, "neither congress nor a state legislature can, by any law or regulation, impair it or restrict it." States could pass legislation only strengthening masters' ability to capture potential runaways: indeed, he believed that states had a duty to do so. Taney remained in the minority. Only Thompson and Daniel agreed that the states possessed a concurrent authority to aid masters, and neither justice claimed a position as extreme as Taney's.[11]

Although they divided on some points, the rest of the justices demanded that state authority yield to federal power in all matters pertaining to fugitive slaves. The Constitution, Story stated in his controversial opinion for the majority, secured a "positive and unqualified recognition" of a master's common-law right to seize fugitive slaves anywhere in the Union in a manner "unaffected by any state law or legislation whatsoever." The Fugitive Slave Clause, he continued, contemplated "an absolute, positive right and duty, pervading the whole Union with an equal and supreme force."[12] Such uniformity required that regulatory authority over fugitive slaves vest exclusively in Congress, and the states therefore could not constitutionally pass any laws on the subject. Congress, however, could not compel state officers to assist in the apprehension of fugitives, and states could even pass legislation prohibiting them from doing so. Joseph Story and even more forcefully William W. Story, the justice's son and biographer, cited this point as a "triumph of freedom" because it allowed the states to withdraw from enforcing the Fugitive Slave Law. As numerous historians have noted, the argument most likely emerged in response to abolitionist criticism. When he wrote *Prigg*, Story probably considered the lack of officers a problem to be remedied in future legislation. Shortly after delivering his opinion, the justice urged an ally in Congress to amend a pending bill in a way that would allow the federal courts to appoint officers for the job.[13]

Story's *Prigg* opinion deliberately mixed antiabolitionist and antislavery arguments. His ruling steadfastly supported the Fugitive Slave Law and was coldly insensitive to free blacks endangered by that legislation. Story embraced these implications. In his manuscript, Story changed his initial argument that the Fugitive Slave Clause enjoyed the Constitutional Convention's "unanimous consent" and instead stressed the clause's function as a break on shifting public opinion. "Its true design, was," his new sentence read, "to guard against the doctrines and principles prevalent in the non-slave-holding states, by preventing them from intermeddling with, or obstructing, or abolishing the rights of the owners of slaves."[14] Story's opinion thus incorporated the Taney Court's antiabolitionism as well as antislavery positions. *Prigg*'s release of state officers from enforcing the Fugitive Slave Law may have been unintentional, but the justice emphasized that any obligation to the South ended with the Fugitive Slave Clause. Slavery was a product of local, municipal law that "no nation [or state] is bound to recognize . . . when it is in opposition to its own policy." Story here drew on the theory, developed in his *Conflict of Laws*, that no state was bound to apply a foreign law that ran contrary to the state's policy. He also incorporated the doctrine—albeit a conservative version—of *Somerset v. Stewart* (1772), an English decision that was a central text in antislavery legal discourse. McLean had attempted the same thing in *Groves*, but Story's effort generated more support among his colleagues, probably because he employed the *Conflict of Laws* framework that Taney Court justices found appealing.[15]

Story may have hoped subtly to push the court in an antislavery direction. Story's son, his most recent biographer, and some of his harshest critics all agree that although Story was no abolitionist, he was a lifelong opponent of slavery. He spoke publicly against its expansion during the Missouri Crisis, assailed the slave trade from the bench, and opposed Texas's annexation.[16] He even modified Huber's theory in *Conflict of Laws* so that it could accommodate *Somerset*.[17] Story's opposition to slavery led him to advocate a rather flexible construction of the Fugitive Slave Clause. Taney spoke of the master's right as if it were a strict exception to power at all levels of the government: no legislature could "impair . . . or restrict" the apprehension of fugitive slaves. Story maintained that the clause merely recognized a master's common-law right of recaption. "When any one . . . wrongfully detains one's wife, child or servant," Blackstone wrote, "the husband, parent, or master, may lawfully claim and retake them, wherever he happens to find them." Remedies associated with recaption remained subject to a wide range of legislative discretion. In providing remedies, legislatures could enact statutes of limitation, establish modes of proof, specify what actions were usable, and so on. Precisely because this discretionary power, if left to the states, would undermine a uniform policy, the Constitution placed fugitive slaves under exclusively federal jurisdiction. That discretionary power now resided in Congress, and Story hinted that the Fugitive Slave Act of 1793 did not "exhaust" the possible remedies. He did not pursue the point, but his vision of the right secured by the Fugitive Slave Clause could accommodate alternatives other than those heretofore "deemed expedient or proper."[18]

Prigg's schizophrenic stance toward slavery highlighted the concessions that Story made to gain the four votes that allowed him to speak for the court. Story's primary goal in this case centered not on protecting or undermining slavery but rather on frustrating Taney and his associates' agenda. *Prigg* split the justices on the issue of whether the Constitution stripped the states of all power to supplement the Fugitive Slave Law. And the case embraced many of the same choices concerning federal exclusivity, unaccountable police powers, and concurrent exercises of sovereign authority that confronted the court in Commerce Clause cases. Story considered the emphasis on unaccountable police powers or federal-state concurrency that his colleagues advocated to be disturbing departures from the vital constitutional doctrines set out under Marshall. Story had tried both open dissent and a pained, silent acquiescence in response to the court's changing inclination, but neither strategy appealed to him, and he ultimately concluded that resignation was the only viable option. In *Prigg*, however, Story pulled together a faction committed to upholding federal exclusivity against Taney and Daniel's efforts to ground Fugitive Slave (and Commerce) Clause doctrine in an uncompromising defense of slavery. *Prigg*'s use of both antislavery and antiabolitionist arguments not only stemmed from the interaction between the Fugitive Slave Law and Story's personal sensibilities but also arose because he needed to appeal to the differing interests of four other justices. Story's antislavery probably attracted McLean, the court's most outspoken critic of human bondage and the only justice to voice any concern about the rights of free blacks under the Fugitive Slave Law.[19]

Yet Story crafted his argument in a manner that secured the support of Wayne, Catron, and John McKinley, all of whom owned slaves and held little sympathy for antislavery arguments. This coalition of supporters and opponents of human bondage underscored the justices' understanding of the stakes involved in *Prigg* and other slavery cases. Divisions on the court centered not on whether the federal government would support slavery (every justice accepted that) but rather to what extent it would do so. Court members split, therefore, over whether the states possessed an inherent right of self-preservation that trumped federal power in any matter touching on slavery. In *Prigg*, the court said no. Historians criticize Story for conceding too much to slavery interests, but a softer position might have shattered his coalition. Only McLean and Wayne shared Story's nationalist commitment. Catron and McKinley considered the full extent of national power open to negotiation, and they might have gravitated toward Thompson, Daniel, or Taney without such concessions. Those justices, especially Daniel and Taney, advocated a subordination of federal power to the perceived needs of the slaveholding states, and that position might have become the opinion of the court if Story had increased his argument's antislavery content.[20]

Story's success came at a high cost, for his concessions ultimately sub-verted both *Prigg*'s antislavery and its nationalism. Story moved almost im-mediately against his opinion's most significant antislavery implication. He asked his congressional connections to remedy the federal government's in-ability to require state officers to participate in the apprehension of fugitive slaves. Why Story took this action is not clear—perhaps to pacify Catron and McKinley—but his effort failed, and northern states took advantage of *Prigg* until the passage of a new fugitive slave law. Story also conceded that the Fugitive Slave Clause and the 1793 law did not shut out all state action. States retained authority under the police power "to arrest and restrain runaway slaves, and remove them from their borders, and otherwise to secure them-selves against their depredations and evil example, as they certainly may do in cases of idlers, vagabonds and paupers." The states never surrendered this ability to protect their populations, and they could exercise it as long as they did not affect the rights of masters to recapture their slaves. Story's language sounded similar to that used by the majority in *Miln*, from which he had dissented in 1837. It also contrasted sharply with the arguments of Wayne and McLean, who in their concurring *Prigg* opinions discussed the Fugitive Slave Clause as if it were a complete surrender of sovereign author-ity on the part of the states.[21] Story's invocation of state police powers, to which he had previously given lip service, allowed him to insist on federal exclusivity without presenting it as an undue imposition on the states. His position probably allowed him to secure the votes of Catron and McKinley, but it also provided an opening that the court would use against *Prigg* ten years later.[22]

Despite its ultimate futility, the strategy in *Prigg* met Story's immediate goal: Taney found himself forced into the minority. After *Prigg*, advocates of an inherent state power of self-preservation faced a coalition of justices biased toward the defense of federal exclusivity. The *Prigg* majority chose national uniformity over the increased security for masters' property rights that Taney and Daniel demanded. Given the divisions within his coalition, which consisted of a mix of antislavery and slaveholding justices and two men without a strong commitment to federal exclusivity, Story's opinion for the court in *Prigg* represented a remarkable achievement. Story's blending of antislavery and antiabolitionist themes and simultaneous recognition of federal exclusivity and state police power let him maneuver around those divisions and pull together a nationalist coalition. This coalition remained the dominant force in cases dealing with the balance of state and federal power throughout the 1840s. Its members' persistence eventually convinced Taney that his insistence on states' inherent power of self-preservation was an institutional dead end. He could never convince his colleagues to join him, and Taney consequently abandoned his position in 1851 and joined the majority in a relatively moderate conceptualization of state power.

Taney's moderation, however, worked itself out in a context of doctrinal disarray and bitter division among the justices that enticed Catron to abandon his support for federal exclusivity. Story's *Prigg* coalition held together throughout the 1840s and retained its majority position in constitutional cases, but its success owed more to the shifting membership and consequent disorganization in its opposition than it did to its members' ability to formulate compelling arguments. Following Story's resignation and death in 1845, the coalition possessed no justice capable of shaping court doctrine in a manner that could negotiate the divisions among McLean, Wayne, Catron, and McKinley. All of these justices were lawyers of average ability who rarely, if ever, spoke for the court in matters of constitutional law. With the loss of Story, the judicial defense of exclusive federal authority became increasingly disordered. Coalition justices, although united regarding the outcome of particular cases and in their rejection of Taney's position, provided separate justifications for their conclusions. The net effect of these developments was cacophony as the justices debated the relative merits of federal exclusivity and state self-preservation. Questions involving slavery only increased the volume of these deliberations. By 1849, a majority of the justices had come to realize that neither position was workable and began signaling a willingness to stand behind a new compromise that would settle their differences on both the exclusivity and slavery questions.

The divisions over the exclusivity question cemented in *Prigg* emerged again, although in a disorganized fashion, in the *License Cases* (1847). In this decision, the justices confronted an issue in which they largely agreed about the outcome. Even so, seven of the eight justices sitting in the case wrote their own opinions. The *License Cases* involved three suits questioning the constitutionality of temperance legislation in Massachusetts, Rhode Island, and New Hampshire. Each state possessed a law assessing stiff penalties for the sale of liquor without a license. These statutes, moreover, imposed no obligation on local governments to grant such licenses and explicitly stated that governments possessed the option of granting no licenses at all, effectively creating prohibition in the area. Both Massachusetts and Rhode Island designed their legislation to avoid conflict with the Commerce Clause by requiring licenses only for the sale of quantities suited for local consumption. All seven justices writing opinions in these cases agreed that the license laws constituted an appropriate use of the police power. States passed such laws to protect their citizens from the dangers intoxicating beverages posed to health, safety, and morality. McLean, himself a temperance advocate, went further and used language that generally emerged in Taney's and Daniel's defenses of slavery. License laws, he wrote, were "essential to self-preservation." All the justices, despite their differences, considered these laws matters of local legislative discretion. [23]

The fragmentation pattern that emerged in the *License Cases* underscored the contentious nature of Commerce Clause issues independently from any other question and revealed that, for some justices, arguments over the extent of federal power were merely vehicles for their larger jurisprudential agendas. McLean, for example, abandoned his usual commitment to federal exclusivity in support of the license laws, which had "a salutary tendency on society" and rested on "the highest moral considerations." [24] Although Daniel—joined by Story's replacement, Woodbury—maintained a position supportive of exclusive state authority, Taney, along with Catron, toyed with a concurrent-sovereignty conception of federal relations. New Hampshire's law, because it failed to take into account federal power over interstate commerce, was potentially unconstitutional, but since Congress had passed no legislation on the subject, the law could stand until that body did so. [25] This unusual pattern emerged primarily because the justices perceived in the *License Cases* no serious implications for slavery. Counsel baited them. Daniel Webster, Samuel Ames, and John Whipple, who represented the liquor dealers, hinted that rejections of federal exclusivity functioned only to protect the peculiar institution and drew comparisons between the licensing laws and the Negro Seamen Act. Only Woodbury responded; the other justices focused on what they considered the real issues in the case. Rather than arguing about slavery—which, as *Groves* and *Prigg* revealed, they were not reluctant to do—the justices went on for pages lecturing counsel on the correct reading of court precedent and debating among themselves the point at which goods ceased to be articles of interstate commerce. [26]

The refusal to engage the slavery issue was telling. If nothing else, the positioning of Taney and Daniel pointed toward divisions among the advocates of unaccountable state authority. Daniel's commitment to state power constituted part of a larger vision rooted ultimately in the theory of the Virginia school of politics that belied reduction into a narrow effort to protect slavery. Taney's overtures toward concurrent sovereignty, however, indicated that his insistence on an unlimited power of self-preservation bore a more direct connection to the slavery question. He believed that slavery required protection. Before 1850, he was willing to sacrifice federal power to the perceived needs of the South to ensure its safety, but he saw no need to do so when slavery did not face an immediate threat.

Taney did perceive a threat in the *Passenger Cases* (1849), the next major Commerce Clause case to come before the court. As the justices confronted questions of federal exclusivity and slavery, the *Prigg* coalition reconstituted itself, with Robert C. Grier of Pennsylvania providing the crucial fifth vote in the place of the departed Story. Again, the court split into rough factions favoring federal power or increased security for slavery. And again, the nationalists won. This time, however, no justice pulled together a majority, and all nine of the court's members wrote opinions (and some wrote more than one). The *Passenger Cases* involved New York and Massachusetts laws that levied a tax on every ship passenger landing in their major ports. Counsel for the states, citing the *Miln* decision, defended this legislation as police regulations that defrayed the expenses generated by the increasing number of immigrants entering New York City and Boston. Most justices considered the laws as simply mechanisms to raise tax revenue and thus unacceptable regulations of commerce. Either way, the *Passenger Cases* concerned the states' ability to control (in the name of self-preservation) the migration of persons into their territories, raising issues similar to those generated by the Negro Seamen Act. These implications made the suits inherently divisive, and the court probably would have split whenever it heard them, but the final arguments occurred in the midst of the sectional controversy set off by the introduction of the Wilmot Proviso a few years earlier. The justices therefore gave their opinions at a moment when their political counterparts had become deadlocked over the slavery issue. The crisis placed the *Passenger Cases'* issues in sharp relief, although the justices did not divide neatly along a North-South axis. [27]

Taney, with Samuel Nelson of New York concurring, reasserted his arguments from *Prigg, Groves,* and his manuscript on the South Carolina Negro Seamen Act. Massachusetts and New York possessed the exclusive authority to levy these taxes as incident to their inherent sovereign power of self-preservation. A state had a right to bar entry to or remove from its juris-diction anyone "it may deem dangerous or injurious to the interests and welfare of its citizens." A state, moreover, held an "exclusive right to deter-mine, in its sound discretion, whether the danger does or does not exist, free from the control of the general government."[28] This issue, Taney be-lieved, had been settled by his *Groves* concurrence, which had the explicit assent of a majority, and by Story's acknowledgment in *Prigg* of a state's authority to remove, through its police power, persons perceived to be ob-jectionable. Yet now the court's majority argued that this taxation unconsti-tutionally violated federal commercial power. Immigrants brought, he con-tinued, "a fearful amount of disease and pauperism," and states' handling of those problems represented matters of sovereign discretion into which the court had no right to inquire.[29] Stripping the states of this power en-dangered the South. If New York's and Massachusetts's passenger taxes vio-lated the Commerce Clause, then southern laws barring entry to free blacks were unconstitutional as well. "The emancipated slaves of the West Indies have at this hour the absolute right to reside, hire houses, and traffic and trade throughout the Southern States," Taney warned, and their presence would bring "the most serious discontent and . . . the most painful conse-quences." His hyperbole aside, Taney considered a claim to exclusive federal control over noncitizens migrating from Europe an issue that raised serious questions about the states' ability to control their free black populations (al-legedly domestic noncitizens). Power over the one, implied Taney in a point echoed in the separate opinions of Daniel and Woodbury, conferred power over the other.[30]

McLean, Wayne, Catron, Grier, and McKinley—the *Prigg* coalition—remained unconvinced and ruled the New York and Massachusetts laws un-constitutional. A tax on disembarking immigrants, these five justices agreed, constituted a regulation of commerce. McLean and Wayne, both staunch nationalists, stressed Congress's exclusive power over commerce, which pre-cluded all state legislation on the subject. They conceded that states pos-sessed a limited control over immigrants to contain disease and pauperism, but levying a tax on healthy immigrants crossed the line between legitimate police powers and blatant regulations of commerce. Catron and Grier took a concurrent-sovereignty position, arguing that Congress had already passed immigration legislation—naturalization policies—that trumped any com-peting state laws. As Grier wrote, "It is the cherished policy of the general government to encourage and invite Christian foreigners of our own race to seek an asylum within our borders, and . . . add to the wealth, population, and power of the nation." Apparently undisturbed by their incompatibility, McKinley embraced both arguments.[31]

As they did in *Prigg*, McLean, Wayne, Catron, and McKinley refused to ground federal policy in an uncompromising defense of slavery. Yet Grier's reference to federal policies geared toward "foreigners of our own race" indicated that the majority's members shared some of the dissenters' concerns. Catron and McKinley did not address these concerns, but other justices did. McLean took the least conciliatory position, conceding only that the states could deny residence to diseased and pauperized immigrants and to slaves brought into their jurisdictions as merchandise (as per *Miln* and *Groves*, respectively). The Ohio justice considered that authority incident to the states' powers of self-preservation, which he construed quite narrowly. Both Wayne and Grier assured the dissenters that they intended no infringement on state power to control their free black populations. Dismissing as utter nonsense Taney's hyperbole about the dangers of West Indian immigration into the southern states, Wayne spoke confidently that the court could handle differently immigrants and African Americans. Grier made similar overtures. If they wanted the support of these justices, Taney and his dissenting associates would have to rest their arguments on something more substantial than the nebulous power of self-preservation.[32]

A sense of frustration with the increasingly counterproductive exclusivity debate emerged in the *Passenger Cases*. Both extremes still had fervent partisans. McLean and Wayne defended Congress's exclusive power over commerce as stringently as ever, and Daniel and Woodbury countered with vigorous assertions that the laws belonged exclusively within the bounds of state police power. These arguments generally became mired in seemingly interminable lectures on the proper readings of court doctrine. Grier considered the debate "of little practical importance," especially since Congress had actively exercised its authority in the area. Catron likewise saw no reason to argue the point. Even Taney found the argument tiresome. A portion of his opinion addressed the concurrent-authority position, although he maintained that none of Congress's legislation touched the subject at issue. As they struggled through the *Passenger Cases*, therefore, a growing number of justices began moving toward the middle ground that Thompson had marked out in his *Miln* concurrence more than a decade earlier and with which most justices had subsequently flirted.[33]

The fragmentation in the *License Cases* and the *Passenger Cases* generated little except confusion on the court and among the public. To commentators, a five-four decision marked by eight separate opinions exposed disturbing ambiguities in constitutional law. Southern partisans worried about the *Passenger Cases'* implications for slavery. A correspondent for the *Charleston Mercury* argued that the ruling swept away southern laws that barred "free colored persons—'citizens of Massachusetts' or whatever abolition region—from entering our ports and cities." Federal law would "strip the South of all power of self-protection, and make submission to its rule equivalent to ruin and degradation." Campbell's criticism of the court also emphasized these decisions as a threat to the South.[34]

Such pessimism was unfounded; the Supreme Court's members did not intend to destroy the southern slave regimes. A majority wanted the South protected, but its members did not know exactly how to do so without sacrificing their commitment to federal power. The ensuing cacophony may have even soured the justices' personal relationships. Taney criticized Wayne in the *Passenger Cases* for revealing (private) information from conference that challenged the legitimacy of *Miln*. A month later, Daniel reported to his daughter that he had lately seen little of Wayne's family, with whom he had previously often socialized. He blamed the Waynes' coolness on "an unfortunate collision . . . between Wayne and the Chief Justice; one in which there is some approach to bitterness." Daniel claimed no part in the dispute, but since he stayed in the same boardinghouse as Taney, Daniel believed Wayne was suspicious of him as well. "Certainly I have not been so much pressed to visit the family as I have been." Doctrinal confusion and deteriorating personal relationships, however, may have combined to convince some justices that the solution to this problem required the removal of the slavery issue from Commerce Clause litigation (again) and a context-sensitive vision of federal-state relations that privileged neither pole.[35]

In the early 1850s, the court developed a jurisprudential structure that effectively negotiated the divisions of the 1840s. A critical component of this development came when Taney abandoned his self-preservation argument. His tempered views allowed him to protect slavery within the constraints limned out by his colleagues, and he thus joined the majority. A settlement of the court's Commerce Clause doctrine quickly followed. These changes did nothing to compromise the Taney Court's antiabolitionism.

Even so, the justices sought, through their decisions, to reconcile the Union's free-labor and slaveholding regimes within its governing structure. Many of them experienced, in a practical sense, what Eugene Genovese has termed the "Slaveholders' Dilemma": a deeply felt need to protect slavery for the sake of social and political order as well as a contradictory but perhaps equally compelling desire to reap the benefits of liberal capitalism.[36] In the court's jurisprudence, those benefits remained connected intimately to federal commercial power, corporate law, and diversity jurisdiction. After the *Passenger Cases*, most Taney Court members worked through this dilemma by developing an increasingly sophisticated doctrinal web that maintained a series of partitions allowing the court to preserve a protective stance toward slavery without sacrificing the benefits of federal power, commerce, and capitalism.

A concept of concurrent sovereignty occupied the center of this web: both the state and federal government were supreme and independent within their spheres but also mutually limited in their authority because of their place within the constitutional order. This idea represented no conceptual innovation: the balancing was implicit in the Constitution and in much of court doctrine. Taney Court justices merely found a renewed emphasis on concurrency a useful strategy in the wake of the *License Cases* and *Passenger Cases*. They could now circumvent the exclusivity debate and manage the slavery question, thereby checking the court's tendency toward incoherence. *Strader v. Graham* (1851) represented the decisive move toward this position. *Strader* concerned the freedom claims of three Kentucky slaves—skilled musicians—who voluntarily returned to that state after their master had sent them to work for a few days in Ohio and Indiana. Although Kentucky case law generally recognized such claims, the state's highest court held that a brief stay in free territory accompanied by a "voluntary" return to the state created no claim to freedom. Entry into free states, the court admitted, suspended the master's authority for the duration of the slaves' stay, and they could have remained forever in Ohio or Indiana as free persons. Yet when they returned to Kentucky, the master's power revived, and the slaves' status remained unchanged.[37.]

The losing party appealed to the U.S. Supreme Court, arguing that the Kentucky ruling was erroneous. Speaking for the court (for the first time in a slavery decision), Taney dismissed the case for want of jurisdiction. "Every state," he wrote, "has an undoubted right to determine the *status*, or domestic and social condition, of the persons domiciled within its territory." His statement sounded similar to those in his manuscript on the Negro Sea-men Act as well as in his opinions in *Groves*, *Prigg*, and the *Passenger Cases*. Perhaps recognizing his colleagues' disapproval of his self-preservation ar-gument, Taney added a qualification: "except in so far as the powers of the states in this respect are restrained, or duties and obligations imposed upon them, by the Constitution of the United States."[38] To abolitionists such as Birney and subsequent historians, this passage sounded invidious—a pos-sible signal that Taney and his colleagues considered those "duties and obli-gations" a mechanism to force slavery into the northern states. The argu-ment goes too far. Taney's qualification probably conceded the limitations on state authority limned out in *Prigg* and the *Passenger Cases* and indicated the chief justice's willingness to pursue his agenda within the constraints established by his colleagues.[39]

With his newly moderated stance, Taney articulated a general approach to the slavery question. Although it accepted federal supremacy over matters such as immigration and the reclamation of fugitive slaves, Taney's formu-lation presumed that the vast majority of matters fell into state jurisdiction and pointed toward a strategy in which the court would vigorously assert a lack of jurisdiction until litigants proved otherwise. Refusal of jurisdic-tion in effect forced all but a handful of slavery questions down to the states and permitted their courts to address the matters as they saw fit. Indeed, Taney outlined a doctrinal foundation he hoped would handle most such cases. *Strader*'s fact situation really raised only the question concerning the status of an allegedly enslaved person of color "voluntarily" returning to a slave state after a stay in a free one. Taney's opinion, however, encompassed returns from territories covered by federal antislavery provisions, like the legislation enacting the Missouri Compromise or recognizing the force of the Northwest Ordinance. The court's stance therefore remained staunchly supportive of slavery. Its members set aside an early motion to dismiss the case for want of jurisdiction and allowed counsel to proceed to the merits, and Taney went out of his way to express satisfaction with the substance of Kentucky's ruling, although the merits of the case were technically not before the court.[40] Scholarly emphasis on proslavery constitutionalism has obscured the shift in Taney's attitude that underlay *Strader*. No longer did he invoke an absolute and unlimited state power of self-preservation. He now signaled a willingness to allow both state and federal authority the potential to expand to their constitutional limits. His argument implied, moreover, that the court would handle the determination of whether slavery questions fell into federal or state jurisdictions on a case-by-case basis, albeit with an unambiguous presumption toward the states.

One year later, the court made its commitment to the concurrent-sovereignty position explicit and closed the exclusivity debate among its members. This move came in *Cooley v. Board of Wardens of the Port of Philadelphia* (1852), where Woodbury's recent replacement, Benjamin Robbins Curtis, ruled that the states could pass commercial regulations until Congress legislated. "I expect the decision will excite surprise," Curtis wrote to his uncle, "because it is adverse to the exclusive authority of Congress and not in accordance with the opinion of McLean and Wayne, who are the most high toned federalists on the bench." Nevertheless, the decision fully satisfied Curtis, "and it has received the assent of five justices out of eight, although for twenty years no majority has ever rested their decision on either view of this question." Pilot laws hardly generated the level of emotion that regulations concerning temperance, immigration, and slavery did, but Curtis deftly avoided raising the issues that had fragmented the court in the past. His ruling made no mention of contested precedents, of quarantine and health laws, or even of the police power. Curtis merely noted that the bewildering scope of commercial regulation called for a case-by-case approach rather than sweeping statements of exclusivity. With that argument, he laid down a doctrine that held for nearly a century and cemented the reconfiguration of the court's majority that followed in the wake of *Strader*. The ruling did not please everyone. Catron reported to the future president James Buchanan a sense of elation, but McLean and Wayne dissented, as Curtis reported to his uncle, and Daniel wrote a concurring opinion that rejected the court's reasoning. McLean and Daniel both retained their insistence on exclusivity (of federal and state power, respectively), but, after *Cooley*, these positions remained decidedly in the minority. Although individual justices occasionally joined either McLean or Daniel at the court's poles, the majority, as a whole, favored the case-by-case approach that the emphasis on concurrent sovereignty enabled. Through this method, the court could tailor individual doctrines that protected slavery without resorting to sweeping theoretical positions that threatened to subordinate federal power and its benefits to the perceived needs of the South.[41]

The strategy worked, and the justices revealed in *Moore v. Illinois* (1852) that they had effectively moved beyond the impasse that the intersection of the slavery and exclusivity questions had generated. In 1842, Illinois fined Richard Eells $400, under an 1833 statute, for harboring a fugitive slave who had fled from Missouri. Eells appealed, arguing that the statute violated Congress's authority as expressed in the Fugitive Slave Law of 1793, and the case eventually worked its way before the Supreme Court. *Moore* could have reopened old debates, but the court unanimously and unceremoniously upheld the Illinois law by labeling it a police regulation that only incidentally aided masters. The statute merely levied a fine (for the state's benefit) or brief imprisonment designed to discourage its citizens from harboring fugitives, and it never contemplated masters or slaves. Illinois's law thus came within the police power concessions of Story's *Prigg* ruling. *Prigg*, said Grier, speaking for the court, affirmed the states' authority "to protect themselves against the influx either of liberated or fugitive slaves, and to repel from their soil a population likely to become burdensome and injurious, either as paupers or criminals." Even McLean agreed, but he maintained that the law was unconstitutional because it subjected Eells to double jeopardy (the Fugitive Slave Law already contained a similar provision). "No government, regulated by laws, punishes twice criminally the same act," he wrote. "And I deeply regret that our government should be an exception to a great principle of action, sanctioned by humanity and justice." McLean's disagreement, which again struck at the implications of concurrent sovereignty, proved mild relative to the fragmentation that had appeared on the court in the 1840s.[42]

Moore's placidity indicated that the justices had struck upon a strategy allowing the court to deal with slavery in a Union of concurrent sovereigns. The court's post-1852 policy emphasized that it would throw the majority of issues concerning social status down to the states, and the *Cooley* doctrine assumed that the states possessed the authority to legislate in such matters. Again, this strategy lent strong support to slavery. Grier hinted in *Moore* that the court might reconsider whether states could pass legislation that actively aided masters in apprehending fugitive slaves.[43] A majority of justices, however, agreed to contemplate this policy only after Taney conceded that certain aspects of federal law would not be subordinated to slavery. The settlement of differences achieved by *Strader* and *Cooley* ended the debate that divided the justices throughout the 1840s. A conception of the Union as a relationship among concurrently sovereign governments allowed the formation of doctrinal strategy that protected slavery without sacrificing federal power and the benefits it offered to the perceived needs of the South. Approaching issues concerning the extent of federal power on a case-by-case basis enabled the court to develop a series of doctrinal partitions around slavery that would protect the peculiar institution without undermining the court's agendas in commercial and corporate law. The settlement also functioned to keep the more proslavery justices in check. Taney himself apparently remained mindful of the divisions that had plagued the court in the 1840s, and throughout the 1850s he steadfastly held to the contours of concurrent sovereignty as limned out in *Strader* and *Cooley*.

Between 1842 and 1852, the Taney Court reworked its stance toward slavery. Although it never wavered in its antiabolitionist predisposition, the court developed an increasingly sophisticated approach to slavery that allowed a reconciliation of the justices' commitment to the peculiar institution with their desire to facilitate commercial interaction. Ever since *Groves*, the justices had agreed that commerce and slavery ought to be handled separately, but their consensus made no provision for the deeper divisions concerning the extent of federal power that characterized the court in the 1840s. Underlying disagreements exposed the flimsy nature of the *Groves* consensus when the issues of slavery and exclusivity intersected in *Prigg* and the *Passenger Cases*, and the ensuing fragmentation took the court to the edge of incoherence. The court solved this problem in the early 1850s by placing a renewed emphasis on concurrent sovereignty, which allowed the justices to separate their concerns about security for slavery from the theoretical disputes over federal exclusivity. That this disjunction took place in *Strader* and *Cooley*—two cases that superficially had little to do with each other—symbolized that separation.

The policy limned out in *Strader* and *Cooley* worked a subtle transformation in the Supreme Court's approach toward slavery. A presumption that state authority controlled issues of social status and standing qualified by an assertion that federal power could trump such authority in particular cases altered the dynamic of Taney Court jurisprudence. Disputes among the justices over slavery no longer centered on the theoretical limits of federal power and usually did not take place in slavery cases. Rather, the slavery debate shifted to areas such as corporate law, where the justices argued, without ever explicitly saying so, over the proper ways in which to separate the peculiar institution from other areas of judicial concern. An unintended consequence of this changing emphasis was a heightened attention to matters of race. The slavery cases that preceded *Dred Scott*—*Moore* being the last of them—never rested explicitly on considerations of black inferiority. They centered primarily on whether the states possessed an inherent power of self-preservation that trumped federal authority. A working assumption of white superiority, of course, ran latently through the court's discourse and constantly influenced its members' thinking. The background presence of this assumption, however, exerted little overt influence on the court's rulings. As late as 1855, in fact, a unanimous court ruled that the Treaty of Guadalupe Hidalgo incorporated nonwhite Mexicans as citizens of the United States.[44] Efforts to keep slavery separate from other issues, however, encouraged the justices to seek ways to draw proper distinctions between free blacks and other legal subjects. That process culminated in *Dred Scott*'s denial of federal citizenship to blacks, but the perceived need for that denial arose in the context of an internal debate over the proper way to reconcile the protection of slavery with the emerging corporate order.

CHAPTER FIVE

The Limits of Judicial Partisanship

Corporate Law and the Emergence of Southern Factionalism

IN 1856, THE RECENTLY APPOINTED Justice John A. Campbell, supported by his colleagues Peter V. Daniel and John Catron, issued a scathing dissent against the court's decision in *Dodge v. Woolsey*. The court had just ruled that Ohio possessed no authority to abolish the tax exemptions it had previously granted to its banking corporations. Earlier decisions declared that Ohio could not change corporate tax rates through ordinary legislation, and now the court asserted that Ohio could not do so by amending its constitution. The court's ruling, Campbell wrote, placed "this court between these corporations and the government and people of Ohio, to which they owe their existence." In doing so, the court raised the specter of class conflict by supporting a "caste" of elites "who will habitually look beyond the institutions and the authorities of the State to the central government . . . to maintain them in the enjoyment of their special privileges and exemptions." Such protection threatened to increase "alienation and discord between the different classes of society" and introduce "a fresh cause of disturbance in our distracted political and social system." "In the end," Campbell concluded, "this decision may lead to a violent overturn of the whole system of corporate combinations."[1]

Campbell spoke for a faction of southern justices (himself, Daniel, and Catron) who had come together, shortly after the Taney Court had implemented its strategy for dealing with slavery, to mount a sustained attack on the court's corporate doctrine as it had developed since 1819. On the surface, the faction expressed concern with the unintended consequences of sustaining the Marshall Court's constitutional protection of corporations. When the Taney Court formed in 1837, its members curbed procorporate precedent and prevented the formation of an elite based on constitutionally protected corporate privileges. Under Taney's lead, the court achieved this goal through the rigid construction of charter language. Strict construction functioned to protect the people's sovereignty both by forcing corporations to remain within the confines of their charters and by ensuring that the people need only adhere to those obligations articulated in explicit statutory language. By 1853, however, the Supreme Court's corporate jurisprudence shifted its emphasis, as corporate litigants learned to work within the parameters of Taney Court doctrine. Rulings increasingly sustained corporate privilege against state efforts to meet changing social demands, and by 1855 the court had unintentionally transformed itself into a defender of corporate power against popular will as it was legislatively and even constitutionally expressed. Threatened by the limitations on state sovereignty contained in this doctrine, Campbell, Catron, and Daniel's southern faction demanded a complete rejection of the court's corporate law doctrine and advocated an alternative based on an explicit recognition of the states' inherent power of self-preservation. This division, although superficially remote from the slavery question as the court generally confronted it, formed the immediate doctrinal context in which the *Dred Scott* case emerged.

The Taney Court's difficulties with corporate privilege began with the doctrinal legacy of the Marshall Court. Federal and state judiciaries performed critical administrative functions within the antebellum state by overseeing legislative granting policy. Through the distribution of land and corporate charters, legislatures harnessed acquisitive desire to public ends and encouraged development within their jurisdictions.[2] These distributive policies generated a great deal of conflict, as politicians and citizens debated whether corporations benefited the community generally or merely a small number of politically connected investors. Beneath these debates lay a question of whether governmental policy should foster a guiding elite that would promote orderly social development or whether such development should occur haphazardly according to the interests of equally privileged individuals. The Marshall Court by no means remained neutral in this discourse. Its members saw the protection of corporate privilege as a means to sustain (Federalist) elite power in the wake of the egalitarian impulses unleashed by the revolution and expressed in antielitist sentiment. Marshall Court intervention into corporate law set the parameters of its successor's jurisprudence.

The Taney Court's handling of corporate charters proceeded under the constraints imposed by *Fletcher v. Peck* (1810) and *Dartmouth College v. Woodward* (1819). *Fletcher* involved a suit over a title to land granted by

Georgia's legislature to a group of speculators who promised legislators some of the land after its conveyance. That was bribery, and the succeeding legislature promptly repealed the grant. Chief Justice John Marshall declared the repeal unconstitutional because the state violated the obligation of contracts, which the Constitution expressly forbade. Legislative corruption was, of course, deplorable, but Marshall discerned no clear standards for judicial remedy. A determination of what constituted an actionable amount of corruption—which a court could define as "undue influence of any kind"—impinged on questions of legislative discretion that Marshall believed, like Taney after him, lay beyond judicial cognizance.[3]

Yet Marshall stripped from the Georgia legislature any power to remedy the situation. A grant, he said, reviewing Blackstone, "is a contract executed." If Marshall had followed Blackstone, Georgia could have repealed the grant (because execution ended a contractual relationship and transformed the grant's object into the property of another), but the chief justice apparently misread the English jurist. A grant of property, Marshall wrote, extinguished the right of the grantor by creating an implied contract "not to reassert that right." Parties, such as Fletcher, who purchased the land from the grantees without knowledge of the corrupt circumstances surrounding the original transaction did so under the expectation that Georgia would stand by those obligations. Marshall's error may have been innocent, for *Fletcher* predated the antebellum legal profession's rediscovery and systemization of the common law. Mistaken or not, however, the equation of property and contracts ensured that the Marshall Court would curb redistributionist state legislatures.[4]

Almost one decade later, *Dartmouth* brought grants of corporate charters under the protection of the Obligation of Contracts Clause. In 1816, New Hampshire's legislature, having recently come under Jeffersonian-Republican control, placed the management of Dartmouth College, a Federalist stronghold, under the governor's oversight. Dartmouth's trustees, to whom the original charter gave administrative authority, challenged the law, and the Supreme Court upheld their claim. Constitutional protection, Marshall argued, applied to all contracts involving property—those agreements whose breach "weakened the confidence of man in man, and embarrassed all transactions between individuals, by dispensing with a faithful performance of engagements." Many corporate charters fell into this category, and they were, following *Fletcher*, contracts executed with which a state could not interfere. As Justice Joseph Story wrote in his influential concurring opinion, a completed grant "involved a contract, that the grantees should hold, and the grantor should not re-assume the grant." Dartmouth College's charter, Story continued, lay beyond the reach of the legislature, and states could not alter a charter unless it contained a clause authorizing them to do so. New Hampshire's law was therefore unconstitutional.[5]

Both *Fletcher* and *Dartmouth* represented maneuvers in a class struggle with cultural dimensions. Legal historians have generally focused on the economic implications of the court's protection of vested rights.[6] Such focus is warranted, but the point need not be labored here. A curb on legislative redistribution among whites—Marshall Court doctrine offered little protection to property held by Native Americans beyond the assertion that dispossession rightfully took place under federal rather than state oversight—probably encouraged investment and fueled development in a capital-scarce economy. Story, after all, explicitly placed banks and insurance companies under constitutional protection. Market forces, however, do not explain all things. Control over an educational institution such as Dartmouth remained vital to the representatives of the Union's embattled Federalist elite. These schools provided training grounds for the younger generation and instilled the elitist values perceived to be appropriate to their class. There was a reason New Hampshire's legislature considered Dartmouth a threat: the college produced powerful and articulate opponents bent on frustrating Jeffersonian-Republican agendas.[7]

Marshall understood the stakes. Dartmouth's original trustees "were among the most eminent and respectable individuals in New Hampshire." Such "learned and intelligent men," Marshall assumed, "would select learned and intelligent men for their successors" and would be "as well fitted for the government of a college as those who might be chosen by other means." "Should this reasoning ever prove erroneous," he added, "public opinion . . . would correct the institution." One may well wonder how: Marshall's court had just undercut the most powerful vehicle for expressing public opinion. A popularly elected legislature possessed no authority to alter the college's charter. Under this newly asserted independence, colleges chartered before 1819 could become centers for the reproduction of an elite hostile to the changes taking place around it. Harvard, with which the ubiquitous Story was deeply involved, capitalized on the *Dartmouth* protections and established itself at the center of an institutional matrix devoted toward the aggrandizement of national power for Boston's elite. More economically oriented corporations played a role in this network, but they comprised only part of the elite's wider effort to secure their power through these ancient charters.[8]

The Marshall Court's rulings in *Fletcher* and *Dartmouth* limited state legislatures' ability to rectify grants later perceived as improvidently given and provided a doctrinal foundation that sustained elite privilege in the face of more egalitarian alternatives. Through these mechanisms, the Marshall Court set itself up as a guiding elite that protected the Union from the actions of what its members considered irresponsible state legislatures. Marshall and his colleagues also promoted a regime in which economic development would take place under the stewardship of those reared in protected institutions such as Dartmouth and thus ensure that social change took place in an ordered fashion. Taney Court members reacted strongly against these features of Marshall Court jurisprudence and rejected their predecessors' elitism. Yet *Fletcher* and *Dartmouth*, for all their political implications, were unquestionably legitimate rulings. They had been argued in open court and determined according to known rules, and they had become precedent in subsequent cases. Their status as precedent, in fact, would profoundly shape the contours of the Taney Court's reaction to the Supreme Court's earlier corporate jurisprudence.

A Taney Court majority never challenged either *Fletcher* or *Dartmouth*, although the Democratic justices promptly curbed the latter decision. With the ascension of President Andrew Jackson's appointees, the perceived beneficiaries of Supreme Court rulings changed. No longer did a majority of the court link the Union's fate to the vested rights of an elite threatened by irresponsible legislatures. The Union's fate lay with the sovereign people, who had to be self-governing. A shift in perceived beneficiaries brought a marked change in the court's corporate law doctrine, which immediately rejected the role of guiding elite for both corporations and the court itself. The justices' desire to transform popular sovereignty from a theoretical postulate to a lived social relationship embraced deep currents in the court's jurisprudence. Indeed, one of the most significant features of its rulings in this area—the strict construction of charters—sought not only to mitigate the potentially elitist tendencies of corporations and the court but also to maintain a distinction between popular sovereignty and legislative authority.

Jackson's appointees understood the stakes involved in corporate law, and they wasted no time in curbing *Dartmouth*. In the 1837 *Charles River Bridge* decision, a divided court conceded the contractual nature of corporate charters but maintained that such grants required a strict construction that applied any ambiguities against the grantees and in favor of the public. *Charles River Bridge*'s origins lay in the Massachusetts Legislature's 1827 chartering of the Warren Bridge Corporation, which would build an (ultimately) toll-free bridge spanning the Charles River, linking Boston to Charlestown. Warren Bridge's course was essentially contiguous with that of the older Charles River Bridge, which had a 1785 charter authorizing it to collect tolls mostly for the proprietors' benefit. Toll collection along this route was apparently quite lucrative. By 1814, according to Stanley Kutler, the company's stock had risen to more than 600 percent of its original value. Because the older bridge's value rested on the tolls collected, its proprietors accurately perceived the chartering of an adjacent free bridge as a taking. After unsuccessful struggles in the legislature, the proprietors of the Charles River Bridge took their competitors to court and eventually worked their way to the U.S. Supreme Court. There, counsel for the Charles River Bridge argued that the charter contained an implied contract between grantees and the state that the latter would not reduce the value of the charter by creating a competitor.[9]

Charles River Bridge, a wide range of legal historians concede, represented a contest between contrasting modes of economic development. The Warren Bridge (and Taney Court) position favored a dynamic use of property encouraging economic growth through competition, whereas the Charles River Bridge (and Story's dissenting) stance promoted a vision of legal certainty and predictability as fundamental for maintaining an environment attractive to investors.[10] Once again, the focus on economics only partially explains the decision. Both Taney and Story, although quite conscious of the economic implications, conceived the problem before them in political terms. *Charles River Bridge* hinged on whether the court would extrapolate intentions from charter grants that in effect illegitimately imposed obligations on the sovereign people. The chief justice and the majority of his colleagues believed that this policy would allow persons of perceived aristocratic pretension to claim protection for implied contractual rights and impose a regime of development more congenial to their interests. Resorting to implication would also force the people to stand to obligations not clear at a charter's creation and consequently subordinate the sovereign but unarticulated will to the judicial, and inherently elitist, determination of legislative intent.

Taney flatly refused to move his court in those directions. "The continued existence of a government," he wrote, "would be of no great value, if, by implications and presumptions, it was disarmed of the powers necessary to accomplish the ends of its creation, and the functions it was designed to perform, transferred to the hands of privileged corporations."[11] The Charles River Bridge's charter constituted a "grant of certain franchises, by the public, to a private corporation, and in a matter where the public interest is concerned." Drawing on a relatively small sample of English and American precedent, Taney insisted that the rule governing the case was "that in grants by the public, nothing passes by implication." The charter allowed the proprietors to build a bridge and to collect the tolls but said nothing about barring the construction of competing bridges or conferring an exclusive right to Boston-Charlestown traffic. Thus, a future legislature, acting out of its concern for the public good, could charter competing franchises, even if they effectively destroyed the value of older corporations.[12]

Taney's argument powerfully articulated the Democratic justices' vision of judicial authority. He read the charter as the court would any other statute, and he refused to extrapolate legislative intention from textual silences. His behavior anticipated the court's stance in *Bank of Augusta v. Earle* and *Swift v. Tyson* because it treated the words of a statute as the only relevant evidence of the people's will. Through the strict construction of those documents, moreover, the Taney Court fashioned itself as an antielitist facilitator of popular sovereignty. A rejection of more liberal patterns of interpretation worked on two levels. First, it underscored the justices' refusal to become a guiding elite that used the authority of its institution to save the Union and corporations from potentially irresponsible legislatures, and it thus constituted a direct reaction against the politics of *Fletcher* and *Dartmouth*. On the second, and ultimately more significant, level, the vision of judicial authority in *Charles River Bridge* employed strict construction to maintain a distinction between the sovereign people and the legislatures that spoke for them. Court members presumed an identity between popular will and statutory language but simultaneously recognized a disjunction between the people's sovereignty and the legislature itself. In Taney Court discourse, sovereignty rested in the people, which the court imagined as an undifferentiated mass of white men generally lacking in individual influence, and the legislature constituted the mere representative of this sovereign. A tendency toward strict construction in the court's jurisprudence represented a necessary consequence of this disjunction, for legislatures always remained subordinate to their sovereigns. Taney Court justices enforced that subordination by resorting to strict construction, which required that legislatures speak for their people only through explicit statutory wording.

Taney infused this vision of judicial authority with an intense, partisan approval of its policy implications, a combination that made his argument compelling. The implied contract claimed by the Charles River Bridge's proprietors involved the rights of the whole community, which would be adversely affected by the privileges claimed. Implying a contract in this case, he said, demanded "a strong exertion of judicial power, acting upon its own views of what justice required, and [what] the parties ought to have done." Such an exercise of "judicial coercion" would strip from the states a "portion of that power over their own internal police and improvement, which is so necessary to their well-being and prosperity." Taney and his court thus freed the states to charter new corporations without fear of running against vested rights under implied charter-contracts and diminished the protection that *Dartmouth* offered to corporations and the elites who composed them. Justices John McLean and Joseph Story found those features profoundly disturbing. Despite its policy-oriented elements, however, Taney's *Charles River Bridge* opinion touched deeper jurisprudential concerns that rendered his argument difficult to resist. McLean, for example, lambasted Massachusetts's legislature for what he believed to be an unjust taking, yet he could see no way around the court's ruling, and he uncomfortably concurred with the majority.[13]

Only Story possessed both the politically inspired outrage and the capability to challenge Taney's melding of policy goals and jurisprudential assumptions. The common-law rule governing this case, Story argued, demanded that grants from the legislature receive the same construction as grants from individuals, meaning that any ambiguities worked in favor of the grantees. A grant, moreover, implied all the rights necessary for its enjoyment and thus required no explicit enumeration in the charter. Story staked out a reasonable position. The Charles River Bridge's value rested solely on the tolls granted to the proprietors under the charter. Constructing the bridge was a major architectural achievement at the time, and the proprietors, Story speculated, most likely would have rejected a charter that did not guarantee the tolls in exchange for such a risky and expensive undertaking. They almost certainly would have rejected a charter reserving the legislature's right to create contiguous bridges with the same termini. No sound person would accept such a deal, and the court, by reading the charter so strictly, not only sustained an unconstitutional impairment of contractual obligations but also threatened to discourage investment. "The very agitation of a question of this sort," Story said, "is sufficient to alarm every stockholder in every public enterprise of this sort, throughout the whole country."[14]

Story also challenged what he incorrectly perceived as the majority's equation of sovereign and legislative will and argued that the court had essentially freed the legislatures from all restraint. The rule for strict construction against grantees, he wrote, was completely unsuited to American institutional conditions. At common law, the rule applied to royal grants, which rested on monarchical prerogative. Taney assumed an analogous relationship between legislative and royal grants, but the latter type stood "upon the divine right of kings, or, at least, upon a sense of their exalted dignity and pre-eminence over all subjects" by which their grants merited special treatment. Grants of Parliament, the authority of which state legislatures had assumed after the revolution, received treatment just like those made between individuals, and legislatures possessed no grounds to claim royal authority. Indeed, the "legislature of Massachusetts is," Story noted, "in no just sense, sovereign." The legislature legitimately exercised only that authority given to it by the sovereign people through the state constitution. By that document, the legislature possessed unlimited authority to bestow grants but retained only a limited ability to resume one, because taking property (or destroying its value) for public use required compensation. The Warren Bridge's charter was therefore void under Massachusetts's constitution as well as the U.S. Constitution as interpreted in *Fletcher* and *Dartmouth*.[15]

Story harbored deep, if misplaced, concerns about the corrosive implications he perceived in *Charles River Bridge*. "Will the people awake to their rights and duties," he asked rhetorically in a letter to McLean. "I fear not," Story answered. "They have become stupefied, and are led on to their ruin by the arts of demagogues and the corrupted influences of party." He then predicted that the Supreme Court would never again declare a state or federal law unconstitutional.[16] Yet Taney and his Democratic colleagues had no desire to release legislatures from their constitutional obligations, any more than they desired to liberate individuals from their commercial responsibilities. Taney recognized, however, that the contractual dynamic introduced by *Fletcher* and *Dartmouth* into the policing of legislative grants rendered unworkable a strict application of common-law doctrine. Obligation of contracts doctrine—and a Taney Court majority never challenged its extension to grants of property or charters—provided corporations with a powerful mechanism against legislative intervention. Bringing implied contracts, even reasonable ones, under this protection placed the court on a slippery

slope, forcing it to develop an arbitrary rule that would manage these undefined rights. Any such rule, Taney argued, would unjustly fetter legislatures
and stifle state internal improvement schemes, since no one would know
without litigation what obligations bound the parties. The management of
undefined rights would also transform the court into a guiding elite and
perhaps sustain efforts by persons of aristocratic pretension to pursue their
interests through silently granted corporate privileges, which the legislature
might well have denied if it had fully articulated the people's will.[17]

The Taney Court's commitment to popular sovereignty brought about
a shift in the Supreme Court's corporate doctrine. Rejecting the Marshall
Court's use of the Obligation of Contracts Clause to bolster the position of
the Union's established elites, Taney and his colleagues introduced a strict
constriction of corporate charters. This interpretive strategy represented
part of the court's antielitism, and it sought to check the ability of corporations, the justices, and to some extent state legislatures to constitute themselves as a guiding few within the social order. The court's qualification of
Dartmouth gave state legislatures relatively more freedom of action in their
dealings with corporations, especially those chartered before 1819 and others
that lacked charter clauses allowing legislative revision. By permitting states
to create competing companies, *Charles River Bridge* allowed the formulation of policy designed specifically to put older corporations out of business.
Beneath the immediate policy concerns and overt partisan implications of
Charles River Bridge, however, lay a deeper commitment to a jurisprudence
of popular sovereignty that sought the preservation of the people's power
through the strict construction of charter language. By adhering strictly to
the words of a charter, the court forced legislatures to state explicitly what
they were giving away before they could create any obligations that bound
the people.[18] The consequent disjunction between popular sovereignty and
legislative authority effectively limited state as well as corporate power, and
by the 1850s, this feature of the court's corporate jurisprudence had become
a matter of serious contention among the justices.

In the years immediately preceding *Dred Scott*, in fact, court members divided bitterly over corporate law's implications for state sovereignty. Most
justices perceived institutional limitations on their policing of privileges
granted to corporations, although the fervor of their rhetoric sometimes
obscured this recognition. After *Charles River Bridge*, the justices considered
Dartmouth to be good law, and they applied it with little hesitation when a

corporation claimed protection through an express charter grant. Obligations of contract doctrine thus became a powerful bar on legislative intervention into the workings of corporations when the latter remained within the confines of their charters. Yet *Charles River Bridge* also curbed most court members' legal imagination. Their emphasis on forcing corporations to remain within the confines of explicitly granted and rigidly construed charter provisions prevented the court from providing remedies when doctrinally proper grants barred state legislatures from adjusting their policy to changing social demands. This problem came into sharp relief in the mid-1850s, when the court confronted a series of cases pitting express grants against changing popular will as it was legislatively and even constitutionally expressed. By continuing to adhere to *Dartmouth*—even as mediated by *Charles River Bridge*—a fragmented, sometimes uncomfortable majority suddenly became defenders of corporate privilege. That majority faced a coherent and persistent opposition mounted by three southern justices who advocated a complete rethinking of the court's corporate doctrine because it had become an unconscionable limitation on state authority. This division formed the immediate background for the *Dred Scott Case*.

Dartmouth's power lay in its treatment of corporate charters as contracts, which brought them under the protection of the Constitution's obligation of contracts provision. Following the Marshall Court's 1819 ruling in *Sturges v. Crowninshield*, the court applied a rigid rule barring state intervention into the obligations of contracts (as distinct from contracts found in grants) already made.[19] In 1843, for example, the court instructed a lower federal court to ignore an Illinois law retroactively preventing creditors from selling foreclosed lands unless the sale would yield two-thirds of the property's appraised value. Speaking for the court, Taney declared the law unconstitutional because it deprived a creditor "of his pre-existing right to foreclose the mortgage by a sale of the premises" and imposed "upon him conditions which would frequently render any sale altogether impossible." Illinois thus transcended its legitimate authority.[20] Eight years later, a divided court ordered an officer of the state of Arkansas to accept payment of debts owed to the state in the depreciated paper issued by the Bank of Arkansas. The bank's 1840 charter declared that the state would accept such currency for the payment of debts, although the legislature repealed that provision five years later. Arkansas, McLean argued for the court, had struck a contract with the holders of the notes, and it incurred an obligation to accept the worthless paper for any debt contracted between 1840 and 1845. Obligation of contracts doctrine provided a powerful bar to state intervention into contractual relationships, and litigants constantly sought—not always successfully—to bring their suits under its protection.[21]

When they convinced the court that they remained within the bounds of their charters, corporations enjoyed a powerful federal shield against state encroachment. A unanimous court held in 1845 that Maryland could not tax the Union Bank of Maryland beyond what its charter specified. The state had granted the bank a charter extension in exchange for its contribution to the funding of roads and schools and said explicitly that it would levy no further taxes on the franchise for the duration of the charter. When it paid the required taxes, Justice James M. Wayne wrote, the Union Bank tendered valuable consideration and struck a contract with the state, and the Obligation of Contracts Clause barred any further tax on the franchise. Further taxation would in effect increase the contract's price beyond that agreed upon by the original parties. As Justice Levi Woodbury said in 1848, a major test for violations of the Obligation of Contracts Clause centered on whether legislative activity altered the value of a contract. On those grounds, a divided court struck down an 1840 Mississippi statute forbidding its banks from transferring any negotiable paper coming into their possession. Such transactions formed a sizable amount of the banking business, and the state had explicitly granted that privilege in the Planters' Bank of Mississippi's charter. The court therefore would not allow the new act to stand.[22]

Before 1853, the justices apparently found nothing disturbing about the obligation of contracts doctrine. A shifting majority recurrently ruled that corporations with explicit grants in their charters received the full benefits endowed by the court's rigid construction of the Obligation of Contracts Clause, although justices frequently differed over whether a particular charter should receive such protection.[23] After Story's resignation, in fact, only Daniel possessed a vision of state-corporate relations that differed significantly from that of his colleagues. A hint of his outlook emerged in 1848, when he rebuffed a Vermont bridge company's invocation of the Obligation of Contracts Clause. The company's 1795 charter granted an exclusive right to the bridge tolls for one hundred years, but about fifty years later, the state took the bridge (after giving compensation) for use as part of a free, public road. Daniel defended the state's action in language similar to the self-preservation argument employed by Taney throughout the 1840s: "In every political sovereign community there inheres necessarily the right and the duty of guarding its own existence, and of protecting and promoting the interests and welfare of the community at large." Daniel spoke here of eminent domain, a power so deeply connected to considerations of "the interior polity and relations of social life" that the court would not consider it given away by implication, especially when its exercise served the public good. In the course of his argument, however, Daniel broke with court's corporate doctrine and equated the people's sovereignty with legislative authority. Eminent domain, he wrote, was "paramount to all private rights vested under the government, and these last are, by necessary implication, held in subordination to this power, and must yield in every instance to its proper exercise." Although he spoke for the court here, Daniel anticipated a rift that would develop suddenly in the 1850s.[24]

This rift became apparent between 1854 and 1856, when the court confronted three Ohio cases involving the states' ability to grant away their taxing authority. Because *Charles River Bridge* merely tempered *Dartmouth's* protection of corporations, a majority of justices found themselves upholding the constitutionality of explicit legislative grants that clearly ran against changing popular will as statutorily and even constitutionally expressed. These cases pitted the justices' desire to recognize state authority to break the power of privileged corporate elites against their effort to protect the people's sovereignty from state legislatures as well as corporate grantees through the strict construction of charter language. The issue split the court along roughly sectional lines. A divided majority, adhering to the court's strategy of strict construction and defending its position in the name of federal supremacy, precedent, and the perceived morality of contractual fulfillment, grudgingly recognized the legitimacy of the grants. Those rulings, however, prompted a faction of southern justices to attack the court's use of the obligation of contracts doctrine to hinder the states' regulation of their internal affairs. Only a complete repudiation of *Dartmouth*, they argued, would remedy the situation.

Because these three decisions rested on the same set of laws and embraced similar factual circumstances, the analysis here will treat them as if they were one case. The justices did so. Some began their opinions in later cases precisely where they left off in previous cases, and some claimed that their opinions in one case covered the issues in the others. At any rate, *Piqua Branch of the State Bank of Ohio v. Knoop* (1854), *Ohio Life Insurance and Trust Company v. Debolt* (1854), and *Dodge v. Woolsey* (1856) all involved corporate resistance to an 1851 Ohio law (and, in the last case, a provision in the state's new constitution) subjecting corporations to the same tax rate as individuals. All three of the corporations traced their charters to an 1845 general incorporation statute passed in response to a statewide banking shortage. To encourage banking, the legislature inserted a provision setting a tax rate of 6 percent on profits in lieu of all other taxes. A number of entrepreneurs took advantage of this provision. Ohio's policy changed in 1851, when the legislature imposed the same tax rate on both corporations and individuals and when a contemporaneous constitutional convention inserted a similar provision into the state's new constitution. The corporations claimed that Ohio violated the Obligations of Contracts Clause and sued. A popularly elected state court, not surprisingly, proved unsympathetic, so the cases moved into federal court.[25]

A majority of justices, although considerably fragmented, held unequivocally that a state could grant away its taxing authority and therefore ruled in *Knoop* and *Dodge* that Ohio had violated the U.S. Constitution. (A majority rejected contractual status for the grant in *Debolt.*) According to McLean in *Knoop*, incident to their sovereignty, states unquestionably possessed authority to make contracts (charter grants). "A state, in granting privileges to a bank, with a view of affording sound currency, or of advancing any policy connected with the public interest, exercises its sovereignty, and for a public purpose, of which it is the exclusive judge." Charters created a set of vested rights that "can no more be disregarded nor set aside by a subsequent legislature, than a grant for land," for the federal Constitution "inhibited the exercise of such a power."[26] A new state constitution, moreover, had no effect on these contracts: "Moral obligations never die," Wayne stated in *Dodge*. "If broken by states and nations, though the terms of reproach are not the same with which we are accustomed to designate the faithlessness of individuals, the violation of justice is not the less." The Constitution, wrote the Georgia justice, was supreme "over all who made themselves parties to it; States as well as persons." Under this supreme law, states possessed no authority to impair the obligations of contracts, and any law or constitutional provision doing so was therefore void.[27]

McLean and Wayne's opinions followed squarely along the line of precedent established by *Dartmouth* and *Charles River Bridge*. Legislatures possessed the discretionary authority to create corporations as they felt necessary, and any ambiguities in the charter worked against the grantee. And no state could alter the value of a charter resting on an express agreement without giving compensation. Court members had invested a great deal of energy and ideological commitment in this doctrine, and it had become quite influential in the state courts. Still, some justices perceived in *Knoop, Debolt,* and *Dodge* a direct threat to the states' ability to rule themselves through their legislatures. Although its author dismissed such objections as nonsense, McLean's opinion implied that the states could grant away their taxing authority in perpetuity. Wayne proved a bit more cautious, but his opinion offered little guidance on the issue.

Taney attempted a clarification in *Debolt,* where the justices agreed on the ruling but remained too divided for anyone to speak for the court. His effort only underscored the limitations of the court's corporate jurisprudence. Repeating the view of federal relations he had first announced in *Strader v. Graham* (1851), Taney asserted that with the exception of the powers ceded in the Constitution, "the people of the several States are absolutely and unconditionally sovereign within their respective territories." Consequently, he wrote, "they may impose what taxes they think proper upon persons or things within their dominion, and may apportion them according to their discretion and judgement." The states thus possessed full authority to exempt corporations from taxation and to throw the burden to another segment of the population, and they could do so by contract if they wished. Legislatures might use this power "indiscreetly and injudiciously," and "experience may prove that [a particular contract] is a public injury." "When the contract is made," the chief justice continued, "the Constitution of the United States acts upon it, and declares that it shall not be impaired, and makes it the duty of this court to carry it into execution." "That duty," Taney added in words that did not appear in his manuscript, "must be performed."[28] In a passage inserted into the manuscript after he had written his larger argument, Taney explained that what he advocated was merely a continuation of the *Charles River Bridge* doctrine, which sustained the states' power to grant away their taxing authority. Even so, he displayed some discomfort with his conclusion and sought a way to soften it. Legislatures held their power in trust, he argued, and thus could perform no act binding their successors unless the constitution of the state authorized them to do so. No state could enter a contract depriving the legislature of its taxing authority, even for a specified time, unless its constitution allowed it—as Ohio's earlier document did. Taney's argument satisfied only Robert C. Grier, and the majority proved so fragmented that the court could give no indication about how it would address the problem.[29]

Three southern justices—Daniel, Catron, and the newly appointed

John A. Campbell of Alabama—found the Ohio tax cases profoundly disturbing. As Daniel said, "I can never believe in that . . . suicidal doctrine, which confers upon one legislature, the creatures and limited agents of the sovereign people, the power . . . to bind forever and irrevocably their creator, for whose benefit and by whose authority alone they are delegated to act."[30] The taxable property involved in these cases, Catron and Campbell argued, amounted to millions of dollars in Ohio alone, and the implications embraced millions more. Under the court's rulings, successive legislatures could lock up the vast majority of the state's property in contractual arrangements placing it beyond the reach of the taxing authority, thereby creating an aristocracy that would stifle the states' ability to serve their populations. The court's assumption that legislative motivation rested in a concern for the public good, Campbell added, ensured that the states possessed no remedy for contracts originating in corrupt bargains and thus brought the court back to the problem of *Fletcher*. Obligation of contracts doctrine as applied to corporate charters rendered government essentially useless to state populations and benefited no one except the charter's holders.[31]

The Framers, Campbell stated, never intended to limit the states in this manner. A power to change tax rates in response to shifting policy goals, all three justices contended, constituted part of the states' inherent power of self-preservation.[32] The court's rulings placed illegitimate fetters on that power and required repudiation. Sometime after he wrote his *Debolt* opinion, Catron inserted a rejection of *Dartmouth* into his manuscript (perhaps in response to Taney's addition of a defense of that decision). "I have become entirely convinced," Catron wrote, "that the protection of State legislation and independence, supposed to be found in a liberal construction of State laws in favor of the public and against monopolies, as asserted in the Charles River Bridge Case, is illusory and nearly useless." Courts could construe "almost any beneficial privilege, property, or exemption, claimed by corporations or individuals in virtue of State laws," into a contract. Tempering *Dartmouth* offered no protection, and the only proper response was a complete rejection of the obligation of contracts doctrine as it applied to corporate charters.[33]

By 1855, therefore, the court's corporate doctrine had become a highly contested matter. A majority of justices seemed satisfied with *Dartmouth* after its qualification in *Charles River Bridge*, although the resulting doctrine increasingly sustained corporate power as lawyers became more proficient in negotiating advantageous privileges. Obligation of contracts doctrine prevented the states from adjusting policy to changing social needs and thus allowed corporations to benefit at the expense of the community. An emphasis on forcing corporations into the confines of their charters ensured that its doctrine provided no conceptual tools to handle such unintended consequences. Daniel, Catron, and Campbell's solution—a reconfiguration of corporate doctrine based on the explicit recognition of an inherent power of self-preservation within the states—attempted to remedy that limitation, but the dissenters employed an argument that the court's majority had repeatedly rejected in slavery cases. Its treatment of the argument's revival in corporate law would not differ. A reemergence of the self-preservation argument, however, underscored the primary fissure on the Supreme Court on the eve of *Dred Scott*. The justices divided not into sectional factions over direct manifestations of the slavery question but rather into a southern faction and a relatively loose cross-sectional coalition over the implications of corporate law for states' rights.

Catron, Daniel, and Campbell exposed a real limitation in the court's corporate rulings. *Charles River Bridge* had originated as a facilitator of popular sovereignty and a constraint on the potential abuses of would-be aristocrats, but by the 1850s Supreme Court doctrine again sustained corporate power and blocked legislative attempts to remedy the situation. These consequences were largely unintended. Yet the Taney Court justices built them into corporate law as they reconciled the Marshall Court's *Fletcher* and *Dartmouth* rulings with its successor's partisan commitments, a combination that left intact the unfortunate association of charter and land grants with contracts. With that doctrine undisturbed, the court's partisanship meshed with its fidelity to federal supremacy and stress on the fulfillment of contractual obligations to allow the court to drift into a stance of procorporate formalism. As with the *Swift* doctrine, business interests found these rulings congenial and flocked to the federal courts. Indeed, *Dodge* came to the court through diversity because the agents of the bank involved wanted to avoid the hostile Ohio courts.[34] Disarmed by the logic of their court's rulings, the majority perceived little alternative beyond treating corporations as normal litigants. Despite their loud outcries, the members of the southern faction offered little remedy. Their opinions read as if inspired by an agrarian (or prebourgeois) fear of northern corporate power, but only the ideological purist Daniel sincerely desired a complete revision of the court's corporate doctrine.[35] Campbell and Catron merely used their extreme stance as a bargaining chip to force their colleagues to address a weakness in the court's larger strategic approach toward the slavery question. The weakness they saw centered on the access of corporations created by state law to the federal courts; such access potentially gave free blacks, if recognized as citizens by state law, an opportunity to enter the federal courts and avoid state laws designed to keep them in submission. Both Campbell and Catron were fully prepared to risk a complete gutting of the court's corporate law to ensure that the court addressed their concerns.

CHAPTER SIX

The Sources of
Southern Factionalism

Corporations, Free Blacks, and the Imperatives of Federal Citizenship

IN A CRITIQUE OF THE *PASSENGER CASES*, a correspondent for the *Charleston Mercury* argued that the Supreme Court had stripped the South of laws that could bar free blacks recognized as citizens in northern states from coming into the region under federal protection. The Supreme Court, of course, had done no such thing. Indeed, abolitionist James G. Birney condemned the ruling in *Strader v. Graham* for precisely the opposite reason. *Strader* held that slave states need not recognize the freedom claims of enslaved African Americans who had spent time in free territory; such questions were best left to state discretion. By asserting that states held nearly complete control over matters of social status within their boundaries, Birney contended, the court violated the predisposition toward freedom of both the Constitution and the Framers. The Framers hoped to bring slavery to an end, and one way of doing so was to recognize the freedom of any enslaved person that a master voluntarily took into free territory. Such persons not only became free but became citizens entitled to all the rights held by white citizens, whether naturalized or native-born. Moreover, these free black citizens also held the right to go into the South and claim all rights held by white citizens. "Any other interpretation of the constitution . . . would annul that portion of the instrument which declares, that 'the citizens of each State shall be entitled to all the privileges and immunities of citizens in the several States.'" Birney was well aware that his account of the law did not explain current practice, but that was because passion, interest, and a misunderstanding of popular opinion obscured the court's ability to see the Constitution's correct interpretation. Both Birney and the *Mercury*'s correspondent discussed a turn of events that never came to pass during the antebellum period. Yet they discussed a scenario that was certainly plausible in the context of federal citizenship law and one that the court's southern faction, through its maneuvers in corporate law cases, prepared to counter.[1]

As they assailed corporations, members of the southern faction continually revisited the question of corporate jurisdiction. *Dodge v. Woolsey* (1856) placed the issue in sharp relief. The case, which involved an Ohio constitutional provision judged to be a violation of the Obligations of Contract Clause, entered the federal courts through diversity jurisdiction, because previous decisions allowed corporations to claim citizenship in the state in which they were chartered. Allowing corporations access to this jurisdictional avenue, Justice John A. Campbell argued, did nothing except gratify "the most morbid appetite for jurisdiction among all their various members" and sustain corporate privilege at the expense of the states' ability to provide for their citizens' welfare through legislation.[2] The underlying concern of members of the faction, especially Campbell and John Catron, may have had less to do with corporate access to diversity jurisdiction per se than with the fact that in the court's understanding of citizenship law, the status of corporations and free blacks were conceptually identical. Both gained citizenship through the recognition of particular states, and if the court recognized corporations as citizens for the purposes of jurisdiction, then it might do so for free blacks as well. Corporations, as *Dodge* demonstrated, benefited immensely from the federal protection this recognition granted, and free blacks might likewise use their access to the federal courts to undermine the southern slave regimes. Because corporate access to diversity jurisdiction offered analogies that could be useful to free black litigants, the southern faction treated it as a potential threat, and the faction's maneuvers would form the immediate doctrinal context for *Dred Scott*.

For the southern faction, the central problem of American citizenship lay in its duality. "Every citizen of a State," Justice William Johnson wrote in 1820, "owes a double allegiance; he enjoys the protection and participates in the government of both the State and United States." At law, *citizenship* signified a legal relationship in which purportedly free individuals gave their allegiance to a sovereign community in exchange for the protection of their rights to life, liberty, and property. Citizens thus agreed to obey laws that in turn safeguarded for them a bundle of rights that varied significantly according to race, gender, and jurisdiction. In the United States, citizens effectively belonged to two sovereign communities, creating, in Justice Samuel

Chase's words, a "two-fold political capacity" that provided citizens with two bundles of rights. As Chase wrote in 1798, "In relation to the state, [a citizen] is subject to the various municipal regulations founded on the State Constitution and policy, which do not affect him in his relation to the United States." This duality raised the possibility that citizens' claims to federal protection could justify judicial intervention in state affairs. Members of the southern faction apparently believed that the court's corporate rulings signaled the beginning of such intervention, especially in cases such as *Dodge*, where they witnessed a corporate litigant enter the federal courts through diversity jurisdiction and successfully invoke the obligation of contracts provision against a state constitution. Again, their fears probably centered on the possible adoption of these strategies by free black litigants, but their understanding of the perceived threat remained inextricably linked to their assumptions concerning the structure and function of federal citizenship within the Union's polity.[3]

American citizens' two political capacities served different purposes. Most rights to which American citizens laid claim stemmed from state citizenship, although states had few qualms against limiting access to these rights for women and people of color. Massachusetts's high court, for example, declared in 1805 that women, because of their subordination to their husbands in marriage, could not be citizens. No other state went that far, but the practice of coverture was only beginning to break down during the Taney Court's tenure. Likewise, many states, North and South, maintained legal regimes committed to the continued subordination of blacks with methods ranging from denial of franchise to separate schooling to barring entry to the state. Through the selective protection of certain inhabitants' rights, state citizenship functioned to preserve liberties deemed necessary to the continuance of the social order in a particular jurisdiction. Federal citizenship, however, concerned a much smaller body of liberties that the Framers incorporated into the Constitution and its amendments to ensure the Union's stability.[4]

Constitutional protection for selected rights arose from the Framers' desire to preserve the federal structure, not from a libertarian concern for individual freedoms. Article 1, section 9 prohibited Congress from undertaking a number of actions, including closing the slave trade (for a limited time), passing ex post facto laws, and granting titles of nobility. Alexander Hamilton argued in the *Federalist* that the convention had inserted this clause to protect individual rights, but such reasoning at best explained only why

Congress could not legitimately suspend habeas corpus in peacetime or pass bills of attainder. Rather, the clause removed from Congress the ability to use its delegated powers to harm the states. Taking Congress's power to tax exports, for example, prevented the legislature from levying heavy taxes on the products made in hostile states. Those few individual rights that received protection in the section served a similar function, for the empowerment of individuals worked to protect the states. A prohibition of ex post facto laws and bills of attainder ensured that Congress would not use such mechanisms against state leaders who opposed federal views. Similar logic applied to the Bill of Rights, which prevented the federal government from using its power to crush state opposition. Protection of rights concerning assembly, petition, and bearing arms combined with limitations against quartering soldiers in private houses and imposing excessive fines reduced the federal government's power to use force or intimidation to coerce states to acquiesce to its policy and ensured that it would stay within its bounds. Federal liberties functioned to reinforce the federal structure. They represented strict exceptions to power: the federal government simply possessed no legitimate authority to qualify or regulate these rights in any manner, although states remained free to do so. Those people who possessed federal rights had the ability to exercise them with no fear of (federal) government intervention.[5]

Federal protection of certain liberties served another function as well: it secured rights designed to promote good relations among the states. "Whatever practices may have a tendency to disturb the harmony between the states," Alexander Hamilton wrote in *Federalist* 80, "are proper objects of federal superintendence and control." He spoke specifically about people's access to the federal courts through diversity jurisdiction. Such access certainly merited attention, but Hamilton and the other authors of *The Federalist* neglected several large bodies of rights far more substantial than the one providing diversity jurisdiction. The Constitution secured these rights under a single clause: "The Citizens of each State shall be entitled to all the Privileges and Immunities of Citizens in the several States." Exactly what this language meant was a matter of some debate in antebellum America. At a minimum, the clause required that states not treat citizens from other states as aliens, an obligation that ensured federal citizens the right to own property and to access courts outside of their home state. Yet Michael Kent Curtis has argued that the public, or at least newspaper editors, understood the clause to provide broad protection for a wide range of rights. Some abolitionists went even further, arguing that the language provided all persons—

white, black, slave, and free—the right to vote and to equal protection under the law.[6]

Taney Court justices, not surprisingly, construed the clause more narrowly. *Corfield v. Coryell*, an 1823 circuit ruling, most likely informed their assumptions. In *Corfield*, Justice Bushrod Washington expressed "no hesitation" in confining the Privileges and Immunities Clause to fundamental liberties, "which belong, of right, to the citizens of all free governments." Those rights fell into several general categories:

> Protection by the government; the enjoyment of life and liberty, with the right to acquire and possess property of every kind, and to pursue and to obtain happiness and safety; subject nevertheless to such restraints as the government may justly prescribe for the good of the whole. The right of a citizen of one state to pass through, or to reside in any other state, for the purposes of trade, agriculture, professional pursuits, or otherwise; to claim the benefit of the writ of habeas corpus; to institute and maintain actions of any kind in the courts of the state; to take, hold and dispose of property, either real or personal; and an exemption from higher taxes or impositions than are paid by the other citizens of the state; may be mentioned as some of the particular privileges and immunities of citizens, which are clearly embraced by the general description of privileges deemed to be fundamental: to which may be added the elective franchise, as regulated and established by the laws of constitution of the state in which it is to be exercised.

Washington presented a long but not exhaustive list. Some rights, such as the right of a citizen of one state to fish in the waters of another, did not merit inclusion with rights essential to republican governments and thus received no federal protection.[7]

From the Taney Court's perspective, however, the protection federal citizenship did provide went far enough to carry unwelcome implications. The Privileges and Immunities Clause offered a potential mechanism for resisting the patterns of racial discrimination within the states. Some abolitionists in fact maintained that this clause rendered slavery unconstitutional. Taney Court justices would flatly reject such radical interpretations, but even Washington's moderate reading of the provision could become controversial if it embraced people of color. If free blacks could access the rights enumerated in *Corfield*—the ability to pass through or reside in the state unhindered, to demand habeas corpus, to maintain suits in court—they might undermine the states' ability to control their subaltern racial populations. At least since the Missouri controversy, a number of northern politicians had argued that black citizens of their states should enjoy the same rights under the Privileges and Immunities Clause as their white counterparts. This argument also constituted one of the critiques against the Negro Seamen Act. With the exception of John McLean and perhaps Benjamin Robbins Curtis, the Taney Court justices opposed this position, although they had not yet discovered how to address it. In his 1832 manuscript on the Negro Seamen Act, Roger B. Taney, then serving as U.S. attorney general, developed an argument based on legislative discretion and the states' inherent power of self-preservation, but he had little luck persuading the court to follow him during the 1840s.[8]

By 1850, Taney had given up on the self-preservation argument, but Catron, Campbell, and Peter V. Daniel had not: they merely shifted the grounds of the debate. In the 1840s, the internal debate over slavery took place mainly in the context of Commerce Clause litigation. Following the closing of that pathway in *Strader*, *Cooley*, and *Moore*, Daniel, Catron, and Campbell moved the debate into corporate law, where they implicitly pondered free blacks' ability to use diversity jurisdiction to subvert state law. This shift in emphasis proved to be quite perceptive, for it anticipated a strategy used in antislavery litigation. One of the Scott family's lawyers, Roswell Field of Missouri, advised his clients to proceed in diversity jurisdiction. Such an approach not only counteracted the court's effort to push the majority of slavery cases down into the state courts but also circumvented discriminatory legislation. "If in fact . . . a black man may sue his master in the Federal courts," Field wrote to another of Scott's lawyers, "the right of a *trial by jury* is still left to the slave in an action at common law, which if brought into the Federal courts may be enforced in the judgement throughout the Union." Field believed that such a holding could even undermine the Fugitive Slave Law of 1850, since a diversity jurisdiction recognized in the Constitution would trump any congressional law, "and this may be a strong argument against allowing black men to sue as citizens."[9]

Daniel, Catron, and Campbell began their critique of corporate citizenship shortly before the Scott family executed Field's strategy, but the justices probably perceived the same opening as Field did and addressed it in the context of current litigation. This issue emerged as a consequence of the structure of federal citizenship itself. The federal Constitution created a new body of citizens and secured to these people a new body of rights. The Framers' decision to protect these rights represented not an act of civil libertarianism but rather a desire to see the Union function properly. By investing federal citizens with certain rights, the Constitution precluded attempts by the general government to use its powers to quash any state-based opposition. Many of these rights also limited the instances in which states came into conflict with each other. The form of federal citizenship thus supported the primary function of the federal Constitution. It sustained a government strong enough to hold together a union of different states and limited enough to allow them to remain independent policy centers. At the same time, the dual character of national citizenship made it the site of fierce struggle within the Union's racial and sectional politics.

Questions of dual citizenship became problematic because members of the Union's political class widely assumed that possession of state citizenship implied the enjoyment of federal citizenship. And that assumption could sanction precisely the type of federal intervention on behalf of free blacks that abolitionists such as Birney advocated and that southern partisans such as the *Charleston Mercury*'s correspondent feared. The issue centered on the reach of the Constitution's Privileges and Immunities Clause, which extended protection to "the citizens of each state," raising the question of whether each state possessed the authority to create federal citizens merely by recognizing certain persons as citizens within their own jurisdictions. An 1843 House report criticizing the southern Negro Seamen Act revealed the implications of this argument. "Now, it is well understood that some of the states of this Union recognize no distinction of color in relationship to freemen," the report read. "Their citizens are all free; their freemen all citizens." Such recognition entitled the citizens of those states, regardless of their color, "to all the privileges and immunities of a citizen in the several states." In 1844, the Taney Court extended at least partial recognition to this argument when it declared that a corporate charter created not only an artificial person but also a new state citizen that the courts would treat as a federal citizen at least for the purposes of jurisdiction. Corporate doctrine revealed a possibility that the rule might extend to free blacks. Members of the southern faction, therefore, may have mounted their crusade against corporate citizenship because they understood that the federal government's working assumptions about dual citizenship threatened the South's perceived needs.[10]

Legal communities in the early and antebellum republics (abolitionists excepted) remained curiously silent on the relationship between federal and state citizenship.[11] Scholars who have closely studied this issue attribute the silence to the specter of sectional conflict. Their arguments contain merit but do not explain why the legal community exhibited so much more restraint on this question than on others.[12] Taney Court members, as their behavior in *Groves*, *Prigg*, and the *Passenger Cases* indicated, showed little reluctance to engage such questions when the need arose. Their reticence probably had rather banal origins. Because state citizenship embraced so many basic rights relative to federal citizenship, jurists may have merely assumed the primacy of the former. For the question even to matter, moreover, cases needed to involve a fact situation that accommodated ornate technical issues.

Dred Scott was one of the few cases to meet those criteria, and it was certainly the first that squarely confronted the issue. Both Taney, the author of the court's official opinion, and Curtis, the case's most significant dissenter, conceded the primacy of state citizenship. Before the Constitution's ratification, Taney argued, a citizen of one state possessed no rights in any other, except by comity (rights acknowledged as a courtesy by a host jurisdiction). Ratification, however, made every citizen of every state—and no one else—a citizen of the United States and bestowed on "each citizen rights and privileges outside of his State which he did not before possess," placing "him in every other State upon a perfect equality with its own citizens." Despite his sweeping terms, Taney quickly stated that the citizens to whom he referred were those inhabitants within the states not targeted by any discriminatory legislation. Curtis disputed that aspect of Taney's argument, but he agreed that the states determined access to federal citizenship. "The whole matter," he wrote, "was left to stand upon the action of the several States." Both Taney and Curtis concluded that federal citizenship derived from state citizenship; consequently, the latter was primary. Neither justice cited any evidence for his contentions: both men assumed their correctness and moved on. There was in fact no precedent on this issue, and both the Constitution and the Judiciary Act of 1789 said nothing concerning the matter. The silence was significant, for the omission of a definition of citizenship in these carefully drafted documents suggested that it was defined elsewhere. James Wilson, a member of the Constitutional Convention and later a Supreme Court justice, drew out this implication in a lecture he delivered in the 1790s: "A citizen of the United States is he, who is a citizen of at least some one state in the Union."[13]

The Supreme Court's treatment of areas within the United States but outside the boundaries of any state—that is, the District of Columbia and the federal territories—reinforced Taney, Curtis, and Wilson's assumptions about the primacy of state citizenship. Although inhabitants of the District of Columbia were federal citizens, for example, they lacked state citizenship (and consequently the right to sue in diversity). Inhabitants of the district occupied a legally anomalous position, but under court doctrine, their status posed little conceptual difficulty. According to an 1805 decision, the district's inhabitants held citizenship in either Virginia or Maryland until those states ceded the land that became the District of Columbia. At that time, the inhabitants lost their state citizenship and joined a new political community over which Congress held sole authority. This ruling implicitly spelled out the source of federal citizenship within the district. Inhabitants became federal citizens in their capacity as citizens of Virginia and Maryland before the District's creation. When the District formed, its inhabitants already possessed federal citizenship, and they lost only their state capacity. But their former capacity as state citizens ensured their standing as federal citizens, and they would pass this status on to their descendants.[14]

The citizenship status of the federal territories' inhabitants also supported Taney and Curtis's suggestion. Unlike the residents of the District of Columbia, many people in the territories never possessed state citizenship, although they enjoyed, according to Chief Justice John Marshall, "the privileges, rights, and immunities of the citizens of the United States." Marshall explained this anomaly in *American and Ocean Insurance Companies v. Canter* (1828), which, until *Dred Scott* set it aside, represented the leading case on the relationship between the territories and the United States. According to Marshall, international law and treaties governed the status of people living in the federal territories. Under international law, the inhabitants of a ceded territory dissolved their relationship with their former sovereign and entered a relationship with a new one. Treaties determined the manner by which this transfer of allegiance occurred. In *Canter*, Marshall discussed a clause, which appeared regularly in cession treaties, stipulating that inhabitants of the Florida territory become citizens as soon as possible and that, in the interim, they had access to the privileges and immunities of those citizens.[15]

This provision did not immediately bestow U.S. citizenship but merely admitted "the inhabitants of Florida to the *enjoyment* of the privileges, rights, and immunities of the citizens of the United States." Floridians "do not, however, participate in political power; they do not share in the government, till Florida shall become a state."[16] Marshall then dropped the issue and discussed the federal government's authority to establish territorial courts. He said enough to demonstrate that territorial inhabitants were not federal citizens. After the 1810s, both state and federal courts interpreted such provisions to mean that territorial inhabitants did not become U.S. citizens until their territory entered the Union as a state. Those treaties, however, provided inhabitants with "the enjoyment of the privileges, rights, and immunities of the Citizens of the United States," and they need not wait for citizenship to attain those privileges. Because treaties formed part of the "supreme law of the land," people in the territories—although many of them were not American citizens—possessed, at least formally, many of the same rights that U.S. citizens did. In 1835, for example, Benjamin Butler, Taney's successor as U.S. attorney general, reminded the secretary of state of that point, discouraging him from proceeding against the inhabitants of the Arkansas Territory when they began organizing a state government without permission. "I am not prepared to say, that all proceedings on this subject, on the part of the citizens of Arkansas will be illegal," Butler wrote. "They undoubtedly possess the ordinary privileges and immunities of citizens of the United States. Among these is the right of the people 'peaceably to assemble and to petition the government for the redress of grievances.'"[17]

Although no single document defined the relationship between federal and state citizenship, a clear pattern emerged. The Constitution explicitly said little about the nature of the relationship between state and federal citizenship, but this silence indicated that questions regarding the access to and character of citizenship were to be handled within the states. Cession treaties revealed a consistent assumption among senators and executives of the primacy of state citizenship, and the opinions of Marshall in *Canter* and Taney and Curtis in *Dred Scott* revealed that the courts agreed. To be a citizen of the United States, then, one must first be a citizen of a state.[18] The federal Constitution created a new form of citizenship that people possessed along with their state citizenship. In this dual relationship, state citizenship retained its primacy and became the prerequisite for federal citizenship. Yet the question raised by the 1843 House report criticizing the Negro Seamen Act remained: did a state's recognition of corporations or free blacks as citizens within its jurisdiction also make such persons federal citizens entitled to protection under the Privileges and Immunities Clause? In the mid-1850s, the Supreme Court's southern faction would force this issue to the center of judicial discourse.

This debate took place within the confines of corporate law, especially with regard to corporations' ability to sue in diversity. The debate took place here because court doctrine invited analogies between corporate and free black citizens. Advocates of African American legal rights contended that free people of color recognized as citizens in their home states were entitled to legal protection through access to the federal courts and especially through the Privileges and Immunities Clause. (The provision, after all, entitled the "Citizens of each State . . . to all Privileges and Immunities of Citizens in the several States.")[19] They argued, in other words, that the states possessed the authority to create federal citizens. In its corporate rulings, the Taney Court had given partial recognition to that argument. Between 1839 and 1844, the justices developed a doctrine allowing a corporation to claim citizenship for the purposes of diversity jurisdiction in the state where it was chartered. When it chartered a corporation, a state legislature in effect created a kind of federal citizen. The court developed this doctrine with surprisingly little internal dissention, but beginning in 1852, the southern faction suddenly demanded the abandonment of this doctrine because the implications of corporate citizenship potentially threatened the states' ability to control their internal populations.

The Taney Court inherited an unusually poor Marshall Court precedent concerning the ability of corporations to sue in diversity. In *Bank of the United States v. Deveaux* (1809), Marshall rejected contentions that a corporate charter conferred state citizenship and thereby would allow suits involving citizens from outside the chartering state to proceed in diversity jurisdiction. Access to the federal courts through that avenue depended on citizenship. "That invisible, intangible, and artificial being," Marshall wrote, "that mere legal entity, a corporation aggregate, is certainly not a citizen; and, consequently cannot sue or be sued in the courts of the United States." The court would take jurisdiction of a suit involving a corporation only if all the members composing the entity came from a different state than the opposing party. This ruling set a high threshold for corporate diversity cases and became a source of trouble for the justices and of aggravation for litigants, especially since corporations could avoid the federal courts by selecting members from jurisdictions in which legal difficulties might arise.[20]

The Taney Court chafed under this precedent and eventually struck it down. Taney qualified *Deveaux* at the first opportunity. In *Bank of Augusta v. Earle* (1839), he limited the potential scope of Marshall's ruling. Although Taney maintained that the rule still applied for jurisdictional purposes, the court would not look beyond the charter to the individual members for any other reason. Counsel for the bank argued that because the federal courts treated corporations as a group of individuals conducting business under a corporate name, its client should therefore receive protection under the Privileges and Immunities Clause. Under that clause, the Bank of Augusta could certainly conduct business in Alabama. Taney agreed that corporations could transact their affairs in places beyond the borders of their home states, but they did so through comity rather than through the Privileges and Immunities Clause. If the court extended the individuating principle of *Deveaux* so that it embraced a corporation's normal operations, the court would destroy the character granted by the charter. Placing individual members of a corporation under the Privileges and Immunities Clause, Taney argued, would give them not only individual rights but also individual liabilities. It would reduce the corporation to a mere business partnership and destroy the limited liability that made corporate organization so valuable. Taney emphatically rejected the contention that a corporation or any citizen might claim rights under the clause without the concomitant liabilities. "This would be to give the citizens of other states far higher and greater privileges than are enjoyed by the citizens of the state itself." For every other purpose besides jurisdiction, therefore, the court would treat a corporation as a citizen of the state in which it was chartered, except that rights it claimed originated in its charter, not by virtue of its citizenship.[21]

Five years later, the court overturned *Deveaux*, holding that it would now treat corporate litigants, for the purposes of diversity jurisdiction, as if they were citizens of the state in which they were chartered. Writing for a unanimous court in *Louisville, Cincinnati, and Charleston Railroad Company v. Letson* (1844), Justice James M. Wayne completely rejected the precedent. For years, he wrote, the court had adhered to *Deveaux* merely "because the decision had been made, and not because it was thought to be right." The bar never liked the ruling, and the justices, including Marshall, had become increasingly dissatisfied with it. According to Wayne, "It was in the knowledge of several of us, that he repeatedly expressed regret that those decisions had been made, adding . . . that if the point of jurisdiction was an original one, the conclusion would be different." Invoking a recent congressional statute, Wayne declared that it was time to strike down the precedent. From this point on, "a corporation created by and doing business in a particular state, is deemed to be . . . a person, although an artificial person, an inhabitant of the same state, for the purposes of its incorporation, capable of being treated as a citizen of that state, as much as a natural person." No one dissented. Catron and Daniel both sat on the court at the time when it handed down *Letson*, but they said nothing against it for eight years.[22]

In 1853, however, Daniel suddenly attacked corporate citizenship, and Catron and the newly appointed Campbell joined the assault the following year. Daniel's about-face came in *Rundle v. Delaware and Raritan Canal Company*. *Rundle* involved a suit by a New Jersey citizen against a Pennsylvania corporation whose canal works had allegedly damaged the former's Delaware River land. The court held him to be without remedy. Although he agreed with the result, Daniel dissented, arguing that the court should have never taken jurisdiction. Corporations, the Virginian argued, were artificial beings, not citizens, and therefore had no place in the federal courts. Marshall's ruling in *Deveaux* was incorrect because it enabled corporations to circumvent this barrier, and Wayne's ruling in *Letson* constituted an even more egregious violation of the Constitution because it confounded citizenship with residence. "But . . . the Constitution does not make inhabitancy a requisite of suing or being sued; that requisite is citizenship." Citizenship, Daniel continued, implied a right of residence, but residence in a state by no means implied citizenship.[23] Catron, who had advocated a revival of the *Deveaux* doctrine in *Rundle*, initiated his critique of *Letson*, with the support of Daniel and Campbell, during the next term. That ruling, as Catron understood it, did not recognize corporate citizenship but merely held that litigants need not maintain a suit against all the stockholders, who were too numerous and transient to include in a single suit. Catron left little ambiguity about where he stood: "I view this assumption of citizenship for a corporation as a mere evasion of the limits prescribed to the United States courts by the Constitution." Incorporation allowed people with means to gain charters anywhere, even in states different from the one in which the corporations actually conducted business. *Letson* allowed such persons to "sue their next neighbors of their own State and city" in the federal courts and thus illegitimately to place the federal government between a state and its citizens.[24]

When the majority responded with a defense of *Letson*, the southern faction intensified its critique. The defense came in a particularly unsavory case involving a contract that attempted to bribe Virginia's legislature into granting corporate privileges. Justice Robert C. Grier, speaking for the court, held the contract illegal under Virginia law, but not before he spent around half his opinion extolling corporate diversity jurisdiction. *Letson* settled the jurisdictional question; no justice dissented at the time it came down, and the federal courts had integrated it into their practice. "If we should now declare these judgements to have been entered without jurisdiction or authority," he wrote, "we should inflict a great and irreparable evil on the community." In cases touching jurisdiction, the principle of stare decisis was "absolutely necessary to the peace of society." Moreover, Grier continued, the recognition of corporate citizenship secured an important right, because it allowed litigants an appeal to a neutral federal court. "The right of choosing an impartial tribunal is a privilege of no small practical importance, and more especially in cases where a distant plaintiff has to contend with the power and influence of great numbers and the combined wealth wielded by corporations in almost every State." Asserting jurisdiction over the corporations allowed litigants to move their cases into jurisdictions less susceptible to corporate influence and gave the corporations a like privilege in states "where local prejudices or jealousy might injuriously affect them." There was no need, Grier concluded, to construe the Diversity Clause as a "penal statute." Even as he issued this defense, however, Grier backed away from *Letson* and conceded that corporations could not be citizens per se. Rather, the court merely assumed their residency in the state in which they were chartered for the purposes of jurisdiction.[25]

Daniel and Campbell, with Catron concurring, welcomed the concession but yielded no ground. Daniel found unconvincing Grier's appeal to convenience and stare decisis. Invoking a rigid formalism, Daniel claimed that the court possessed no discretion over the meaning of constitutional language: "Wherever the Constitution commands, discretion terminates. Considerations of policy or convenience, if ever appealed to, I had almost said if ever imagined . . . , become an offence. Beyond the Constitution or the powers it invests, every act must be a violation of duty, an usurpation." As for the stare decisis argument, *Letson* wrongfully overturned the decisions that preceded it, and the court faced no obligation to follow it. The majority's argument, Daniel concluded, amounted to nothing more than this: "The abuse has been already put in practice; it has, by practice merely, become sanctified; and may therefore be repeated at pleasure." Campbell maintained that the Framers never contemplated the inclusion of corporations under diversity jurisdiction. Arguing that state courts might be partial in their dealings with corporations, "soothing as it is to the official sensibilities of the federal courts," offered no excuse for ignoring those intentions. Campbell's problem with *Letson*, however, stemmed not so much from the illegitimate assertion of jurisdiction over corporations as from how the language of that decision shifted the terms of the debate. Before that case, state courts had handled out-of-state corporations on comity principles. *Letson*'s claim that corporations were citizens like natural persons now forced the state courts to confront whether that character gave corporations rights under the Privileges and Immunities Clause, which would limit the states' regulatory authority. The court's interpretation of the word *citizen*, Campbell concluded, drew on principles of interpretation that "will undermine every limitation in the Constitution, if universally adopted."[26]

Again, the dissenters' concern extended beyond the corporation. The subtext of their argument, although never explicit, centered on the implications of this doctrine for the security of slavery. Specifically, their interest focused on free black litigants' ability to use corporate jurisdiction cases as analogies for their situation. No one ever expressed the matter in those terms, perhaps because meeting the issue squarely would appear to be an unwarranted departure from the cases at hand, but the dissenters structured their arguments so that they could speak to the question. The southern faction advocated a denial of jurisdiction for corporations not only because those entities were artificial persons but also because they were at best merely "*quasi*-citizens."[27] Corporations, Daniel wrote in *Rundle*, possessed only those rights and privileges enumerated in their charters, and that limitation placed them on a level below that of the citizen. "Each citizen," he continued, "certainly does, under our system of polity, possess the same rights and faculties, and sustain the same obligations, political, social, and moral, which appertain to each of his fellow citizens."[28] If the term encompassed corporations, then those organizations could hold office, just as any true citizen could. In the case of corporations, the contention was absurd. Yet their inclusion as citizens within the meaning of the Constitution, despite their limited rights, could serve as a precedent for free blacks, who, like corporations, received recognition as citizens in some states despite having limited rights.

At this level, corporate doctrine potentially threatened the state's ability to regulate its internal populations. At the same time that the justices wrestled with questions of corporate diversity jurisdiction (1852–55), the court demonstrated in *Knoop* and *Dodge* that the Constitution would sustain corporate rights in the face of changing policy considerations within the states. The court justified this intervention through the Obligation of Contracts Clause as interpreted in *Fletcher*, *Dartmouth*, and *Charles River*

Bridge, but the members of the southern faction, especially Campbell, wondered whether the court's enforcement of the Privileges and Immunities Clause would sustain similar interventions. In the context of the court's corporate rulings, *Letson*'s imprecision notwithstanding, the issue hardly proved compelling. No justice intended to treat corporations as natural persons and to give them access to the Privileges and Immunities Clause. Corporate rights began and ended with the charter, and the majority backed away from Wayne's sweeping formulation as soon as the southern faction pressed it. But free blacks, if embraced as citizens, had no charters; they were natural persons, and the argument citing the charter as a barrier to the Privileges and Immunities Clause thus fell apart. The court's rulings on corporate citizenship opened the racist policies employed by the states, especially the southern ones, to potential challenge in the federal courts. "A single instance of this kind awakens apprehension," Campbell wrote, "for it is regarded as a link in a chain of repetitions."[29] Campbell, Daniel, and Catron hoped to break that link by shutting corporations out of diversity jurisdiction, and they revealed themselves willing to undermine the entire structure of corporate law to do so.

As they had done before, the majority—this time with Taney among its ranks—resisted efforts to subordinate court doctrine to the defense of slavery. Still, the southern faction's behavior proved problematic, for its members routinely challenged doctrines that the majority regarded as settled. Moreover, Campbell, Catron, and Daniel addressed the questions with little or no prompting from counsel. Such activity among the justices invited litigation strategies challenging the court's jurisdiction and forced a continual revisiting of old questions that clogged an already crowded docket. A solid faction of three dissenting justices caused other problems as well. The court could accommodate isolated crusaders such as McLean or Daniel, who usually dissented alone, because their arguments rarely appealed to the other justices and faced little prospect of becoming majority opinion. Dissent by three justices acting in concert over a period of years, however, changed the dynamic of the court's internal criticism. A sudden change in the court's composition could carry momentous consequences and transform court doctrine. For those reasons alone, the challenge presented by Catron, Daniel, and Campbell demanded response.

Moreover, the southern faction identified a significant problem. With *Strader*, the court had implemented a strategy that handled questions of slavery coming on appeal from the state courts. That policy left unresolved the way in which the court planned to address issues proceeding through the federal courts, and this problem became more pressing in the 1850s. Catron, Daniel, and Campbell advocated a drastic response: a complete closure of the diversity jurisdiction to so-called quasi-citizens—corporations and implicitly people of color. The three judges' colleagues considered that strategy too extreme, so the southern faction's opinions remained dissenting ones. By 1855, the court had polarized. Despite the majority's resistance, its members in general sympathized with the subtextual aspects of the dissenters' arguments. Indeed, Taney would soon reveal that he was merely waiting for a case that would present them with an opportunity squarely to confront the issue.

Despite its general attacks on corporate power, the southern faction recurrently focused on a single issue: corporations' access to federal citizenship. This concentration stemmed from the possible analogies that free black litigants could draw between their situation and those of corporations. Both constituted quasi-citizens created by the policy of individual states, and both had a plausible claim to federal citizenship. The widespread assumption concerning the primacy of state citizenship raised the possibility that the states could indeed create federal citizens. The Supreme Court's treatment of corporations since *Letson* had lent support to that position. Corporations' status as artificial persons with rights limited by their charters, however, prevented them from accessing the Privileges and Immunities Clause. Such limitations could not apply to free blacks, who were not artificial persons, and a claim to federal citizenship, if successful, would secure them the protections offered by the Privileges and Immunities Clause. Such protection could provide, as Roswell Field noted, leverage against the southern slave regimes. Members of the southern faction advocated a radical solution to what they perceived as a serious problem. They wanted corporations shut out of the federal courts, and they were willing to risk the destruction of the doctrinal structure that had sustained the emerging corporate order since 1819. By 1855, the southerners' critique had become so persistent that Taney probably felt that he had to respond, and *Dred Scott* provided him with an opportunity to do so.

PART THREE

Inescapable Opportunity

The Supreme Court and the Dred Scott *Case*

WHILE THE SUPREME COURT STRUGGLED with its southern faction over issues of corporate law, the sectional crisis reemerged in electoral politics. A few years of relative calm passed after politicians settled for the Compromise of 1850, but in 1854 Congress organized the Kansas and Nebraska Territories and allowed settlers to determine whether slavery would be permitted in their midst. Enabling settlers to exercise this "popular sovereignty" required that the Kansas-Nebraska Act repeal the thirty-year-old Missouri Compromise restriction, which had closed to slavery the portion of the Louisiana Purchase Territory that lay outside the borders of Missouri and north of 36°30′ longitude. The repeal reopened the debate over slavery's expansion and transformed American politics. With surprising swiftness, the Whig Party collapsed, and the Democratic Party's main competitor became the Republican Party, an organization that drew support exclusively from northern voters and that made opposition to slavery's expansion its central plank. Events over the next two years kept tensions high. Settlers in Kansas split into pro- and antislavery factions, armed themselves, and, for a brief period, killed one another. On the Senate floor, Representative Preston Brooks of South Carolina attacked Senator Charles Sumner of Massachusetts with a cane over remarks the latter had made during the debates over "Bleeding Kansas." During the 1856 presidential election, numerous southern politicians signaled that secession would be the price of a Republican victory. The debate over slavery's expansion had become intractable, and elected politicians had failed to cope effectively with it. In his 1857 inaugural address, however, incoming President James Buchanan suggested that the politicians might no longer need to deal with the problem. Slavery's status in the territories was "a judicial question, which legitimately belongs to the Supreme Court of the United States, before whom it is now pending" in the *Dred Scott* case. "To their decision, in common with all good citizens, I shall cheerfully submit, whatever this may be."[1]

Two days later, the court rendered its decision. Chief Justice Roger B. Taney, speaking for a deeply divided court, passed over an opportunity to avoid the case's controversial aspects under the *Strader* doctrine and issued two sweeping rulings. First, blacks were not citizens within the meaning of the Constitution, and they therefore had no right to bring suit in the federal courts. Second, Congress possessed no authority to limit the expansion of slavery into the federal territories. Submission to the ruling, however, was hardly cheerful. "Instead of quieting the subject," wrote "A Kentucky Lawyer," the decision only worked "further to inflame the controversy, by stimulating the already too highly excited jealousy of northern people."[2] Former Democratic Senator Thomas Hart Benton of Missouri complained that "the opinion itself has become a new question, more virulent than the former!"[3] Numerous critics found the decision weakly reasoned and unconvincing. In a lengthy and dispassionate critique, Massachusetts lawyers Horace Gray and John Lowell pronounced Taney's opinion "unworthy of the reputation of that great magistrate."[4] "A Kentucky Lawyer" found the reasoning "as about the flimsiest and least satisfactory that ever influenced the opinion of any respectable tribunal upon an important question." "By this single act," he continued, the court had "done more to lower the moral tone and standard of our judiciary than any thing that has ever occurred."[5] Other critics saw more sinister forces at work. "We cannot fail to see," wrote Judge Samuel A. Foot of New York, that the ruling gave "the country a new constitution, and a new system of law, on the subject of slavery and the government of our territories."[6] The opinion, in the estimation of a joint committee of New York's Senate and Assembly, was simply "*inhuman, unchristian, atrocious*—disgraceful to the Judge who uttered it, and to the tribunal which sanctioned it."[7]

Dred Scott generated such a harsh reaction among antislavery politicians in part because its rulings were so sweeping but also because the tenor of politics had become rankly antagonistic by the late 1850s. At least since the Mexican War, antislavery members of the northern wings of both the Democratic and Whig Parties had warned that a "slave power"—a conspiracy of southern politicians who would stop at nothing to protect and extend slavery—had captured the federal government. Antislavery politicians had made relatively little headway by the early 1850s, but the repeal of the

Missouri Compromise changed everything. As David Potter has noted, the compromise "had established a kind of national preference for freedom over slavery," and its revocation "established a policy that slavery was a local issue, not a subject of any national preference one way or the other."[8] Northern antislavery politicians also watched in horror as the bill's main supporter, Senator Stephen Douglas of Illinois—who primarily wanted the territory organized to secure a route for a transcontinental railroad—invited proslavery politicians to support his bill as a way to open up territory that had long been closed to their constituents. In 1854, many northern politicians (and voters) believed they saw an effort by the slave power, aided by complicit northern politicians such as Douglas, to embark on a new, aggressive phase of expansionism. And the effort to oppose this expansion forced a realignment in American politics. Antislavery politicians in the North bolted their parties and ultimately coalesced as Republicans. Their shifting allegiances destroyed the Whig Party and weakened the Democrats' northern wing so much that their party would soon lose its national dominance. Republican strategy, however, relied on impugning the motives of those politicians opposed to antislavery on the grounds that they were the self-seeking lackeys of the slave power or, worse, active conspirators in an effort to force slavery throughout the Union.

The Supreme Court's ruling in *Dred Scott* quickly became part of the Republicans' conspiracy theory. A joint committee of New York's Senate and Assembly, for example, could not "omit to notice" the timing with which the court rendered its decision: "A new Pro-Slavery, sectional Administration" had just come to power, and it would be sure to shield "partisan Judges from merited punishment, . . . produce acquiescence in their ultra Pro-Slavery, unconstitutional doctrines," and "consign [Kansas] to the deadly embrace of Slavery."[9] Prominent Republicans on the national level made similar claims. Senator William Seward of New York, a potential Republican candidate for the 1860 election, charged that President-Elect Buchanan "approached or was approached" by the court, which informed him about *Dred Scott*. "The court did not hesitate to please the incoming President, by . . . pronouncing an opinion that the Missouri prohibition was void." In so doing, the court "forgot its own dignity" and enabled Buchanan to promise, knowingly and falsely, that Kansas's voters could reject slavery if they wished.[10] Abraham Lincoln, in his famous "House Divided" speech, claimed that Douglas, Buchanan, Taney, and former president Franklin Pierce were following a plan that had the structural coherence of a building. Every part of the plot—from the Kansas-Nebraska Act to the *Dred Scott Case* to a later effort by a minority of settlers to force a fraudulent, proslavery constitution onto Kansas—"exactly make the frame of a house or a mill, . . . all the lengths and proportions of the different pieces exactly adapted to their respective places." "We find it impossible," Lincoln concluded, "not to believe that Stephen and Franklin and Roger and James all understood one another from the beginning, and all worked upon a common plan or draft drawn up before the first blow was struck."[11] With their detailed descriptions of the slave power conspiracy's activities, Lincoln, Seward, and other Republicans provided a powerful explanation of how *Dred Scott* fit into the complex series of political events that dominated the 1850s.

Such explanatory power ought to give one pause, for the Republicans' account may obscure as much as it explains. The interpretive problem here lay not in the absence, whatever contemporaries may have thought, of any genuine conspiracy dedicated to imposing slavery on the Union; rather, the problem is one of hindsight. Because *Dred Scott* fit so well into the Republicans' framework concerning the expansion of slavery, the court's motivation in framing its rulings must have fit into the framework as well. Thus, *Dred Scott* must be explained as the product of a proslavery agenda and as an attack on the Republican platform. Although there is some evidence to sustain such an account, scholars should keep in mind an observation made by David Potter in his discussion of the Kansas-Nebraska Act: "It should be remembered that most human beings during these years went about their daily lives, preoccupied with their personal affairs, with no sense of impending disaster nor any fixation on the issue of slavery."[12] A similar remark may apply to the Taney Court as well. Although its members were probably more concerned about slavery than were most people, the court had been balancing that concern with its commitments to federal power and commercial expansion for nearly two decades.

And if anything preoccupied the court on the eve of *Dred Scott*, it was the question of how to handle the unintended consequences of this balancing act. By 1857, internal debates taking place among the justices had effectively boxed in the court to such an extent that its rulings in *Dred Scott* appeared both unavoidable and absolutely necessary. They appeared unavoidable because the doctrines developing out of *Swift v. Tyson* had simply destroyed any possible mechanism the court could have had to evade the case's controversial aspects. The rulings appeared absolutely necessary first because breaking the southern faction's challenge to the court's doctrine regarding corporations required devising a way to sever the issues of corporate and free black citizenship and second because the Supreme Court had given very little thought to the quantum of power constitutionally granted to Congress over the territories. These concerns, which external political pressure and the justices' personal partisan agendas no doubt mediated, shaped the court's ruling. *Dred Scott*, therefore, responded primarily to problems of the Taney Court's own making, and those were not the same ones that plagued politicians.

CHAPTER SEVEN

The Failure of Evasion

Dred Scott v. Emerson, Strader v. Graham, Swift v. Tyson, *and* Dred Scott v. Sandford

"HOW MUCH MORE WEIGHT of authority and general acqui-escence this decision would have commanded," Massachusetts lawyers Horace Gray and John Lowell briefly wondered in a lengthy critique of *Dred Scott*, "if the majority of the judges had confined themselves to the point necessary to the judgment."[1] Gray and Lowell raised a valid point, for Chief Justice Roger Taney and his associates had an opportunity to dispose of the case on very narrow grounds, which would have allowed them to avoid ruling on the citizenship and territorial questions. Part of *Dred Scott*'s fact situation involved a Missouri master who took an enslaved person to a free state (Illinois), stayed a few years, and then returned to Missouri with his slave. Missouri's Supreme Court had ruled, albeit recently, that a stay in free territory accompanied by a "voluntary" return created no claim to freedom. In *Strader v. Graham*, moreover, the Taney Court had declared that it would defer to the state courts in such matters.[2] Under such circumstances, the Supreme Court could have easily pronounced Dred Scott a slave without addressing any other issue. Gray and Lowell offered little speculation about why the court went on to the other issues, but other commentators were not as circumspect. A writer for the *North American Review* bluntly stated the matter:

> Two years' residence in a free State, with the consent of his master, did not make him a free man. . . . This was the whole principle in dispute, on the merits, and the court have now decided it. . . . What more is to be done?
> . . . Do they stop here? or is other work to be done? Does deciding the merits end the case? By no means. "There is still much land to be possessed."[3]

That land, of course, was the territory covered by the Missouri Compromise restriction. When they addressed the other issues, the justices transformed *Dred Scott* into "a political manual or text-book, an authorized registration of the political heresies" of the Democratic Party.[4]

Taney and his associates had numerous reasons for addressing all the questions involved in *Dred Scott*. Some were certainly partisan; others were more closely linked to the debates that had dominated the court in the 1850s. Taney, for example, found that the citizenship question provided an opportunity to respond to the southern faction and sever the connection between black and corporate quasi-citizenship. Yet scholars should not overlook the justices' genuine effort to avoid these issues and to decide *Dred Scott* on the narrowest possible grounds. By the time it had reached the Supreme Court, the case had already become laden with politically charged questions, and a short-lived majority opted to avoid them by invoking *Strader*. After a great deal of internal debate, the court's initial majority maintained, through Justice Samuel Nelson, that the court was bound to follow the Missouri Supreme Court's ruling in *Dred Scott v. Emerson* (1852), which had denied Scott's claims to freedom.[5] This strategy failed, but not primarily because the justices gave in to their partisan urges and judicial agendas. Instead, it failed because Dred and Harriet Scott, together with their lawyers, pursued a litigation strategy designed to avoid *Strader*, which controlled cases coming out of state supreme courts. Dred and Harriet Scott proceeded in diversity jurisdiction, where the application of *Strader* was not as clear. Recent rulings in diversity jurisdiction had only rendered *Strader*'s relevance more uncertain, since in the years following *Swift v. Tyson* the Supreme Court had become increasingly less deferential to state court rulings. By the eve of *Dred Scott*, the Supreme Court had even claimed the right to ignore rulings with which it disagreed. The Scotts' litigation strategy, aided by Justice John McLean's willingness to invoke the court's recent rulings in diversity against Nelson's argument, ultimately forced the justices to abandon a narrow ruling in favor of the sweeping ones that made *Dred Scott* infamous. Leaving behind that initial strategy, however, probably owed more to the court's accidental undermining of its own evasive mechanisms than to anything else.

Originating in the 1840s as an effort by Dred and Harriet Scott to hold their family together, the *Dred Scott* case transformed in the hands of the Missouri Supreme Court into an overtly political repudiation of its policy toward slaves who had resided in free territory. Dred and Harriet Scott had both spent a number of years living in either the free state of Illinois or the federal territory closed to slavery under the Missouri Compromise agreement. Since the 1820s, the Missouri Supreme Court had enforced the antislavery provisions of other jurisdictions, and under its rulings, the Scotts appeared to have a strong case. Despite the ostensible liberalism of the court's precedents, the judges who developed the doctrine extending comity to antislavery law made it contingent on the free states' recognition of slavery's legitimate place in the Union. When the peculiar institution's place within the expanding Union became contested in the mid-1840s, the Missouri Supreme Court reformulated its policy. Unfortunately for Dred and Harriet Scott—who, like all of the litigants involved in their suit, had no political motivation—the judges found their case to be a useful medium for their own agendas. When the court finished with *Dred Scott*, Missouri had a new judicial policy toward antislavery law, and the members of the Scott family remained enslaved.

The facts involved in the *Dred Scott* case began taking shape in 1832, when Dr. John Emerson purchased a slave named Dred Scott to accompany him on a military tour of duty. Emerson, a physician, had been working as a civilian at Jefferson Barracks near St. Louis, and he soon received a commission as assistant surgeon in the U.S. Army. One year later, the army moved Emerson—and Dred Scott—to Fort Armstrong in the free state of Illinois, where they remained for the next two and a half years. Although military records, such as post returns, say nothing about Scott's presence, Miles H. Clark, who was stationed at the fort with Emerson, later stated in a deposition that the doctor claimed and used Scott as a slave throughout this period. In April 1836, the army closed Fort Armstrong, and Emerson received orders to report at Fort Snelling in the Iowa Territory (now in the state of Minnesota). The doctor brought Scott along, even though his new post lay deep within the territory that the Missouri Compromise restriction had closed to slavery. Emerson was not the only officer to do so; other officers brought enslaved persons with them as well. Indeed, Dred Scott met and married his wife, Harriet, at Fort Snelling. Harriet's owner, Major Lawrence Taliaferro, had brought her from Virginia in the early 1830s, and she had resided at the fort for two or three years before Scott and Emerson arrived. Sometime in 1836 or 1837, Taliaferro sold Harriet to Emerson and married the couple in a civil ceremony. (Taliaferro was a justice of the peace for the territory.) Dred and Harriet's marriage produced four children, although two died in infancy.[6]

Dred Scott claimed to have resided at Fort Snelling for five years, although the record is not clear on that point. Emerson himself maintained a discontinuous residence at the post. On October 8, 1837, the doctor wrote that he had orders to report at Jefferson Barracks, but his orders changed a few weeks later, and Emerson found himself heading south to Fort Jesop, Louisiana. His two slaves stayed behind under the charge of the officers to whom Emerson had hired them out. The documents say little concerning why Emerson left the Scotts behind, but his subsequent behavior indicated that he intended only a temporary absence. (Emerson regularly complained to his superiors about his new post, hoping for a transfer back to Fort Snelling.) While at Fort Jesop, Emerson married Eliza Irene Sanford, the daughter of a Virginia manufacturer and recent immigrant to Missouri named Alexander Sanford. Emerson also sent for Harriet Scott, who most likely came south to maintain the household for the new Mrs. Emerson. Dred Scott apparently remained at Fort Snelling. Catherine Anderson, the woman who had exploited Harriet's services until Emerson sent for her, stated that Dred was still at the post when she left, at least two months after Harriet had departed for Louisiana. Emerson's litany of complaints must have paid off, however, for in October 1838, he, Irene, and Harriet Scott returned to Fort Snelling, where they remained until 1840. In May of that year, Emerson received orders to proceed to Florida. Before he did so, however, Emerson left his wife and the Scotts around St. Louis. He worked at various posts in Florida for roughly the next two years, complaining all the while. Emerson's time in the army ended in September 1842, and he eventually settled in Davenport, Iowa, and died on December 29, 1843.[7]

When he left the Scotts under the control of others and departed to Florida and then Iowa, Emerson's role in what was to become the *Dred Scott* case ended. By that time, his travels with Dred and Harriet had given them cause to bring actions for their freedom. Emerson had exercised his authority as the Scotts' master almost entirely on free soil. Dred had spent most of his time as the doctor's slave either in Illinois or the Iowa Territory, both of which possessed laws declaring slavery illegal. Although Harriet had gone to Louisiana to wait on her owners, she also spent the majority of her time on free soil. Emerson in fact purchased her within free territory, and he had hired out the Scotts on free soil and even left the territory without them. Emerson may have believed that his military status exempted him from the operation of local antislavery laws. Missouri Supreme Court decisions, however, rejected such contentions, and its doctrine provided the Scotts with a strong case for freedom.

Missouri's Supreme Court had vigorously enforced extrajurisdictional antislavery laws since the 1820s, and its rulings covered every aspect of the Scotts' case. The court's enforcement began in *Winny v. Whitesides* (1824). Winny, an enslaved woman, sued for her freedom because before her masters brought her to Missouri, they held her for several years in Illinois Territory, in violation of the Northwest Ordinance, which had closed the area to slavery in 1787—at least in theory. A unanimous court recognized her claim to freedom, arguing that the ordinance governed property held in common by the states and that the Union's members consequently had a duty to enforce its terms. National policy outlawed slavery in the territory, and violations would carry a heavy penalty in Missouri: the destruction of a property interest in the slave. As soon as a slave owner breached an antislavery provision by taking an enslaved person into free territory and establishing a residence, the slave received a permanent claim to freedom, and nothing could change that—not even a return to a slaveholding state such as Missouri. Twelve years later, in *Rachael v. Walker* (1836), the court applied the same reasoning to the Missouri Compromise restriction. *Rachael*, in fact, lent strong support to the Scotts' case, for she had been held as a slave by a military officer at Fort Snelling. In addition to rulings covering masters' decisions to hold slaves in Illinois (whether the state or territory) or the area covered by the Missouri Compromise, the Missouri Supreme Court had also decided that the hiring of slaves in free territory, except under the strict conditions specified in the Illinois Constitution of 1818, created a claim to freedom. Missouri court decisions thus covered the places at which the Scotts resided during their time with Emerson as well as his decision to hire them out and provided the Scotts with strong grounds for a lawsuit.[8]

On April 6, 1846, Dred and Harriet Scott filed separate actions for freedom against Irene Emerson, John Emerson's widow. Although they filed separate suits with differing factual claims, the Scotts always filed at the same time and employed the same litigation strategies. Their behavior, Lea VanderVelde and Sandhya Subramanian have argued, gave every indication that the couple worked together as a family unit whose actions centered on preventing the separation of themselves and their children. Despite the strength of their suits, the Scotts lost their cases because their lawyer, Samuel Mansfield Bay, failed to establish that Irene Emerson owned the slaves in question. After the Scotts moved for a new trial, Emerson's counsel, perhaps aware that his client had a weak case under Missouri law, pursued a strategy centered on delaying a final decision. In 1850, the Scotts finally received a new trial, and their lawyers established conclusively that both Dred and Harriet lived in areas where the introduction of slavery had been outlawed and that Irene Emerson had kept them in servitude after their return. Emerson responded with an argument that the Missouri Supreme Court had rejected years earlier in *Rachael*: that John Emerson's military service exempted him from the antislavery provisions of the Illinois Constitution and the Missouri Compromise restriction. The judge rejected the argument, and the jury found for the Scotts. Emerson's counsel promptly appealed, delaying a final judgment for another two years. Such delays must have been frustrating to the Scotts, but the lengthy process had at least one advantage. Missouri law barred Emerson from selling or removing any slave involved in the case. The Scotts could therefore keep their family intact for as long as they could maintain their suit. Yet the long process also permitted time for events to move against them.[9]

Unfortunately for the Scotts, the Missouri Supreme Court never based its rulings upholding extrajudicial antislavery laws on a desire to favor liberty over slavery. Although *Winny*'s author, Judge George Tompkins, abhorred slavery and even expressed a desire to free every slave that came before him, no evidence suggests that his colleagues shared his sentiments.[10] Court members, in fact, never posed the questions before them in terms of liberty and slavery: they thought about the issues in terms of acceptable use. As lawyers working in a slaveholding jurisdiction, the judges considered slaves to be a form of property, which the state regulated as its agents deemed necessary. Such regulations focused on all aspects of slaveholding. The legislature and courts developed policies that set (largely unenforceable) standards for disciplining enslaved blacks, addressed issues of warranty for buyers of sick or injured slaves, limited masters' abilities to manumit enslaved persons, and punished (with increasing severity) the owners and officers of boats that allowed fugitives to escape on their vessels. Missouri's legislature had also committed to abide by the terms of the agreement that brought the state into the Union as a slaveholding jurisdiction in exchange for closing the federal territory north of 36°30' to the expansion of slavery.[11]

Missouri's Supreme Court vigorously enforced this policy, and its members considered a breach of extrajudicial antislavery provisions to be a misuse of one's slave property so egregious that only a complete forfeiture would remedy the situation. The court, however, repeatedly signaled that its policy was contingent on the free states' policies toward slavery, particularly on the question of slave transit. Missouri's judges insisted on slaveholders' right to pass through free jurisdictions when traveling from one slave state to another. As Judge Mathias McGirk wrote in 1828, "The ordinance was intended as a fundamental law for those who may choose to live under it, rather than as a penal statute to be construed by the letter against those who may choose to pass their slaves through the country." Even so, slaveholding travelers could not tarry in the free states; they could stop only for necessary delays: floods, serious illness, broken wagons, and the like. Stops for "mere convenience" constituted a wrongful introduction of slavery and created a freedom claim. On these grounds, the court freed a woman named Julia because her owner had held her for a month in Illinois before hiring her out in Missouri. It also freed Rachael, whose owner was a military officer stationed at Fort Snelling, because her owner, although he had no control over where the army sent him, brought her along for his convenience, not out of necessity. [12]

By the time the Scotts began their suit, members of Missouri's high court had started to reconsider their support for extrajurisdictional antislavery provisions. The court had regularly asserted that its policy rested contingently on northern states' recognition of slavery's legitimate place in the Union, a recognition that they could display by permitting the direct, unhindered movement of slaveholders through their states and into some portion of the federal territory. But developments in important free states and in Congress during the 1840s would signal to court members that northern policy makers were no longer willing to accept a legitimate place for slavery within the Union. In both Ohio and Illinois—states through which many travelers bound for Missouri passed—the right of slave transit became murkier. Ohio's supreme court, as Paul Finkelman has demonstrated, declared in 1845 that slaves entering the state with the consent of their masters automatically went free. Illinois did not go nearly as far, but in the 1840s its high court completely reevaluated its stance toward slavery and insisted, like Missouri, that any establishment of a domicile in the state would create a freedom claim. Its court said little about slaveholders' ability to travel through the state and thus rendered ambiguous the right of slave transit on which Missouri's high court insisted. Missouri's Supreme Court indicated a sense that the ground was shifting in 1846 when Judge William Scott wrote that only a river border separated Missouri from "a non-slaveholding

State, inhabited by many who are anxious, and leaving no stone unturned to deprive us of our slaves." The Wilmot Proviso (1846)—a congressional proposal to bar the expansion of slavery into any territory acquired during the then ongoing war with Mexico—intensified this sense of defensiveness, and the political fallout within Missouri generated a new set of resolutions in which the General Assembly repudiated the terms of the Missouri Compromise. By 1848, the Missouri Supreme Court was ready to do the same for its previous rulings on slave transit.[13]

A combination of judicial elections, disagreements over the best way to frame the issue, and a lack of law books containing a key precedent prevented the court from moving quickly, but in 1852 it finally announced its new policy. Scott v. Emerson, which handled Dred and Harriet's cases under a single set of facts, completely and bitterly rejected the court's previous stance toward extrajudicial antislavery law. Earlier decisions, Judge William Scott wrote for the majority, assumed that the court possessed a duty "to carry into effect the constitution of other States and territories, regardless of the rights, policy or institutions of the people of this State." To Scott, the practice of "confiscating the property of her own citizens by the command of a foreign law" presented a "humiliating spectacle," bordering on the absurd. Some older decisions, he maintained, held that a "hiring for two days" in free territory would work an emancipation. If two days was sufficient, then so was one day, or even six hours. There was no principled difference between holding a slave in free territory for two days rather than one. Judge Scott overstated the rigidity of Missouri's case law here—there was no decision resting solely on a two-day hire in free territory—but his argument underscored the tenacity with which the court had previously applied antislavery laws, a tenacity that Judge Scott regarded as a sign of weakness. "Times now are not as they were when the former decisions on this subject were made," he continued. While the court adhered to the policy set out in Winny v. Whitesides, "a dark and fell spirit in relation to slavery" had gripped the northern electorate, which pushed for measures "whose inevitable consequence must be the overthrow and destruction of our government." "Under such circumstances," he concluded, "it does not behoove the State of Missouri to show the least countenance to any measure which might gratify this spirit."[14]

Judge Scott's ruling politicized Scott v. Emerson. Until near the end of the proceedings, when Emerson's counsel began questioning the legitimacy of the Missouri Compromise restriction, no litigant had used the suit as a vehicle for political agendas. The only relevant issue through the early phases of the suit was whether Irene Emerson or the Scott family controlled the bodies and labor of Dred, Harriet, and their two daughters. In the court's hands, however, the case became a proslavery manifesto that wreaked havoc with the court's previous decisions. Judge Scott not only dismissed nearly thirty years of precedent as wrongheaded but embraced arguments that his predecessors had explicitly rejected. Thus, because John Emerson had been a military officer, he had no control of where he resided and therefore could not be held responsible for taking slaves into free territory. The court had rejected that argument in *Rachael*. Judge Scott also asserted that even if the Scotts' residences in Illinois and Minnesota had created a valid freedom claim, their decision to return "voluntarily" to a slave state such as Missouri restored their former status as slaves. Missouri's supreme court had dismissed that argument in *Winny*, but the contention had since gained judicial respectability in a number of southern courts.[15]

Despite the ruling's overtly political character, Judge Scott crafted his opinion in a manner that would avoid review by the U.S. Supreme Court. He did not challenge the constitutionality of the Missouri Compromise restriction—doing so would have courted federal review. But he did contend that its antislavery provision had no effect after slaves returned to Missouri from free territory. Scott probably rested on doctrinally safe ground here. In *Strader v. Graham* (1851), Chief Justice Taney had ruled that questions of social standing, except in a handful of instances controlled by the Constitution, belonged exclusively within state jurisdiction. *Strader*, of course, involved a situation in which slaves had "voluntarily" returned to a slave state from a free one, but in dicta, Taney stated that federal antislavery provisions covering the territories possessed only local force, and consequently the court would leave to the states those cases in which slaves "voluntarily" returned from free territory.[16] Judge Scott thus intended to have the last word on the Scott family's case, and his ruling exhausted the family's legal options at the state level. Although their suits had initially shown a great deal of promise, increasing uncertainty over the legitimacy of slavery led to an overtly political ruling that either overturned or simply ignored the previous rulings that sustained the Scotts' claims, and Judge Scott carefully crafted his opinion in a way he hoped would avoid federal review. He did not fail completely. The Scott family would move its case into the federal court, but not by directly challenging Judge Scott's ruling. Rather, the Scotts would enter the U.S. courts through diversity jurisdiction, precisely as the Supreme Court's southern faction had feared.

Despite their defeat before the Missouri Supreme Court, the Scotts remained intent on litigating for their freedom, a process that, if nothing else, held the family together as long as it lasted. The *Emerson* judgment was not a final decision. The court remanded the case back to the circuit court for more proceedings that would inevitably result in a jury verdict against the Scotts.[17] Legally, the only option left to the Scotts centered on getting their case reviewed by the U.S. Supreme Court, which would probably defer to the state ruling. Their bleak prospects aside, the Scotts pushed on, although they seemed to lose any control they might have had over their case. As the case moved through the federal courts, new lawyers offered their services, hoping to address the wide array of issues involved. These lawyers brought to the fore the place of black citizens within the Union, the impact of positive antislavery law on slaves traveling with their masters, and the constitutionality of Congress's efforts to limit slavery's expansion in the territories. A majority of the Supreme Court's members, however, proved reluctant to confront those issues, opting instead to focus on arcane technical matters before they finally attempted to evade all of the *Dred Scott* case's larger questions.

Prospects for the Scotts brightened when they came under the claim of a new owner and found a new lawyer. The record for the federal phase of the *Dred Scott* case stated that John Emerson had sold the Scott family to John F. A. Sanford (which the case misspelled as Sandford), but the statement was an oversimplification. Sanford, a citizen of New York and the brother of Irene Emerson, held a questionable claim to the Scotts. John Emerson had died before the state suit began, so Sanford could not have bought the Scotts directly from Emerson. No record indicates that he purchased them at all. He apparently claimed them through his status as Emerson's executor, but even that claim, as Walter Ehrlich has demonstrated, remains open to suspicion. Even so, no one challenged Sanford's ownership of the Scotts, and Sanford, who could have quickly ended the case by admitting that he did not own them, never denied his claim. Roswell M. Field, the Scotts' new lawyer and a sincere opponent of slavery, saw an opportunity in Sanford's claim, and he developed a strategy that he hoped would force the federal courts to decide whether a stay in free territory worked a permanent emancipation.[18]

At Field's suggestion, the Scotts filed against Sanford in federal diversity in November 1853, alleging—fictitiously—that the New Yorker assaulted and imprisoned Dred Scott, a Missouri citizen. A suit in diversity, Field believed, offered the Scotts a better chance at victory than simply appealing the state decision directly to the Supreme Court. Moving the suit directly to the Supreme Court, Field later explained, would bring it squarely within the confines of *Strader*, which would provide grounds to dismiss the ruling. Proceeding in diversity jurisdiction circumvented *Strader* and permitted the court to address the merits. Field hoped to convince the court that the antislavery provision in Illinois's constitution worked an instant and permanent emancipation on Dred Scott as soon as he entered the state. A claim to freedom so created, Field believed, trumped the reattachment argument made in *Emerson*.

Although the Scotts enjoyed some early success, the federal circuit court under Judge Robert Wells ruled against them. Sanford opened the case with a plea in abatement challenging the court's jurisdiction. Scott was, Sanford's counsel argued, a black man descended from slaves and not a citizen of the United States. He could not therefore sue in diversity. Judge Wells rejected the argument. Citizenship, for the purposes of diversity jurisdiction, rested on residence and the ability to own property, not on race. The parties then proceeded to the merits, and the court, following *Strader*, ruled against the Scotts, who promptly appealed.[19]

Like the early phases of *Emerson*, the initial stages of *Sandford* did not focus on the case's larger political implications, but that changed as *Dred Scott* headed toward final judgment in the Supreme Court. Recognizing the case's potential to challenge congressional authority over slavery in the territories—an issue that had reemerged in the debates over the Kansas-Nebraska Act—two distinguished southern lawyers, Henry Geyer and Reverdy Johnson, volunteered their services to Sanford. Geyer was a leading Missouri lawyer and a U.S. senator, and Johnson was a Maryland attorney reputed to be one of the best lawyers in the country. Montgomery Blair, a free-soil Democrat and political enemy of Geyer's, agreed to argue the Scotts' case in Washington. *Scott v. Sandford* entered the Supreme Court's docket late in the 1854 term, but the justices did not hear arguments until February 1856. Blair followed Field's strategy, arguing that *Emerson* wrongly ignored the effect of Illinois's constitution on Scott's status. He devoted the majority of his brief to the jurisdictional question of whether Scott could bring a case in a federal court, probably anticipating that the question would arise since the Supreme Court attached considerable attention to the scope of federal jurisdiction. Johnson and Geyer filed no brief (or none has survived), but newspaper accounts reveal that in addition to arguments against the court's jurisdiction and a reliance on *Strader*, they raised objections to the constitutionality of the Missouri Compromise. Again, *Dred Scott* was becoming politicized.[20]

Even so, the justices revealed little inclination to confront the case's larger issues and instead stalled on a technical matter. A few months after initial arguments, the court ordered a reargument, delaying the case until the next term.[21] Some contemporary observers believed that the justices wanted to avoid ruling before the 1856 presidential election. Yet McLean, who was a serious contender for the Republican nomination, made no objection to the postponement, although a strong defense of the Missouri Compromise given from the bench might well have enhanced his prospects. Court members more likely put off a ruling simply because they had reached an impasse over the plea-in-abatement and citizenship questions. In letters written many years later, Justice John A. Campbell detailed the court's divisions. He, McLean, John Catron, and Robert C. Grier believed that the plea-in-abatement and citizenship issues were not before the court. Taney, James M. Wayne, Peter V. Daniel, and Benjamin Robbins Curtis thought otherwise. Samuel Nelson remained undecided. Campbell described the debates on the matter as "repeated and protracted" and the parties as "animated and earnest" on the one side and "unwavering" on the other.[22]

The justices' reported opinions underscored the technical nature of this division. McLean and Catron argued that by proceeding to the merits, Sanford waived any objections to the jurisdiction, and Scott, who brought the case for review, understandably did not ask for the issue to be reopened. Taney and Curtis conceded that their colleagues had identified the correct practice for common-law courts, but the Supreme Court, as part of a government of limited and enumerated authority, worked according to a different set of jurisdictional rules. Sanford, said Curtis, possessed no choice but to proceed to the merits when the plea in abatement failed. If he had brought a writ of error, the Supreme Court would have dismissed the case because the Judiciary Act allowed the court only to take jurisdiction over final judgments. Taney agreed, and, although there were no federal cases directly on point, he and his colleague from Massachusetts probably had the stronger argument. The court routinely dismissed cases for lack of final judgment in an effort to police its jurisdiction. Although the majority eventually sided with Curtis and Taney, its members perhaps remained uncertain on the issue. Little wonder that no one objected when Nelson requested that the plea-in-abatement and citizenship questions be argued more thoroughly.[23]

The reargument took place in December 1856. Geyer and Johnson argued that the court must inquire into the plea in abatement to ensure that the lower court had not been mistaken, which, they contended, it had in fact been (because blacks were not citizens within the meaning of the Constitution). On the merits, they argued, *Strader* required the court to follow *Emerson* whatever the effect of Illinois's constitution or the Missouri Compromise restriction, which they considered unconstitutional at any rate. Blair, with the assistance of George T. Curtis (Justice Curtis's brother), discussed several ambiguous cases that Blair said demonstrated that Sanford had waived the objection to the court's jurisdiction. Blair also defended Scott's citizenship in more detail and added an argument defending Congress's power to ban slavery in the territories. Moreover, he incorporated a section on choice of law where he contended that the Supreme Court, under *Swift v. Tyson* (1842), worked under no obligation to follow *Emerson.* Blair's reasoning on this point would have a profound impact on the development of *Dred Scott.* The lawyers canvassed a wide range of issues in their arguments, ranging from the relatively uncontroversial citizenship issue to the more politically charged matter of slave transit to the explosive question of slavery in the territories. In conference, the court decided it would address none of them. The reargument convinced Nelson that the plea in abatement was not before the court, and he joined McLean, Catron, Grier, and Campbell in a majority. The court at that time also believed that the constitutionality of the Missouri Compromise legislation was not before it.[24]

At the majority's request, Nelson wrote an opinion for the court. He quickly disposed of the plea-in-abatement problem, stating only that his approach rendered a discussion of the divisive matter unnecessary. He then dropped the issue and proceeded to the merits.[25] He in fact avoided all of *Dred Scott*'s controversial aspects—including the challenge to the Missouri Compromise. Nelson was well positioned to make such an argument. His hedging on the plea-in-abatement issue kept him outside of the coalitions that had developed in conference, and he had maintained a low profile in slavery cases. Unlike Taney, Daniel, McLean, or even Grier, Nelson possessed no outspoken record on the peculiar institution, and the decision to have him deliver the opinion of the court may have indicated the justices' desire to avoid the sectional fray. Moreover, the court's doctrinal emphasis on the Union as a collection of concurrent sovereigns also allowed a handling of *Dred Scott* without breaking new ground. Nelson thus responded to the case before him merely by invoking the court's previous ruling in *Strader*.

According to Nelson, only one question concerned the court: whether slaves residing temporarily in free territory possessed a valid claim to freedom after returning to a slaveholding jurisdiction. State decisions, he wrote, exhibited a great deal of variety because each state held exclusive authority to resolve the matter as it saw fit. "The power flows from the sovereign character of the States of this Union; sovereign, not merely as respects the federal government . . . but sovereign as respects each other." Missouri's Supreme Court had ruled that stays in free territory did not create a valid claim to freedom upon a return to the state, and the U.S. Supreme Court considered itself bound to follow that ruling. "Except in cases where the power is restrained by the Constitution of the United States," Nelson wrote, paraphrasing *Strader*, "the law of the State is supreme over the subject of slavery within its jurisdiction." With those words, Nelson left the Scotts at the mercy of Missouri's Supreme Court.[26]

Nelson's opinion constituted a classic example of the Taney Court's slavery jurisprudence. The opinion asserted the concurrent nature of sovereignty within the Union's state structure and expressed a determination to defer to the states on questions of social status. It also protected slavery without subordinating court doctrine to the perceived needs of the peculiar institution; thus, Nelson avoided ruling on the constitutionality of the Missouri Compromise. Even as he did so, however, the justice maintained the court's hostile stance toward political antislavery. Although he saw no need to address the compromise legislation, Nelson underscored the contested nature of that act. "Many of the most eminent statesmen and jurists of the country," he wrote, "entertain the opinion that this provision of the act of Congress, even within the territory to which it relates, was not authorized by any power under the Constitution."[27] Nelson, as Don E. Fehrenbacher has correctly argued, hardly staked out a neutral position for himself. Yet following Nelson's lead, the court could have avoided ruling on *Dred Scott*'s most divisive issues—if the other justices had chosen to do so.[28]

Nelson soon learned that he would not speak for the court. Sometime between February 14 and February 19, 1857, the court rejected, on Wayne's motion, a narrow resolution and instead selected Taney to write an opinion embracing all the issues raised by *Dred Scott.* The reasons for the change

in strategy are not entirely clear. Wayne contended, Campbell later recol-
lected, that the reargument had created a public expectation that all the
issues would be discussed. Grier and Catron, each unknown to the other,
told President-Elect James Buchanan that McLean and Curtis forced the
change in strategy by voicing their intentions to dissent.[29] Historians' speculation on the reasons behind the court's shift generally centers on extrajudicial factors—usually the politics of slavery.[30] Such accounts, however,
slight the way in which notions of professional responsibility and doctrinal
fidelity refracted and shaped the court's politics. In their dissents, McLean
and Curtis pierced the veil of Nelson's neutrality and revealed his argument
to be fundamentally out of step with the court's most recent decisions. Their
critique of the New Yorker's position proved sufficiently powerful to convince the other justices, already under a great deal of pressure to address all
the issues, to change their strategy.

What Wayne described as "public interest and expectation" certainly
weighed heavily on the justices. In the late 1840s and early 1850s, members
of Congress had urged the court to handle the seemingly intractable slavery
question, and party leaders throughout the Union signaled that they would
honor the ruling. When the justices began hearing arguments in *Dred Scott*,
Congress had again become embroiled in the territorial question, and politicians again called for judicial intervention.[31] Justices also faced more direct
urgings. Senator Alexander Stephens of Georgia told his brother in late 1856
that he was pushing the court toward a quick decision, and Catron solicited
Buchanan's aid to pressure Grier into siding with the majority. Other people
probably tried to influence the court as well, and some justices certainly discussed the case among their friends and allies. A correspondent for Horace
Greeley's *New York Tribune*, for example, kept a roughly accurate running
account of the justices' positions in conference, and Stephens knew enough
to predict correctly the case's outcome two months before the decision was
rendered.[32] A number of the justices, Campbell recalled, believed they had
an obligation to confront all the questions. "The Court," he remembered
these justices saying, "would not fulfil public expectation or discharge its
duties by maintaining silence on these questions." Several of his colleagues,
he correctly speculated, had begun work on their own opinions before the
court took up the case in conference.[33]

These pressures surely influenced the decision to address all the issues
in *Dred Scott*, but McLean and Curtis's critique of Nelson may have neces-
sitated the change in strategy. The dissenters questioned the New Yorker's

interpretation of *Scott v. Emerson*, which presented the case as if it were a culmination of a settled line of case law. Under *Strader*, Nelson contended, the court would defer to the latest rulings of a state's highest court on questions of social status. Missouri's rulings showed "some diversity of opinion," but such matters were of no consequence "unless the first decision of a principle of law by a State court is to be permanent and irrevocable."[34] Nelson then attempted to depoliticize *Emerson* by asserting that six of the eight cases heard before 1852 were consistent with the later ruling. Each involved a situation where slaveholders went to Illinois to establish a permanent residence (domicile). Emerson, because he was a military officer, never intended to establish a permanent residence, and Missouri's supreme court had thus ruled consistently with its own decisions as well as those of other southern courts.[35] Nelson acknowledged that *Rachael v. Walker*, which held that military service offered no exemption from antislavery law, was one of the decisions in conflict with *Emerson*, but he lamely admitted his inability to explain the inconsistency and moved on.[36]

Nelson's reading of *Emerson* did not merely conflict with decisions such as *Rachael* but also contrasted sharply with the reasoning of Judge William Scott, who proudly proclaimed that his court was overturning the state's previous case law. Missouri's supreme court had never attached much importance to whether slaveholders established permanent residences or to drawing distinctions between sojourning and domicile, as some other southern courts had. Its decisions instead employed an idiosyncratic notion of wrongful introduction of slavery into free territory that rendered the threshold for freedom much lower than it was in the standards on which Nelson drew. Nelson couched his argument in terms that were largely alien to Missouri's jurisprudence. His use of such terms diminished the Scotts' prospects for freedom and allowed him to pretend that his court deferred to an application of known law rather than a politically motivated decision.

Yet Nelson's argument was vulnerable. In the context of the court's recent rulings, *Emerson* was not law but rather what the long-dead Story would have called "at most, only evidence" of what the law was.[37] Montgomery Blair took advantage of this vulnerability in his brief, and he put forth an argument that probably forced the court to change its strategy. The Scotts lost in the circuit court because Judge Wells believed himself bound by *Strader*. Yet that case, argued Blair, came to the Supreme Court directly from Kentucky's highest court under the claim that the court had violated a right based on federal law (the Northwest Ordinance). Taney and his associates found no violation of federal law and consequently had no jurisdiction under the terms of the Judiciary Act of 1789. Kentucky's ruling was thus "final and conclusive." *Scott v. Sandford*, however, came to the court through diversity jurisdiction where the Supreme Court considered state decisions binding only when they involved matters of real property or statutory construction. *Swift v. Tyson* controlled the procedure for this case, and *Emerson*, Blair contended, "is of no weight at all, beyond what is due the research, reason and authority which the opinion . . . displays, or which may be due to the court which pronounces it." With this argument, Blair turned the court's commercial rulings against *Strader* and presented the scenario that had most likely motivated the southern faction's attack on corporate diversity jurisdiction. Even worse, from their perspective, Blair's contention—as McLean's dissent would make obvious—was completely plausible in the context of the court's most recent rulings.[38]

Since 1842, the Taney Court had steadily broadened the *Swift* doctrine, which both imposed uniformity within federal jurisdiction and coerced citizens into standing by the obligations they incurred in the market while allowing court members to style themselves as facilitators of self-rule who did not declare policy in the place of the states. The expansion began in 1842 when Story, with the unanimous consent of his colleagues, declared that *Swift*'s principles embraced insurance contracts. Two years later, Story reversed a jury instruction given by a federal court because it conflicted with the general commercial law. He emphasized that the general commercial law came into play because the state in which the case arose (Mississippi) possessed no statute stating that its courts should follow a different procedure. If Mississippi had such a statute, Story claimed, the court would follow it without hesitation.[39]

Taney Court justices maintained an image of scrupulous adherence to state statutes when they drew on general commercial-law principles. "With all due respect for that distinguished tribunal," Justice John McKinley wrote of Louisiana's high court in 1846, "we are constrained to dissent from the general proposition they have laid down on the subject of demand and presentment, and from all their reasoning in support of it." Demand and presentment—collection procedures for bills of exchange—belonged to the general commercial law, but before he reached this conclusion, McKinley carefully analyzed the state's relevant statute to be sure that the legislature had enacted no change in those procedures.[40] Even those justices most concerned with the preservation of state authority drew on this extrajurisdictional body of law. In 1850, Daniel did so in a case involving a contract both made and sued on in Alabama. "Although the legal principles and inquiries involved in this cause are to a great extent local in their character and operation," he wrote, "it will be found to embrace rules . . . extending in some respects beyond the influence of merely local jurisprudence."[41]

Despite repetitious claims to the contrary, the concern for commerce and jurisdictional uniformity embodied in *Swift v. Tyson* eroded the court's deferential stance toward state law. As early as 1845, the court, speaking through McLean, refused to follow the state courts in their construction of wills "or any other instrument" and thus backed away from previous assertions that the federal courts were bound to follow state decisions concerning real property. Taney dissented, but his disagreement centered on a particular application of *Swift*.[42] Two years later, he showed a lack of deference when he rejected the ruling of Mississippi's high court that the state's provision banning the importation of slaves for sale was self-executing. The Supreme Court, Taney argued, had already ruled on that issue in *Groves v. Slaughter*, and the justices would not reverse the decision to bring it in accordance with changing state law. Such actions would subordinate federal policy to the wills of the state courts. Taney declared that the cases growing out of *Groves* were anomalous, but the court was in fact gradually moving into a position from which it could ignore state law for a number of different reasons.[43]

By the eve of *Dred Scott*, the justices felt safe to ignore state courts' statutory construction and even statutes, although *Swift* considered both binding. Two days after it ordered *Dred Scott's* reargument, the court assertively rejected a construction of a Michigan statute by the state's supreme court in *Pease v. Peck* (1856). *Pease* involved an action of debt between a creditor from New York and a debtor from Michigan who claimed protection under his state's statute of limitations. Although the period specified in the statute had passed, the New Yorker contended that the law did not apply to people living "beyond the seas," a technical phrase meaning outside of the state's jurisdiction.[44] The debtor denied that the language appeared in the statute. The printed version contained the phrase, but Michigan's high court had ruled that a recently discovered manuscript, which lacked the crucial words, controlled these cases. Justice Grier, speaking for the majority, refused to follow such a decision. Michigan had used the printed version for thirty years, yet now the state's courts declared that the will of the legislature was embodied in a "document reposing in the crypts of the secretary's office." Members of the legislature probably never saw the document, or, if they did, their decision to print a different version revealed their intention. Either way, an adoption of a version different from the printed one "would be, in our opinion, judicial legislation, and arbitrary assumption." The court therefore would not follow the ruling, especially since diversity jurisdiction rested on the premise that state courts would favor their citizens over those from other states. Campbell and Daniel dissented, but they offered little disagreement with Grier in principle; they objected only to the application. Michigan's courts had never provided an interpretation of the language in question, and counsel had cited no cases showing a conflict with the recent ruling. The court should consequently follow the latest rulings.[45]

Daniel revealed his acceptance of these developments when he wrote an 1856 opinion in which a unanimous court ignored a statute because it was in conflict with the general commercial law. A Mississippi law prevented creditors, "upon no principle of reason or justice," from suing debtors in accordance with the procedures of the general law.[46] Under *Swift*, the adjudication of negotiable instruments in the federal courts rested on the "law . . . of the commercial world," and the states possessed no authority to dictate otherwise. "The general commercial law," Daniel argued, was "circumscribed within no local limits," and its administration did not belong "to any peculiar jurisdiction." "The constitution and laws of the United States," he continued, "conferred upon the citizens of the several States, and upon aliens, the power or privilege of litigating and enforcing their rights acquired under and defined by" those doctrines. Consequently, "any state law or regulation" impairing those rights or limiting the federal court's cognizance of them, "in their fullest acceptation . . . , must be nugatory and unavailing." The federal courts would simply ignore such laws.[47] Daniel wrote this opinion while *Dred Scott* was pending before the court and while he, Campbell, and Catron stood in vocal opposition to the court's policy of extending diversity jurisdiction to corporate quasi-citizens. Their membership in the majority in many of these cases and their complete lack of systematic opposition to *Swift* underscored the plausibility of Blair's argument for the Scotts.

In his *Dred Scott* dissent, McLean took full advantage of the *Swift* doctrine. As Blair argued, the court did not consider itself bound to follow state court decisions unless they involved constitutional or statutory construction or the law of real property. *Emerson* involved neither. The decision overturned thirty years of settled case law because a majority of the state court's members resented—and they said so explicitly—"the excitement against the institution of slavery in the free States."[48] The court had no obligation at all to follow the ruling. A majority of justices in *Pease* confirmed that the court could adhere to previous rulings. "When the decisions of the State court are not consistent," said McLean, quoting the ruling, "we do not feel bound to follow the last, if it is contrary to our own convictions." That sentiment became stronger in cases "where, after a long course of consistent decisions, some new light suddenly springs up, or an excited public opinion has elicited new doctrines subversive of former safe precedent."[49] McLean quoted Grier, who now sided with the majority, as did several others who had acquiesced in that ruling.[50] McLean, together with Curtis's relatively weak contribution on this point, revealed the court's use of *Strader* to be an unabashedly policy-oriented strategy that in no way closed the discussion of *Dred Scott*'s larger issues.[51]

McLean made a powerful argument, and no one in the majority directly confronted it. The majority justices stood by Nelson. Catron, for example, called his New York colleague's opinion "the most conclusive argument on the subject within my knowledge." Taney assailed the Scotts for bringing their case in diversity jurisdiction, which he considered a breach in proper procedure designed to circumvent *Strader*. Grier explicitly concurred with Nelson; Wayne said nothing on the subject. Daniel and Campbell squirmed and devoted some pages to attacking the contention that a slave's stay in free territory created a valid freedom claim.[52] This behavior was strange for justices certain that they had the rules of jurisdiction on their side. Yet the justices' subsequent behavior revealed a sense that Nelson's opinion could not stand alone, because the policy laid out in *Strader* did not adequately address the issues of *Dred Scott*. The court had hoped that *Strader* would force all but a handful of cases—those dealing with fugitive slaves and perhaps unnaturalized immigrants—back to state and territorial forums, and its policy was to insulate slavery without complicating the court's agendas in commercial and corporate law. The way in which *Dred Scott* entered the federal courts combined with the myriad questions concerning the state court ruling, however, made the larger issues in the case impossible to ignore, especially when the dissenters pushed the issue.

The policy set out in *Strader v. Graham* proved incapable of dismissing a slavery case brought before the court in the manner *Scott v. Sandford* was. A majority of justices hoped that they could avoid involvement in the issues the case raised with an assertion that *Emerson* bound their actions.

The strategy failed. *Dred Scott v. Emerson*, whatever its status in the Missouri court system, constituted a profoundly flawed ruling, as Curtis and McLean demonstrated. The Supreme Court's reflexive resort to it through *Strader* compromised northern antislavery law and the court's fidelity to its own rulings. The *Strader* strategy thus offered evidence of judicial bias, especially since the court seemed content to pass over these issues with dubious arguments about *Emerson*'s consistency with Missouri's previous decisions. Moreover, the court surely had the authority, through the *Swift* doctrine, to ignore *Emerson* and come to its own conclusions on the law. McLean must have been convincing on this point, because his colleagues in the majority thereafter did exactly that, although neither he nor Curtis liked the answers that resulted. The majority's decision to address *Dred Scott*'s larger issues indicated its members' sense that Nelson's arguments could not stand alone: the dissenters made that plain. Even so, the failure of the *Strader* strategy by no means implied (as Curtis and McLean believed) that Scott should go free. That question depended on whether Scott received a valid claim to freedom under the Missouri Compromise legislation, and that in turn required the court to query whether blacks could sue under diversity jurisdiction.

CHAPTER EIGHT

The Political Economy of Blackness

Citizenship, Corporations, and the
Judicial Uses of Racism in Dred Scott

CHIEF JUSTICE ROGER B. TANEY RESPONDED to the fail-
ure of *Strader* with a jurisdictional ruling that denied Dred Scott access to
the federal courts on the basis of his race. No black person, whether slave or
free, could lay claim to U.S. citizenship because, at the time of the founding, blacks "had no rights which the white man was bound to respect." The
opinion was striking in its sheer excess. Taney devoted twenty-four of his
fifty-five pages to a doctrinal and historical discussion of his position, and he
embellished his argument with, by A. Leon Higginbotham's count, twenty-
one separate references to either black inferiority or white superiority. The
jurisdictional issue, although important, was not that difficult—the plea in
abatement was more so—and it did not require such a laborious approach.
Taney's critics again saw partisanship at work. As one Republican member
of Congress said, Taney's arguments on citizenship had become "political
and judicial truths, the contemplation of which the modern Democrat finds
his richest consolation." Abolitionist Frederick Douglass called the ruling a
"judicial incarnation of wolfishness" and challenged the veracity of Taney's
citizenship ruling. "As a man, an American, a citizen, a colored man of both
Anglo-Saxon and African descent, I denounce this representation as a most
scandalous and devilish perversion of the Constitution, and a brazen mis-
statement of the facts of history." Douglass expressed a recurrent criticism
of *Dred Scott*'s citizenship ruling and one that recent historians have embraced. Like Douglass, they view Taney's opinion as an attempt to strike out
against the antislavery movement, and they underscore its partisan nature
by emphasizing that its substantive arguments were doctrinally and historically incorrect. Yet this focus on Taney's "mutilation of fact [and] subver-
sion of the law," to borrow a phrase from one of Justice Benjamin Robbins

Curtis's correspondents, has both downplayed the ambiguity of the historical record, which rendered Taney's claims at least plausible, and obscured the extent to which Taney was responding to divisions on his court.[1]

Without question, Taney's citizenship ruling was agenda-laden, and it pursued two policy goals. It closed the federal courts to free blacks and thereby frustrated antislavery litigation strategy. Critics such as Douglass were therefore correct to see the ruling as a challenge to their movement. Yet Taney took care to close off this avenue in a manner that left the courts open to corporate litigants. Here lay the purpose of Taney's excess. His stress on the racist aspects of federal law underscored that blacks' historical and legal experience placed them in a category different from that of other quasi-citizens. The court could thus treat corporate litigants differently than free black ones, and the court would in fact begin to do so shortly after *Dred Scott*. Taney's ruling also drew heavily on the court's understanding of the nature of federal power, a feature that placed the opinion on a firm doctrinal basis and rendered it difficult to challenge within the constraints of Taney Court discourse—as the powerful dissents of John McLean and Curtis demonstrated.[2]

The breakdown of the *Strader* strategy allowed Taney an opportunity to discuss the vexing issues that the *Dred Scott* case raised and to address the divisions that had developed in the court since 1853. Taney's ruling on African American federal citizenship proceeded on two fronts. It blocked free blacks from suing in diversity, an avenue that *Strader* left open, but did so in a way that conveyed to Taney's southern colleagues that the court could close itself to blacks without shutting out corporations. Both aspects of this strategy hinged on the racism that the chief justice perceived to be ingrained in constitutional law. Yet Taney's arguments remained in a state of development when he delivered them on March 6, 1857. He spent several months revising his opinion after the decision was rendered, an unusual practice that angered some of his colleagues. He later wrote a supplement for the opinion and tried unsuccessfully to have it included in the *U.S. Reports*.[3] Because Taney extensively revised his opinion, the reported decision provided an inaccurate portrayal of what Taney said from the bench, and newspaper accounts, as Don E. Fehrenbacher notes, are too sketchy to allow comparison.[4] The most reliable pieces of evidence concerning the substance of Taney's arguments in March 1857 are the two sets of Taney's heavily revised page proofs housed in the National Archives. Those documents—particularly the earlier one—reveal that the chief justice delivered an opinion of considerable sophistication in which he channeled racist elements inherent within constitutional law toward the fulfillment of his immediate policy goals.

Dred Scott marked a departure from the court's previous rulings on slavery because the decision rested explicitly on considerations of black inferiority. The discussions in Groves, Prigg, the Passenger Cases, and Strader all centered primarily on whether the states possessed an inherent power of self-preservation that trumped federal authority. A working assumption of white superiority, of course, ran latently through the court's discourse and influenced its members' thinking. In Prigg, Joseph Story ignored the plight of kidnapped free blacks, and Robert C. Grier praised the Union's immigration policy for its attraction of white Christians. A lawyer once lectured the court on the enormity of incest by comparing it to miscegenation.[5] Despite its background presence, this assumption exerted little overt influence on the court's rulings. Even Taney, who argued in his opinion on the Negro Seamen Act that the Constitution existed for the benefit of whites only, refrained from deploying such arguments on the bench and relied instead on discussions of inherent state authority. One exception appeared in 1846 when Taney, speaking for a unanimous court, upheld a murder indictment against John Rogers, a white man protesting the court's jurisdiction because of his membership in the Cherokee Nation. Taney rejected the argument. "He was still a white man, of the white race, and therefore not within the exemption in the act of Congress." This racist conception of the polity usually remained latent. As late as 1855, a unanimous court ruled that the Treaty of Guadalupe Hidalgo incorporated nonwhite Mexicans as citizens of the United States.[6]

In Dred Scott, Taney reasserted his racist conception of the polity in the form of a specifically antiblack federal citizenship. As numerous scholars argue, he surely planned to shut blacks out of the federal courts, but his motivation stemmed from more than opposition to the antislavery movement.[7] Taney constructed his ruling so that it realized that goal without requiring major revisions of the court's rulings on corporate standing. His strategy depended on a rhetorical isolation of blacks from not only white males (normative citizens) but also other subaltern segments of the population, such as white women and minors and other nonwhites in general. Taney explicitly exempted both Native Americans and women from his citizenship ruling. Different rules applied to Indians because they generally lived under the jurisdiction of separate tribal groups. White women and minors also suffered under various disabilities, but *Dred Scott* did not apply to them; their status derived from their husbands and fathers.[8] Taney did not provide wholly satisfactory explanations on these points. Still, the construction of federal citizenship along an (oversimplified) black/white (male) binary allowed a focus on what Taney considered the primary factor barring blacks from the federal polity: their history of enslavement and subsequent degradation within American legal culture. This background explained why some quasi-citizens had access to the federal courts while others did not.

Before he took up that issue, however, Taney elaborated a theoretical framework that sustained his antiblack vision of federal citizenship. This aspect of the opinion generally eludes scholars, who focus on its partisan and racist character. Such emphasis is neither surprising nor unwarranted. Yet the chief justice made the work of subsequent readers more difficult because he silently relied on Daniel's concurring opinion for an important part of his ruling's conceptual framework. Without Daniel's concurring opinion, Taney's argument is not readily understandable. The chief justice, in fact, insisted that his ruling first appear alongside the other opinions given in the case, and he prohibited anyone—his colleagues included—from gaining access to the document until it had been published in the *U.S. Reports.*[9] Taney issued the order around the time Curtis initiated inquiries about Taney's revisions, and the rule was certainly self-serving. Still, the chief justice's insistence may have stemmed in part from his dependence on the concurring opinions. Most analyses of *Dred Scott* slight these documents and generally cite them to show that Taney's ruling had very little support even among the majority. Yet separate opinions need not always imply disagreement; sometimes they elaborate issues that the majority has neglected to discuss in detail. Such tactics allow the majority to retain focus on a case's most important (or occasionally least controversial) issues. Taney, for example, said very little about the impact of Illinois law on Scott's status but relied on Samuel Nelson's concurrence for that. Likewise, Taney wrote little about the nature of state citizenship but simply began his analysis where Peter V. Daniel left off. No discussion of Taney's opinion, therefore, should begin without consideration of the argument presented by the chief justice's Virginia colleague.

Daniel contributed to the conceptual underpinnings of Taney's vision of antiblack citizenship by examining the ways in which the master-slave relationship limited free blacks' prospects for state citizenship. Daniel, a member of the southern faction and a more proslavery justice than any of his colleagues, pursued this subject with alacrity. His critique of the court's corporate rulings rested heavily on his contention that corporations were quasi-citizens and hence not entitled to diversity jurisdiction. A similar analysis underlay his objection to Dred Scott's attempt to use the same avenue. Daniel's arguments concerning citizenship drew on what James Kettner has termed the doctrine of election. This doctrine became a basic premise of American citizenship law as jurists, roughly between 1776 and 1830, conceptualized the polity as a sovereign community of equal (white, male) citizens who voluntarily subordinated themselves to the law in exchange for the protection of their liberties. Citizens, in other words, chose their sovereign.[10]

Daniel grounded his argument on this premise, but he emphasized the sovereign community's power to choose the citizens it incorporated. Counsel for the Scott family assumed that free blacks held citizenship in their states of residence, but that belief failed to account for the ways in which the current or former possession of slave status shaped blacks' opportunities to consent to the governments that ruled them. Citizenship, Daniel contended in language similar to that he used with regard to corporations, conveyed "ideas of connection or identification with the State or Government, and a participation of [sic] its function." It implied the possession and enjoyment of a body of rights on an equal basis with the other members of society, and it further presupposed that this equality promoted the population's general welfare. Moreover, the doctrine of election asserted that citizens consented to the social and political arrangements under which they lived, and it rested on two further assumptions. First, all members who formed the society possessed the ability to give and withhold their consent. Second, the people whom the citizenry embraced as equals posed no threat to the constituted social order.[11] Counsel for the Scott family contended that emancipation, whether brought on by the master's voluntary act or not, instantly produced a citizen. They suggested, according to Daniel, that manumission transformed the slave "from a mere subject of property, into a being possessing a social, civil, and political equality with a citizen." Daniel perceived dangerous implications in the argument, especially for a state's ability to regulate the social standing of its inhabitants. The Scotts' counsel in effect asserted that an individual held the power to incorporate a new citizen into a state's body politic, "without cooperation or warrant of the Government" and "perhaps in opposition to its policy." A power to create new citizens, they implied, lay beyond of the control of the government.[12]

State policies, however, revealed that governments in the United States maintained a tight control over whom they admitted as citizens. Many states refused to incorporate free blacks at all. Illinois, Indiana, and Iowa barred free blacks from entering their borders, although masters retained the right to bring their slaves into those states.[13] Other states allowed free blacks to live within their borders but not as citizens. Georgia's Supreme Court asserted that any rights that free persons of color enjoyed within the boundaries of the state stemmed from the whim of the legislature rather than from such persons' free status.[14] North Carolina, Massachusetts, Pennsylvania, and Louisiana had no difficulty in declaring free blacks citizens but placed restrictions on that portion of the population. Massachusetts forced the children of its free black citizens to attend different schools than whites, and the Supreme Court of North Carolina held that white citizens possessed the right to beat that state's citizens of color for insolence. Emancipation by itself guaranteed little beyond freedom, and any rights that free blacks enjoyed rested on the whims of the white-dominated governments under which free blacks lived.[15]

Taney's discussion of federal citizenship drew heavily on the doctrine of election as Daniel described it. The argument that the creation of black state citizens required a two-step process—emancipation and a subsequent incorporation into the polity—infused Taney's opinion. Daniel's influence emerged clearly in the chief justice's discussion of the relationship between citizenship and discriminatory legislation targeting blacks. Such laws demonstrated that whites associated free blacks with the so-called slave race and underscored that whites considered this segment of the population a threatening presence rather than fellow citizens. Taney incorporated Daniel's stance while revising the opinion, for the chief justice modified all of his references to black citizenship to emphasize that free blacks held their rights at the whim of the white population.[16] Taney probably found this aspect of Daniel's argument useful because it allowed him simultaneously to achieve his two policy goals. Daniel's focus on the way in which the election doctrine accommodated racial distinctions provided Taney with a conceptual foundation justifying the exclusion of free blacks from the federal courts. It also allowed him to argue, in terms acceptable to his southern colleagues, that the court could do so without shutting itself to all quasi-citizens. Taney implicitly met the latter goal by stressing that policies of black exclusion reflected a widespread assumption, held since the founding, that free blacks constituted a threat to the Union's white-dominated social orders. That assumption, Taney argued, required that the court treat free blacks differently from all other quasi-citizens.

Before making that argument, Taney elaborated on the conceptual structure that Daniel had provided and put forth the main legal point: federal law excluded blacks from citizenship, even while some state laws did not, because state and federal citizenship constituted starkly different forms of political association. States possessed governments of inherent authority and bore the responsibility for regulating the health, safety, and morality of the American people. States held the power to incorporate anyone they wished into their own body politic. If they wished to extend rights of citizenship to recent immigrants or newly emancipated slaves, states were free to do so. If they saw these groups as a threat, they could deny access to such rights. A state's power to create new citizens stopped at its borders and conferred no legal standing within any other state. Federal citizenship provided those who possessed it with rights outside of their home state as well as the right to sue in federal court.[17]

Only the federal government could confer this type of citizenship, and it recognized, for the most part, only two ways to attain this status. Citizens either traced their descent to a person who had become a citizen at the time of the Constitution's ratification, or they—or their ancestors—had subsequently become naturalized according to the provisions of federal law. States, Taney contended, held no power to "introduce a new member into the political community created by the Constitution of the United States." They could not create federal citizens by recognizing them as state citizens, and they certainly could not "introduce any person, or description of persons, who were not intended to be embraced into this . . . political family . . . but were intended to be excluded from it." This position was fully consistent with the Supreme Court's vision of a union composed of concurrently sovereign governments, and it meshed well with the actual practice of federal citizenship policy, which claimed exclusive authority over naturalization and more or less linked access to citizenship with one's line of descent. Perhaps this explains why a constitutional amendment was required to overturn *Dred Scott* and why few of Taney's critics challenged this aspect of his argument.[18]

The next part of Taney's opinion attracts a large amount of criticism. Through historical analysis, Taney demonstrated to his satisfaction that the Framers intentionally excluded blacks from the federal polity and that the federal government had maintained a strict line of racial division since that time. No government in the United States, state or federal, had embraced racial equality either before or after the founding, and none of them extended the same rights to blacks as to whites. This perception of inferiority combined with legislation designed to perpetuate racial subordination, Taney asserted, relegated blacks to a second-class or quasi-citizenship that locked them out of the federal polity. In this portion of his opinion, Taney employed a level of detail that many scholars find excessive if not offensive. He had strategic reasons for this approach. He hoped on one level to compromise the dissenters' critiques of his position. He admitted to Curtis that after hearing his and McLean's arguments, he added references to "proofs & authorities . . . regarding the historical facts & principles of law which were stated in the opinion as too well established to dispute."[19] Taney's use of detail worked on another level as well. Through his laborious account of discriminatory legislation targeting free blacks, he could explain why federal policy excluded free blacks but implicitly not other types of quasi-citizens.

After a litany of references to black inferiority—including the opinion's infamous phrase that blacks "had no rights which the white man was bound to respect"—Taney came to the point of all this detail. States impressed these "deep and enduring marks of degradation" on blacks because racial equality was considered dangerous to social stability. Free blacks' claims to federal citizenship threatened to undermine those discriminatory policies. Federal citizenship recognized a political equality among those who possessed it, and for that reason only members of the highest class of citizens in each state received its blessings. "It cannot be supposed," Taney wrote, that the states "intended to secure to [free blacks] rights, and privileges, and rank, in the new political body throughout the Union, which *every one of them denied* within the limits of its own borders." The Framers understood, he contended, that federal citizenship would enable blacks to escape the laws that held them in submission. Under the Privileges and Immunities Clause, free blacks could enter any state in the Union and demand the same treatment that white citizens received. These visitors could come to a state "whenever they pleased, singly or in companies, without pass or passport, and without obstruction, to sojourn there as long as they pleased, to go where they pleased at every hour of the day or night without molestation." A state could do nothing to stop this influx unless a free black person committed a crime for which a white would be punished. Federal citizenship, moreover, would have allowed blacks the rights to "the full liberty of speech in public and private upon all subjects upon which its own citizens might speak; to hold meetings on political affairs, and to keep and carry arms wherever they went." [20]

In this passage, Taney broadly constructed the Privileges and Immunities Clause and treated it as if it were a color-blind provision that secured blacks (if they were federal citizens) the same rights as whites. He had strategic reasons for doing so. The southern faction's criticism of the extension of citizenship to corporations, for the purposes of diversity, rested on an equally broad construction of the clause. John A. Campbell had warned in 1854 that the policy would "undermine every limitation in the Constitution, if universally adopted." [21] Taney met the southerners' critique by applying their broad interpretation of the clause to free blacks. He then asserted that the consequences of their inclusion into the polity could be so devastating to the southern states that they would have never joined a union in which blacks could be citizens. Taney, of course, read contemporary southern concerns back into the past and most likely projected into the minds of the Framers his own fears about a black-led abolition movement in the South. Even so, his argument possessed a solid doctrinal foundation, for the Framers probably did intend the provision to be color-blind. During the drafting of a nearly identical clause for the Articles of Confederation, as Curtis pointed out in his dissent, the delegates explicitly rejected an attempt to limit it to "free white inhabitants" only. Taney accepted Curtis's argument but did not agree that color-blindness implied a possession of federal citizenship. [22]

Rather, Taney maintained that the discriminatory legislation of the ratification era pointed toward an assumption that the newly created federal polity would not embrace free blacks. There is no evidence that the Framers had much concern for members of that group. If the treatment of enslaved blacks provides any indication, the Framers considered free blacks wholly expendable to the needs of the federal system. The Constitution left free blacks at the mercy of the states in which they lived and made no provision, barring amendment, to incorporate free blacks later. Again, Taney confined his opinion solely to blacks. Although other segments of the population also held a sort of quasi-citizenship—women, children, corporations—only blacks found themselves completely excluded from the federal polity. This exclusion, Taney argued, originated in a historical experience that had placed them at the bottom of the social order. Only blacks belonged to a racial group that had been forcibly removed from another continent and transported to the United States to work as slaves. Only the members of that race suffered under the nearly total deprivation of legal rights that sustained slavery as an institution. The perceived needs of that institution, which undoubtedly shaped the minds of the Framers, demanded that free blacks likewise be kept in a state of subordination. Yet excluding free blacks from federal citizenship did not aid only the South. It also allowed states in the North and West to pursue their own policies of racial subordination.

Taney's combination of the election doctrine, a federal citizenship dependent on state citizenship, and an emphasis on the racism inherent within constitutional law allowed him to meet his two immediate policy goals. He closed the jurisdictional gap left open by *Strader*, a decision that Taney believed should have controlled *Dred Scott*. Yet the Scott family's "indirect and circuitous way" of avoiding that ruling required a different strategy.[23] The denial of black federal citizenship thus represented a continuation of *Strader*'s effort to force all questions of social status, with the exception of the handful of instances covered by *Prigg* and the *Passenger Cases*, back to the states. At the same time, Taney implicitly responded to the southern faction's critique of corporate diversity jurisdiction. His stress on discriminatory legislation as a restraint on the perceived threat that free blacks posed to the social order, especially in the South, allowed him to distinguish free blacks from other quasi-citizens. Taney's invocation of a specifically antiblack form of federal citizenship embodied the stance toward slavery to which a majority of the justices had clung since the 1840s (and which Taney himself adopted around 1850). His court would protect slavery—the justices perceived a constitutional duty to do so—but would not do so in a manner that subordinated its doctrine to southern interests. Taney's detailed account of these "marks of degradation" thus sought a justification for a seemingly inconsistent approach to quasi-citizens.[24] The court accepted corporate claims to diversity jurisdiction while rejecting those of blacks because the latter group, unlike the white men who benefited from corporate organization, possessed a legal history rooted in slavery and continuing racial subordination. That history, Taney argued, demanded that the court treat free blacks differently from all other litigants, but there was no need to close the courts to all quasi-citizens.

As they did with Nelson's opinion, Curtis and McLean offered a critique of Taney's argument, but their efforts underscored Taney's plausibility. A combination of deep-seated racism within American constitutional law and the antiabolitionist constraints of the Taney Court's jurisprudence rendered exceedingly difficult the development of a judicially convincing alternative to Taney's ruling. Neither Curtis nor McLean spoke to *Dred Scott*'s corporate implications, which at any rate remained latent in the opinion. The dissenting justices focused on the immediate issue and assailed the majority's rejection of black federal citizenship. In their dissents from the majority opinion, McLean and Curtis drew heavily on antislavery constitutional arguments to justify blacks' incorporation into the federal polity. Numerous historians praise Curtis's opinion, but he failed in his effort to fuse political antislavery with a jurisprudential framework that was both inherently racist and intentionally shaped by his colleagues to push antislavery legal thought to the margins of federal judicial culture. Unlike his predecessor and teacher, Joseph Story, Curtis made no effort to pull together a coalition against Taney's position. Curtis's opinion sought little common ground with his colleagues, who surely found it not only politically unappealing but also doctrinally radical.

Curtis seemed an unlikely candidate to write a strong dissent in a case such as *Dred Scott*. He had never advocated antislavery, and he believed that the Union's survival depended on resisting the abolition movement. Before coming to the bench, he had defended slaveholders in high-profile cases and had supported the passage of the Fugitive Slave Law of 1850. Yet his rejection of antislavery did not lead him to conclude that free blacks should be barred from the federal polity. Like Taney, Curtis had already developed views on black citizenship. He had signed a petition protesting the Negro Seamen Act that asked Congress "to render effectual in [free blacks'] behalf the privileges of citizenship secured by the Constitution of the United States."[25] Faced with the majority's oppressive vision of black citizenship, Curtis hoped to discover the existence of an alternative policy that was more in line with what he assumed to be the Framers' intentions. Throughout his argument, Curtis filtered his evidence through an assumption that the Framers planned for slavery to pass eventually from the American scene and that they intended that federal legal protection to extend to all (male) persons, regardless of their present or former status under state law. He did not make such assumptions without warrant. The first idea had an undoubted, if ambiguous, foundation in the documents of the founding era and was becoming increasingly influential in northern political circles. Curtis's second assumption—the idea that free blacks had a claim to equal protection under the law—remained a hotly contested issue even among some antislavery advocates, but it infused Curtis's entire opinion.[26]

Curtis rejected the core assertion of the majority's argument: that federal law protected only persons privileged enough to have white skin. Taney and Daniel produced a large body of evidence showing that the governments of the United States had discriminated against blacks since before the founding, but Curtis dismissed as "monstrous" any idea that such regulations mandated a perpetual exclusion from the federal polity. He simply rejected them out of hand and ignored two—the election doctrine and discriminatory legislation—of the three bodies of legal rules that the majority considered relevant to the citizenship question.[27] He then reworked the third so that his conclusion would not conflict with his assumptions. Along the way, he groped for data on which to rest several tenuous assertions. Most importantly, Curtis contended that birth on a nation's soil automatically made a person a citizen and that constitutional law recognized a necessary link between suffrage and citizenship. Neither of these positions was well established in federal law, and they would not become so until after the ratification of the Fourteenth and Fifteenth Amendments. Curtis therefore worked extremely hard to make his case, and federal law—quite possibly because it had developed under the stewardship of a Supreme Court hostile to antislavery—offered his positions little favor.

Curtis began with a creative use of precedent. Citing John Marshall's opinion in *Gassies v. Ballon* (1832), Curtis argued that "a citizen of the United States, residing in any State of the Union, is, for the purposes of jurisdiction, a citizen of that State."[28] Yet Marshall spoke only of naturalized citizens and said simply that when aliens became citizens of the United States, they acquired citizenship in the states in which they lived as well. He made no mention of natural-born citizens. With no discussion of these issues, Curtis extended *Gassies* to cover Dred Scott's situation and attacked the majority opinion at what he considered its weakest point. Scott resided in Missouri at the time the suit was brought, and he was consequently a citizen of that state and entitled to sue in federal court—provided, of course, that he was a citizen of the United States. According to John F. A. Sanford's plea, Curtis wrote, only Scott's slave ancestry barred him from federal citizenship. If the court found evidence that *any* person with such a background had become a citizen of the United States, however, then Sanford's contentions provided no bar, and Scott was a federal citizen with the right to sue in federal court.[29]

Curtis put the plea to the test and rigorously attacked the historical portion of Taney's argument. Because Taney had revised his opinion so extensively, Curtis was at a disadvantage. In all probability, Taney did not argue that no African Americans possessed state citizenship in 1787, but he may have presented his contentions with little or no supporting evidence. Curtis would claim later that the chief justice added eighteen pages designed to refute his colleague's arguments (whether Curtis meant handwritten or typeset pages is not clear). The proof sheets in the National Archives account for only around ten (handwritten) pages, but Taney may well have made additional revisions before submitting the opinion to the printer.[30] Whatever the reason, Curtis set out to refute an argument less sophisticated than the one Taney printed, and the associate justice thus failed to account for the full subtlety of the majority opinion. Curtis identified five states in which free blacks held the vote, which implied that they were considered citizens. He then argued, based on a 1838 North Carolina ruling, that American law recognized no distinctions at all between citizens and free inhabitants. At first glance, Curtis successfully compromised Sanford's plea, and Curtis's reasoning seemed devastating to Taney's opinion. Closer inspection renders problematic Curtis's arguments. He made no effort to account for the discriminatory legislation that targeted free blacks; he just ignored it (and said nothing about why both he and Taney could use two of the same states as examples). Curtis's entire contention on this point rested on an equation between suffrage and citizenship, a formula that he admitted was imperfect because states disenfranchised many citizens—"native-born women, or persons under age or under guardianship because insane or spendthrifts." Yet all voters, he insisted, certainly possessed state citizenship.[31]

The matter was not so clear-cut. Antebellum legal theory saw no necessary relationship between citizenship and suffrage. Responding to Curtis, Taney pointed out that suffrage was too ambiguous to serve as a foundation for citizenship. All states, Taney agreed, held large numbers of citizens within their borders who could not vote. But states, as sovereign entities, also had the authority to extend the franchise to people who were not state citizens. Some states, Taney added, allowed unnaturalized immigrants to vote. (As late as 1873, in fact, the New York District of the U.S. Circuit Court held that citizenship was not a necessary qualification for suffrage.) Voting thus bore no necessary connection to citizenship. "The State," Taney concluded, "may give the right to free negroes and mulattos, but that does not make them citizens of the State, and still less of the United States." Incorporation into the franchise meant that a person could vote but did not necessarily carry any further implications. Curtis assumed that it did.[32]

Curtis then moved on to Taney's jurisdictional argument and asserted that people of color faced no bars to federal citizenship after ratification of the Constitution. Although he did not become any less innovative, Curtis employed a theory of concurrent sovereignty that resembled the one Taney used. The two justices, however, disagreed sharply on where to draw the line between state and federal authority. Before 1787, Curtis wrote, the states controlled access to a national, or "general," citizenship in the United States. People claimed this status through the Articles of Confederation's Privileges and Immunities Clause, which aggregated the citizens of separate states into "the people of the United States." Moreover, the clause's authors had successfully fought off southern attempts to limit it to whites. Curtis quickly deduced the meaning of this action: the provision was to be color-blind. Because the term *free inhabitants* excluded only "paupers, vagabonds, and fugitives from justice," the language clearly implied at the time of ratification that "free colored persons of African descent might be, and, by reason of their citizenship in certain States, were entitled to the privileges and immunities of general citizenship of the United States."[33]

Curtis's reliance on this theory of general citizenship proved important for two reasons. Most obviously, the access of people of color to this type of citizenship further undercut Taney's historical argument by showing blacks receiving the same rights under this provision as whites. Indeed, Taney's own rendering of the Privileges and Immunities Clause indicated that he could find this argument convincing. More importantly, Curtis used this theory to counter the argument that the Constitution conferred no power to make African Americans citizens. There was essentially no evidence on this issue, so Curtis had a great deal of interpretive freedom. Yet his theory of general citizenship made little sense on a consideration of the different institutional structures that the Articles and the Constitution had created. Curtis gave the matter scant attention and maintained that before 1788, the states had possessed the power to grant U.S. citizenship. If this was the case, he wrote, the states retained this power unless the Constitution expressly took it away. The states, therefore, held the power to make blacks federal citizens and thereby give them access to the federal courts and the Privileges and Immunities Clause.

From the perspective of post–Fourteenth Amendment jurisprudence, Curtis's argument appears unremarkable. Access to federal citizenship rested on one's birth in a state. "Every free person born on the soil of a State, who is a citizen of that State by force of its Constitution or laws," in other words, "is also a citizen of the United States." Even so, Curtis contended, the Framers never intended for every person born within the jurisdiction of a state to become a federal citizen, and the states thus retained authority to determine who became a state citizen and who became a citizen of the United States. Curtis again resorted to his equation between suffrage and citizenship to determine which inhabitants became citizens. Although the franchise was not an essential characteristic of citizenship, the constitutional provisions allowing people to vote provided decisive evidence of which persons a state considered citizens. Curtis then made his conclusion. Every person that both had been born in and held the franchise in a particular state possessed federal citizenship, and all of them, whether black or white, received the right to sue in federal court and to find protection in the Privileges and Immunities Clause.[34]

The implications of Curtis's argument, as Stuart A. Streichler has noted, were staggering, and they directly challenged the Union's long-standing policies of racial subordination.[35] Curtis did not contend that a free black traveling from one state to another should receive the same amount of legal protection that a black inhabitant of the latter state received. Rather, he maintained that a free African American would receive the same rights and privileges that the latter state conferred on the voting citizens within its jurisdiction. In essence, he asserted that the Constitution gave each state a certain degree of direct influence over the manner in which the other states regulated social status within their borders. Curtis's interpretation constituted a boldly innovative argument on both the doctrinal and policy levels; it also represented precisely the type of scenario that underpinned the southern justices' critique of corporate jurisdiction. Under this formulation, free black litigants could access the Privileges and Immunities Clause through the federal courts and undermine the southern states' black codes and the western states' bans on black migration, especially if the courts had the authority under *Swift v. Tyson* to ignore those laws.

Constitutional law offered very little support for this position, and Curtis proceeded only by knitting together scraps of data. He offered no evidence that the states retained the power to choose which of their citizens entered the federal polity. Although he drew explicitly on the court's doctrine of concurrent sovereignty, he did not present a court decision, statute, or even one of the Framers' writings to prove that the Constitution divided the authority to create federal citizens. His assertion that federal law recognized a definite link between citizenship and birth rested on a firmer but still quite scanty foundation: the requirement that the president be a "natural-born citizen."[36] Use of this term, Curtis argued, connected the document to a principle of public law referring citizenship to one's place of birth, establishing "the rule that persons born within the several States are citizens of the United States."[37] Maybe. Anglo-American jurisprudence had long recognized a connection between birth and citizenship, but the doctrinal test for citizenship asked not whether one was born on the soil but rather whether one had been born into the allegiance of the sovereign. Citizenship thus followed bloodlines, and the language of the provision Curtis cited supported that position. "No person except a natural born Citizen," it read, "or a Citizen of the United States at the time of the Adoption of this Constitution shall be eligible to the Office of President." Curtis quoted only the first part of the clause, and the omission was important. The major category in the clause was the latter one, for it encompassed the population of United States at the time of ratification. The category of natural-born citizen was exceptional in that it handled citizens to be born in the future, not yet alive. These people became natural-born citizens because they were the descendants of the people encompassed in the second category. Use of the term, therefore, did not imply an equation between citizenship and birth on the soil and offered no guarantee of black citizenship.[38]

Curtis's colleagues lacked the disposition to accept his argument, but its innovative character probably did not help matters. Even Curtis backed away from his opinion's more radical implications. He conceded that the Privileges and Immunities Clause's color-blindness raised significant problems for the Union's patterns of racial regulation, and he offered his own solution. Although he maintained that birth on the soil combined with possession of the franchise constituted decisive proof of citizenship, Curtis insisted that this formulation did not encompass all citizens. "The truth is, that citizenship . . . is not dependent upon the possession of any particular political or even of all civil rights; and any attempt so to define it must lead to error." It rather depended on the possession of a bundle of core liberties to which every free male—black or white—in a state could lay claim. States, however, held full discretion over which rights constituted the bundle associated with "mere naked citizenship." Some states might have neglected to exclude blacks from access to this bundle, and the federal courts could not remedy the problem with a claim that "the Constitution was made exclusively by and for the white race." Federal judges instead had to confront the issues case by case, determine which rights a particular state attached to citizenship, and enforce those rights accordingly, even if that would allow some travelers to escape the black codes and migration restrictions.[39]

Although this ruling could have set the legal stage for Taney's worst-case scenario—the possibility that free people of color, under the protection of the Privileges and Immunities Clause, would flood the southern states and destroy their slave societies—Curtis, perhaps unwittingly, provided an escape. Under the logic of his opinion, states could reduce "naked citizenship" to the possession of that bundle of liberties associated with the threshold of freedom: the ability to have an officially recognized family life and release from the master's constant threats of violence and sale. This action would place all citizens under the restrictions formerly placed on only free blacks. States enacting such a policy could then allow those citizens who met certain requirements, such as being white, to avoid these restrictions. Curtis thus left the rights of citizens of color to the mercy of the state governments.[40]

Curtis did not stop to ponder this possibility. To his own satisfaction, he refuted Taney's contentions that African Americans never belonged to the people of the United States and that no government possessed any authority to incorporate them. Yet Curtis made this argument only by totally rejecting the status distinctions that weighed so heavily in the majority's argument and by selecting pieces of constitutional law that matched his assumptions. When read in the light of existing federal law, none of Curtis's opinion withstands scrutiny. There were no necessary links between citizenship and either birth on the soil or suffrage. Federal citizenship itself did not exist before 1788, and so there was absolutely no evidence that the states had retained the right to create federal citizens after ratification. The majority opinion, probably because Taney revised it to take the dissents into account, largely explained away any evidence that Curtis could muster. Curtis's dissent, despite its popularity among historians, represented little more than a failed attempt to produce an antislavery ruling within a hopelessly antiabolitionist legal structure.

Doctrinally and historically, Taney had the more plausible argument. His contentions rested on long-established practices within the Union. American law, since the founding of the republic and more intensely thereafter, sought the continued subordination of free blacks, and Curtis addressed this point only by ignoring it. Within the confines of his opinion, moreover, Taney pursued two related goals. He worked for the complete exclusion of free blacks from the federal polity by closing the gap that *Strader* left open, and he tried to do so in a manner that did not jeopardize corporations' standing before the federal courts. This strategy centered on an identification of blacks as a social group perceived to be so threatening that the court could handle their cases in a fashion completely different from that of other quasi-citizens. Taney's strategy would work, but his success was not immediately obvious. Curtis and McLean fervently rejected the chief justice's contentions, and John Catron maintained that Sanford, because of the plea in abatement, had waived having the issue considered.[41] Only Daniel and James M. Wayne explicitly agreed with Taney; the others remained silent and thereby supported Taney, whatever they may have thought of his opinion.[42] Within a year, however, the court's rulings concerning corporate diversity jurisdiction became sedate. Before that shift occurred, however, the justices had to confront the central constitutional issue of the 1850s.

CHAPTER NINE

Looking Westward

Concurrent Sovereignty and the Answer to the Territorial Question

"IF DISUNION TAKES PLACE," Massachusetts jurist Joel Parker wrote in 1861, "it will be occasioned . . . by this unhallowed interference . . . with the great political question of the day." Parker referred to the court's intervention into the territorial issue and its ruling that Congress possessed no authority to limit slavery's expansion into the western territories. Critics immediately denounced the ruling as an illegitimate use of judicial power. "We have no longer a Constitution," insisted Justice Benjamin Robbins Curtis in his dissent, "we are under the government of individual men, who for the time being have power to declare what the Constitution is, according to their own views of what it ought to mean." Curtis initiated a tradition of criticism that the court had taken on a political issue that it was not equipped to address. "Political reasons have not the requisite certainty to afford rules of juridical interpretation," he wrote. "They are different in different men. They are different in the same men at different times." Former senator Thomas Hart Benton of Missouri made a similar point: "These decisions being political, are dependent upon moral considerations for their effect. They cannot be enforced. . . . Influence—not authority—is the only power the Court can wield." In their effort to further a prosouthern partisan agenda, the majority had overstepped its bounds, meddled in a matter that was not part of the court's official business, and made the sectional crisis even worse. Parker bluntly stated the position: "Evil was the hour; . . . when six judges of the supreme court . . . united in a sheer usurpation of the powers of Congress."[1]

The Taney Court's critics had a point—its territorial ruling had an obviously partisan dimension—but the focus of their critiques, which were not free of partisanship themselves, obscured the extent to which the court, through Chief Justice Roger B. Taney, may have been using *Dred Scott* to integrate the territories more securely within the constitutional system. Taney's opinion approached slavery in the territories in precisely the same manner the court had handled slavery in the states: it forced the issue into the local courts. As he did in *Strader*, Taney emphasized the U.S. character as a union of concurrent sovereigns, and he sought to integrate the territories into this framework. His strategy also allowed the court to declare unconstitutional the antislavery restriction in the Missouri Compromise. Yet Taney's maneuvers were not political in any simplistic sense; he in fact rejected all available partisan arguments on the territorial question. He also set aside the court's ambiguous case law and drew on his perception of constitutional language and history to develop a novel and controversial approach to the territorial question. His ruling barred any congressional prohibition of slavery in the territories but did so in a manner that would require a complete rethinking of territorial policy. Taney sought not only to break congressional deadlock by forcing legislators to formulate prosouthern policy but also to break with nearly sixty years of territorial governance. His radical approach disturbed Justice John Catron, a member of the majority, and brought strong protests from the two dissenters, John McLean and Curtis, who merely confirmed Congress's possession of an authority that it had proven itself incapable of exercising effectively since the 1840s. Despite its unsavory character, Taney's opinion for the court at least attempted to place the territories on a sound legal footing. And given the parameters of Supreme Court jurisprudence, he put forth a plausible argument.

Much criticism directed at Taney's opinion concerned the propriety of handling the territorial question at all. "Such an exertion of judicial power," Curtis wrote in his dissent, "transcends . . . the authority of the court." When it ruled that Scott lacked citizenship, the court likewise ruled that it had no jurisdiction, and it should have dismissed the suit at that point. Instead, it proceeded to discuss "a great question of constitutional law, deeply affecting the peace and welfare of the country." Taney's entire discussion was improper and therefore not binding. Curtis's argument quickly became a central feature in the criticism of *Dred Scott*. Discussions of the case before the 1970s, in fact, generally refrained from substantive analysis and offered instead complex accounts concerning which issues were before the court and the related quandary over what the court really decided. As David Potter has demonstrated, this argument became influential because it allowed antislavery politicians a way to repudiate the court's ruling on the territories without preaching overt defiance of the law. Critics of the decision thus received Curtis's remarks as a godsend. Even so, his contentions had little basis in the court's jurisprudence.[2]

Curtis maintained that everything the court said after its ruling on Scott's citizenship constituted obiter dicta. If the case had come directly from a state court, Curtis would have had a strong argument: court doctrine clearly stated that a ruling against the court's jurisdiction barred a consideration of the merits. *Dred Scott v. Sandford*, however, originated in the federal courts, and Curtis cited no case showing that correcting a lower federal court's jurisdictional error prevented the Supreme Court from going to the merits. He did produce some decisions in which the Supreme Court refused to inquire into the merits after resolving a jurisdictional question, but those cases involved situations in which lower courts allowed litigants to mix the merits with jurisdictional issues.[3] *Dred Scott* did not fall into that category. Judge Robert W. Wells considered such proceedings to be poor practice, and he insisted that questions concerning jurisdiction be handled separately. The litigants in *Dred Scott* therefore addressed the citizenship question through a plea in abatement and proceeded to the merits only after the court found that it had jurisdiction. All of this was proper form, despite the Supreme Court's conclusion that both rulings were erroneous. Curtis's claim of obiter dicta thus had little foundation in court doctrine.

Taney thought the argument a devious undermining of the court's authority. Although his first version of page proofs contained only a brief response to Curtis on this point, Taney later added another few pages after Curtis privately published his dissent. Taney used Curtis's publication as an excuse to bar the dissenter from access to the chief justice's revised opinion before its publication, and he used his new pages to challenge the dissenter's contentions.[4] Curtis made a "manifest mistake," Taney argued, confusing the proceedings appropriate to cases originating in the state courts with those originating in the federal circuits. When cases came up from the circuits (on a writ of error), the court possessed "not only the right, but . . . the judicial duty . . . to examine the whole case as presented by the record." Correcting one error—even those concerning the jurisdiction of the lower courts—did not prevent the court from fixing any others that it found in the course of its review.[5]

Such activity formed "the daily practice of this court, and of all appellate courts where they reverse the judgment of an inferior court for error."

The court "always" perceived a duty to correct mistakes made by the lower courts, especially when its silence "might lead to misconstruction or future controversy." Words such as *daily* and *always* may have represented hyperbole, but Taney accurately described the court's approach toward the circuits. Supreme Court justices maintained their litigious constituency by imposing a regime of consistency on the lower courts, and one way to do so involved reviewing the entire record of the cases that came before the court. Taney cited no decisions to support his argument. He probably placed the issue among those he considered "too well established to dispute," and he was correct. The court had repeatedly and regularly examined the whole record for errors and occasionally remanded cases for mistakes counsel failed to address.[6]

Moreover, Taney argued, the territorial issue raised a jurisdictional question. According to the record, Dred Scott "was born a slave." Yet if he was a slave, he could not sue in diversity because a slave could not be a citizen, and the court must therefore inquire into whether he had a valid claim to freedom. Resolution of that issue required an investigation of the merits. "If the facts upon which he relies have not made him free," Taney wrote, "then it appears affirmatively on the record that he is not a citizen." Consequently, he could not have sued John F. A. Sanford in diversity, and the lower court erred by ruling in the owner's favor since "the court had no authority to pass any judgment between the parties." By going to the merits, as Edward Corwin noted long ago, Taney continued his examination of the jurisdictional question. A conclusion of this issue, Taney admitted, had little direct relevance to the parties—a dismissal of the case or a judgment for Sanford essentially resulted in the same outcome. Yet the duties imposed on the court by its position within the Union's state structure impelled the court to go beyond a mere resolution of the case. His court would not, by upholding a lower court's judgment, sanction an error that was "patent on the record" and that "might be drawn into precedent, and lead to serious mischief and injustice in some future suit."[7]

Curtis's denunciation of the opinion as obiter dicta therefore had little merit. *Dred Scott*'s closest students generally concur on this point. They agree that the court possessed a right to address the territorial question, although they maintain that the justices' decision to do so was at best unwise and at worst an abdication of judicial responsibility.[8] Their conclusions assume that evading the territorial issue was a viable option by the time the court rendered its final judgment. Yet with the abandonment of the strategy outlined in *Strader*, which every justice except Samuel Nelson willingly rejected, the court lost all of its evasive mechanisms—the roots of which lay in practices established for the review of state court decisions. They now treated *Scott v. Sandford* as it should have been treated: as a case arising in federal jurisdiction from a forum over which the Supreme Court held full power of review. Court members perceived a duty to police the circuits for errors even in the most mundane cases. The politically charged territorial question must have sharpened that perception, and the clamor from the Union's political class for a judicial resolution of an issue it had found intractable probably intensified the justices' sense of duty. When we add to those factors the partisan sensibilities of a majority in which most of the members opposed congressional regulation of slavery in the territories, it should come as no surprise that the justices felt compelled to address the issue. Indeed, they might have perceived themselves as remiss had they dodged the territorial question.

Under the Constitution, Congress held the "Power to dispose of and make all needful Rules and Regulations respecting the Territory or other Property belonging to the United States." Federal officers and others worked under the understandable assumption that this clause conferred full regulatory power over the territories. Congress regularly, although not systematically, governed the territories by overseeing their laws, redrawing their borders, planning and funding their internal improvements, and organizing their governments. Exercising this power generated little controversy among federal officers, except when the slavery question intervened. The Supreme Court, however, had never subjected this aspect of congressional power— the Needful Rules Clause—to rigorous constitutional analysis. By the time of *Dred Scott*, only a handful of decisions dealt with the territories, and they generated only minor and ambiguous rulings that offered the justices little guidance.[9]

Arguments of counsel in *Dred Scott* underscored the paucity of the court's case law. Discussion centered on three cases: an 1840 ruling that equated the word *territory* with "lands" and thus determined that Congress could lease territorial lands; an 1819 ruling where Chief Justice John Marshall acknowledged Congress's right to establish territorial governments; and an 1828 ruling where Marshall stated that Congress combined state and federal powers when it legislated for the territories.[10] Counsel on both sides in *Dred Scott* quickly moved from these cases to a more general discussion of slavery in the territories. One of Sanford's attorneys, Henry Geyer, contended that such decisions in no way sustained a congressional power to close the territories to slavery, while Montgomery Blair, one of Scott's attorneys, contended that they did. The cases could sustain neither interpretation, although Blair could at least rely on the fact that Congress had until the 1850s assumed that it held full governing authority over the territories and that this power included the ability to restrict slavery's expansion.[11] With the exception of the 1828 ruling, which became a point of dispute between Taney and McLean, the justices found the cases counsel cited useless, citing none of them. Yet Congress's long legislative history of prohibiting slavery in the territories, on which Blair relied extensively, also offered little to the justices. The question before them concerned the constitutionality of this legislation. Blair demonstrated only that Congress had assumed and exercised this authority, but assumption and exercise did not prove constitutionality. Doctrinally, therefore, the justices had an open field before them.

Although there was no controlling precedent, the Taney Court had given some thought to the territories. Between 1845 and 1853, it had produced a disaggregated series of minor rulings that somewhat anticipated the majority's opinion in Dred Scott by invoking its own common-property doctrine, recognizing the Constitution's extension over the territories, and applying the bill of rights against territorial governments. Taken together, these rulings revealed a pattern of thinking that would emerge starkly in the court's 1857 opinion. These rulings, moreover, displayed little evidence of politicalization. The court had developed its common-property doctrine, for example, about a year before the appearance of the Wilmot Proviso and about two years before John C. Calhoun responded with his own common-property doctrine. Calhoun and the court agreed that the United States held the territories in trust for the people of the United States, but Calhoun then asserted that any act of Congress that discriminated against slaveholders in those areas was therefore unconstitutional. Such a conclusion by no means followed, as future justice John A. Campbell told Calhoun in 1848. Calhoun had merely identified a "moral obligation upon Congress" not to discriminate against a portion of the Union, but that did not create an enforceable legal right for slaveholders.[12]

Taney court justices never drew such conclusions from the common-property doctrine invoked in Pollard v. Hagan (1845), which determined that Alabama, not the federal government, possessed alluvial lands that had been submerged during the state's territorial phase. According to Justice

John McKinley, in his only notable opinion, title to lands submerged beneath navigable waterways belonged to the sovereign—the people of the state. Despite its oversight during the territorial phase, "the United States never held any municipal sovereignty, jurisdiction, or right of soil in and to the territory, of which Alabama, or any of the new states were formed; except for temporary purposes." Rather, the federal government exercised its authority in accordance with the "trust" created by the cessions of territory by Virginia, Georgia, and France, which instructed the United States to govern the area until statehood. These cessions invested the United States "with the eminent domain of the country ceded, both local and national, for the purposes of a temporary government." By *eminent domain*, McKinley meant "the right which belongs to the society, or to the sovereign, of disposing, in case of necessity, and for the public safety, of all the wealth contained in the state." He said nothing concerning the larger implications of federal power over the territories, but there was nothing inherently proslavery about his position. Indeed, Campbell in 1848 saw no such implications. "When you admit that Congress may form a *government,*" he told Calhoun, "you concede the right to define what shall be property and how it may be enjoyed transferred or inherited."[13]

In *Dred Scott*, the court circumvented this difficulty by asserting constitutional restrictions against Congress's power to form territorial governments. Free-soil Democrat Thomas Hart Benton, in a lengthy critique of the decision, accused the court of Calhounism for this argument. Congress, he insisted, governed the states only through the Constitution; it ruled the territories through its inherent power of sovereignty. Benton's position had few adherents in 1857—even among the late Calhoun's enemies—and only one member of the Supreme Court, the long-dead Henry Baldwin, had ever offered similar arguments.[14] Most Taney Court justices, however, agreed that the Constitution applied to the territories. In *Flemming and Marshall v. Page* (1850), Taney held that the Constitution, not the law of nations, provided the rules by which any territory acquired during the Mexican War would be governed. Three years later, in *Cross v. Harrison* (1853), James M. Wayne argued loosely that the Needful Rules Clause endowed the United States with the sovereign authority to rule California until it became a state. Both of these cases held only minor importance; they involved only matters relating to the collection of customs duties and did not examine the larger issue of federal rulership of the territories.[15]

In 1851, McLean, writing for a unanimous court, underscored the Constitution's applicability to the territories when he reversed an Iowa decision in part because it rested on a territorial law that violated the Seventh Amendment. Iowa's territorial legislature had passed a law empowering a group of commissioners to dispossess the Sac and Fox Indians of 190,000 acres of land that Congress had granted the territory. The act forbade a trial by jury, permitted the commissioners to sue all the owners in one suit without naming any individual, and deemed an announcement in the *Iowa Territorial Gazette* eight weeks before the trial sufficient notice of process. Two lawsuits promptly stripped the Indians of their land. McLean reversed the rulings. Iowa's law did not allow sufficient notice, and it violated the Seventh Amendment's guarantee of a jury trial in civil suits over twenty dollars. "The organic law of the Territory of Iowa, by express provision and by reference," McLean wrote, "extended the laws of the United States, including the Ordinance of 1787, over the Territory, so far as they are applicable."[16] The reference to both the Seventh Amendment and the Northwest Ordinance displayed a characteristic lack of precision in McLean's constitutional thinking but also underscored the ambiguity in which the legal aspects of the territorial question were shrouded. All of the justices agreed that Congress ruled the common property embodied in the territories through the Constitution, but they remained deeply divided over the exact source of that authority as well as its full scope. The court's minor and ambiguous rulings prior to *Dred Scott* offered essentially no guidance on these matters and therefore provided little check against the justices' larger political agendas.

When the justices took up *Dred Scott*, they were of course well versed in the debate swirling around the question of slavery in the territories, and almost certainly they had formed their own opinions on the matter. We know positively that some of them did. Peter V. Daniel told Martin Van Buren in 1847 that he believed the Missouri Compromise unconstitutional. McLean had issued public statements against opening the territories to slavery, and he continued to discuss the issue, in general terms, with his correspondents as the case was pending. Campbell, as already noted, found Calhoun's arguments wanting but also considered unacceptable the conclusion that the federal government could limit the expansion of slavery into the territories. As the Alabama justice's recent biographer has demonstrated, Campbell spent the next few years after his exchange with the South Carolinian searching for a more judicially convincing argument against Congress's authority.[17] He would present the fruits of his labor in *Dred Scott*, where he gave an argument similar to Taney's. The other justices had remained quiet on the matter, perhaps because they knew the day would come to rule on the territorial question. That day did come, and when it did, a loose majority, under Taney's lead, found the field open for a sweeping decision that legitimately made their political vision the law of the land.

Taney took advantage of the opportunity but hoped to do more than merely further a southern partisan agenda. Congressional deadlock over the slavery question and the violent outbreaks in Kansas underscored a genuine need to rethink federal territorial policy. With no definitive Marshall Court ruling constraining them, the majority could give free rein to its policy goals. Yet Taney rejected simplistic formulations that simply translated the arguments of southern legislators into legal doctrine. By contrast, Justice Daniel did precisely that as he stated a policy excluding slavery from the territories could not "be rationally imputed to the patriotic or the honest, or to those who were merely sane."[18] In the space of two pages, he restated Calhoun's common-property doctrine and declared the Missouri Compromise unconstitutional. Neither Taney nor any of the other justices who addressed the territorial question displayed Daniel's lack of sophistication. They all considered the matter a complex legal issue that required resolution in accordance with their understandings of the Union's structure. Indeed, Taney, aided somewhat by Campbell, embarked on a larger strategy in *Scott v. Sandford*. In addition to protecting slavery, the chief justice's ruling elaborated a framework that might have integrated the territories into the system of concurrent sovereignty that the court had carefully elaborated over the preceding two decades. That effort required a confrontation with two daunting theoretical questions. First, the court needed to sort through the state-structural implications arising from the replacement of the Articles of Confederation with the Constitution. Second, the justices faced the problem of how federal power, rigidly construed in Taney Court discourse and possessing an enumerated character designed to manage a union of semi-independent and sovereign states, applied in regions where no states yet existed.

Taney's resolution of these questions led him to conclude that Congress, under the Constitution, possessed no power to close the territories to slavery. His account proved plausible and even compelling, although his focus on those two theoretical issues generated silences that disturbed even members of the majority. He began by explaining away the Needful Rules Clause, which he considered irrelevant to territory added to the United States after 1789. Counsel for the Scotts, along with Curtis, McLean, Catron, and numerous legal commentators, considered the clause a grant of plenary authority over the territories. As Joseph Story wrote in his *Commentaries on the Constitution* (1833), the clause granted Congress an "exclusive and universal" power over the territories that included the authority to end slavery. Story accurately described territorial policy as Congress had understood it at least since the first decade of the nineteenth century.[19] Taney rejected the argument as a rationalization of a constitutionally suspect policy, and he emphasized that the words "power to dispose of and make all needful rules and regulations respecting the territory or other property belonging to the United States" represented awkward phraseology for a general grant of sovereign authority. Terms such as *rule* and *regulate* generally appeared in the Constitution to confer on the federal government "some particular specified power" rather than "general powers of legislation." So, Taney argued, the document granted authority "to establish an uniform *rule* of naturalization" or "to *regulate* commerce." These passages gave Congress a great deal of power over specific matters, but they sounded distinctly different from the clause referring to the ten-square-mile area that would become the District of Columbia, where Congress exercised "exclusive legislation in all cases whatsoever," language that signified unambiguously a general grant of sovereign authority over a particular territory.[20]

According to Taney, the Needful Rules Clause did not confer a grant of plenary authority to govern the territories; rather, it provided for the disposal of public lands over which Congress had oversight. The clause's language pointed to a specific object: the western territory acquired from Great Britain during the Revolution. The Constitution, Taney wrote, "does not speak of any territory, nor of *Territories*" but rather of "the Territory or other Property belonging to the United States." By his interpretation, the word *territory* referred to that region organized under the Northwest Ordinance in 1787, and the phrase *other property* signified certain claims to western land held by Georgia and North Carolina but expected to be ceded to the United States. This provision, which closed with a statement that the Constitution would not prejudice the claims of either the United States or any particular state, centered on transferring the property of the United States from the old confederation government to the new federal one. Indeed, the clause provided for the continuation of the Confederation Congress's solution to a crisis that had dogged federal policy makers throughout the 1780s. Ownership of the western lands became a focus of contention among the states, as smaller states such as Maryland demanded that the lands should be held in common to pay off the Revolutionary War debt while larger states resisted the effort. Division over the issue delayed the ratification of the Articles and thereafter threatened to dissolve the newly formed Confederation. Eventually, the states worked out an agreement. Virginia ceded its western lands, and other states—except Georgia and North Carolina—followed suit. These states ceded not only their land but also their powers of sovereignty and eminent domain over them, and the Confederation Congress organized a government for them that provided for the sale of land and the creation of new states. With those developments, the Confederation Congress had put to rest what Taney described as a "disturbing element of the time."[21]

As these events took place, the members of the Philadelphia Convention devised a new government designed to remedy the defects of the Confederation. Under the Constitution, Taney wrote, the states would "surrender a portion of their independent sovereignty to a new government, which, for certain purposes, would make the people of the several States one people, and which was to be supreme and controlling within its sphere of action throughout the United States." Because it "was to be carefully limited in its powers" and could "exercise no authority beyond those expressly granted by the Constitution, or necessarily to be implied from the language of the instrument," the federal government could not merely assume power over the newly organized Northwest Territory. Convention members thus made special provisions for it by inserting the Needful Rules Clause, which provided the authority to sell the western lands but conferred on Congress no general power to govern the territories. There was no need to do so. The Northwest Ordinance had already handled the issue in a manner that most policy makers found satisfactory, and the Constitution imposed on the new government an obligation to stand by "all Debts contracted and Engagements entered into" by the old government. In Taney's opinion, the Needful Rules Clause appeared in the Constitution "to meet a present emergency, and not to regulate its powers as a government."[22]

Sources from the Philadelphia convention and the ratification debates supported his contentions. On August 18, 1787, for example, James Madison proposed that powers "to dispose of unappropriated land," to establish temporary governments in federal territory, to regulate Indian relations, and "to exercise exclusively Legislative authority at the Seat of Government" be added to the Constitution's working draft. Only the clause referring to temporary governments failed to appear. Madison's timing suggests why. He submitted the clause for addition to a draft constitution that said nothing about the new government assuming the obligations of the old one. When the latter clause became part of the Constitution, a provision for temporary governments became superfluous because the Northwest Ordinance already provided for them. The power for which he contended, even if it had explicitly appeared in the final document, hardly called for a grant of plenary authority over the territories. Language such as "to institute temporary governments" remained a far weaker description of governance than "to exercise exclusively legislative authority." Madison made the two proposals at the same time, and the difference in language surely indicated a different quantum of power over the two areas.[23]

Madison's Publius certainly thought so about the finished Constitution. *Federalist* 48 devoted roughly one page to explaining the "indispensable necessity of complete authority at the seat of government." It covered the Needful Rules Clause in nine lines, saying only "this is a power of great importance . . . rendered absolutely necessary by jealousies and questions concerning the Western territory." Madison said nothing about the clause as a source of legislative power over the territories. Nor did anyone else engaged in the struggle over ratification.[24] Such silence indicated, as Taney said, that the provision extended to the territory held in 1787 and did not grant a general power of legislation. "We put aside," he wrote, "any argument, drawn from precedents, showing the extent of the power which the General Government exercised over slavery in this territory, as altogether inapplicable to the case before us."[25]

Even so, an expansionist constitutional republic unquestionably possessed the power to govern the territory acquired after 1787. That authority did not stem from the Needful Rules Clause but rather constituted a necessary implication of Congress's power to admit new states. Taney could have located a better constitutional source of this power, such as in the power to declare war or negotiate treaties.[26] All the territory added to the United States had in fact been acquired through either treaty negotiations or naked military aggression (subsequently confirmed by treaties). His decision reflected his vision of American expansion and probably that of most of his colleagues. "The genius and character of our institutions are peaceful," Taney wrote in 1850, "and the power to declare war was not conferred upon

Congress for the purposes of aggression or aggrandizement." In an apologetic discussion of the legal implications for the recent conquest of northern Mexico, Taney contended that the federal government made war "to vindicate by arms . . . its own rights and the rights of its citizens." Territorial gains, however, proceeded through the treaty power: "a war . . . can never be presumed to be waged for the purpose of conquest or the acquisition of territory."[27] In *Dred Scott*, Taney added that the United States acquired territory solely for the creation of new states; the Constitution granted "no power . . . to acquire a territory to be held and governed" as a colony.[28] New territories, he admitted, generally entered the possession of the United States ill suited for immediate statehood, and they required governance in the interim. No specific provision controlled this aspect of federal authority. So "the court must necessarily look to the provisions and principles of the Constitution and its distribution of powers, for the rules and principles by which its decision must be governed."[29]

Taney stressed that the nature of the federal government set the parameters of territorial governance. Because the Constitution created a government of enumerated and limited authority, migrating citizens could not "be ruled as mere colonists, dependent upon the will of the General Government." Moreover, Congress worked under a moral obligation to manage the territory "for the benefit of the people of the several States who created it." Taney thus reasserted his court's version of the common-property doctrine in which the federal government exercised its authority as a trustee using its delegated powers on behalf of "the whole people of the Union." Yet Congress possessed an undoubted right to organize society in the territories through the creation of a government. This power was necessarily incident to the acquisition of territory and preparation for statehood. Taney spoke of this authority in terms reminiscent of his discussion in his manuscript on the Negro Seamen Act of Congress's power to create a national bank. Such matters fell within the bounds of congressional discretion and were beyond the courts' scope of inquiry. "Some form of civil authority would be absolutely necessary to organize and preserve civilized society; . . . and the choice of mode must depend upon the exercise of a discretionary power by Congress acting within the scope of its Constitutional authority." For the most part, Taney concluded, these issues remained "a question for the political department of the Government, and not the judicial."[30]

Yet Congress exercised only enumerated authority over the territories. Its discretionary authority remained starkly limited because the Constitution protected individual rights by specifying them as exemptions to federal power. "The Federal Government," Taney wrote, "can exercise no power over [a territorial inhabitant's] person or property, beyond what that instrument confers, nor lawfully deny any right which it has reserved." Because of the Bill of Rights, he continued, Congress could not restrict religious liberty, freedom of the press, or access to a jury. Such powers were "in express and positive terms denied" to Congress. Slave owning also fell within these exceptions to power, because the master's property right received protection under the Fifth Amendment, which barred the taking of property without due process. Antislavery provisions like the one found in the Missouri Compromise were therefore unconstitutional because a law that "deprives a citizen of the United States of his liberty or property, merely because he came himself or brought his property into a particular Territory . . . could hardly be dignified with the name of due process of law."[31]

Taney's invocation of the Fifth Amendment underscored his understanding of the nature of federal power. Modern commentators cite this passage as an early example of the substantive due process doctrine—the idea that the Constitution's Due Process Clause protected an irreducible bundle of individual rights from arbitrary legislative interference.[32] Yet such ideas did not take hold among American judges until after the ratification of the Civil War–era amendments. During the antebellum period, these concepts generally circulated in the writings of radical abolitionists who argued that slavery itself violated the Fifth Amendment because it stripped enslaved Americans of their liberty without due process. Taney Court justices, generally dismissive toward antislavery jurisprudence, unsurprisingly paid no heed to such arguments.[33] Likewise, the court did not mention the few substantive due process decisions that did emerge in late antebellum state courts. As William Novak has demonstrated, several states had passed new antiliquor laws that banned the manufacture and sale of alcohol, gave state officials broad powers of search and seizure, placed the burden of proof on the alleged owners of confiscated liquors, and restricted judges' discretionary authority. Courts in Massachusetts, Indiana, and New York responded to the development of increasingly centralized regimes of morals regulation by ratcheting up procedural requirements and protection for individual rights found in state constitutional provisions. New York's Supreme Court even declared the laws to be a violation of the state constitution's Due Process Clause.[34] Although the New York decision appeared in 1856, Taney probably formulated a similar argument for different reasons. State court judges made their rulings in an institutional setting where legislatures exercised the police power and deployed protections of individual rights against a novel application of legitimately held state authority.

A complete absence of police power, however, characterized the institutional context in which Taney and his associates worked. As Taney and his colleagues had said numerous times, the federal government consisted of limited powers and exercised only those plainly given to it or necessarily implied within the Constitution's language. Even as it exercised its granted authority, the federal government still faced the rigid exceptions to power contained in the Constitution. Thus, as Taney argued in 1853, Congress possessed a discretionary authority "to promote the progress of science and useful arts" by granting patents and copyrights, but it could not later pass a law divesting the holders of such grants without violating due process of law.[35] Likewise, Congress could set up a territorial government but could not overturn the vested property rights of slaveholders as it did so. The protection Taney perceived at work in these cases underscored the differences that he and most of his colleagues perceived between state and federal governance. State police power, as long as its exercise did not violate the obligation of contracts doctrine, could run roughshod over vested rights if the will of the people, as legislatively expressed, demanded such action. Yet the federal government, with its enumerated and starkly limited authority, possessed no power to do so, regardless of any expression of popular will short of a ratified constitutional amendment.

Taney therefore found the antislavery provision of the Missouri Compromise unconstitutional, but his argument left the exact configuration of territorial governance unclear. His focus on the limitations of federal authority diminished the powers that Congress could exercise over the territories beyond the critical task of organizing a government. He also said little concerning the powers that territorial governments exercised within their own jurisdictions. He did mention in passing that Congress could not legitimately authorize a territorial government to perform actions, such as closing a region to slavery, that Congress could not undertake. Because of the enumerated nature of its authority, Congress "could confer no power on any local government, established by its authority, to violate the provisions of the Constitution."[36] Catron, McLean, and Curtis all believed that Taney had in effect rejected most—perhaps all—sorts of legislative control over the territories. Although his narrow ruling invited such a reading, Taney probably did not intend to leave the territories ungoverned. He may have, as he did in the citizenship portion of his ruling, relied silently on the work of one of his colleagues—Campbell this time—to fill in his arguments.

Campbell put forth an argument very similar to Taney's except that the associate justice worked through court precedent (while ignoring its ambiguity). In *Dred Scott*, Campbell finally reconciled to his satisfaction Calhoun's political conclusions with Campbell's understanding of the relevant legal doctrine. His analysis retained the Needful Rules Clause, but he denied that the powers to dispose of land or to organize a government implied a "corresponding authority to determine the internal polity, or to adjust the domestic relations, or the persons who may lawfully inhabit the territory." Local control of internal policy, Campbell argued, represented the essence of the American revolutionaries' struggle with Great Britain, and the principle received recognition in the Tenth Amendment. Federal antislavery provisions violated this principle by allowing Congress to dictate the social condition of future states, a question that properly belonged to the people who constituted those states. Campbell exhibited little dispassion in his argument. Advocates of free soil fell in with tyrants and interpreted constitutional language like "the Norths, the Grenvilles, Hillsboroughs, Hutchinsons, and Dunmores—in a word, as George III would have."[37] His hyperbole aside, Campbell's emphasis on Congress's inability to determine domestic policy raised a valid issue and pointed toward the location of the police power over the territories.

Campbell drew on McKinley's 1845 ruling in *Pollard* to handle this matter. According to that decision, land ceded to the United States, either by a state or a foreign nation, brought with it full jurisdiction over the soil. Because Congress's enumerated character allowed it to make only "needful rules and regulations," it exercised only a power of "eminent domain" over the territory. It did not function as a municipal (fully sovereign) government.[38] The federal government, said Campbell, rephrasing his predecessor's argument, held the territory in trust for the people of the United States, and the people restricted their trustee "to such administrative and conservatory acts as are needful for the preservation of the public domain." Such authority permitted Congress to provide land surveys, protection from trespassers, and organized governments as well as "schools, internal improvements, military sites, and public buildings." Congress could, of course, also exercise all of the other powers granted to it in the Constitution as long as it did not overstep the limitations specified in that document. Congress therefore possessed no police power over the territory; such municipal authority rested in the hands of the people that the territorial government served. Taney may have had this argument in mind when he stated that Congress could not rule citizens in the territory as colonists. American citizens ruled themselves, and they did so through their local (state or territorial) governments more directly than they did through the federal one.[39]

Taney and Campbell's effort to force the federal government back within its perceived constitutional limits opened a space in which the court could contemplate the position of the territories and their inhabitants within a union of concurrent sovereignties. *Dred Scott* may have constituted a starting point in this project, and both justices conceded that the relationship between federal power and territorial municipal authority involved complex issues. Those matters awaited future cases, and some of them, such as the quantum of municipal power Congress would allow a territory to wield, lay beyond the court's jurisdiction. The laborious character of Taney's ruling, with its precise specification of the source of federal power over the territory and thorough discussion of its limits, may have indicated that the chief justice intended *Dred Scott* to be the starting point for future adjudication over the territories. Indeed, the implications of the majority's rejection of the federal police power over the territories called for a complete reconsideration of congressional rule over the West. Future cases might have allowed the court to integrate the territories into the Union more thoroughly than had previously been the case. The political implications of Taney's ruling, however, prevented a materialization of that agenda. His argument that the Constitution established a government that could not assume power on the basis of changing popular expectations seemed to his critics to be little more than a naked defense of the aristocratic pretensions of the slave power.

Criticism of Taney's ruling began on the court itself. Catron, McLean, and Curtis all agreed that the majority opinion called for a radical shift in territorial governance. Their assessment was correct, but the recurring deadlock in Washington and open warfare in Kansas underscored a radical failure in the reigning approach. Whether the majority's decision constituted the proper response was a different question, but Taney and his colleagues at least attempted to provide legislators with a structure for future deliberations. McLean and Curtis merely sought a defense of the status quo, and Catron did the same while ruling the Missouri Compromise restriction unconstitutional. McLean and Curtis offered a strong defense of the power that Congress had exercised for decades, but neither man attempted to cater to the assumptions of the loose majority. McLean was too honest a man and too mediocre a judge to play the game that Story did in *Prigg*. Curtis might have done so if he was willing to make the necessary concessions. He would most likely never have swayed Taney, Daniel, Catron, and Campbell, but he might have been able to pit himself, McLean, Nelson, Wayne, and Robert C. Grier against them. Yet Curtis's opinion revealed no effort to do so. He focused rather on subverting Taney's territorial ruling, first by questioning whether the court could address the issue and then by demonstrating that it ran contrary to settled legislative precedent. His argument, like those of Catron and McLean, began with the premise that the federal government could assume the power to rule the territories because Congress perceived a necessity to do so, an unacceptable argument by the standards of Taney Court jurisprudence. The three critics thus took a position at the outset of their opinions that ensured they would remain in the minority.

Although Catron agreed with *Dred Scott*'s outcome, he disagreed sharply with Taney's description of federal power over the territories. He denied that the transition from the Articles to the Constitution caused a radical change in the quantum of federal power over the territories. "Congress," he wrote, "is vested with power to govern the Territories of the United States by the" Needful Rules Clause. Taney's argument offended Catron's sense of professionalism: "It . . . is asking much of a judge, who has for nearly twenty years been exercising jurisdiction, from the western Missouri line to the Rocky Mountains, and, on this understanding of the Constitution, in-flicting the extreme penalty of death for crimes committed where the direct legislation of Congress was the only rule, to agree that he had been all the while acting in mistake, and as an usurper."[40] Congress had ruled the ter-ritories by direct legislation for more than sixty years, and the court could not suddenly question that power. As late as 1854, in *Cross v. Harrison*, the court declared that Congress exercised sovereignty over California through the Needful Rules Clause. In a letter, Catron expressed disappointment with Wayne, who wrote the *Cross* opinion but then sided with the *Dred Scott* ma-jority.[41] Unlike his colleagues, Catron would not contradict himself and ig-nore *Cross*. Yet he mentioned none of the court's previous renderings of the Needful Rules Clause, thereby making *Cross* appear merely to be the most recent decision in an inconsistent line of cases. He also did not note that the court probably would not have chosen Wayne, who, as *Letson* demon-strated, had a penchant for making problematic overstatements, to render a definitive statement on the clause's meaning. Catron merely declared the question settled and recognized in Congress a general governing authority over the territories.

Congress's power over the territories, Catron contended, by no means gave it the authority to exclude slavery in the Louisiana Purchase territory, and he provided two reasons why. His first just restated a Calhounian version of the common-property doctrine; his second was more creative but still problematic. Under the 1803 treaty with France, the United States was to incorporate the inhabitants of the territory acquired through the Louisiana Purchase in a timely manner and in the interim protect their "free enjoyment of the liberty, property, and the Religion which they profess." Because the settled portions of the territories rested on a plantation economy, slaves consequently constituted some of the most valuable property protected under the treaty. A law that arbitrarily prohibited the migration of enslaved inhabitants into a portion of the territory violated the treaty because it could as easily be drawn through New Orleans as it could at 36°30'.[42] McLean and Curtis effectively deflated this argument. According to McLean, the admissions of Louisiana and Arkansas accounted for all of the inhabited territory at the time of the cession. Because the United States had fulfilled its treaty obligations, the Missouri Compromise in no way violated them. Moreover, Curtis contended, the protections secured in the treaty with France could by no means have stripped the federal government of its general power over the portion of territory uninhabited by nonnative settlers. Both France and Spain had regulated these areas and determined the terms under which nonnative Americans would settle them. Catron's reading of the treaty, Curtis implied, was simply wrong: no reasonable interpretation of the treaty would strip the United States of a governing power that France surely possessed and ceded.[43]

Curtis's argument was itself problematic, since it assumed the treaty gave to Congress a plenary authority over the territory, but his assumption pointed toward the two dissenters' immediate concern: the defense of Congress's traditional claim to a general governing authority over the territories. Closing an area to slavery, they maintained, remained a legitimate exercise of this power anywhere within the federal territories. McLean provided a weaker set of arguments than did Curtis but raised one point that elicited a lengthy response in Taney's revised opinion. McLean claimed that the Needful Rules Clause merely provided for Congress's assumption of the power the Confederation Congress exercised over the territories. Congress quickly exercised this authority by providing for the organization of the Northwest

Territory under the Constitution and then organizing the southwest territories along the same lines with the exception of the antislavery provision.
The Supreme Court, moreover, had recognized this authority in *American
and Ocean Insurance Companies v. Canter* (1828). "In legislating for them,"
Marshall said of the territories, "Congress exercises the combined powers
of the general, and of a state government." Taney's predecessor, McLean admitted, wavered on the source of this power, but Marshall considered the
possession of authority over the territories to be "unquestioned." "If the
power be unquestioned," McLean concluded, "it can be a matter of no importance on which ground it is exercised." *Canter* recognized a complete,
though not absolute, power of legislation over the territories. Thus, McLean
concluded that if Congress "on any . . . ground connected with the public
interest" considered the introduction of "slaves or free colored persons injurious to the population of a free Territory," Congress could prohibit their
entry. It of course had no power do so within the states, but in the territories,
necessity compelled an exercise of the "combined powers of the Federal and
State Governments."[44]

Although he initially set aside all precedents on the issue, Taney later
inserted twelve handwritten pages into his revised proofs responding to
McLean's use of *Canter*.[45] Taney responded so vigorously because McLean,
whose opinion went into circulation long before Taney's, created the impression that the chief justice had ignored a controlling precedent. Taney
exposed several flaws in McLean's argument, but Taney's attempt to appropriate *Canter* for his own purposes also proved wanting. The chief justice
rejected the argument that Marshall had left open the question concerning
the source of federal power over the territories because it did not matter.
A determination of the character and limits of federal power required an
eventual answering of that question, but Marshall thought that the case before them did not require it and therefore left the matter for future consideration.[46]

Taney found more troubling Marshall's statement that Congress combined federal and state powers when it legislated for the territories. The
chief justice accused McLean of taking the passage out of context and asserted that Marshall's argument essentially matched Taney's. *Canter* centered on whether Congress could delegate the power to establish courts of
admiralty to a territorial legislature, and Marshall ruled that it could. Such
a narrow opinion hardly justified the expansive vision McLean saw in it.
Taney even argued that Marshall's opinion anticipated that of his successor,

since Marshall spoke only of an issue related to Congress's discretionary power to establish a territorial government. In this contention, Taney went too far: Marshall's references to "combined powers" and "the general right of sovereignty" indicated that his vision of federal territorial power differed from Taney's. Nearly two decades before *Canter*, Marshall had asserted that the Needful Rules Clause conveyed "the absolute and undisputed power" to govern the Orleans Territory. Perhaps Marshall's wavering in *Canter* indicated that he was moving away from that stance; perhaps not. Whatever he meant to do in that case, he did not do it clearly enough to support fully either McLean's or Taney's argument. The decision was useless as precedent on this issue.[47]

Curtis offered a more sophisticated critique of Taney's position, including a challenge to the chief justice's conception of due process. Curtis offered an alternative to Taney's opinion in a manner that defended Congress's traditional assertion of governing authority over the territories while fusing it within a larger aspirational framework. Yet Curtis's project built on assumptions about the nature of federal power that his colleagues would have found unacceptable independent of the slavery question. He spoke as if the government possessed an inherent authority to address social needs as they arose rather than one rigidly limited by a set of enumerated powers and restrictions. Like the rest of his colleagues, Curtis recounted the history of the western lands, and, as McLean and Catron did, Curtis argued that the Needful Rules Clause transferred to Congress the power that the Confederation had exercised over the territories. "Any other conclusion would involve the assumption that a subject of the gravest national concern . . . was nevertheless overlooked; or that such a subject was not overlooked, but designedly left unprovided for." Curtis considered this position, which he implied was Taney's stance, unthinkable given the Framers' overall foresight. Records from the Constitutional Convention revealed that the Framers made proposals for the governance of the territories, and all the justices agreed that Congress could govern the territories to some extent. Curtis saw no reason why the court should draw this power from implication when the Constitution possessed a provision "manifestly intended to relate to the territory, and to convey to Congress some authority concerning it."[48]

Despite his references to the convention debates, Curtis rested ultimately on an assumption that the Framers *must* have provided for the governance of the territories through the Needful Rules Clause. His evidence hardly supported his assertion. The debates he cited centered on the admission of new states and the possibility of the federal government dividing existing ones.[49] No one but Madison had mentioned territorial governance, and the convention rejected his sole proposal on the issue. Taney explained the rejection by invoking the Northwest Ordinance. Curtis, by contrast, fell back on the Framers' aspirations: "We must take into consideration not only all the particular facts which were immediately before them, but the great consideration . . . that they were making a frame of government . . . under which they hoped the United States might be . . . a great and powerful nation, possessing the power to make war and to conclude treaties, and thus to acquire territory." The Needful Rules Clause thus applied both to the land the United States held at ratification as well as to that subsequently acquired. After ratification, Congress organized the territory acquired from North Carolina and Georgia, and it exercised the same authority over the territory acquired in 1803. Six states had formed in that territory, and the time for quibbling over the source of congressional governance had long passed. Curtis avoided the technical problem raised by the replacement of the Articles with the Constitution by contending that the source of Congress's power over the territories was identical both before and after 1803. For Curtis, such technical considerations were not important, but the Framers' overall vision was. Taney's narrow reading of the Needful Rules Clause seemed "to be an interpretation as inconsistent with the nature and purposes of the instrument, as it is with its language, and I can have no hesitation in rejecting it."[50]

The Needful Rules Clause granted a general power of legislation over the territories. "It must be remembered that this is a grant of power to the Congress—that it is therefore necessarily a grant of power to legislate— and, certainly, rules and regulations respecting a particular subject, made by the legislative power of a country, can be nothing but laws." Congress claimed sweeping powers under its authority to regulate commerce; it even permitted the use of the death penalty as a consequence for violating some of its regulations. And the Needful Rules Clause conferred a similar authority over the territories. Congress's power under this clause was not unlimited; it could not pass ex post facto laws or perform other prohibited actions. Beyond those limitations, however, the only restriction that applied was that the rules and regulations be needful. Whether a law was needful, Curtis rightly claimed, constituted a matter of legislative discretion into which the court could not inquire. Nothing in the language of this clause barred Congress from closing the territories to slavery. Between 1790 and 1848, Congress prohibited slavery eight times and allowed it six. Fourteen separate exercises of this discretion over five decades, Curtis believed, should "be entitled to weight in the judicial mind on a question of construction," and the court should recognize Congress's full discretion over this matter. If the court ruled otherwise, then it rejected "the fixed rules which govern the interpretation of laws" and allowed "the theoretical opinions of individuals . . . to control [the laws'] meaning."[51] Moreover, organizing a government for a territory predisposed a determination of its social character: Congress could not perform one without performing the other. The federal government, therefore, must have such discretionary authority.

Curtis then turned to the provision on which Taney rested his denial of that authority, the Fifth Amendment. Before addressing that issue, Curtis noted, citing Prigg, that slavery was a product of municipal law. In the territories, Congress established these municipal laws at its discretion. Exercising such laws against slavery hardly violated due process, which had been part of Anglo-American law since the Magna Carta. Every state constitution contained a Due Process Clause, and no jurist had ever asserted a conflict between those clauses and antislavery provisions. If Taney was correct, then not only did the Missouri Compromise violate due process protection but so did the Northwest Ordinance, Congress's prohibition of the international slave trade, and limitations on the internal slave trade enforced in the southern states. Curtis's argument rested on an assumption that Congress exercised a combination of state and federal power in the territories. Such a stance implied that the federal government could regulate slavery in the territories exactly as the states did in their jurisdictions and that questions of freedom could be handled on the conflicts-of-law principles recognized in Prigg, Strader, and the other parts of Dred Scott.[52]

Curtis's position raised two difficulties. First, the Constitution contained no clear grant of municipal authority over the territories. One need not accept Taney's argument to realize that Curtis conclusively demonstrated merely that Congress had assumed a municipal authority: he only asserted that the practice represented the Framers' intention. Taney pointed out the second problem. Curtis's argument that slavery constituted a special—that is, municipally defined—form of property rested on comity principles. The argument implied that the law of nations intervened between the federal government and its citizens, much as it did between two nations or two states. Such a contention was simply incorrect. The Constitution specified the rights of citizens, and the federal government could not resort to any other body of laws to add or to subtract from them. Constitutional law, moreover, did not distinguish between slaves and other forms of property. It distinctly recognized that some jurisdictions allowed slavery and some did not, and it had no power to change the definition specified by the states. The limited character of federal power and its complete lack of municipal authority outside of the District of Columbia accounted for the rigid protection it extended to slavery in the territories.[53]

Curtis, McLean, and Catron's arguments rejected the assumptions about the nature of delegated power that generally shaped the Taney Court's constitutional decisions. Their contentions centered on their belief that the federal government needed a discretionary authority over the territories and on the fact that the federal government had actually exercised such power for decades. From the standpoint of the majority, these arguments were clearly unacceptable, for they effectively recognized Congress as the arbiter of its own authority in the territories. Yet the dissenters raised a valid point. Congress's assertion of a sovereign authority over the territories had proven largely beneficial to the Union (a conclusion that ignored, of course, expansion's destructive impact on Native American populations), and numerous states had entered the Union under Congress's guise. "What do the lessons of wisdom and experience teach, under such circumstances, if the new light, which has so suddenly and unexpectedly burst upon us, be true?" McLean asked. "Acquiescence," he answered, "acquiescence under a settled construction of the Constitution for sixty years, though it may be erroneous; which has secured to the country an advancement and prosperity beyond the power of computation."[54] Sound advice perhaps, but Curtis and McLean's argument offered little of the help for which Congress clamored. The policy of discretion that the dissenters advocated had become unworkable by 1848; the possession of discretionary authority by then empowered Congress only to deadlock itself. Although morally more praiseworthy than Taney's and Campbell's opinions, the dissenters' arguments provided Congress with no way around that gridlock.

Taney's opinion at least closed off some of Congress's options and provided the legislature with a new point of departure. Under the circumstances, the justices would have been remiss in their duties if they had dodged the issue. One of the court's main functions within the Union's state structure, after all, centered on keeping federal and state power within the spheres established by the Constitution. The court's recent showing in the Ohio bank cases, which spawned the southern faction, showed that the justices could treat the states heavy-handedly if such a need was perceived, and *Dred Scott* revealed that the court would treat Congress in the same manner. For sixty years, the federal government had assumed the power to rule the territories without constitutional authorization, and now the court demanded that the legislature bring itself within the parameters that *Dred Scott* set out. Taney's unabashedly prosouthern tenor, however, prompted the two dissenters to issue powerful denunciations of the court's strategy. Although the arguments failed to convince the dissenters' colleagues (if they were ever intended to do so), their circulation through the Union's northern political subculture allowed them to become elements in a larger discourse that utterly destroyed *Dred Scott*'s credibility.

United Court, Divided Union

Judicial Harmony and the Fate
of Concurrent Popular Sovereignty

WITH *DRED SCOTT*, Chief Justice Roger B. Taney settled the internal divisions that had plagued the justices, but the decision also undermined the amoral union of concurrent popular sovereigns that the Taney Court had defended since its formation. Historians have repeatedly recounted the narrative of *Dred Scott*'s reception. Works by David Potter, Don E. Fehrenbacher, and Michael Morrison have told the story well, and there is no need to handle it in detail here.[1] The decision engendered mixed reactions in the press, generally along partisan lines, and the court—or, more accurately, its current membership—lost prestige in Republican circles. Antislavery advocates, of course, had little faith in the Taney Court to begin with. However, historians overlook the extent to which *Dred Scott* resolved the issues that had so bitterly divided the justices between the 1852 and 1855 terms. After 1857, the court witnessed none of the fragmentation of the previous years, although the justices confronted the same issues of corporate citizenship and slavery that had previously troubled them. Harmony came at a cost. Taney and his associates' opinions, along with signifiers like his whispers to President-Elect James Buchanan on Inauguration Day or the call for reargument, entered a public sphere charged with paranoia, fear, and hatred. His ruling offered partisans a powerful device through which they could express group allegiances, and in the hands of Republicans and prosouthern Democrats both opposition and fidelity to *Dred Scott* became vehicles for expressing discontent with the constitutional order advocated by the Taney Court.

Only Benjamin Robbins Curtis rejected the arrangement taking shape among the justices. His dissenting opinion conveyed an impression that the majority manipulated settled law to its own ends, and he perceived that manipulation continuing as the opinions awaited their official publication. Volume 19 of *Howard's Reports* was scheduled to be published in early April 1857, but Taney delayed its publication so he could further revise his *Dred Scott* opinion. Upon hearing this news, Curtis believed that he might also need to revise his opinion, which more or less responded directly to Taney. On April 2, he asked the court's clerk, William Carroll, for a printed copy of the majority opinion. Four days later, Carroll denied the request, citing an order given by Taney, and signed by Justices James M. Wayne and Peter V. Daniel, forbidding anyone to access Taney's opinion. The order, which bore the suspicious date of April 6, noted that the opinion had "been greatly misunderstood and grossly misrepresented in publications in the newspapers," and Taney did not want to give them any more fuel. The chief justice had a point. Antislavery and Republican papers significantly overstated the reach of *Dred Scott*, but Taney's order was clearly self-serving, especially since he instructed Carroll to apply it to members of the court. Curtis believed denial of access to a justice was unthinkable, and he contacted Taney for an explanation.[2]

Taney responded by accusing Curtis, who, like Taney, generally held himself aloof from party politics, of partisanship. According to the chief justice, he issued the order verbally, "soon after the decision was given," to keep the opinion out of the hands of "irresponsible reporters" and under the control of the officer appointed to print the court's decisions. One of Curtis's relatives had asked for a copy of the opinion, which he planned to publish alongside Curtis's dissent. Carroll denied the request, and Taney later instructed Carroll to deny the justice's request as well on the assumption that he was only trying to get a copy for his relative.[3] Taney told a problematic story. He may have never given a verbal order, but he apparently offered such a suggestion to some of his colleagues. On March 10, for example, Justice John A. Campbell told Carroll not to let anyone see his manuscript, noting, "the Chief Justice advises me to adopt this course."[4] Carroll never mentioned the order to Curtis's relative, although the clerk did quote a price for the copy. Nor is there any evidence that Justice Curtis and his relative were working together. Taney might have simply fabricated the story from the materials on Carroll's desk. But Taney did not stop there. He told Curtis that his membership on the court in no way entitled him demand a copy of the majority opinion. If he wished to use the document for official duties, he would surely have that right; yet, Taney asserted, that was not Curtis's intention. "You announced from the Bench that you regarded this opinion as extra-judicial and not binding upon you or anyone else." Curtis wanted the opinion "for some other unexplained purposes," and such desires rendered his request identical to any other person's. He had no right to use his position to subvert the court's "judicial character and standing—and more especially the judicial character and standing of the members of the court who gave opinions."[5]

Taney leveled serious and quite probably baseless charges at his colleague and fully expected him to back down.[6] Curtis fired back a letter clarifying his intentions and hinting at the chief justice's impropriety. Curtis denied that he acted on his relative's behalf, but he saw no reason why a member of the court should explain himself to the clerk. More disturbing was Taney's suggestion that Curtis wanted the opinion for "unexplained purposes." His duties involved writing dissenting opinions on important legal questions, and he had responded to the opinion that Taney read in conference. "After I returned home," he continued, "I was informed that this opinion . . . had been revised and materially altered." "I thought I have a right to know . . . whether any alterations material to my dissent, had been made." Curtis then questioned the propriety of Taney's order. The court had not discussed it, and it bore the signatures of only three justices, who signed it when the court was out of session. Keeping the opinion from the public, Curtis continued, only increased the probability of distortion by the press.[7]

One month later, Taney harshly dismissed the charges of unwarranted revisions and wrongly holding his opinion from the public. He devoted the most space to the latter charge, as he explained that all the excitement surrounding the court had occurred before. "Whole states have been agitated upon constitutional questions of the deepest interest, at the very moment they were before the Supreme Court and there decided." In those cases, the justices often disagreed, and the press misrepresented the court's rulings. All of that came along with judicial duties. Early publication of Curtis's opinion ensured that many people would learn of the majority opinion through his critique rather than by reading the decision itself, an action that encouraged partisan attacks on the court. Taney blamed Curtis for subverting the court's authority. "This is the first instance in the history of the Supreme Court in which the assault was commenced by the publication of a dissenting judge: carrying with it the weight and influence of a judicial opinion delivered from the Bench in the presence and hearing of the Court." Taney admitted to revising his opinion but denied making any substantive changes. "There is not one historical fact, nor one principle of constitutional law—or common law—or chancery law—or statute law in the printed opinion that was not distinctly announced and maintained from the bench." Taney added only "proofs and authorities" supporting the "historical facts and principles of law" that he had believed "too well established to dispute" until he heard them challenged by the dissenters.[8]

Taney employed what might today be considered a type of Oval Office honesty. His claim that he added nothing to the opinion except "proofs and authorities" represented an accurate statement. None of his revisions—or at least none of those contained in the proof sheets—indicated a shift in the lines of the argument that he had presented from the bench. Court members, of course, expected an opportunity to revise their opinions before publication. An investigation of nine hundred surviving manuscripts and page proofs housed in the National Archives, however, reveals that revisions beyond mundane proof reading were rare. Significant alterations appeared in fifty-eight opinions. Almost every justice made at least one such revision during his tenure (and Joseph Story made more than ten). These cases included both important and forgettable opinions. *Prigg v. Pennsylvania* (1842), for example, numbered among Story's revised cases, and *Strader v. Graham* (1851) appeared on Taney's list. Curtis's only revised case was nothing less than *Cooley v. Board of Wardens of the Port of Philadelphia* (1852).[9]

Yet the scale of Taney's revisions in *Dred Scott* was unique. He said he added only "proofs and authorities" to his opinion, and such revisions may have been an acceptable practice. Alterations in manuscripts and proof sheets frequently elaborated on points already made or added discussions of precedent or statute law. Thus, in *Cooley*, Curtis inserted a brief passage explaining that Congress had structured its regulations concerning pilots in a manner that left the states free to pursue their own piloting regulations. Taney once added an explanation of the policy behind a ruling, but he generally cited additional cases or legislation with explanations in his revisions, as he did in *Strader*. Other justices followed suit. These changes tended to be brief—often a few notes in the margin or perhaps half a page. The two pages that Justice John McLean added to one set of proofs, in fact, made it one of the most heavily revised documents to appear in the search.[10] Taney's revisions in *Dred Scott*, which Curtis calculated at around eighteen pages, made everything else seem mild by comparison. No document in the Taney Court's files matched this one, and his battering of Curtis revealed that he knew it. Curtis believed the revisions were a direct response to his opinion, but he overstated his case.[11] Taney spent much of his time addressing McLean as well, but he surely took his revisions beyond acceptable bounds. If he had pursued this issue, Curtis could have exposed Taney to considerable embarrassment.

Curtis instead backed away. His next letter read as if he realized that his inquiries had led him into an affair of honor with Taney. Curtis's queries, Taney said, carried an implication that he had acted unprofessionally, that he had used his position for his own ends. Curtis had said no such thing: he mentioned the revisions guardedly, and he carefully avoided any accusation of wrongdoing. Taney, whose handling of *Dred Scott* after the revisions was at best questionable, simply pounced on Curtis to frighten him off. The strategy worked. Curtis spent the majority of his final letter fending off Taney's accusations and resigned from the court shortly thereafter. His exact reasons for doing so remain open to speculation. He may have left the bench because the position paid too little and the travel associated with judicial duties burdened his family life—his official reason for doing so. His exchange with Taney, which both men agreed had become "an unpleasant correspondence," no doubt also shaped the decision to resign.[12]

Curtis did not depart to make a partisan statement. As he told Taney in his final letter, "I have no connection with any political party and have no political or partisan purpose whatever save a determination to avoid misconstruction and misapprehension." Despite the popularity of his dissent in Republican circles, Curtis kept his distance from the party. About one year after his resignation, he reminded a supporter that if he ran for the state senate, he would not submit to party discipline. "I am not a member of the Republican Party and could not accept the nomination of one of its conventions." In 1860, he spoke against Massachusetts's personal liberty law, calling it a violation of the state's constitutional obligations and winning the praise of his former colleagues, Samuel Nelson and John Catron. As late as 1863, Curtis considered Abraham Lincoln "shattered, deranged, and utterly foolish."[13]

The reaction of Curtis's colleagues to his resignation was mixed. In a short, formal reply, Taney told Curtis that leaving the bench for a more lucrative private practice was a good idea; Daniel sent no letter at all. Curtis had maintained good relations with his other colleagues, and they expressed sincere regret. Campbell thought the timing bad: "There are public considerations which in my judgement made your decision a misfortune to the country." McLean expressed little surprise but a great deal of regret.

Supreme Court justices, he told his fellow dissenter, had a difficult job. The review of legislation touching even mundane matters represented a duty of "very great responsibilities." "But when it touches public questions involving interests and passions of the whole nation, the responsibility is fearful." He could not blame Curtis for declining such duties.[14]

Curtis probably objected not so much to the duties of office as to the terms under which he believed he would have to perform them. As his colleagues noted, Curtis was a lawyer and judge above all else, and no one except a defensive chief justice had accused him of placing partisanship above principle. Yet judging on the Taney Court, at least in the cases that truly mattered, never involved mere principle. Rather, the justices struggled to reconcile doctrine with their sometimes conflicting political and ideological commitments while maintaining a professional decorum that made the court appear above partisanship. *Dred Scott* shattered that image in Republican circles, and Curtis's ensuing exchange with Taney revealed that adjudication in the Union's highest court could be a very sordid affair indeed. Although Curtis would have none of it, the court's strategy proved to be quite effective. In particular, Taney's handling of the citizenship question put to rest the issues that had divided the justices in the mid-1850s. McLean and Daniel, both consistent critics of the court, still had misgivings, but in the 1857 term the southern faction collapsed. The next two major cases involving slavery also passed with little controversy, at least among the justices. In *Dred Scott*, therefore, Taney reconciled the justices' desire to protect both slavery and corporate capitalism.

Taney's strategy showed signs of success in the term immediately following his infamous decision. In *Covington Drawbridge Company v. Shepherd* (1858), Taney, who before *Dred Scott* had remained silent on these issues, reasserted the court's position in *Letson*. Corporations were, for the purposes of diversity jurisdiction, citizens of the state that chartered them. As he reviewed the case law, however, he subtly shifted the doctrinal emphasis away from the corporation itself to the members who composed those entities. "Now, no one," he stated, "ever supposed that the artificial being created by an act of incorporation could be a citizen of a State in the sense in which that word is used in the Constitution of the United States." Taney did not mention that Wayne's *Letson* opinion was quite susceptible to such a reading. The court now merely presumed that the members of a corporation all held citizenship in the chartering state. In practical terms, this shift changed nothing, but ideologically, Taney had redirected the focus from corporate quasi-citizens to the white males who (more than likely) composed them. This emphasis combined with the previous term's invocation of anti–black federal citizenship undermined the perceived need for further conflict over corporate diversity jurisdiction. In contrast to their behavior before *Dred Scott*, both Catron and Campbell joined the majority; the latter even explicitly concurred in the result. Only Daniel, an ideological purist, dissented. The court, he argued, "wholly failed to bring conviction to my mind, that a corporation can be a citizen." [15]

Daniel, who died in 1860, spent his remaining time on the bench as a lone dissenter against corporate diversity jurisdiction. His former partners became staunch members of the majority. By the 1858 term, both Catron and Campbell were speaking for the court in diversity cases involving corporations. [16] In contrast to their posturing before *Dred Scott*, the two justices lost their concern for the corporate threat to states' rights. They now followed the example of the rest of their colleagues and treated corporations no differently than they did other litigants. Taney's handling of the citizenship question in *Dred Scott* thus allowed the federal courts to close themselves to free blacks without making any major alterations in the treatment of corporations.

By eliminating the idea that the states could make federal citizens out of either black people or corporations, Taney cleared the way for an uncontroversial corporate diversity jurisdiction based on the citizenship of the corporate stockholders. This strategy continued the court's policy of protecting slavery without subordinating its doctrines to perceived southern needs, but it also provided a boon to emerging corporate interests. Lawyers became increasingly aware that their corporate clients could use federal diversity jurisdiction to avoid state laws that did not work to the clients' favor. Indeed, avoidance of an inconvenient state law was exactly what was happening in the Ohio tax cases around which the southern faction had formed. The Scott family employed a similar strategy as well. This practice, as Tony Freyer and Edward Purcell have demonstrated, became more widespread (and judicially acceptable) after the Civil War, but it relied on several doctrinal developments spearheaded by the Taney Court. [17] One of the critical innovations in this process—indeed, the one on which the others hinged—involved the right of corporate litigants to access diversity jurisdiction. With his citizenship ruling in *Dred Scott*, Taney implicitly transformed that issue from a sharply contested matter to a largely unquestioned right. The rule announced in *Letson*, protected in *Dred Scott*, and reaffirmed in *Covington*

Drawbridge has in fact stood to this day.[18] Taney's denial of black federal citizenship, in other words, contributed to the development of a legal regime in which corporations could flourish.

In the wake of *Dred Scott*, the court also unanimously maintained its supportive stance toward slavery, but its position remained tightly linked to the justices' conception of a limited federal supremacy within a union of concurrent sovereignties. In *Ableman v. Booth* (1858), the justices reasserted their position when the court demanded that Wisconsin's state courts stop undermining the controversial Fugitive Slave Law of 1850. Sherman M. Booth, an abolitionist editor, suffered arrest and imprisonment for inciting a riot that resulted in the rescue of a fugitive slave in Milwaukee, a federal crime under the 1850 law. Following his arrest by federal officers, Booth applied to the state courts for a writ of habeas corpus. Because they considered the law unconstitutional, the state courts set him free. Wisconsin's Supreme Court initially submitted to federal review of its decision, but it soon refused to comply with or even officially acknowledge the U.S. Supreme Court's writ of error.[19]

Wisconsin thus effectively nullified the Fugitive Slave Law and declared itself the final interpreter of the Constitution within its borders. Speaking for a unanimous court, Taney wrote that the state judges acted as if their decision were final and binding not only on the courts of the state but also on the federal courts. Wisconsin's refusal to comply with a federal writ of error—the Supreme Court, under Chief Justice John Marshall, had conclusively established that it possessed this power of review—undermined the federal government's supremacy within its sphere.[20] Like all the other states in the Union, Wisconsin was a sovereign entity, but it possessed no right to assert its power within the jurisdiction of another government. States possessed no authority to intervene in the proceedings of the federal government. If they did, then the federal government could not exercise its powers without the permission of the state in which it acted, and there would be no uniformity in federal law. Federal courts held their powers of review precisely to enforce uniformity. Wisconsin possessed no legitimate authority to intervene on Booth's behalf, and he should serve his sentence.[21] Despite their initial resistance, Wisconsin's courts eventually drifted into compliance.

As in many of its slavery cases, the court in *Booth* lent its support to the peculiar institution, but its primary interest lay in maintaining the perceived proper distribution between federal and state authority. The concern emerged again in the 1860 term, when the Supreme Court confronted a situation where Ohio's governor refused to extradite to Kentucky a person accused of aiding an escaping slave. In *Kentucky v. Dennison* (1861), Taney, again speaking for a unanimous court, upheld the governor's action. Governors, he wrote, worked under a moral obligation to extradite alleged criminals. States, although united for some purposes, stood as sovereigns in relation to one another. The Constitution, he continued, functioned as more than a mere treaty that created obligations only on the subjects specifically listed. Rather, it implied a stance of goodwill among the states and an obligation to support one another's governments. Ohio's action, of course, generated ill will and hostility, but the federal government possessed no power to coerce it into compliance. Congress's statute on the subject certainly did not authorize it, and the Framers, Taney wrote, probably never intended for the exercise of such a power. Federal enforcement of state extradition procedures would in effect subordinate state officers to the federal government, even in matters of exclusively local concern. The governor of Ohio, therefore, could refuse to comply if he wished.[22]

In this case as in *Ableman*, the court's major concern lay with the policing of boundaries, not with the protection of slavery at all costs. If the court had pursued the latter course, it would have ruled the other way and thus embarked on a course that might have realized the Republicans' worst nightmares.[23] The Taney Court's behavior between 1857 and 1861 revealed an effort to maintain the balance among the concurrently sovereign entities that composed the Union. Taney used *Dred Scott* to prevent his southern colleagues from undermining that balance, and he tried later to do the same with the Supreme Court of Wisconsin and the governor of Kentucky. "The Constitution," he wrote in *Ableman*, "was not formed only to guard the states against danger from foreign nations, but mainly to secure union and harmony at home."[24] Yet Taney's constitutional enforcement secured harmony only on his own bench, and even that came about in part by driving away the court's most dissatisfied member. Within the larger political culture, the court's position brought no harmony at all.

After Taney read the decision from the bench, *Dred Scott* entered a public sphere saturated with sectional and partisan animosity. Institutionally insulated from the public and mired in conventions that refracted their partisan sensibilities, the justices produced the opinion they did for reasons that did not easily reduce to a prosouthern political agenda. They rejected an evasive reliance on *Strader v. Graham* (1851) because the court's most recent case law could not convincingly accommodate a deferential and neutral stance toward state law in a diversity case. Taney's citizenship ruling settled internal differences that had threatened the standing of the emerging corporate order in the federal courts. Even the most unambiguously partisan aspect of the decision addressed a genuine failure in federal territorial policy. None of those intentions mattered after March 6, 1857. *Dred Scott* no longer belonged to the Supreme Court; it belonged to the public, and its meaning became sharply contested. At this point, *Dred Scott* became part of what Stephen Greenblatt might term the mimetic capital of American political culture. It fell into a stockpile of symbols, images, and representations circulating through the social order and constituting the material for the production of new symbols, images, and representations that expressed group allegiances within a given cultural space.[25] *Dred Scott* provided rich material for this process by contributing to the articulation of a privileged white identity and by providing a mechanism allowing both Republicans and southern Democrats to criticize the constitutional order that the court defended.

Taney's citizenship ruling quickly fed into the developing discourse that linked the possession of white skin with social and political privilege. In 1859 and 1860, for example, Taney's opinion appeared in publications alongside the scientific writings of Samuel A. Cartwright, a New Orleans physician who specialized in the treatment of slaves. Cartwright theorized that blacks were biologically conditioned for subordination because, among other things, they consumed less oxygen and thus had less brain development.[26] Like Taney, Cartwright sought a justification—although in his case biological rather than legal—for American race relations. Their writings, however, remained confined to their respective professional concerns, and they were not written primarily as political addresses. Yet in the hands of editors, their writings became precisely that. In *Cotton Is King* (1860), E. N. Elliot, the president of Mississippi's Planters' College, placed Taney's and Cartwright's writings together with other major works defending slavery from every conceivable angle from economics to theology to politics to science to law. Likewise, John H. Van Evrie of New York, an advocate of the controversial theory of polygenesis, which argued that all human beings did not descend from Adam and Eve because God had created the races separately, published a pamphlet containing Taney's opinion and one of Cartwright's essays. In his introduction, Van Evrie attacked the specter of racial amalgamation. *Dred Scott*, he argued, gave legal confirmation to a biological truth.[27]

Texts such as these created an impression that blacks' perceived inferiority demanded legal discrimination. That these impressions became forged in a public sphere undergoing a partisan reorganization only intensified those impressions. Claiming whiteness, as Noel Ignatiev and others have noted, provided different ethnic groups—the Irish, for example—with a mechanism for demanding status and treatment similar to that expected by Anglo-Saxon Protestants. The power of this appeal did not get lost among politicians, who saw in the invocation of a monolithic white identity a useful tool for negotiating an ethnically diverse electorate in which the precise lines of racial division remained sharply contested. Thus, Stephen A. Douglas in his 1858 debates with Abraham Lincoln for a seat in the U.S. Senate repeatedly trumpeted the racial implications of *Dred Scott.* "I hold that a negro is not and never ought to be a citizen of the United States," he told an audience in Jonesboro, Illinois. "I hold that this government was made on the white basis, by white men, for the benefit of white men and their posterity forever, and should be administered by white men and none others. I do not believe that the Almighty made the negro capable of self-government." Douglas even went further than Taney, who limited his ruling only to blacks. Douglas juxtaposed whiteness against all degrees of nonwhiteness. The Declaration of Independence, he said, embraced "white men, men of European birth and European descent, and had no reference either to the negro, the savage Indians, the Fejee, the Malay, or any other inferior and degraded race." [28]

This white identity proved compelling to Americans of European descent, although it was not monolithic. Douglas occasionally received taunts from the audience when he tried to link the Republican Party to an agenda of racial equality, and reformers in New York and Ohio led efforts to lessen discriminatory laws against blacks. [29] In the 1850s, however, these challenges proved unsuccessful, and racist sentiment carried the day. Abolitionist Susan B. Anthony considered *Dred Scott*'s citizenship ruling "a reflection of the spirit and practice of the American people, North as well as South." Indeed, Lincoln ceded the citizenship issue in his debates with Douglas. The future president believed that the Declaration of Independence embraced blacks, but he thought that they should not be citizens. Before he made that concession, Lincoln made clear his stance on white superiority: "There is a physical difference between the white and black races which I believe will forever forbid the two races living together on terms of social and political equality . . . and I as much as any other man am in favor of having the superior position assigned to the white race." [30]

Dred Scott thus facilitated the articulation of a politically and socially privileged white identity, but its significance did not stop there. Lincoln's comments on the decision pointed toward a widespread disillusionment among both Republicans and southern Democrats with the deferential and amoral vision of a union of concurrent popular sovereignties that the Taney Court had advocated throughout its tenure and had recently extended to the territories. The Lincoln-Douglas debates provide a powerful document for examining this process, for they focused squarely on the potential implications of *Dred Scott* both for the territories and the free states. These debates, of course, by no means constituted the only forum for those issues. The partisan press and members of Congress also wrestled with the difficult questions that *Scott v. Sandford* posed. In these venues, however, discussions of the case often became mixed into the discussion of sectional controversies of equal importance, such as the struggle over the Lecompton Constitution, an effort to force a proslavery constitution on Kansas despite the known wishes of its people. The increasingly popular stance among Republicans and legal intellectuals that Taney's decision constituted primarily dicta also cut off the need for analysis. Lincoln's strategy against Douglas required different tactics. Douglas's opposition to the Buchanan administration's support for the Lecompton Constitution had made the senator an acceptable figure among some Republicans, so Lincoln had a reason to downplay the issue.[31] Lincoln likewise implicated Douglas in a slave-power conspiracy in which *Dred Scott* constituted a step toward forcing slavery into the free states. Rather than avoid the decision, Lincoln showed a determination to drag his opponent through it, forcing him to grapple with the ruling's implications. Douglas, quite comfortable with the amoral jurisprudence that shaped *Dred Scott*, offered plausible answers to Lincoln's queries both on the stump and in an 1859 essay published in *Harper's Magazine*, but his answers proved morally and politically unacceptable to both Republicans and southern Democrats.

Lincoln pushed two questions relevant to the discussion here. He first asked whether Douglas would support a second Dred Scott decision that barred the free states from abolishing slavery. This question played into Lincoln's charging of Douglas with conspiracy, a charge that Lincoln had limned out a few weeks earlier in his "House Divided" speech. Douglas offered a correct but hardly satisfactory answer: "I tell him that such a thing is not possible," he said. "It would be an act of moral treason that no man on the bench would ever descend to." The rhetoric was overblown—Daniel might have taken such a descent—but the prospect that the court as a whole would do so remained unlikely. Yet Douglas spoke like a student who knew the answer without understanding how to defend it. To Lincoln and other antislavery advocates, *Dred Scott* looked ominous. He correctly pointed out that no justice in the case said that a state *could* abolish slavery, although the justices had said repeatedly in other cases that the states could do so subject to the limitations of the Constitution.[32] The phrase "subject to the limitations of the Constitution" probably referred to the limitations on state power outlined in *Prigg* and the *Passenger Cases*, but these words too carried a disturbing ring in antislavery circles, since the court never spelled out what they meant.

Douglas ought not to have dismissed the argument so quickly. His fierce protest against the question played into Lincoln's charge that the senator was merely trying to lull northerners into a political stance that would allow the slave power to push forward unopposed. Moreover, as Harry Jaffa and Paul Finkelman have argued, Lincoln's assertion that the court would go further than it had in *Dred Scott* remained a possibility. Neither Lincoln nor these two scholars made a judicially persuasive case for the nationalization of slavery. Lincoln, in a position admirably elaborated by Jaffa, put forward a syllogistic, rights-oriented, constitutional argument that underscored the alleged proslavery tendency of the court's thinking:

> Nothing in the Constitution or laws of any State can destroy a right distinctly and expressly affirmed in the Constitution of the United States.
> The right of property in a slave is distinctly and expressly affirmed in the Constitution of the United States.
> Therefore, nothing in the Constitution or laws of any State can destroy the right of a property in a slave.[33]

Lincoln, of course, rejected the minor premise but maintained that the syllogism held for anyone, like Douglas or Taney, who did not. Lincoln's logic, as Jaffa noted, exposed a constitutional niche in which slavery was to receive protection no less than any other form of property and quite possibly was entitled to a greater amount.[34] Lincoln's syllogism might explain accurately the use to which southern Democrats put *Dred Scott*, but it remained a poor reading of the court's decision and its members' motivations. Taney's argument centered not on individual rights but on the lack of federal power either to incorporate blacks as citizens or to close the territories to slavery. The delegated and enumerated character of federal power constituted Taney's major premise, and that shaped the court's rulings. Taney's discussion of the right to hold slaves, in fact, rejected Lincoln's minor premise that the Constitution entitled slavery to special protection (Fugitive Slave Clause excepted); the chief justice argued that slaves did not differ from any other kind of property. If he had believed otherwise, Taney probably would have ruled the other way in *Dennison.*

Even so, the possibility remains that the court might have gone further in protecting the rights of masters than it did in *Dred Scott.* In his "House Divided" speech, Lincoln noted that a New York case challenging masters' ability to pass through free states with their slaves as they traveled from one slave state to another had begun moving through the judicial system.[35] The New York courts ruled that any slaves brought into New York went free under the state's constitution. The U.S. Supreme Court might have overturned those rulings or perhaps instructed lower federal courts to ignore them, but whether the Constitution—or, more precisely, the Privileges and Immunities Clause—protected a master's right to travel through free states with slaves was not at all clear. Lemuel Shaw of Massachusetts left the question open in his celebrated opinion in *Commonwealth v. Aves* (1836).[36] Nelson likewise left the question open in *Dred Scott.* His brief discussion, however, hinted that the court considered questions concerning masters' right to travel with their slaves through free states to be a complex matter. Indeed, the court might have perceived a need to draw distinctions among masters who traveled "on business or [for] commercial pursuits" and those who did so "in the exercise of a Federal right, or the discharge of a Federal duty."[37] Such a distinction most likely would have allowed masters with apprehended fugitives to travel through free states on their way back to their home states but perhaps would not have protected masters, like the one involved in the New York case, who took their slaves through free states for other reasons.[38] Whatever, if anything, they planned, the justices left the question for further determination, but they almost certainly had no plans, as Lincoln alleged, to use a right of transit as the basis for the nationalization of slavery.

Douglas's response to Lincoln's second query, although weakly theorized, proved far stronger. At the Freeport Debate, Lincoln asked how Douglas could reconcile *Dred Scott* with his popular-sovereignty position that allowed the people of a particular territory to decide for themselves whether they would become a slave or a free state. The question, of course, rested on the assumption that the court considered slavery a specially protected form of property and further that the court had ruled that a territorial legislature possessed no power to close itself to slavery. Taney, in his opinion for the court, never made those contentions. His reference to territorial legislatures said emphatically, but in dicta, that Congress could not instruct a territorial legislature to do so, but his opinion left open the issue whether a territory, in the exercise of its municipal authority, could assume that authority on its own. Douglas's answer, which he had already given before he announced his so-called Freeport Doctrine, took advantage of that silence. A territorial legislature, he said, could frustrate slaveholders' settlement efforts by enacting "unfriendly legislation" that would in effect render a nullity the right to hold a slave in a particular territory. The exercise of this sort of authority differed in no respect from laws prohibiting the sale and consumption of alcohol in the territories.[39]

Douglas offered a plausible reading of *Dred Scott* that understood Taney far better than Lincoln did, but the senator's answer underscored the fundamental amorality of the constitutional order that so disturbed Lincoln and his fellow Republicans. Survival of the Union, Douglas argued, depended on the people of each state minding their own business. Illinois had tried slavery in its territorial days and found it wanting; Missouri had had a different experience. The latter became a slave state, and the former did not. Each had a right to do so. "I am now speaking of rights under the Constitution, and not of moral or religious rights," Douglas said. "I do not discuss the morals of the people of Missouri, but let them settle the matter for themselves." Douglas stood on firm constitutional ground. The delegated and enumerated character of federal power took shape in part to keep morally sensitive issues such as slavery or religious establishment out of national politics, although the Jeffersonian-Republican and Democratic Parties perhaps intensified that character more than the Framers had anticipated. Lincoln articulated a simple but powerful response to this argument. Slavery, he argued, represented "a moral, a social and a political wrong" that required (eventual) eradication. Douglas, who cared not "whether slavery is voted up or voted down," did not perceive the wrong, and he thus ensured slavery's perpetuation. His amorality sustained a great evil and would do nothing to stop its spread.[40] Lincoln, of course, lost the election but transformed himself into a leading Republican representative, and he and his supporters would eventually mobilize antislavery or at least antisouthern sentiment to produce a presidential victory in the 1860 election.

Republicans benefited from southern Democrats' growing disenchantment with the amoral constitutional order that Douglas and the Taney Court defended. In 1859, Douglas elaborated his position on the territories in a widely read essay published in *Harper's Magazine.* Again, Douglas was not a constitutional thinker of any particular talent, but he still put forth a plausible argument. The Framers, he wrote, considered the power "to exercise exclusive legislation in respect to all matters pertaining to their local polity—slavery not excepted"—to be an inalienable right of the people constituted into a political community. The people had fought the revolution for this control and had enshrined it in the nation's early territorial policy, although Douglas's analysis conspicuously made no mention of the Northwest Ordinance. Adopting Taney's *Dred Scott* argument, Douglas invoked a narrow reading of the Needful Rules Clause that limited it to the territory held at the time of ratification. The power to acquire territory came through the new states or the Necessary and Proper Clause, but these conferred no municipal power over the territories. Indeed, the Supreme Court struck down the Missouri Compromise because the federal government, under the proper understanding of the Constitution, had "no right to interfere with the property, domestic relations, police regulations or internal polity" of the territories. The court's ruling, Douglas continued, did not establish slavery in the territories but rather confirmed the principles already recognized in the Kansas-Nebraska Act of 1854. The territories possessed full control over their domestic institutions, and the federal government's lack of municipal authority conferred no right and no power to bar or protect slavery in the territories. Nonintervention constituted the federal government's only legitimate stance.[41]

Douglas's essay generated a number of responses, but the critique offered by Jeremiah S. Black of Pennsylvania stands out as particularly interesting. Black worked as Buchanan's attorney general and fully supported the administration's increasingly prosouthern stance and its effort to destroy Douglas for his repeated opposition to that tendency since Lecompton. In a short pamphlet, Black attacked Douglas's popular-sovereignty formula. The attorney general correctly noted that slaveholders did not lose title to their human property simply by crossing into a territorial jurisdiction. Only a law passed by a sovereign state could produce that effect. Black failed to note, however, that a territorial government, through the exercise of its municipal authority, might radically alter the rights and remedies associated with such titles within their jurisdictions. This contention formed the core of Douglas's "unfriendly legislation" argument. Bypassing this problem, Black pronounced popular sovereignty a muddle: Douglas treated territorial governments as if they differed in no respect from sovereign states, while the Supreme Court in *Dred Scott* had declared such governments provisional and temporary. Black exaggerated Douglas's argument: Douglas would surely have distinguished between state and territorial governments. Citizens in the territories, for example, had no control over the way in which their governments were framed or which rights their constitutional laws privileged because Congress did the framing. Douglas did, however, believe the people in the territories to be sovereign and thus to be in possession of the police power—an amorphous authority to regulate on the behalf of health, safety, and morals—which they could turn against slavery. The court had been manifestly unclear about what powers territorial governments held, and Douglas's contention was therefore as reasonable a reading as any other one. Black found it positively alarming, especially since he overstated the argument. According to the attorney general, under Douglas's formula, the territorial governments possessed an unlimited sovereign authority akin to that of a "Russian Autocrat." Such an authority, Black continued, enabled a handful of immigrants from Europe and America to rule the territories with "a rod of iron."[42]

At this point, the Republican and prosouthern critiques of Douglas's reading of *Dred Scott* converged. The people in the territories could not exercise an unfettered municipal authority because they could not be trusted: they would use their power to do wrong. The remedies differed. Republicans wanted the decision overturned and the territories closed to slavery. Southern Democrats proposed a territorial slave code, which, because it employed the same federal municipal authority required to prohibit slavery, would have required an overturning or, more likely, a glossing of *Dred Scott*.[43] Both remedies revealed a disillusionment with the amoral vision of concurrent popular sovereignty that the Taney Court had promoted since its formation and that it (and Douglas) probably hoped to extend to the territories. Unlike the court's ruling on black citizenship, which underscored the widespread racism that contributed to the Reconstruction Era failure to rebuild the Union on a foundation of racial equality, the territorial ruling exposed no consensus among the partisans. Rather, it forced a final struggle for control of the federal government that brought a Republican election victory and Southern secession. *Dred Scott*, albeit indirectly, stimulated a double rejection of the Taney Court's and the Democrats' deferential constitutional order. In the North, the electorate revealed its sentiment that Douglas's amoral "don't care" policy played into the hands of the slave power, while in the South secession conventions demonstrated that southerners could no longer trust the people of the United States to protect southern interests.

With *Dred Scott*, Taney articulated a plausible interpretation of the Framers' intentions and used his constitutional argument to resolve the issues that divided his court and to place the territories on a new foundation. Taney succeeded in settling the internal difficulties that plagued his court, but the justices' actions set into motion a series of events that compromised the constitutional order that Taney had spent his career elaborating and defending. Ironically, the reaction against the court took the same form that he had advocated nearly thirty years earlier in his manuscript on the Negro Seamen Act. In that document, he argued that the proper response to oppressive governmental action rested with the vote.[44] The future chief justice referred to the Jacksonian resistance to the Second Bank of the United States, and he did not contemplate the Republicans' resistance to what they perceived as the slave power. To Republicans, federal policies like that embodied in *Dred Scott* looked threatening and oppressive. Lincoln quite legitimately registered his and his party's opposition to the decision. Republicans thought it wrong and sought, through victory at the polls, to appoint new justices who would overturn the decision and prevent its extension.[45] Douglas, of course, assailed Lincoln for this position, but Lincoln remained firmly within the bounds of partisan conflict. The Republicans' strategy left the chief justice quite bitter. The new party had beaten the Democrats at their own game and had done it so decisively that the Union had split. Sometime in 1860, in fact, Taney produced a manuscript blaming free-state aggression and especially the Republicans for driving the South from the Union. The surviving document, which contains no beginning, end, or clear indication of the purpose for which Taney wrote it, also exposed the limitations of the Taney Court's constitutionalism. Secession, Taney wrote, represented an unconstitutional action, but the Constitution conferred no power on the federal government to coerce the states into remaining within the Union. The Union therefore could not preserve itself, and at a moment of a very real constitutional crisis, Taney's vision of concurrent popular sovereignty, no doubt intensified by his own partisan sympathy, proved all but useless.[46] He, as Lincoln said of Douglas, offered little more to the Union than an official sanction of the people's ability to do wrong.

Note on Method

DRED SCOTT DEVELOPED WITHIN a dense network of concerns formed by the Taney Court justices' differing agendas, anxieties, and senses of obligation, and this study employs an analytical framework that places the case in broad perspective. Although the preceding pages have described *Dred Scott* in its judicial context, the argument makes no effort to deny that the Supreme Court's work was not, in many senses, political. Taney Court discourse formed a part of American political culture, and the justices drew heavily from the symbolic universe so carefully described by historians of the early American republic.[1] Like many other Americans before and since, the court's members wrestled with the implications of popular rule: the definition of "the people," the nature and limits of their authority, the moral implications of public policy. Jacksonian jurisprudence, moreover, described certain aspects of social and political life and asserted specific forms of class and racial domination. Taney Court discourse helped perpetuate the U.S. commitment to hierarchical relations among the races and helped bolster if not legitimate new forms of hierarchy among whites, especially those relationships increasingly dependent on wage labor and corporate organization.[2] Despite the relationships between Taney Court jurisprudence and other aspects of antebellum American culture, however, this study has focused on *Dred Scott*'s development as a legal problem that involved the tracking of four separate but related elements.

The first of these centers on precedent and takes a vertical view of legal development. *Dred Scott*, as historians are well aware, was not the first U.S. Supreme Court decision to confront slavery and was no aberration. Scholars who have traced the line of cases culminating in *Dred Scott* consider the court's 1857 ruling to have been the product of at least twenty years of doctrinal, political, and social development.[3] Understanding these cases comprises an important part of this study, because understanding the central legal issues and the history of those issues remains an indispensable aspect of any analysis of *Dred Scott*. Yet this study rejects the current tendency to portray this line of cases as a more or less coherent line of staunchly proslavery decisions. American slave law did not form a coherent body of rules. It was a mixture of statutory police regulations designed to manage people and common-law doctrines that governed property, and the tension between the two has long fascinated observers.[4] Cases involving slavery, moreover, emerged in a number of different doctrinal contexts and often had little in common aside from their ultimate impact on the body of an enslaved person somewhere in the United States. Such variety ensured that the court's members encountered slavery in conjunction with a range of other issues. Because slavery, both as an idea and as a concrete social relationship, resonated on numerous levels, its presence in a case often put the implications of other questions into sharp relief. Taney Court justices recurrently encountered cases that linked slavery to matters that they already considered important and that therefore took on a heightened significance. Although its rulings generally favored masters' interests, the slavery cases' most interesting aspect is not their proslavery character but rather the justices' efforts to balance their concerns for the security of slavery with commitments to federal power and economic development. The Supreme Court's position as the highest court in a national judicial forum required its members to struggle with a dimension of what Eugene Genovese has termed "the slaveholders' dilemma": a deeply felt need to protect slavery for the sake of social and political order and a contradictory but perhaps equally compelling desire to reap the benefits of liberal capitalism. Unlike the conservative intellectuals that Genovese holds dear, however, none of the Taney Court's members officially advocated secession as a solution.[5] Instead, their effort to protect slavery coexisted with an effort to bolster both federal power and the spread of market relations, and each of these facets of the court's work accommodated the others.

This feature of Taney Court discourse points to the second element of this study's analytical framework: the interrelationships and interplay among various lines of precedent, or what might be termed a horizontal view of legal development. For the past few decades, historians of American law have generally conceptualized their subject along horizontal lines. Most of the leading work has analyzed the way in which changes largely external to the legal system have forced a number of roughly parallel developments across a wide range of doctrinal areas. These studies have offered numerous insights

concerning the law's relationship to shifts in the U.S. political system, social structure, economic organization, cultural sensibility, and intellectual
context, and this book draws extensively on these insights.[6] Emphasis on
external factors, however, has shifted historians' attention away from doctrinal considerations and led to a working assumption that legal doctrines
emerged along parallel lines that developed more or less independently of
each other in response to larger social forces. As Barry Cushman argues,
legal historians have not explored the ways in which various strands of doctrine interacted with one another and became intertwined in "an interde-
pendent *web* of constitutional thought."[7]

Cushman confines his discussion to students of modern constitutional
law, but his observation applies equally well to historians of the antebellum
legal order. Scholars in this field have produced important work on the legal
system's relationship to both slavery and capitalist economic development
but have allowed an analytical partition to develop between the two areas
of inquiry. Historians interested in what Morton Horwitz has termed the
"transformation of American law" pay scant if any attention to the interrelationships between slavery and the legal aspects of economic development.[8] A few scholars investigating the law of slavery have been more sensitive to these relationships, but their investigations thus far have centered on
cases that directly involved both slaves and the market.[9] Historians have thus
made little effort to explore cases in which slavery's connection to questions
of economic development were not immediately apparent.[10] On the Taney
Court, however, seemingly disconnected bodies of law moved in relation
to one another. Developments in the court's slavery rulings could shape
changes in commercial and corporate law, which in turn could influence
the justices' approach to slavery cases. This doctrinal interplay no doubt
emerged in part from slavery cases' tendency to raise difficult questions
that the justices believed to be important in their own right as well as from
the justices' sincere but occasionally unsuccessful efforts to remain doctrinally consistent while balancing their court's conflicting priorities. The justices may not have always been fully conscious of their participation in this
process—they certainly never said so. But the overlap of doctrinal concerns,
the timing of particular developments in the court's slavery rulings relative
to those in other lines of cases, and the ebb and flow of factionalism among
the justices strongly suggests that slavery occupied a developmentally inter-
dependent position in a larger web of jurisprudential concerns.[11]

The third element of this study's analytical framework connects this web to larger patterns of cultural, economic, political, and social changes within the antebellum United States. Following the examples of C. F. C. Milsom, Robert C. Palmer, and Mark M. Carroll, this study examines the often unintended consequences of legal change that the clashing agendas of different legal actors—judges, lawyers, litigants, and legislatures—generated as they responded in varying ways to legal and social change.[12] A central burden of this analysis rests on the exploration of the court's doctrinal web by interrogating the network of assumptions about litigation, governmental power, political economy, social order, and judicial authority that ran throughout Taney Court discourse. Such an approach entails significant challenges. "History is difficult," Milsom cautions, "because people never state their assumptions or describe the framework in which their lives are led."[13] In this respect, the Taney Court's members differed little from Milsom's medieval subjects. The justices at times stated their assumptions with clarity, but they often held other assumptions so deeply that they felt no need to express them, and the justices' adherence to such assumptions must ultimately remain a matter of speculation. Some of this study's conclusions, therefore, can lay no claim to absolute proof, since the justices, despite the Taney Court's relative laxity concerning the secrecy of its deliberations, left much unsaid or at least unrecorded. Gaps and silences thus permeate the court's records, and historians' failure to bridge these gaps has contributed to the disaggregated view of legal development that characterizes current writing about antebellum legal history.

Rather than reproduce that unsatisfactory perspective, this account offers a reading of those silences by tracking closely the discursive movements of individual justices as they worked through more than sixteen hundred reported cases in the two decades under study. The analysis in this volume devotes extended attention to the arguments of concurring and dissenting justices not merely as statements in opposition to the majority's position—although they were on occasion precisely that—but also as indicators of the competing assumptions and commitments that ran through the court's discourse. This study also draws on the justices' personal papers and the court's working records, especially the extant manuscript and galley versions of the justices' opinions housed at the National Archives. Some of those documents contain revisions that, when read carefully, reveal much about the court's various commitments. By examining these materials together, this book confronts not only the issues the justices talked about but also those issues that the justices talked around. Its argument highlights the ways in which these silences emerged in lines of cases that seemingly had little to do with one another—for example, corporate and slave law. The mapping of these silences within the court's discourse, moreover, provides an opportunity to hypothesize about the common political, cultural, and legal assumptions that sustained the justices' reticence. This line of analysis requires a sustained sensitivity to the doctrinal, social, and partisan contexts in which the court worked. This book, therefore, approaches the court's decisions as both legal statements and ideological expressions. Following David Brion Davis's usage, the term *ideology* refers to "an integrated system of beliefs, assumptions, and values, not necessarily true or false, which reflects the needs and interests of a group or class at a particular time in history."[14] Taney Court rulings, even abstruse or highly technical ones, often had as much to do with the justices' effort to fashion their court as a facilitator of democratic self-rule as they did with the law itself.

Neither court doctrine nor ideological assumptions, however, fully explain the dynamics that ultimately produced *Dred Scott*, and this study therefore incorporates a fourth element into its analytical framework: a focus on the justices' crucial role as officers in a larger state structure. Students of the Taney Court have, for the most part, treated its rulings primarily as expressions of partisan ideology, class and racial domination, or sectional interests—and in many ways they were. Yet recent work in the social sciences has emphasized the irreducibility of state activity and the behavior of state functionaries to the play of economic, social, and cultural forces. "Both appointed and elected officials," writes Theda Skocpol, "have ideas and organizational and career interests of their own, and they devise and work for policies that will further those ideas and interests, or at least not harm them."[15] On the Taney Court, two aspects of the justices' office powerfully influenced the court's approach to cases. The first centered on an individual's appointment to the Supreme Court not only as a reward for loyal partisan service but also as recognition of genuine legal ability. Legalistic thought dominated the Taney Court. Judicial writing could be technical and abstruse, and its connections to larger social processes were sometimes oblique, but the patterns of thought it embodied were central to the court's internal dynamics. As Cushman has stressed, judges do not simply look at a case, formulate a policy goal suited to the interests they favor, and then translate that position into legal language. Rather, judges perceive the world in the terms of their professional discourse and become heavily invested in the jurisprudential framework that they articulate over a period of years and in hundreds of decisions.[16] Supreme Court justices who wanted to be influential among their colleagues faced professionally imposed constraints that pressured them to maintain at least an appearance of consistency with both precedent and the accepted meanings of common-law terminology.

The second factor emerged as a consequence of the Supreme Court's organization as an institution that consisted of a panel of members. Writing about the Taney Court has typically treated its rulings as if they were solely the product of the individual justices who wrote them. Justices who wrote dissenting opinions and especially those members who wrote concurring opinions or remained silent tend to get relegated to the margins. There is, of course, an obvious utility to this approach, but it understates the nature of the Supreme Court's official opinions as the product of group deliberation. Although the "opinion of the court" usually appeared under the name of a single justice, those documents gained their status after they had received the assent of a majority of justices in conference. Justice John McLean of Ohio described the process in a draft letter he contemplated sending to an editor of a Methodist paper in the mid-1850s. Following arguments of counsel, he wrote, the justices met privately, and each stated his view of the law. At that point, the chief justice tallied votes and assigned a member to write the court's opinion, which would be read in a later conference and subjected to another vote. If a majority of justices approved of the document, then it became the opinion of the court.[17] A primary—perhaps *the* primary—audience for a Supreme Court justice was, therefore, his colleagues on the bench, and the need to secure a majority of votes among them appears to have influenced the justices' writing and the law they both expounded and made. Any justice hoping to carry the court had to couch his arguments in language that not only appeared consistent with court precedent and common-law terminology but also appealed to the larger policy and doctrinal concerns of a number of his colleagues. Such a process impelled justices who ranked the protection of slavery first among the court's priorities to respond to the concerns of colleagues who rejected extreme states'-rights positions as the proper mechanism for protecting the South's perceived needs. At the same time, justices who ranked federal supremacy over the security of the South's peculiar institution had to take into account the views of their relatively more proslavery colleagues. A focus on the context of the justices' cynical horse-trading allows an examination of the Taney Court's most difficult cases in a new light.

Unfortunately, little evidence remains that would allow historians to track this process with mathematical certainty. A few letters, memos, and discussions by individual justices, like McLean's, survive and provide a direct glimpse into the court's internal workings, but such material is limited to isolated cases and provides an incomplete picture of the dynamics at play. This study draws on that evidence yet also places a heavy emphasis on the justices' concurring and dissenting opinions by approaching them as indicators of the possible bounds of judicial consensus. By tracking members' shifting positions through the Taney Court's history, this volume analyzes the ways in which the authors of majority opinions responded to colleagues' concerns and built coalitions that furthered a particular configuration of doctrinal and policy goals. The argument here has benefited from an examination of the National Archives' collection of the extant manuscript and galley versions of the justices' opinions. These documents sometimes contain revised portions that allow a glimpse into the internal dynamics of the court and provide a basis for speculation about a particular justice's efforts to build a winning coalition. When read together, these sources reveal a great deal of negotiation taking place among the justices as they managed their partisan and professional agendas and those of their court.

This book, therefore, has examined *Dred Scott* from a number of angles. It is, above all, a work of legal history, and its argument delves into technical matters without apology when such analysis is necessary for the thesis. The argument's concern with the development of various lines of precedent—most notably the court's doctrines concerning slavery, corporations, and state citizens' access to the federal courts—does not constitute matters of esoteric interest. In a very real sense, the justices' perception of the world in which they lived and worked followed the lines of precedent that they and their predecessors created. The vertical analysis employed by this study becomes crucial not only for understanding the issues that the justices believed to be before the court but also for uncovering the justices' underlying assumptions about slavery, the market, democratic governance, judicial authority, and social order. Because lines of precedent could not, either singly or even in the aggregate, capture the Taney Court's concerns in their totality, this book also examines the justices' work from a horizontal perspective that reveals patterns of development that historians have missed. Elements of Taney Court doctrine, even when they superficially had nothing to do with one another, moved in tandem as the justices struggled to reconcile their and their court's various commitments and agendas. A horizontal approach likewise provides another window into the assumptions that infused judicial writing and allows opportunities to explore the connections between legal discourse and other aspects of antebellum American culture. This study's focus on the multiplicity of judicial commitments and agendas also highlights the critical importance of coalition building and the dynamics of factionalism on the Taney Court. *Dred Scott* represented the court's answer to problems plaguing the Union in the 1850s, but the justices did not design their solution to solve the sectional crisis as it had developed in congressional and presidential politics. Rather, the court's solution arose out of divisions that had developed in the relatively insular world of judicial debate, and its response ultimately left few people, aside from a majority of the court's members, satisfied with the outcome. By tracking these four elements of the case, however, this study seeks to contribute a considerably more textured analysis of *Dred Scott* than previous scholars have offered.

Notes

ABBREVIATIONS

Blair, Plaintiff's Brief I   [Montgomery Blair], *Dred Scott v. Sandford*, Brief of
Plaintiff (U.S. Sup. Ct., December Term, 1855), Blair
Family Papers, Manuscript Division, Library of Congress,
Washington, D.C.

Blair, Plaintiff's Brief II   *Dred Scott v. Sandford*, Argument of Montgomery Blair,
Counsel for the Plaintiff in Error (U.S. Sup. Ct.,
December Term, 1856), Blair Family Papers, Manuscript
Division, Library of Congress, Washington, D.C.

Curtis Papers   Benjamin Robbins Curtis Papers, Manuscript Division,
Library of Congress, Washington, D.C.

Daniel Papers   Daniel Family Papers, Virginia Historical Society,
Richmond.

McLean Papers   John McLean Papers, Manuscript Division, Library of
Congress, Washington, D.C.

OAC #[File Number]   Opinions in Appellate Cases [file number], Records of the
U.S. Supreme Court (RG 267), National Archives and
Records Administration, Washington, D.C.

Supreme Court Records   Records of the U.S. Supreme Court (RG 267), National
Archives and Records Administration, Washington, D.C.

Taney, Dred Scott Proofs I   *Dred Scott v. Sandford*, Taney's page proofs, version I (U.S.
Sup. Ct., 1857), Opinions in Appellate Cases #3230,
Records of the U.S. Supreme Court (RG 267), National
Archives and Records Administration, Washington, D.C.

Taney, Dred Scott Proofs II   *Dred Scott v. Sandford*, Taney's page proofs, version II
(U.S. Sup. Ct., 1857), Opinions in Appellate Cases #3230,
Records of the U.S. Supreme Court (RG 267), National
Archives and Records Administration, Washington, D.C.

Taney, MS-NSA I   Roger B. Taney, Manuscript Opinion on the Negro
Seamen Act I (Taney to State Department, Attorney
General's Office, May 28, 1832), Opinions on Legal
Questions, General Records of the Attorney Generals,
Records of the Department of Justice (RG 60), National
Archives and Records Administration, College Park, Md.

| Taney, MS-NSA II | Roger B. Taney, Manuscript Opinion on the Negro Seamen Act II (Taney to State Department, June 9, 1832), Miscellaneous Letters, Records of the State Department (RG 59), National Archives and Records Administration, College Park, Md. |

INTRODUCTION. Beyond the Sectional Crisis

1. *Dred Scott v. Sandford,* 60 U.S. 393 (1857).
2. *New York Tribune,* March 7, 1857.
3. Potter, *Impending Crisis,* 283–84; *New York Journal of Commerce,* March 12, 1857.
4. Johannsen, *Lincoln-Douglas Debates,* 18.
5. Ibid., 14, 19–20.
6. Von Holst, *Constitutional and Political History,* 6:1–46.
7. Corwin, "Dred Scott Decision"; Warren, *Supreme Court,* 2:294–302.
8. Mendelson, "Dred Scott's Case—Revisited"; Mendelson, "Dred Scott's Case—Reconsidered." For later historical accounts, see Ehrlich, *They Have No Rights;* Hopkins, *Dred Scott's Case;* Potter, *Impending Crisis,* 267–96.
9. Fehrenbacher, *Dred Scott Case,* 5, 337, 595.
10. Perhaps the best measure of Fehrenbacher's influence rests in the number of studies that have uncritically accepted the *Dred Scott Case*'s central conclusions. See, e.g., Kettner, *Development,* 324–32; McPherson, *Battle Cry,* 170–80; Wiecek, *Liberty,* 77–80; Stampp, *America,* 83–109; Sunstein, "*Dred Scott v. Sandford*"; McPherson, "Politics and Judicial Responsibility."
For alternative positions, see Levinson, "Slavery"; Higginbotham, *Shades,* 61–67; Meister, "Logic and Legacy"; Rogers M. Smith, *Civic Ideals,* 243–85; Graber, "Desperately Ducking Slavery."
11. For a recent example, see President George W. Bush's mention of *Dred Scott* in his debate with John F. Kerry (FDCH Media, "Transcript: Second Presidential Debate," October 8, 2004, http://www.washingtonpost.com/wp-srv/politics/debatereferee/debate_1008.html (February 25, 2005).
12. Bickel, *Least Dangerous Branch,* 16–23. For critiques of the countermajoritarian difficulty's applicability to the development of American constitutional law, see Ackerman, *We the People,* 3–33; Barry Friedman, "History," 356–81; Graber, "Nonmajoritarian Difficulty."
13. My understanding of the Scott family's approach to the legal struggle for freedom owes a great debt to VanderVelde and Subramanian, "Mrs. Dred Scott."

PART ONE. Beneath *Dred Scott*

1. Jackson, "Farewell Address," 4:1524, 1525; Keyssar, *Right to Vote,* 348; Harry L. Watson, *Liberty and Power,* 101–4, 149, 232.
My understanding of Jacksonianism has benefited from Earle, *Jacksonian Antislavery;* Ellis, *Union at Risk;* Feller, "Brother in Arms"; Hofstadter, *American Political Tradition,* 57–86; Howe, "Evangelical Movement"; Leonard, *Invention of Party Politics;* Pessen, *Jacksonian America;* Richards, *Slave Power;* Wilentz, "Slavery, Antislavery, and Jacksonian Democracy"; Wood, *Radicalism,* 325–47.

2. Jackson, "Farewell Address," 1521; Harry L. Watson, *Liberty and Power*, 237–46; Feller, *Jacksonian Promise*, 187–88.

3. Jackson, "Farewell Address," 1517–18.

4. Ibid., 1526; U.S. Census Bureau, *Historical Statistics of the United States: Colonial Times to 1970*, bicentennial ed. (Washington, D.C.: U.S. Government Printing Office, 1975), 8, 11, 12; Mintz, *Moralists and Modernizers*, 7; Wilentz, "Many Democracies," 213–14.

5. *Swift v. Tyson*, 41 U.S. 1, 18 (1842).

CHAPTER ONE. Realizing Popular Sovereignty

1. "Trial by Jury and the Federal Court," 480.

2. Peter V. Daniel to Elizabeth Randolph Daniel, Washington, D.C., December 23, 1845, Daniel Papers.

3. Henry M. Beeson to James K. Polk, Uniontown, Pa., April 3, 1845, copy in Carl Brent Swisher Papers, Manuscript Division, Library of Congress, Washington, D.C.

4. Ellis, *Union at Risk*, 19–28, 33–40. See also Ashworth, *"Agrarians" and "Aristocrats"*; Ashworth, *Slavery, Capitalism, and Politics*, 289–302; Howe, "Evangelical Movement"; White, *Marshall Court*, 49–75; Ferguson, *Law and Letters*, 11–33.

5. *Pollard et al. v. Hagan et al.*, 44 U.S. 212, 224 (1845); *Wheeler v. Smith et al.*, 50 U.S. 55, 78 (1850).

6. *United States v. Briggs*, 50 U.S. 351, 355 (1850); *U.S. Statutes at Large*, 4 (1831): 472.

7. *Bank of Augusta v. Earle*, 38 U.S. 519, 591–97 (1839) (quotation on 594). For the substance of the circuit ruling, see 38 U.S. 600–604.

8. *Bank of Augusta*, 594.

9. *Groves et al. v. Slaughter*, 40 U.S. 449, 496–503 (1841).

10. *Bank of Augusta*, 594; John Catron to John McLean, n.p., September 14, 1835, McLean Papers; *Brewer's Lessee v. Blougher*, 39 U.S. 178, 198 (1840). See also *Runyan v. Coster's Lessee*, 39 U.S. 122 (1840); *Luther v. Borden*, 48 U.S. 1 (1849); Fehrenbacher, *Dred Scott Case*, 230–33.

11. Taney, MS-NSA I, esp. 7. See also Freehling, *Prelude*, 111–18; U.S. House Committee, *Free Colored Seamen*.

12. Taney, MS-NSA II, 1–2. See also Taney, MS-NSA I, 12–13.

13. John Catron to John McLean, n.p., September 14, 1835, McLean Papers; *Worcester v. Georgia*, 31 U.S. 515 (1832).

14. *Mills et al. v. County of St. Clair and Harrison*, 49 U.S. 569, 585 (1850).

15. Taney, MS-NSA II, 3; Harry L. Watson, *Liberty and Power*, 172–97; Howe, "Evangelical Movement"; Altschuler and Blumin, "Limits"; Keyssar, *Right to Vote*, 53–76.

16. *Luther*, 41–42; Gettleman, *Dorr Rebellion*; Dennison, *Dorr War*.

17. Blackstone, *Commentaries*, 1:156; James Wilson, "Speech in the State House Yard," in *Documentary History*, ed. Jensen, Kaminski, and Saladino, 2:167–72; Novak, *People's Welfare*, 19–50; *Chisolm v. Georgia*, 2 U.S. 419, 453–65 (1793).

18. U.S. Constitution, art. III, sec. 2, cl. 1, art. VI; Haskins and Johnson, *Foundations of Power*, 186–88; Publius [Hamilton], *Federalist* 78, 438–39. On the early history of judicial review, see Goebel, *Antecedents and Beginnings*, 228–30, 236–50; Casto, *Supreme Court*, 19–22, 213–46; Degnan, "William Paterson"; Gerber, "Deconstructing"; Gerber, "Introduction." But see also Bickel, *Least Dangerous Branch*, 1–14.

19. For brief introductions to the Marshall Court, see McCloskey, *American Supreme Court*, 35–52; Wiecek, *Liberty under Law*, 32–55; White, *American Judicial Tradition*, 25–34. See also Palmer, "Obligations of Contracts," 654–67.

20. White, *Marshall Court*, 485–594. See also Fehrenbacher, *Constitutions and Constitutionalism*, 33–56; Newmyer, "John Marshall."

21. *Gibbons v. Ogden*, 22 U.S. 1, 203 (1824); Palmer, "Federal Common Law"; Preyer, "Jurisdiction to Punish"; White, *Marshall Court*, 567–85.

22. *Gibbons*, 187–208 (quotation on 195); *Elikson v. Deliesseline*, 8 F. Cas. 493 (U.S. Cir. Ct. Dist. S.C. 1823); *The Passenger Cases*, 48 U.S. 283 (1849); *The License Cases*, 46 U.S. 504 (1847).

23. *Cooley v. Board of Wardens of the Port of Philadelphia*, 53 U.S. 299, 313, 319 (1852).

24. Cf. the majority opinions in the *Passenger Cases* (392, 410, 437, 452, 455) and the ruling in *Mayor, Aldermen, and Commonalty of New York v. Miln* (36 U.S. 102, 130 [1837]).

25. *License Cases*, 504.

26. Cf. *Fox v. Ohio* (46 U.S. 410 [1847]) and *United States v. Marigold* (50 U.S. 560 [1850]).

27. Cf. *Veazie and Young v. Moor* (55 U.S. 568 [1853]) and *Pennsylvania v. Wheeling and Belmont Bridge Company* (54 U.S. 518 [1852]).

28. U.S. Constitution, art. VI, cl. 2; *Buchanan v. Alexander*, 45 U.S. 20 (1845); *Dobbins v. Commissioners of Erie County*, 41 U.S. 435 (1842).

29. *Keary v. Farmers and Merchants Bank of Memphis*, 41 U.S. 89 (1842); *Reddall v. Bryan et al.*, 65 U.S. 420, 422 (1861).

30. *U.S. Statutes at Large*, 1 (1789): 73–93, 2 (1802): 156–57; White, *Marshall Court*, 164–81.

31. *Mills et al. v. Brown et al.*, 41 U.S. 525 (1842); *President, Directors, and Company of the Commercial Bank of Cincinnati v. Buckingham's Executors*, 46 U.S. 317 (1847); *Grand Gulf Railroad and Banking Co. et al. v. Marshall*, 53 U.S. 165 (1852); *Michigan Central Railroad Company v. Michigan Southern Railroad Company*, 60 U.S. 378 (1857); *Rector, Church Wardens, and Vestry of Christ Church, Philadelphia v. Philadelphia County*, 61 U.S. 26 (1857); *Farney v. Towle*, 66 U.S. 350 (1862).

32. See, e.g., *Dennistoun v. Stewart*, 59 U.S. 565 (1856); *Webster v. Cooper*, 51 U.S. 54 (1850); *Nesmith v. Sheldon et al.*, 47 U.S. 40 (1848); *United States v. Briggs*, 46 U.S. 208 (1847); *White v. Turk et al.*, 37 U.S. 238 (1838).

33. See, e.g., *Mordecai et al. v. Lindsay*, 60 U.S. 199 (1857); *Prentice et al. v. Zane's Administrator*, 49 U.S. 470 (1850); *Knapp v. Banks*, 43 U.S. 73 (1844).

34. On the docket, see Swisher, *Taney Period*, 275–92. For the obscure case, see *Commonwealth Bank of Kentucky v. Griffith et al.*, 39 U.S. 56, 58–59 (1840). In Taney's manuscript, the discussion of the policy behind this case appears on a separate sheet from the rest of the opinion; see OAC #2095. See also *United States v. Stone*, 39 U.S. 524, 525 (1840).

35. *Choteau v. Marguerite, a Woman of Color*, 37 U.S. 507 (1838); *Mills*, 525.

36. *Grand Gulf Railroad and Banking Co.*, 165. See also *Planters' Bank of Mississippi v. Sharp et al.*, 47 U.S. 301 (1848).

37. Bickel, *Least Dangerous Branch*, 16–28.

38. Publius [Hamilton], *Federalist* 78, 439; Ackerman, *We the People*, 6–7, 67–80.

39. For cases in which the heavily divided justices could not deliver an opinion, see *Passenger Cases*, 283; *License Cases*, 504; *Spalding v. New York ex rel. Backus*, 45 U.S. 21 (1845); *Holmes v. Jennison et al.*, 39 U.S. 540 (1840).

40. Joseph Story to John McLean, Cambridge, Mass., May 10, 1837, August 16, 1844, McLean Papers. See also Newmyer, *Supreme Court Justice Joseph Story*.

41. Joseph Story to Harriet Martineau, Cambridge, Mass., April 7, 1837, in William W. Story, *Life and Letters*, 2:277; Joseph Story, *Conflict of Laws*, secs. 23–28. The court embraced this analysis in *Bank of Augusta*, 519.

42. *Cooley*, 321–25; John McLean to Robert A. Parrish, Washington, D.C., March 3, 1855, McLean to Joseph Vance, Cincinnati, Ohio, May 3, 1857, McLean Papers. See also Weisenburger, *Life*.

43. John McLean to New York Young Men's Christian Association, Washington, D.C., March 2, 1858, McLean Papers; *Groves*, 503–8; *Dred Scott v. Sandford*, 60 U.S. 393, 529–64 (1857); *Proprietors of Charles River Bridge v. Proprietors of Warren Bridge*, 36 U.S. 420 (1837), 554–82; *Fox*, 435–40.

44. John Catron to James Buchanan, Washington, D.C., January 24, 1852, in *Papers of James Buchanan* (microfilm) (Philadelphia: Historical Society of Pennsylvania, 1974).

45. *Cooley*, 325–26.

46. Peter V. Daniel to Elizabeth Randolph Daniel, Washington, D.C., February 15, 1851, Napoleon, Ark., April 17, 1852, Daniel Papers.

47. Peter V. Daniel to Martin Van Buren, Jackson, Miss., June 11, 1844, Richmond, Va., October 17, November 1, 1844, November 19, 1847, in *Papers of Martin Van Buren* (microfilm) (Washington, D.C.: Library of Congress, 1960); *Rundle et al. v. Delaware and Raritan Canal Company*, 55 U.S. 80, 95–102 (1853); *The Genesee Chief*, 53 U.S. 443, 463–65 (1852). See also Frank, *Justice Daniel Dissenting*.

48. Benjamin Robbins Curtis to George Ticknor Curtis, Washington, D.C., February 29, 1852, Curtis Papers.

CHAPTER TWO. Imposing Self-Rule

1. *Philadelphia and Reading Railroad v. Derby*, 55 U.S. 468, 487 (1853).

2. *Philadelphia and Reading Railroad v. Derby*, Grier's Manuscript Opinion (U.S. Sup. Ct., 1852), 7, OAC #2961. Grier's draft contained a great deal of emphasis not reflected in the official report of the case.

3. *Derby*, 487.

4. I have, of course, borrowed and modified Richard Hofstadter's famous phrase; see Hofstadter, *American Political Tradition*, xxxvii.

5. This paragraph draws from Mintz, *Moralists and Modernizers*, 3–11; Wilentz, "Many Democracies"; Rorabaugh, *Alcoholic Republic*; Richards, *"Gentlemen"*; Gilje, *Road to Mobocracy*; Sellers, *Market Revolution*, 103–36, 332–63; Wood, *Radicalism*, 325–47; Wood, "Enemy Is Us"; Montgomery, *Citizen Worker*, 13–61; Hatch, *Democratization*; Taylor, *William Cooper's Town*, 256–91; Harry L. Watson, *Liberty and Power*, 49–51; Altschuler and Blumin, *Rude Republic*, 47–151.

6. *Bend v. Hoyt*, 38 U.S. 263, 263–65, 267–68 (1839) (quotation on 268). For the tariff law, see *U.S. Statutes at Large*, 3 (1823): 729; *Elliot v. Swartwout*, 35 U.S. 137 (1836).

7. *Bend*, 267.

8. Tocqueville, *Democracy in America*, 2:215, 216.

9. Stanley, *From Bondage to Contract*, 1–59.

10. Holt, "Marking"; Gable, "Intention and Structure"; Balbus, "Commodity Form."

11. *Bend v. Hoyt*, Thompson's Manuscript Dissenting Opinion (U.S. Sup. Ct., 1839), addition B, OAC #2087. The added paragraph appeared in the printed version of the case (*Bend*, 275).

12. *Eyre v. Potter*, 56 U.S. 42, 60 (1854). See also Joseph Story, *Commentaries on Equity Pleadings*, secs. 245–46; Verplanck, *Essay*; *Patton v. Taylor et al.*, 48 U.S. 132 (1849).

13. See *Baker et al. v. Nachtrieb*, 60 U.S. 126 (1856); *Goesele v. Bimeler*, 55 U.S. 589, esp. 608–9 (1853).

14. *Bodley et al. v. Goodrich*, 48 U.S. 276, 278 (1849).

15. *Stanley v. Gadsby et al.*, 35 U.S. 521 (1836).

16. See *Bradley v. Washington, Alexandria, and Georgetown Steam Packet Company*, 38 U.S. 89 (1839); *Smith v. Richards*, 38 U.S. 26 (1839). See also Taney's discussion of the court's unanimous rejection of a rehearing (*Smith v. Richards*, Taney's Manuscript Opinion [U.S. Sup. Ct., 1839], OAC #2010).

17. Wyatt-Brown, *Southern Honor*; Ayers, *Vengeance and Justice*; Greenberg, *Honor and Slavery*.

18. Stowe, *Intimacy and Power*, 5–49.

19. *Virginia Argus*, November 15, 1808; *Virginia Herald*, November 9, 1808. The exchange between Taney and Curtis is discussed in the epilogue. Catron, however, struck down a Tennessee law legalizing dueling when he was chief justice of that state's high court. See Catron, "Biographical Letter"; *Smith v. State*, 9 Tenn. 228 (1829); Huebner, *Southern Judicial Tradition*, 45–50.

20. Artemus B. Muzzey quoted in Halttunen, *Confidence Men and Painted Women*, 14.

21. Blumin, *Emergence*, 179–91; Halttunen, *Confidence Men and Painted Women*, 96–99; Mintz, *Moralists and Modernizers*, 10–15.

22. Peter V. Daniel to Elizabeth Randolph Daniel, Washington, D.C., [1851], Daniel Papers.

23. Peter V. Daniel to Elizabeth Randolph Daniel, Washington, D.C., January 3, 1852, Daniel Papers.

24. Peter V. Daniel to Richard B. Gooch, Washington, D.C., December 24, 1847, January 3, 1848, Gooch Family Papers, Virginia Historical Society, Richmond; Peter V. Daniel Jr. to Gooch, n.p., August 28, 1848, Gooch Papers. The tone of Peter Jr.'s letter suggests that Gooch had nearly died during a recent drinking binge.

25. Peter V. Daniel Jr. to Richard B. Gooch, n.p., August 28, 1848, Gooch Papers.

26. *Bend*, 266, 268, 273–77 (Thompson's quotation on 275); Thompson's *Bend* Manuscript, addition A.

27. *Voorhees et al. v. Jackson ex dem. President, Directors, and Company of the Bank of the United States*, 35 U.S. 449, 474–77 (1836).

28. *Brush v. Ware*, 40 U.S. 93, 111 (1841). Technically, the court held Brush to be a purchaser with notice, and according to the law under which the case originated, he was entitled (as the locator of the tract) to one-quarter of the land he claimed (*Brush*, 114).

29. *Bowman et al. v. Walthen and the Mayor and Common Council of Jeffersonville*, 42 U.S. 189, 195 (1843).

30. *Maxwell v. Kennedy et al.*, 49 U.S. 210, 218–21 (1850).

31. Tocqueville, *Democracy in America*, 2:216; Clark, *Lectures*, 225.

32. John Catron to Benjamin Robbins Curtis, Hullatown, Tenn., September 8, 1857, Curtis Papers; Peter V. Daniel to Elizabeth Randolph Daniel, Washington, D.C., February 4, 1847, Daniel Papers.

33. Benjamin Robbins Curtis to Daniel Webster, n.p., October 1851, Curtis Papers; Roger B. Taney to George W. Hughes, Washington, D.C., August 22, 1860, in Samuel Tyler, *Memoir of Roger Brooke Taney, LL.D., Chief Justice of the Supreme Court of the United States* (Baltimore: Murphy, 1872), 406–7. On advice rendered, see, e.g., John Catron to Milton Knox, Washington, D.C., 1846, Subject Files, Clerk's Files, Supreme

Court Records. For McLean and Woodbury's political ambitions, see, e.g., John McLean to John Allison, Chapel Wood, Ohio, July 4, 1856, McLean Papers; Levi Woodbury to Mary Elizabeth Blair, Washington, D.C., December 7, 1847, Blair Family Papers, Manuscript Division, Library of Congress, Washington, D.C.

34. Pound, *Formative Era*, 82–84; Karsten, *Heart versus Head*, 25–127, 147–78.

35. Cf. Daniel's language in *Eyre* (59–60) and *Griffith v. Spratley* (1 Cox Chancery Cases, 383, 389 [1787]).

36. Nelson, *Americanization*, 165–74.

37. Karsten, *Heart versus Head*, 28–31. On legal science, see Milsom, "Nature of Blackstone's Achievement"; Gordon, "Legal Thought and Legal Practice," 81–87; Miller, *Life of the Mind*, 117–85; Wiecek, *Lost World*, 38–41; White, *Marshall Court*, 81–156.

38. Ferguson, *Law and Letters*, 3–84; White, *Marshall Court*, 11–156; Wiecek, *Lost World*, 27–31.

39. On developments within the profession, see Ferguson, *Law and Letters*, 199–304.

40. See *Louisville, Cincinnati, and Charleston Railroad Company v. Letson*, 43 U.S. 497 (1844), overturning *Bank of United States v. Deveaux*, 9 U.S. 61 (1809); *The Genesee Chief*, 53 U.S. 443 (1852), overturning *The Thomas Jefferson*, 23 U.S. 428 (1825).

41. *New York ex rel. Cutler et al. v. Dibble*, 62 U.S. 366 (1858); *Fellows v. Blacksmith and Parker*, 60 U.S. 366 (1856).

42. *Walker v. Taylor et al.*, 46 U.S. 64, 67 (1846). G. Edward White, *American Judicial Tradition*, 109–28, has explored this dynamic in the context of postbellum state courts, but the point applies nicely to the Taney Court as well.

43. For the emphasis on change, see Horwitz, *Transformation*; Nelson, *Americanization*. These studies must be read against Karsten, *Heart versus Head*, which stresses the importance of established doctrine.

44. *Dred Scott v. Sandford*, 60 U.S. 393, 465–66 (1857).

45. Thoreau, "Civil Disobedience," 102.

46. *Gordon v. Longest*, 41 U.S. 97, 104 (1842); Publius [Hamilton], *Federalist* 79, 447.

47. Horwitz, *Transformation*, 211–52; Freyer, *Harmony and Dissonance*, 4–17, 45–75; Freyer, *Forums*. On the court's jurisdiction and enforcement of it, see *U.S. Statutes at Large*, 1 (1789): 73; *Parker v. Overman*, 59 U.S. 137 (1856); *Erwin v. Lowry*, 48 U.S. 172 (1849); *Shelton v. Tiffin*, 47 U.S. 163 (1848); *McNutt v. Bland*, 43 U.S. 9 (1844); *Gwin v. Breedlove*, 43 U.S. 29 (1844); *Bradstreet v. Thomas*, 37 U.S. 174 (1838).

CHAPTER THREE. Evidence of Law

1. Blair, Plaintiff's Brief II, 18; *U.S. Statutes at Large*, 1 (1789): 73–94, sec. 34; Warren, "New Light," 86–88.

2. Horwitz, *Transformation*, 245; *Swift v. Tyson*, 41 U.S. 1 (1842).

3. Two other scholars have noted the relation of *Swift* to *Dred Scott*, although both fail sufficiently to develop the insight. See Streichler, "Justice Curtis's Dissent"; Dean, "Reassessing *Dred Scott*."

4. For clear, brief discussions of negotiable instruments, see *Black's Law Dictionary*, 719; Hall, *Magic Mirror*, 122. On negotiability, see Freyer, *Forums*, 36–52.

5. Freyer, *Forums*, 53–57.

6. Atack and Passell, *New Economic View*, 102. The best work on the economics of the Panic of 1837 remains Temin, *Jacksonian Economy*.

7. *Swift*, 2–3; Freyer, *Forums*, 57–68.

8. See *Rosa v. Brotherson*, 10 Wendall 85 (N.Y., 1833); *Ontario Bank v. Worthington*, 12 Wendall 593 (N.Y., 1834); *Payne v. Cutler*, 13 Wendall 605 (N.Y., 1835). New York courts held the other way both before and after these cases. See *Bay v. Coddington*, 5 Johnson's Chancery Reports 54, 56–57 (N.Y., 1821); *Bank of Salina v. Babcock*, 21 Wendall 499 (N.Y., 1839); *Bank of Sandusky v. Scouville*, 24 Wendall 115 (N.Y., 1840).

9. On the moral implications, see LaPiana, "*Swift v. Tyson*," 792–96.

10. *Swift*, 18–19.

11. *Erie Railroad Co. v. Thompkins*, 304 U.S. 64, 78–80 (1938). Brandeis's reading of *Swift* still informs debates over federal common-law authority among legal academics. See Young, "Last Brooding Omnipresence"; Kramer, "Lawmaking Power"; Redish, "Federal Common Law"; Weinberg, "Federal Common Law," 822–27.

12. See Freyer, *Harmony and Dissonance*, 45–55; Frank, *Justice Daniel Dissenting*, 168–69; *Withers v. Greene*, 50 U.S. 213 (1850).

13. On the Commerce Clause, see chap. 4. On corporate law, see chaps. 5, 6. On admiralty, see *Jackson et al. v. The Magnolia*, 61 U.S. 296 (1858); *The Genesee Chief*, 53 U.S. 443 (1852); *New Jersey Steam Navigation Company v. Merchants' Bank of Boston*, 47 U.S. 344 (1848); *Waring et al. v. Clarke et al.*, 46 U.S. 441 (1847).

14. I have found the following studies of *Swift* useful: Bridwell, "Theme v. Reality"; Dickinson, "Law of Nations"; Freyer, *Forums*; Freyer, *Harmony and Dissonance*; Horwitz, *Transformation*, 245–52; LaPiana, "*Swift v. Tyson*"; [Tushnet], "*Swift v. Tyson*."

15. *Swift*, 20.

16. Ibid. On the lower federal courts, see Freyer, *Forums*, 26–29, 80–89. On credit markets, see Bodenhorn, "Capital Mobility"; La Croix and Grandy, "Financial Integration."

17. See esp. *Van Reimsdyk v. Kane*, 28 F. Cas. 1062 (U.S. Cir. Ct., Dist. R.I., 1812); *United States v. Coolidge*, 25 F. Cas. 619 (Cir. Ct., Dist. Mass., 1813).

18. *Clark's Executors v. Van Riemsdyk*, 13 U.S. 153 (1815); *United States v. Coolidge*, 14 U.S. 415 (1816).

19. Freyer, *Harmony and Dissonance*, 31–33.

20. *Wheaton et al. v. Peters et al.*, 33 U.S. 591, 658 (1834).

21. Bridwell, "Theme v. Reality"; LaPiana, "*Swift v. Tyson*," 782–89.

22. See *Lee v. Dick et al.*, 35 U.S. 482 (1836); *Coolidge et al. v. Payson et al.*, 15 U.S. 66 (1817).

23. *United States v. Henfield*, 11 F. Cas. 1099 (U.S. Cir. Ct., Dist. Pa., 1793); *Respublica v. De Longchamps*, 1 U.S. 111 (Pa., 1784); Palmer, "Federal Common Law," 290–99.

24. *Smyth v. Strader et al.*, 45 U.S. 404 (1845).

25. *Swift*, 18.

26. *Bank of Augusta v. Earle*, 38 U.S. 519 (1839).

27. Lawrence M. Friedman, *History*, 127, 371.

28. Horwitz, *Transformation*, 248–50.

29. Freyer, *Forums*, 77, 90–91; Freyer, *Harmony and Dissonance*, 20–21, 40–41; Wiecek, *Lost World*, 37–54; *Erie*, 74–75; [Tushnet], "*Swift v. Tyson*."

30. The relevant cases, which arose around the time of *Dred Scott*, are discussed in chap. 7.

31. *Stalker v. McDonald*, 6 Hill 93 (N.Y., 1843). See also Freyer, *Producers versus Capitalists*, 85.

32. On state debtor laws, see Freyer, *Producers versus Capitalists*, 57–91.

33. [Tushnet], "*Swift v. Tyson*," 295.

34. *Walker v. Taylor et al.*, 46 U.S. 64, 67 (1846).

35. Freyer, *Forums*, 110–12, 119 n.160. See also Purcell, *Litigation and Inequality*, 59–88.

36. Docket of the Supreme Court of the United States, E:2273, Supreme Court Records.

37. Blair, Plaintiff's Brief II, 18.

38. Joseph Story, *Commentaries on the Conflict*, secs. 18–28; *Bank of Augusta*, 588–97.

39. Taney, MS-NSA I, 4–7.

40. Story, *Commentaries on the Conflict*, 62–95. On Story's shaping of comity doctrine, see Leslie, "Influence," 211–12; Finkelman, *Imperfect Union*, 13–14. For an interesting but not entirely plausible argument that Story misapplied Huber's theory by simple mistake, see Alan Watson, *Joseph Story*. See also Huber, *Jurisprudence*, 1:11–17.

41. See esp. *The Passenger Cases*, 48 U.S. 283 (1849); *The License Cases*, 46 U.S. 504 (1847); *Wilson et al. v. Black Bird Creek Marsh Co.*, 27 U.S. 245 (1829); *Brown et al. v. Maryland*, 25 U.S. 419 (1827); *Gibbons v. Ogden*, 22 U.S. 1 (1824).

42. New York Legislature, *An Act Concerning Passengers in Vessels Coming to the Port of New York* (Albany, 1824), 27–29, secs. I–III; *Mayor, Aldermen, and Commonalty of New York v. Miln*, 36 U.S. 102, 109, 139, 142, 153–61, 143–53 (1837).

43. *Groves et al. v. Slaughter*, 40 U.S. 449, 496–503, 517, 505, 508 (1841); Wiecek, "Slavery and Abolition." See also Wiecek, *Sources*, 71, 114, 117, 271; Mississippi Constitution (1832) and Amendments to the Constitution of 1832 in Thorpe, ed., *Federal and State Constitutions*, 2150–74.

44. *Groves*, 510, 508. Historians rarely note this aspect of *Groves*.

45. Wiecek, "Slavery and Abolition," 52.

46. *Groves*, 510–17.

47. Ibid., 449, 503–17, esp. 510.

PART TWO. Toward *Dred Scott*

1. Peter V. Daniel to Elizabeth Randolph Daniel, Washington, D.C., May 18, December 16, 1849, January 26, February 8, 1850, Daniel Papers.

2. U.S. Census Bureau, *Historical Statistics*, 518; Berlin, *Generations of Captivity*, 161.

3. Butler, *Becoming America*, 50–88; Lamoreaux, "Rethinking."

4. Foner, *Free Soil*, 11–72.

5. U.S. Census Bureau, *Historical Statistics*, 624; Bodenhorn, "Capital Mobility."

6. Larson, *Internal Improvement*.

7. Peter V. Daniel to Elizabeth Randolph Daniel, Washington, D.C., January 18, 1849, Daniel Papers.

8. Larson, *Internal Improvement*, 224.

9. Potter, *Impending Crisis*, 93–95.

10. Campbell, *Rights*, 43; Peter V. Daniel to Elizabeth Randolph Daniel, Washington, D.C., February 15, 1851, Daniel Papers.

CHAPTER FOUR. Moderating Taney

1. Campbell, *Rights*, 29; Birney, *Examination*, 42.

2. Wiecek, "Slavery and Abolition"; Bestor, "State Sovereignty"; Fehrenbacher, *Dred Scott Case*; Hyman and Wiecek, *Equal Justice*, 101–14, 172–91, 197–202; Finkelman, *Imperfect Union*, 236–84; Brandon, *Free in the World*, 85–115.

3. Fehrenbacher, *Slaveholding Republic*; Richards, *Slave Power*; Feller, "Brother in Arms"; Wilentz, "Slavery"; Earle, *Jacksonian Antislavery*.

4. Peter V. Daniel to Elizabeth Randolph Daniel, Richmond, Va., September 9, 1851, Daniel Papers. On the proslavery constitution, see Lynd, *Class Conflict*, 3–21, 153–213; Fehrenbacher, *Slaveholding Republic*, 15–47; Finkelman, *Slavery and the Founders*. On the importance of oaths to antebellum officeholders, see Orren, " 'War between Officers,' " 354–55.

5. Taney, MS-NSA I, 3–5, 7; *Prigg v. Pennsylvania*, 41 U.S. 539, 576–87, 602–5, 616–22 (1842); *Jones v. Vanzandt*, 46 U.S. 215, 231 (1847).

6. *The Amistad*, 40 U.S. 518, 549, 587–97 (1841); Chase, *Argument*, 77, 93–94; *Jones*, 231.

7. *United States v. Rogers*, 45 U.S. 567, 573 (1846); *U.S. Statutes at Large*, 2 (1801): 103–8; *Rhodes v. Bell*, 43 U.S. 397 (1844); *Williams v. Ash*, 42 U.S. 1 (1843); *Miller v. Herbert et al.*, 46 U.S. 72 (1847); *Vigel v. Naylor*, 65 U.S. 208 (1861).

8. See *Pemberton v. Lockett*, 62 U.S. 257 (1859); *Union Bank of Louisiana v. Stafford et al.*, 53 U.S. 327 (1852); *Fowler v. Merrill*, 52 U.S. 375 (1851); *McClanahan v. Davis et al.*, 49 U.S. 170 (1850); *Truely v. Wanzer*, 46 U.S. 141 (1847); *Ventress v. Smith*, 35 U.S. 161 (1836); *Hogan v. Foison*, 35 U.S. 160 (1836).

9. *Bennett et al. v. Butterworth et al.*, 53 U.S. 367, 369–70 (1852).

10. Taney, MS-NSA I, 2–5 (quotations on back of 3); Taney, MS-NSA II, 1; *Groves v. Slaughter*, 40 U.S. 449, 508 (1841).

11. *Prigg*, 626. For Daniel and Thompson, see *Prigg*, 633–36, 650–58. On fugitive slaves and personal liberty law, see *U.S. Statutes at Large*, 1 (1793): 302–5; Morris, *Free Men All*, 19–22, 42–58, 71–93; Leslie, "Pennsylvania Fugitive Slave Act."

12. *Prigg*, 613, 623. There is some scholarly disagreement concerning exactly what *Prigg* held, although the debate is not relevant to the discussion presented here. See Wiecek, "Slavery and Abolition," 45; Burke, "What Did the Prigg Decision Really Decide?"; Finkelman, "Story Telling," 252–55; Fehrenbacher, *Dred Scott Case*, 43–45; Fehrenbacher, *Slaveholding Republic*, 219–20.

13. *Prigg*, 622; Joseph Story to John McPherson Berrien, Cambridge, Mass., April 29, 1842, in McClellen, *Joseph Story*, 262 n.294. William W. Story's *Life and Letters*, 2:381–98, remains the best presentation of the "triumph of freedom" thesis. For historians' criticism, see, e.g., Wiecek, "Slavery and Abolition," 46–47; Holden-Smith, "Lords"; Newmyer, *Supreme Court Justice*, 370–78.

14. *Prigg v. Pennsylvania*, Story Manuscript (U.S. Sup. Ct., 1842), OAC #2181.

15. *Prigg*, 611; *Somerset v. Stewart*, 1 Lofft 1 (K.B., 1772). On *Somerset*, see Wiecek, *Sources*; Davis, *Problem*, 469–552.

16. William W. Story, *Life and Letters*, 1:335–69, 332, 381–98; Newmyer, *Supreme Court Justice*, 345–58; Cover, *Justice Accused*, 238–43; Finkelman, "Story Telling," 292–93. But see Holden-Smith, "Lords," 1090–1116.

17. Alan Watson, *Joseph Story*, 67–70.

18. *Prigg*, 41 U.S. 613, 617 (Story), 626 (Taney); Blackstone, *Commentaries*, 3:4.

19. *Prigg*, 670–73. On Story's relation to the court, see Newmyer, *Supreme Court Justice*, 220–36, 308–16.

20. On Story's concessions, see, e.g., Holden-Smith, "Lords," 1128–34; Fehrenbacher, *Dred Scott Case*, 43.

21. *Prigg*, 625 (quotation), 643, 661–64; *Mayor of New York v. Miln*, 36 U.S. 102, 153–61 (1837). On *Prigg*'s use in the North, see Finkelman, "*Prigg v. Pennsylvania*"; Morris, *Free Men All*, 107–47.

22. *Moore v. Illinois*, 55 U.S. 13 (1852).

23. *The License Cases*, 46 U.S. 504, 589 (1847). For a discussion of these laws in a wider context, see Novak, *People's Welfare*, 171–89.

24. *License Cases*, 588–89.

25. Ibid., 578–86 (Taney), 607–9 (Catron), 611–18 (Daniel), 624 (Woodbury).

26. Ibid., 545–46, 605–8. The assumption that the fragmentation in the *License Cases* had something to do with slavery strikes me as unfounded. For arguments accepting that assumption, see Novak, *People's Welfare*, 176–77, 324 n.154; Hyman and Wiecek, *Equal Justice*, 24, 80–81.

27. *The Passenger Cases*, 48 U.S. 283 (1849). To be specific, the justices gave their opinions in the apprehensive period between John C. Calhoun's failed effort to unify southern members of Congress and Zachary Taylor's inauguration as U.S. president. See Docket of the Supreme Court of the United States, E:2454, 2527, Supreme Court Records; Potter, *Impending Crisis*, 82–89.

28. *Passenger Cases*, 467.

29. Ibid., 466–68 (quotation on 466); *Prigg*, 625; *Groves*, 508–10. See also *Passenger Cases*, 518 (Nelson).

30. *Passenger Cases*, 474 (quotation), 482–83 (Taney), 508–9 (Daniel), 525–30, 542–43, 550 (Woodbury).

31. Ibid., 393–404 (McLean), 411–24 (Wayne), 438–42, 464 (Catron), 452 (McKinley), 455–64 (Grier, quotation on 461).

32. Ibid., 400, 406 (McLean), 425–29 (Wayne), 457 (Grier).

33. Ibid., 393–409 (McLean), 410–11, 415–37 (Wayne), 446–47 (Catron), 462 (Grier quotation), 471–74 (Taney), 496–511 (Daniel), 520–72 (Woodbury); *Miln*, 143–53.

34. Warren, *Supreme Court*, 2:178–82; *Charleston Mercury*, February 14, 1849, quoted in Swisher, *Taney Period*, 393; Campbell, *Rights*, 29.

35. *Passenger Cases*, 283, 430–36 (Grier), 487–90 (Taney) (1849); Peter V. Daniel to Elizabeth Randolph Daniel, Washington, D.C., March 3, 1849, Daniel Papers.

36. Genovese, *Slaveholders' Dilemma*.

37. *Strader v. Graham*, 7 B. Monroe 635 (Ky., 1844); *Graham v. Strader and Gorman*, 5 B. Monroe 173 (Ky., 1844); *The Slave, Grace*, 2 Haggard Admiralty 94 (1827).

38. *Strader v. Graham*, 51 U.S. 82, 93 (1851).

39. Birney, *Examination*, 17–21; Wiecek, "Slavery and Abolition," 53–54; Finkelman, *Imperfect Union*, 271–74; Fehrenbacher, *Dred Scott Case*, 234, 260–62.

40. *Strader*, 94–97; Docket of the Supreme Court of the United States, F:2817, Supreme Court Records.

41. Benjamin Robbins Curtis to George Ticknor Curtis, Washington, D.C., February 29, 1852, Curtis Papers; *Cooley v. Board of Wardens of the Port of Philadelphia*, 53 U.S. 299 (1852); Swisher, *Taney Period*, 406. For the subsequent importance of *Cooley*, see Tribe, *American Constitutional Law*, 324; Currie, *Constitution*, 230–34.

42. *Moore*, 18 (Grier), 22 (McLean); *Eells v. The People*, 4 Scammon 498 (Ill., 1843).

43. *Moore*, 19.

44. *United States v. Richie*, 58 U.S. 525 (1855).

CHAPTER FIVE. The Limits of Judicial Partisanship

1. *Dodge v. Woolsey*, 59 U.S. 331, 373 (1856).

2. On the administrative functions of courts, see Hurst, *Law and Economic Growth*; Skowronek, *Building*.

3. *Fletcher v. Peck*, 10 U.S. 87, 130–31 (quotation on 130); U.S. Constitution, art. I, sec. 10, cl. 1. On the background of *Fletcher*, see Magrath, *Yazoo*.

4. *Fletcher*, 137; Blackstone, *Commentaries*, 2:440; Palmer, "Obligations," 654–63.

5. *Trustees of Dartmouth College v. Woodward,* 17 U.S. 518, 628 (Marshall), 684, 708 (Story) (1819). On the case's background, see Shirley, *Dartmouth College Causes;* Baxter, *Daniel Webster;* Stites, *Private Interest.* See also Hartog, *Public Property,* 192–96.

6. Hurst, *Legitimacy,* 37–41; Kutler, *Privilege,* 67–68; Horwitz, *Transformation,* 111–39.

7. White, *Marshall Court,* 703–40.

8. *Dartmouth College,* 648, 650. Ronald Story, *Forging,* 34, 47–48, 56–57, 64–67, 117–18, 148–49; Newmyer, *Supreme Court Justice Joseph Story,* 237–70; Newmyer, "Harvard Law School."

9. *Proprietors of Charles River Bridge v. Proprietors of Warren Bridge,* 36 U.S. 420 (1837). On the background of the case, see Kutler, *Privilege,* 1–82.

10. For the classic statements, see Kutler, *Privilege,* 3–5; Horwitz, *Transformation,* 130–39.

11. *Charles River Bridge,* 548.

12. Ibid., 544–48 (quotations on 544 and 546).

13. Ibid., 551, 552, 553–82.

14. Ibid., 584–650 (quotation on 608).

15. Ibid., 602, 643–44 (quotation on 643).

16. Joseph Story to John McLean, Cambridge, Mass., May 10, 1837, McLean Papers.

17. *Charles River Bridge,* 552–53.

18. For other cases, see, e.g., *Richmond, Fredericksburg, and Potomac Railroad Company v. Louisa Railroad Company,* 54 U.S. 71 (1852); *Perrine v. Chesapeake and Delaware Canal Company,* 50 U.S. 172 (1850); *Philadelphia, Wilmington, and Baltimore Railroad Company v. Maryland,* 51 U.S. 376, 393–95 (1851); *Mayor, Recorder, Aldermen, and Common Council of Georgetown v. Alexandria Canal Company,* 37 U.S. 91 (1838).

19. *Sturges v. Crowninshield,* 17 U.S. 122 (1819). States, however, retained the power to pass legislation affecting the obligations of contracts made in the future as well as that touching the remedies surrounding a particular obligation.

20. *Bronson v. Kinzie et al.,* 42 U.S. 311, 320–21 (1843).

21. *Woodruff v. Trapnall,* 51 U.S. 190 (1851). For unsuccessful attempts, see *Butler et al. v. Pennsylvania,* 51 U.S. 402 (1851); *Baltimore and Susquehanna Railroad Company v. Nesbit,* 51 U.S. 395 (1851); *Trigg et al. v. Drew,* 51 U.S. 224 (1851); *Paup et al. v. Drew,* 51 U.S. 218 (1851); *Phalen v. Virginia,* 49 U.S. 163 (1850); *Maryland v. Baltimore and Ohio Railroad Company,* 44 U.S. 534 (1845); *Armstrong v. Treasurer of Athens County,* 41 U.S. 281 (1842).

22. *Gordon v. Tax Appeal Court,* 44 U.S. 133 (1845); *Planters' Bank of Mississippi v. Sharp et al.,* 47 U.S. 301 (1848).

23. See *Woodruff,* 209–18; *Planters' Bank,* 334–43; *Bronson,* 322–32.

24. *West River Bridge v. Dix,* 47 U.S. 507, 531–32 (1848).

25. *Dodge,* 331; *Ohio Life Insurance and Trust Company v. Debolt,* 57 U.S. 416 (1854); *Piqua Branch of the State Bank of Ohio v. Knoop,* 57 U.S. 369 (1854). On the politics behind these laws, see Maizlish, *Triumph,* 40–52, 163–65.

26. *Knoop,* 389–90.

27. *Dodge,* 360, 348.

28. *Debolt,* 428, 429.

29. *Ohio Life Insurance and Trust Company v. Debolt,* Taney's Manuscript Opinion (U.S. Sup. Ct., 1853), in OAC #3086; *Debolt,* 427, 431–33.

30. *Debolt,* 443.

31. *Dodge,* 370–78; *Knoop,* 394–404.

32. *Dodge,* 380; *Debolt,* 442, 443; *Knoop,* 400–401, 405–15.

33. *Ohio Life Insurance and Trust Company v. Debolt*, Catron's Manuscript Opinion (U.S. Sup. Ct., 1853), OAC #3086; *Debolt*, 442.

34. *Dodge*, 346–47, 364–69; Swisher, *Taney Period*, 479. On corporate litigants, see Freyer, *Forums*; Rogers M. Smith, *Civic Ideals*, 220–25.

35. This argument conflicts with the usual interpretation. See, for example, Rogers M. Smith, *Civic Ideals*, 224–25; Saunders, *John Archibald Campbell*, 114–20. Swisher noted that the anticorporate commitment did not run too deep, but he made no effort to explore the factors underlying Catron and Campbell's arguments. See Swisher, *Taney Period*, 482.

CHAPTER SIX. The Sources of Southern Factionalism

1. Swisher, *Taney Period*, 393; *Strader v. Graham*, 51 U.S. 82, 93 (1851); Birney, *Examination*, 16.

2. *Dodge v. Woolsey*, 59 U.S. 331, 365 (1856).

3. *Houston v. Moore*, 18 U.S. 1, 33 (1820); *United States v. Worrall*, 28 F. Cas. 774 (U.S. Cir. Ct., Pa. Dist., 1798).

4. *Martin v. Commonwealth*, 1 Mass. 347 (1805); Kerber, "Women's Citizenship"; Rogers M. Smith, *Civil Ideals*, 165–253; Palmer, "Liberties," 55–148.

5. Publius [Hamilton], *Federalist* 79, 473–81; Madison, *Notes*, 500. See also Palmer, "Liberties," esp. 62–67, 82–97, 105–17, 131–38, 146–48.

6. Publius [Hamilton], *Federalist* 80, 447; U.S. Constitution, art. IV, sec. 2, cl. 1; Michael Kent Curtis, "Historical Linguistics"; Wiecek, *Sources*, 268–69. See also *Douglass v. Stephens*, 1 Del. Ch. Rep. 465 (1821).

7. *Corfield v. Coryell*, 6 F. Cas. 546, 551–52 (U.S. Cir. Ct., Dist. Pa., 1823). For the influence of this case on the Taney Court, see *Conner v. Elliot*, 59 U.S. 591 (1856); *Smith v. Maryland*, 59 U.S. 71 (1855).

8. Wiecek, *Sources*, 122–23; U.S. House Committee, *Free Colored Seamen*; Taney, MS-NSA I; Taney, MS-NSA II; *Strader v. Graham*, 51 U.S. 82 (1850); *The Passenger Cases*, 48 U.S. 283 (1849); *Prigg v. Pennsylvania*, 41 U.S. 539 (1842).

9. Roswell M. Field to Montgomery Blair [typescript], St. Louis, January 7, 1855, Dred Scott Collection, Missouri Historical Society, St. Louis.

10. U.S. Constitution, art. IV, sec. 2, cl. 1; U.S. House Committee, *Free Colored Seamen*; *Louisville, Cincinnati, and Charleston Railroad Company v. Letson*, 43 U.S. 497 (1844).

11. There was no shortage of cases noting citizens' dual allegiance. See, e.g., *Buckner v. Finley*, 27 U.S. 586 (1829); *Houston*, 1; *Commonwealth v. Aves*, 35 Mass. 193 (1836); *Abbot v. Bayley*, 23 Mass. 89 (1827). On abolitionists, see Wiecek, *Sources*, 163–67.

12. Kettner, *Development*, 248–49, 264–65; Rogers Smith, *Civic Ideals*, 149–52, 202–3.

13. *Dred Scott v. Sandford*, 60 U.S. 393, 406–7, 572 (1857); Wilson, "Of Citizens and Aliens," 2:573. See also Justice Stephen J. Field's discussion of citizenship in the *Slaughter-House Cases*, 83 U.S. 36, 94–95 (1873).

14. *Reily v. Lamar*, 6 U.S. 344 (1805). See also *Hepburn v. Ellzey*, 6 U.S. 445, 453 (1805); U.S. Constitution, art. I, sec. 8, cl. 17.

15. *American and Ocean Insurance Companies v. Canter*, 26 U.S. 511, 542 (1828); United States and Spain, "Treaty of Amity, Settlement, and Limits [1819]," art. 6, in Bevans, *Treaties*, 11:528–36. For other treaties with similar language, see United States and Mexico, "Treaty of Cession [1853]," art. V, in Bevans, *Treaties*, 9:812–16; United States and Mexico, "Treaty of Peace [1848]," art. IX, in Bevans, *Treaties*, 9:791–806; United States and France,

"Treaty of Cession [1803]," art. III, in Bevans, *Treaties*, 7:818–21; *U.S. Statutes at Large*, 3 (1822): 654–59, secs. 6–10.

16. *Canter*, 542.

17. United States and Spain, "Treaty of Amity, Settlement, and Limits [1819]," art. 6; U.S. Constitution, art. VI, cl. 1; Benjamin Butler to John Forsyth, September 21, 1835 (citing U.S. Const., amend. I), Opinions on Legal Questions, General Records of the Attorney Generals, Records of the Department of Justice (RG 60), National Archives, College Park, Md. See also *Delassus v. United States*, 34 U.S. 117 (1835); *United States v. Laverty*, 3 Martin's Rep. (O.S.) 733 (La., 1813); *Debois's Case*, 2 Martin (O.S.) 185 (La., 1812).

18. At first glance, the federal government's ability to naturalize aliens conflicted with this formulation, but court doctrine held that naturalized citizens simultaneously became citizens of the state in which they resided and of the United States. See *Gassies v. Ballon*, 31 U.S. 761 (1832).

19. U.S. Constitution, art. IV, sec. 2, cl. 1.

20. *Bank of United States v. Deveaux*, 9 U.S. 61, 86 (1809).

21. *Bank of Augusta v. Earle*, 38 U.S. 519, 586 (1839). See also *Irvine v. Lowry*, 39 U.S. 293 (1840); *Commercial and Railroad Bank of Vicksburg v. Slocomb, Richards, and Company*, 39 U.S. 595 (1840).

22. *Letson*, 556, 555, 558; *U.S. Statutes at Large*, 5 (1839): 321–23.

23. *Rundle et al. v. Delaware and Raritan Canal Company*, 55 U.S. 80, 101–2 (1853).

24. *Northern Indiana Railroad Company et al. v. Michigan Central Railroad Company*, 56 U.S. 233, 248–49 (1854).

25. *Marshall v. Baltimore and Ohio Railroad Company*, 57 U.S. 314, 325, 329 (1854); Swisher, *Taney Period*, 468.

26. *Marshall*, 344, 347, 353.

27. Ibid., 345 (Daniel); *Northern Indiana R.R. Co.*, 251 (Catron); *Rundle*, 101 (Daniel).

28. *Rundle*, 101.

29. *Marshall*, 353.

PART THREE. Inescapable Opportunity

1. Buchanan, "Inaugural Address." The best overview of the events discussed in this paragraph remains Potter, *Impending Crisis*, 145–265.

2. Kentucky Lawyer, *Review*, 43–44.

3. Benton, *Historical and Legal Examination*, 5.

4. Gray and Lowell, *Legal Review*, 9.

5. Kentucky Lawyer, *Review*, 43, 44.

6. Foot, *Examination*, 18.

7. *Case of Dred Scott*, 103.

8. Potter, *Impending Crisis*, 172.

9. *Case of Dred Scott*, 103.

10. *Congressional Globe*, 35th Cong., 1st sess., 941.

11. Johannsen, *Lincoln-Douglas Debates*, 18.

12. Potter, *Impending Crisis*, 145.

CHAPTER SEVEN. The Failure of Evasion

1. Gray and Lowell, *Legal Review*, 52.

2. *Strader v. Graham*, 51 U.S. 82 (1851).

3. "The Dred Scott Case," *North American Review* 85, no. 177 (1857): 409.

4. Ibid., 414.

5. *Dred Scott v. Emerson*, 15 Mo. 576 (1852).

6. *Dred Scott v. Irene Emerson*, Deposition of Miles H. Clarke [typescript copy]; *Harriet Scott, a Woman of Color, v. Irene Emerson*, Summons [typescript copy]; *Dred Scott v. Irene Emerson*, Deposition for Catherine A. Anderson [typescript copy], all in Dred Scott Collection, Missouri Historical Society, St. Louis. See also VanderVelde and Subramanian, "Mrs. Dred Scott," 1040–59.

7. The information regarding Emerson's whereabouts during this period rests on the following sources: John Emerson to Thomas Lawson, Fort Snelling, October 8, 1837, October 22, 1838, Fort Jesop, July 10, 1838, Medical Officers' Files (container 180, John Emerson—Letters and Reports, 1833–43), Records of the Adjutant General's Office (RG 94), National Archives and Records Administration, Washington, D.C.; post returns for Fort Snelling, October 1838–May 1840, Fort Lauderdale, November 1840–January 1842, Fort Pickens, March–May 1842, Fort Pike, September 1842, *Returns from United States Military Posts, 1800–1916* (Washington, D.C.: National Archives Microfilm Publications [M 617], 1965); *H. Scott v. Emerson*, Summons; *D. Scott v. Emerson*, Anderson Deposition; Ehrlich, *They Have No Rights*, 22.

8. *Winny v. Whitesides*, 1 Mo. 472 (1824); Finkelman, "Evading the Ordinance"; *Rachael, a Woman of Color, v. Walker*, 4 Mo. 350 (1836); Illinois Constitution (1818), sec. 6; *Vincent (a Man of Color) v. Duncan*, 2 Mo. 214 (1830); *Ralph v. Duncan*, 3 Mo. 194 (1833); *Hay v. Dunky*, 3 Mo. 588 (1834).

9. VanderVelde and Subramanian, "Mrs. Dred Scott," 1060–78; *Rachael*, 350; Allen, "Containing Slavery," 281–91.

10. See Tompkins's statement in *Marguerite v. Chouteau*, 2 Mo. 71, 90 (1828). For differing interpretations, see Fehrenbacher, *Dred Scott Case*, 262; Finkelman, *Imperfect Union*, 217–28.

11. *Ewing v. Thompson*, 13 Mo. 132 (1850); *Wade v. Scott*, 7 Mo. 509 (1842); *Rennick v. Chloe*, 7 Mo. 197 (1841); *Russell v. Taylor*, 4 Mo. 550 (1837); Missouri General Assembly, *Act*; Moore, *Missouri Controversy*, 272–73.

12. *La Grange v. Chouteau*, 2 Mo. 20, 22 (1828); *Julia (a Woman of Color) v. McKinny*, 3 Mo. 270, 275–76 (1833); *Rachael*, 350. See also Allen, "Containing Slavery," 291–304.

13. Finkelman, *Imperfect Union*, 149–55, 165–78; *Eaton v. Vaughn*, 9 Mo. 743, 744–46, 748 (1846); Fehrenbacher, *Dred Scott Case*, 258–60. See also Allen, "Containing Slavery," 304–13.

14. *Emerson*, 582, 584, 586.

15. Finkelman, *Imperfect Union*, 181–235.

16. *Strader*, 94.

17. Dean, "Reassessing *Dred Scott*," 720, 728–29.

18. *Dred Scott v. Sanford*, manuscript record [photocopy] (U.S. Supreme Court, filed December 30, 1854), 11, Appellate Case Files #3230, Supreme Court Records; Ehrlich, "Was the Dred Scott Case Valid?"; Fehrenbacher, *Dred Scott Case*, 276–80; Ehrlich, *They Have No Rights*, 74–81; Kaufman, *Dred Scott's Advocate*.

19. *Dred Scott v. Sanford*, 13 American State Trials 242 (U.S. Cir. Ct., Mo. Dist., 1854); Roswell M. Field to Montgomery Blair [typescript], St. Louis, January 7, 1855, Dred Scott Collection; Ehrlich, *They Have No Rights*, 87–88; Fehrenbacher, *Dred Scott Case*, 276–80.

20. Blair, Plaintiff's Brief I, 2–11; Fehrenbacher, *Dred Scott Case*, 288–302.

21. *Dred Scott v. Sandford*, Order for Reargument [photostat copy] (U.S. Sup. Ct., May 12, 1856), Appellate Case Files #3230, Supreme Court Records.

22. Ibid.; John A. Campbell to Samuel Tyler, New Orleans, November 24, 1870, in Tyler, *Memoir*, 382–84; Campbell to George Ticknor Curtis, Baltimore, October 30, 1879 [typescript copy], Campbell Family Papers, Southern Historical Collection, University of North Carolina, Chapel Hill (the quotations come from this document). For a different account of the division, see John Catron to Samuel Treat, Nashville, May 31, 1857, Samuel Treat Papers, Missouri Historical Society, St. Louis.

23. *Dred Scott v. Sandford*, 60 U.S. 393 (1856). For Catron and McLean's arguments, see *Dred Scott*, 518–19, 529–31. For Taney and Curtis's arguments, see *Dred Scott*, 400–403, 564–67.

24. *Dred Scott v. Sanford*, Case for the Defendant in Error (U.S. Sup. Ct., December Term, 1856), Records and Briefs, U.S. Supreme Court Library, Washington, D.C. (file copies of briefs, 1856, vol. 1851); Blair, Plaintiff's Brief II, 17–18.

25. *Dred Scott*, 458.

26. Ibid., 459; *Strader*, 93–94.

27. *Dred Scott*, 464.

28. Ibid.; Fehrenbacher, *Dred Scott Case*, 390–94.

29. John A. Campbell to Samuel Tyler, New Orleans, November 24, 1870, in Tyler, *Memoir*, 384; John Catron to James Buchanan, Washington, D.C., February 19, 1857, Robert C. Grier to Buchanan, Washington, D.C., February 23, 1857, in Buchanan, *Works*, 106–8.

30. For studies that emphasize, although generally for the wrong reasons, the dissenters' role in expanding the decision, see Warren, *Supreme Court*, 2:293; Hodder, "Some Phases"; Schwartz, *From Confederation to Nation*, 118–19; White, *American Judicial Tradition*, 78–79. For studies placing blame on the southern justices (and not without reason), see Nevins, *Emergence*, 2:473–77; Fehrenbacher, *Dred Scott Case*, 311.

31. Potter, *Impending Crisis*, 270–75; Fehrenbacher, *Dred Scott Case*, 293, 305–14; Mendelson, "Dred Scott's Case—Reconsidered"; Graber, "Nonmajoritarian Difficulty," 46–50.

32. Johnston and Brown, *Life*, 316, 318; John Catron to James Buchanan, Washington, D.C., February 19, 1857, in Buchanan, *Works*, 106–8; *New York Tribune*, February 15, 20, 26, 29, April 19, 10, 11, 12, May 14, 1856.

33. John A. Campbell to Samuel Tyler, New Orleans, November 24, 1870, in Tyler, *Memoir*, 384.

34. *Dred Scott*, 465.

35. Nelson cited *Hay*, 588; *Julia*, 270; *Wilson, a Colored Man, v. Melvin*, 4 Mo. 592 (1837); *Theoteste v. Chouteau*, 2 Mo. 144 (1829); *Merry v. Tiffin*, 1 Mo. 725 (1827); *Winny*, 472. On the law in the southern border states, see *Collins v. America (a Woman of Color)*, 9 B. Monroe 565 (Ky., 1849); *Graham v. Strader*, 5 B. Monroe 173 (Ky., 1844); *Rankin v. Lydia (a Pauper)*, 9 Ky. 467 (1820); *Foster v. Fosters*, 51 Va. 485 (1853); *Mahoney v. Ashton*, 4 Harris and McHenry, 295 (Md., 1799); *Hunter v. Fulcher*, 28 Va. 172 (1829); *Lewis v. Fullerson*, 1 Randolph, 15 (Va., 1821).

36. *Dred Scott*, 466; *Rachael*, 350. See also *Vincent*, 214.

37. *Swift v. Tyson*, 41 U.S. (16 Peters) 1, 18 (1842).

38. Blair, Plaintiff's Brief II, 17–18 (quotations on 18). Only two scholars have noted *Swift*'s importance for *Dred Scott*. See Dean, "Reassessing *Dred Scott*," 734–47; Streichler, "Justice Curtis's Dissent," 512–28.

39. *Burke v. McKay*, 43 U.S. 66, 71 (1844); *Carpenter v. Providence Washington Insurance Company*, 41 U.S. 495, 511 (1842).

40. *Musson et al. v. Lake*, 45 U.S. 262, 276 (1846).

41. *Withers v. Greene*, 50 U.S. 213, 221 (1850).

42. *Lane et al. v. Vick et al.*, 44 U.S. 464, 476, 481–83 (1845).

43. *Rowan et al. v. Runnels*, 46 U.S. 134 (1847); *Groves et al. v. Slaughter*, 40 U.S. 449 (1841). See also *Hardeman et al. v. Harris*, 48 U.S. 726 (1849); *Nesmith et al. v. Sheldon et al.*, 48 U.S. 812, esp. 818 (1849).

44. *Pease v. Peck*, 59 U.S. 595, 596 (1856); Swisher, *Taney Period*, 611.

45. *Pease*, 598–601 (quotations on 598).

46. *Watson v. Tarply*, 59 U.S. 517, 519 (1856).

47. Ibid., 521 (quoting Story in *Swift*, 19).

48. *Dred Scott*, 556; *Emerson*, 586. See also Blair, Plaintiff's Brief II, 17–18.

49. *Dred Scott*, 563 (quoting *Pease*, 599). See also Dean, "Reassessing *Dred Scott*," 734–36; Streichler, "Justice Curtis's Dissent," 512–28.

50. *Dred Scott*, 469 (Grier, concurring); *Pease*, 595.

51. *Dred Scott*, 599–601.

52. Ibid., 519, 453–54, 456, 469, 483–87, 494–519.

CHAPTER EIGHT. The Political Economy of Blackness

1. *Dred Scott v. Sandford*, 60 U.S. 393, 407 (1857); Higginbotham, *Shades of Freedom*, 65; *Congressional Globe*, 36th Cong., 1st sess., 292; Douglass, "Dred Scott Decision," 31, 43; John Appleton to Benjamin Robbins Curtis, Washington, D.C., March 15, 1857, Curtis Papers.

2. Scholars divide over whether Taney ruled correctly on the law. Cf. Potter, *Impending Crisis*, 275–79; Fehrenbacher, *Dred Scott Case*, 276–77, 341–46; Marshall, "Reflections"; Diamond, "No Call to Glory."

Scholars, however, agree overwhelmingly that Taney's historical analysis was flatly incorrect. I have found only two exceptions; both grant the plausibility of Taney's account for the purposes of arguing about legal theory. See Levinson, "Slavery"; Graber, "Desperately Ducking Slavery."

3. For an account of the fallout, see Fehrenbacher, *Dred Scott Case*, 316–21; epilogue to this volume.

4. Fehrenbacher, *Dred Scott Case*, 320. For an opposing view, see Ehrlich, *They Have No Rights*, 144–45.

5. *Prigg v. Pennsylvania*, 41 U.S. 539 (1842); *The Passenger Cases*, 48 U.S. 283, 461 (Grier) (1849); *Brewer's Lessee v. Blougher*, 39 U.S. 178, 183–84 (1840).

6. Taney, MS-NSA I, 4–5; *United States v. Rogers*, 45 U.S. 567, 573 (1846); *United States v. Richie*, 58 U.S. 525 (1855).

7. Rogers M. Smith, *Civic Ideals*, 263–71; Finkelman, "Dred Scott Case"; Fehrenbacher, *Dred Scott Case*, 340–64.

8. Taney, Dred Scott Proofs I, 4, 18–19; Taney, Dred Scott Proofs II, 4. See also *Dred Scott*, 403–4, 422–23.

9. Roger B. Taney to William Carroll, Washington, D.C., April 6, 1857, Official Correspondence: Letters to and from the Justices, Clerk's Files, Supreme Court Records; Taney to Benjamin Robbins Curtis, Baltimore, April 25, 1857, Curtis Papers.

10. Kettner, *Development*, 173–209. See also Rogers M. Smith, *Civic Ideals*, 40–114.

11. *Dred Scott*, 476. Cf. his statement on corporate citizenship: *Rundle et al. v. Delaware and Raritan Canal Company*, 55 U.S. 80, 101 (1853).

12. *Dred Scott*, 477.

13. *Moore v. Illinois*, 55 U.S. 13 (1852); Indiana Constitution (1851), art. XIII, in Thorpe, *Federal and State Constitutions*, 2:1073–95; *Hatwood v. State*, 18 Ind. 492 (1862).

14. *Bryan v. Walton*, 14 Ga. 185 (1853); *Cooper v. Savannah*, 4 Ga. 68 (1848).

15. *Roberts v. Boston*, 59 Mass. 198 (1849); *State v. Jowers*, 33 N.C. 555 (1850); *State v. Harrison*, 11 La. Annual 772 (1856); *Hughes v. Jackson*, 12 Md. Reports 450 (1858); *State v. Manuel*, 20 N.C. 144 (1838); *State v. Edmund*, 15 N.C. 340 (1838); *Hobbs v. Fogg*, 6 Watts 553 (Penn., 1837).

16. Thus, one sentence in Taney's proof sheets initially read, "It does not follow, because he is a citizen of a State, that he must also be a citizen of the United States." Taney edited it so that it read, "It does not follow, *because he has all the rights and privileges of a citizen of a State*, that he must be a citizen of the United States" (Taney, Dred Scott Proofs I, 5).

17. Federal law did recognize some limitations on this power in the case of immigrants. States could not repel healthy immigrants or deny citizenship to naturalized immigrants. See *Passenger Cases*, 283; *Gassies v. Ballon*, 31 U.S. 761 (1832). States could expel people considered likely to become paupers or vagabonds—i.e., elderly and sickly immigrants and all free blacks. See *Moore*, 13; *Mayor, Aldermen, and Commonalty of New York v. Miln*, 36 U.S. 102 (1837).

18. Taney, Dred Scott Proofs I, 5–6 (quotations on 6); U.S. Constitution, art. I, sec. 8, cl. 4; Kettner, *Development*, 214–47; Cushing, "Relation," 7:749.

19. Roger B. Taney to Benjamin Robbins Curtis, Baltimore, June 11, 1857, Curtis Papers.

20. Taney, Dred Scott Proofs I, 7, 14 (emphasis added).

21. *Marshall v. Baltimore and Ohio Railroad Company*, 57 U.S. 314, 353 (1854).

22. *Dred Scott*, 575–76; Taney, Dred Scott Proofs I, 15.

23. The quotation comes from one of several handwritten pages that Taney attached to his first set of proofs, although Taney later crossed it out (Taney, Dred Scott Proofs I, first handwritten page following printed p. 38; Taney, Dred Scott Proofs II, 43; see also *Dred Scott*, 453–54).

24. Taney, Dred Scott Proofs I, 14.

25. U.S. Commerce Committee, *Free Colored Seamen*, 7–8; Swisher, *Taney Period*, 238–40, 628; Maltz, "Unlikely Hero."

26. *Dred Scott*, 574–75; Foner, *Free Soil*, 73–102; Wiecek, *Sources*, 202–27; Wood, "Equality and Social Conflict."

27. *Dred Scott*, 569–70.

28. Ibid., 571; *Gassies*, 762.

29. *Dred Scott*, 571.

30. Undated, handwritten document in Curtis Papers. For more on this issue, see the epilogue.

31. *Dred Scott*, 572–83; *Manuel*, 144.

32. *United States v. Anthony*, 24 F. Cas. 829, 830 (1873); *Dred Scott*, 422.

33. *Dred Scott*, 575–76; Articles of Confederation, art. IV, in Thorpe, *Federal and State Constitutions*, 1:9–17.

34. *Dred Scott*, 576.

35. Streichler, "Justice Curtis's Dissent," 512–28.

36. U.S. Constitution, art. II, sec. 1, cl. 5.

37. *Dred Scott*, 576–77. As evidence of that principle, Curtis cited *McIlvaine v. Coxe's Lessee*, 8 U.S. 209 (1808); *Inglis v. Trustees of the Sailor's Snug Harbour*, 28 U.S. 99 (1830).

38. *Dred Scott*, 576–77; U.S. Constitution, art. II, sec. 1, cl. 5. I am greatly indebted to Bob Palmer for this observation.

39. *Dred Scott*, 580–83 (quotations on 582, 583).

40. This paragraph constitutes what I regard as the implications of Curtis's argument in *Dred Scott*, 583–84.

41. *Dred Scott*, 518–19; John Catron to Samuel Treat, Nashville, May 31, 1857, Samuel Treat Papers, Missouri Historical Society, St. Louis.

42. *Dred Scott*, 455. In his proofs, Campbell crossed out a passage stating that he agreed with Catron. See *Dred Scott v. Sandford*, Campbell page proofs, Appellate Case Files #3230, Supreme Court Records.

CHAPTER NINE. Looking Westward

1. Parker, *Personal Liberty Laws*, 58; *Dred Scott v. Sandford*, 60 U.S. 393, 620–21 (1856); Benton, *Historical and Legal Examination*, 5.

2. *Dred Scott*, 590; Potter, *Impending Crisis*, 279–84.

3. *Wickliffe v. Owings*, 58 U.S. 47, 51–52 (1855); *Sheppard v. Graves*, 55 U.S. 505, 510 (1853) (incorrectly cited as 14 How. 27); *Livingston's Executors v. Story*, 36 U.S. 351, 393 (1837); *De Wole v. Rabaud et al.*, 26 U.S. 476, 498 (1828).

4. Taney, Dred Scott Proofs I, 23–24, and accompanying handwritten pages; Roger B. Taney to Benjamin Robbins Curtis, Baltimore, April 25, 1857, Curtis Papers.

5. *Dred Scott*, 427–28.

6. Ibid., 428, 429; Roger B. Taney to Benjamin Robbins Curtis, Baltimore, June 11, 1857, Curtis Papers. See also *Bradstreet v. Potter*, 41 U.S. 317 (1842); *United States v. Stone*, 39 U.S. 524 (1840); *Commercial and Railroad Bank of Vicksburg v. Slocomb, Richards, and Company*, 39 U.S. 60 (1840).

7. Taney, Dred Scott Proofs I, 24; Corwin, "Dred Scott Decision," 53–59.

8. See Potter, *Impending Crisis*, 279–84; Fehrenbacher, *Dred Scott Case*, 365–66; Ehrlich, *They Have No Rights*, 170–73; Corwin, "Dred Scott Decision," 53–59.

9. U.S. Constitution, art. IV, sec. 3, cl. 1; Benton, *Historical and Legal Examination*, 11–61; Malone, *Opening the West*.

10. *United States v. Gratiot*, 39 U.S. 526, 537 (1840); *McCulloch v. Maryland*, 17 U.S. 316, 422 (1819); *American and Ocean Insurance Companies v. Canter*, 26 U.S. 511, 542 (1828).

11. *Dred Scott v. Sanford*, Case for the Defendant in Error (U.S. Sup. Ct., December Term, 1856), 11–12, Records and Briefs, U.S. Supreme Court Library, Washington, D.C.; Blair, Plaintiff's Brief II.

12. Calhoun, "Speech"; John A. Campbell to John C. Calhoun, n.p., March 1, 1848, in McCormac, "Justice Campbell," 570.

13. *Pollard et al. v. Hagan et al.*, 44 U.S. 212, 221–23 (1845) (Catron, dissenting); John A. Campbell to John C. Calhoun, n.p., March 1, 1848, in McCormac, "Justice Campbell," 569.

14. Benton, *Historical and Legal Examination*, 11–16, 26–30, 35–37, 61; Baldwin, *General View*.

15. *Flemming and Marshall v. Page*, 50 U.S. 603, 615 (1850); *Cross et al. v. Harrison*, 57 U.S. 164, 193–94 (1854).

16. *Webster v. Reid*, 52 U.S. 437, 460 (1851).

17. Peter V. Daniel to Martin Van Buren, Richmond, Va., November 19, 1847, in *Papers of Martin Van Buren* (microfilm) (Washington, D.C.: Library of Congress, 1960); McLean, "Has Congress the Power to Institute Slavery?" See also R. Marsh to John McLean, Steubenville, Ohio, May 23, 1856, John Blunt to McLean, New York, May 22, 1856, McLean to Mr. Tennington, Cincinnati, June 6, 1856, McLean to Joseph C. Hornblower, Cincinnati, June 7, 1856, McLean Papers; Saunders, *John Archibald Campbell*, 69–104.

18. *Dred Scott*, 490.

19. Joseph Story, *Commentaries on the Constitution*, 3:193. See also Blair, Plaintiff's Brief II, 27–40; Kent, *Commentaries*, 1:360; Rawle, *View*, 237; Sergeant, *Constitutional Law*, 389; Hammond, " 'They Are Very Much Interested.' "

20. Taney, Dred Scott Proofs I, 32 (quoting U.S. Constitution, art. I, sec. 8, cl. 3, 4, 17).

21. Taney, Dred Scott Proofs I, 26–30 (quotation on 27); U.S. Constitution, art. IV, sec. 3, cl. 2.

22. Taney, Dred Scott Proofs I, 30–32, 33 (quotations on page 28); U.S. Constitution, art. VI, cl. 1.

23. Madison, *Notes*, 385–96, 477.

24. Publius [Madison], *Federalist* 48, 278–81 (quotations on 279, 281). For the one exception in the ratification debates, see Jensen, Kaminski, and Saladino, *Documentary History*, 10:1319–20, 1387–88.

25. Taney, Dred Scott Proofs I, 33.

26. U.S. Constitution, art. IV, sec. 4, cl. 1; Taney, Dred Scott Proofs I, 33.

27. *Flemming*, 614.

28. Taney, Dred Scott Proofs I, 33. In the proof, Taney inserted the word *permanently* after *governed*. See *Dred Scott*, 446.

29. Taney, Dred Scott Proofs I, 34.

30. Ibid., 34–35.

31. Ibid., 36.

32. Hall, *Magic Mirror*, 232; Potter, *Impending Crisis*, 276–77; Fehrenbacher, *Dred Scott Case*, 378–79, 381–84.

33. See Wiecek, *Sources*; Russel, "Constitutional Doctrines."

34. Novak, *People's Welfare*, 171–89; *Wynehamer v. People*, 13 N.Y. 378 (1856).

35. *Bloomer v. McQuewan et al.*, 55 U.S. 539, 554 (1853) (McLean, dissenting; see esp. 557).

36. Taney, Dred Scott Proofs I, 37. Leading commentators on *Dred Scott* have argued that this passage undercut the popular-sovereignty position on the territorial question. See Potter, *Impending Crisis*, 291–92; Fehrenbacher, *Dred Scott Case*, 379. This conclusion is problematic, as the epilogue discusses.

37. *Dred Scott*, 501, 511.

38. *Pollard*, 221–23.

39. *Dred Scott*, 514 (Campbell quotations); Taney, Dred Scott Proofs I, 34.

40. *Dred Scott*, 519–20, 522–23.

41. *Cross*, 193–94; John Catron to Samuel Treat, Nashville, May 31, 1857, Samuel Treat Papers, Missouri Historical Society, St. Louis.

42. United States and France, "Treaty of Cession [1803]," art. III. Congress did initially contemplate such a step; see Hammond, " 'They Are Very Much Interested.' "

43. *Dred Scott*, 557, 629–33.

44. *Canter*, 546, 543; *Dred Scott*, 541.

45. Taney, Dred Scott Proofs I, manuscript pages beginning with p. B following p. 33. For the final version, see *Dred Scott*, 442–46. This discussion uses the final version.

46. *Dred Scott*, 442–44.

47. Ibid., 444–46; *Canter*, 546; *Sere v. Pitot*, 10 U.S. 332, 337 (1810).

48. *Dred Scott*, 608–9, 610.

49. See esp. Madison, *Notes*, 552–59.

50. *Dred Scott*, 611, 613.

51. Ibid., 614, 619, 621.

52. Ibid., 624–27; *Prigg v. Pennsylvania*, 41 U.S. 539 (1842).

53. Taney, Dred Scott Proofs I, 37; *Dred Scott*, 451.

54. *Dred Scott*, 546.

EPILOGUE. United Court, Divided Union

1. Potter, *Impending Crisis*, 280–93; Fehrenbacher, *Dred Scott Case*, 417–567; Morrison, *Slavery and the American West*, 188–96.

2. Benjamin Robbins Curtis to William Carroll, Pittsfield, Mass., April 2, 1857, Carroll to Curtis, Washington, D.C., April 6, 1857, Taney to Carroll, Washington, D.C., April 6, 1857, Official Correspondence: Letters to and from the Justices, Clerk's Files, Supreme Court Records; Carroll to Curtis, Washington, D.C., April 14, 1857, Curtis Papers.

3. Roger B. Taney to Benjamin Robbins Curtis, Baltimore, April 25, 1857, Curtis Papers; C. P. Curtis to William Carroll, Boston, March 16, 1857, Correspondence (1791–1908), Clerk's Files, Supreme Court Records.

4. John A. Campbell to William Carroll, Washington, D.C., March 10, 1857, Official Correspondence: Letters to and from the Justices, Clerk's Files, Supreme Court Records.

5. Roger B. Taney to Benjamin Robbins Curtis, Baltimore, April 25, 1857, Curtis Papers; Curtis to William Carroll, Boston, March 30, 1857, Official Correspondence: Letters to and from the Justices, Clerk's Files, Supreme Court Records (price quoted on back of April 6, 1857, letter).

6. Fehrenbacher, *Dred Scott Case*, 318.

7. Benjamin Robbins Curtis to Roger B. Taney, Pittsfield, Mass., May 13, 1857, Curtis Papers.

8. Roger B. Taney to Benjamin Robbins Curtis, Baltimore, June 11, 1857, Curtis Papers.

9. *Cooley v. Board of Wardens of the Port of Philadelphia*, Curtis's manuscript (U.S. Sup. Ct., December Term, 1851), OAC #2863–64; *Strader v. Graham*, Taney's proofs (U.S. Sup. Ct., 1850), OAC #2671; *Prigg v. Pennsylvania*, Story's manuscript (U.S. Sup. Ct., 1842), OAC #2181.

10. Curtis, *Cooley* Manuscript, 25–26; *Commonwealth Bank of Kentucky v. Griffith*, Taney's Manuscript (U.S. Sup. Ct., 1840), OAC #2095; *Woodruff v. Trapnall*, McLean's page proof (U.S. Sup. Ct., December Term, 1850), 3, 5, OAC #2632.

11. Undated, handwritten document, Curtis Papers.

12. Roger B. Taney to Benjamin Robbins Curtis, Baltimore, June 11, 20, 1857, Curtis to Taney, Pittsfield, Mass., June 16, 1857, Curtis Papers; Swisher, *Taney Period*, 636–37; Fehrenbacher, *Dred Scott Case*, 318–19.

13. Benjamin Robbins Curtis to Roger B. Taney, Pittsfield, Mass., June 16, 1857, Curtis

to Henry B. Rogers, n.p., October 28, 1858, typescript copy of broadside, Samuel Nelson to Curtis, Washington, D.C., November 25, 1860, Curtis to William Whitwell Greenough, Washington, D.C., January 1, 1863, Curtis Papers.

14. George Ticknor Curtis, *Memoir*, 1:254; John A. Campbell to Benjamin Robbins Curtis, Washington, D.C., September 9, 1857, John McLean to Curtis, Portland, Ohio, September 9, 1857, Curtis Papers.

15. *Covington Drawbridge Company v. Shepherd et al.*, 61 U.S. 227, 233–34 (1858).

16. *Zabriskie v. Cleveland, Columbus, and Cincinnati Railroad Company et al.*, 64 U.S. 381 (1860) (Campbell, for court; Daniel, not sitting); *Philadelphia, Wilmington, and Baltimore Railroad Company v. Quigley*, 62 U.S. 202 (1859) (Campbell, for court; Daniel, dissenting); *Covington Drawbridge Company et al. v. Shepherd et al.*, 62 U.S. 112 (1858) (Catron, for court; Daniel, dissenting). See also *Board of Commissioners of the County of Knox v. Aspinwall et al.*, 62 U.S. 539 (1859) (Nelson, for court; Daniel, dissenting); *Winans v. New York and Erie Railroad Company*, 62 U.S. 88 (1859) (Grier, for court; Daniel, dissenting); *Union Insurance Company v. Hoge*, 62 U.S. 35 (1859) (Nelson, for court; Daniel, dissenting).

17. Freyer, *Forums*, 110–12, 119 n.160; Purcell, *Litigation and Inequality*, 28, 59–86.

18. Hyman and Wiecek, *Equal Justice*, 74.

19. *Ableman v. Booth*, 62 U.S. 506 (1859).

20. *Cohens v. Virginia*, 19 U.S. 264 (1821); White, *Marshall Court*, 494–524.

21. *Ableman*, 514–18.

22. *Kentucky v. Dennison*, 65 U.S. 66, 102–8 (1861).

23. Finkelman, *Imperfect Union*, 296–332.

24. *Ableman*, 517.

25. Greenblatt, *Marvelous Possessions*, 6.

26. Cartwright, "Philosophy," 697–99.

27. Elliot, *Cotton Is King*, 691–728, 741–808; Van Evrie, *Dred Scott Decision*, 1857.

28. Ignatiev, *How the Irish Became White*; Jon Gjerde, " 'Here in America,' " 673–90; Kolchin, "Whiteness Studies"; Johannsen, *Lincoln-Douglas Debates*, 127, 128.

29. Johannsen, *Lincoln-Douglas Debates*, 92–93. On the significance of Douglas's racism and its contested nature, see Roediger, "Pursuit of Whiteness," 585–89; Davis, "Culmination," 774–75.

30. Johannsen, *Lincoln-Douglas Debates*, 162, 198; Anthony quoted in Fehrenbacher, *Dred Scott Case*, 430.

31. Potter, *Impending Crisis*, 297–355; Fehrenbacher, *Dred Scott Case*, 485–89.

32. Johannsen, *Lincoln-Douglas Debates*, 14–21, 79, 91, 251.

33. Ibid., 230–31.

34. Jaffa, *Crisis*, 288–91.

35. *The People, ex. rel., Lewis Napoleon, v. Lemmon*, 5 Standford 681 (N.Y., 1852); *Lemmon v. The People*, 26 Barbour 211 (N.Y., 1860); Finkelman, *Imperfect Union*, 296–332.

36. *Commonwealth v. Aves*, 35 Mass. 193, 224–25 (1836).

37. *Dred Scott v. Sandford*, 60 U.S. 393, 468 (1857).

38. Shaw noted that the Fugitive Slave Clause probably protected a right of transit for masters of apprehended fugitives; see *Aves*, 224.

39. Johannsen, *Lincoln-Douglas Debates*, 79, 147, 150, 88, 217; Fehrenbacher, *Dred Scott*, 490–91.

40. Ibid., 275, 299, 255–57.

41. Douglas, *Popular Sovereignty*, 11–40. See also Johannsen, *Lincoln-Douglas Debates*, 270, 328.

42. Black, *Observations*, 12, 13.

43. Potter, *Impending Crisis*, 401–4.

44. Taney, MS-NSA II.

45. Johannsen, *Lincoln-Douglas Debates*, 255.

46. Roger B. Taney, fragment of a manuscript relating to slavery in the United States (c. 1860), Roger B. Taney Papers, Manuscript Division, Library of Congress, Washington, D.C.

NOTE ON METHOD

1. This study has benefited from the influential and extensive body of work associated with the republican synthesis and its critics. Most helpful in developing my framework were Appleby, *Capitalism*; Bailyn, *Ideological Origins*; Elkins and McKitrick, *Age of Federalism*, 3–29; Hartz, *Liberal Tradition*; Kloppenberg, *Virtues of Liberalism*; McCoy, *Elusive Republic*; McCoy, *Last of the Fathers*; Meyers, *Jacksonian Persuasion*; Shalhope, "Toward a Republican Synthesis"; Shalhope, "Republicanism"; Wood, *Creation*.

2. On the interrelationship between ideas and power, David Brion Davis's work on antislavery and capitalism remains indispensable, as does Michel Foucault's work on prisons. See Davis, *Problem*; Foucault, *Discipline and Punish*; Morgan, *Inventing*.

3. Bestor, "State Sovereignty"; Brandon, *Free in the World*; Fehrenbacher, *Dred Scott Case*, 40–47; Fehrenbacher, *Slaveholding Republic*; Finkelman, *Imperfect Union*, 236–84; Finkelman, " 'Hooted Down the Page' "; Hyman and Wiecek, *Equal Justice*, 101–14, 172–91; Wiecek, "Slavery and Abolition."

4. For a recent work that admirably examines both aspects of slave law, see Morris, *Southern Slavery*.

5. Genovese, *Slaveholders' Dilemma*. Mark M. Smith's study of clock time in the Old South also highlights the ways in which southerners' confrontation with the "slaveholders' dilemma" resulted in consequences quite different than a perceived need for secession. See Mark M. Smith, *Mastered by the Clock*.

6. See, e.g., Nelson, *Americanization*; Horwitz, *Transformation*; Ferguson, *Law and Letters*; Grossberg, *Governing the Hearth*; Freyer, *Producers versus Capitalists*.

7. Cushman, *Rethinking the New Deal Court*, 6.

8. The literature on the "transformation," if any, is extensive. For examples, none of which examine slavery to any significant degree, see Horwitz, *Transformation*; Hurst, *Law and the Conditions*; Nelson, *Americanization*; Novak, *People's Welfare*; Karsten, *Heart versus Head*.

9. See esp. Schafer, *Slavery*; Morris, *Southern Slavery*; Russell, "New Image"; Wahl, *Bondsman's Burden*. See also Finkelman, "Slaves as Fellow Servants"; Schafer, " 'Guaranteed against the Vices and Maladies Prescribed by Law' "; Fede, "Legal Protection"; Cottroll, "Liberalism and Paternalism."

10. Studies of the Commerce Clause constitute an exception to this trend. See Hyman and Wiecek, *Equal Justice*, 55–114; Wiecek, "Slavery and Abolition." See also Finkelman, " 'Hooted Down the Page.' "

11. Again, I am indebted to Cushman on this point; see *Rethinking the New Deal Court*, 6–7.

12. See Milsom, *Historical Foundations*; Milsom, *Legal Framework*; Palmer, "Origins"; Palmer, *Whilton Dispute*; Palmer, "Obligations of Contracts"; Palmer, *English Law*; Carroll, *Homesteads Ungovernable*.

13. Milsom, *Legal Framework*, 1.

14. Davis, *Problem*, 17.

15. Skocpol, *Protecting Soldiers*, 42. See also Orren, " 'War between Officers' "; Skocpol, *States and Social Revolutions*.

16. Cushman, *Rethinking the New Deal Court*, 5, 33–43.

17. John McLean, draft response to editorial on *Smith v. Swormstet*, c. 1854, McLean Papers. See also Benjamin Robbins Curtis to George Ticknor Curtis, Washington, D.C., February 29, 1852, Curtis Papers; Peter V. Daniel to Elizabeth Randolph Daniel, March 7, 1851, Washington, D.C., Daniel Papers.

Bibliography

MANUSCRIPT COLLECTIONS

Adjutant General's Office. Records (RG 94). National Archives and Records Administration, Washington, D.C.
Blair Family. Papers. Manuscript Division. Library of Congress, Washington, D.C.
Campbell Family. Papers. Southern Historical Collection. University of North Carolina, Chapel Hill.
Curtis, Benjamin Robbins. Papers. Manuscript Division. Library of Congress, Washington, D.C.
Daniel Family. Papers. Virginia Historical Society, Richmond.
Gooch Family. Papers. Virginia Historical Society, Richmond.
McLean, John. Papers. Manuscript Division. Library of Congress, Washington, D.C.
Scott, Dred. Collection. Missouri Historical Society, St. Louis.
Swisher, Carl Brent. Papers. Manuscript Division. Library of Congress, Washington, D.C.
Taney, Roger B. Papers. Manuscript Division. Library of Congress, Washington, D.C.
Treat, Samuel. Papers. Missouri Historical Society, St. Louis.
U.S. State Department. Records (RG 59). National Archives and Records Administration, College Park, Md.
U.S. Supreme Court. Records (RG 267). National Archives and Records Administration, Washington, D.C.

PRINTED PRIMARY SOURCES

Baldwin, Henry. *A General View of the Origin and Nature of the Constitution of the United States, Deduced from the Political History and Condition of the Colonies, from 1774 until 1788 and the Decisions of the Supreme Court of the United States.* New York: Da Capo, 1970.
Benton, Thomas Hart. *Historical and Legal Examination of That Part of the Decision of the Supreme Court of the United States in the Dred-Scott Case, Which Declares the Unconstitutionality of the Missouri Compromise Act, and the Self-Extension of the Constitution to Territories, Carrying Slavery along with It.* New York: Appleton, 1857.
Bevans, Charles I., ed. *Treaties and Other International Agreements of the United States of America, 1776–1949.* 13 vols. Washington, D.C.: Department of State, 1968–76.
Birney, James G. *Examination of the Decision of the Supreme Court of the United States, in the Case of Strader, Gorman, and Armstrong vs. Christopher Graham, Delivered at Its*

December Term, 1850: Concluding with an Address to the Free Colored People, Advising Them to Remove to Liberia. Cincinnati: Truman and Spofford, 1852.

Black, Jeremiah S. *Observations on Senator Douglas's Views of Popular Sovereignty, as Expressed in Harpers' Magazine, for September, 1859*. Washington, D.C.: McGill, 1859.

Blackstone, William. *Commentaries on the Laws of England*. 4 vols. 1765–69. Reprint, Chicago: University of Chicago Press, 1979.

Buchanan, James. "Inaugural Address," March 4, 1857. Avalon Project at Yale Law School. http://www.yale.edu/lawweb/avalon/presiden/inaug/buchanan.htm (accessed February 3, 2005).

———. *The Works of James Buchanan: Comprising His Speeches, State Papers, and Private Correspondence*. Edited by John Basset Moore. Vol. 10. New York: Antiquarian Press, 1960.

Calhoun, John C. "Speech on the Introduction of His Resolutions on the Slave Question [February 19, 1847]." In *Union and Liberty: The Political Philosophy of John C. Calhoun*, edited by Ross M. Lence, 511–21. Indianapolis: Liberty Fund, 1992.

Campbell, John A. *The Rights of the Slave States, by a Citizen of Alabama*. N.p.: Southern Rights Association, 1851.

Cartwright, Samuel A. "Philosophy of the Negro Constitution, Elicited by Questions Propounded by Dr. C. R. Hall, of Torquay, England, through Prof. Jackson of Massachusetts Medical College, Boston to Saml. A. Cartwright, M.D., New Orleans." In *Cotton Is King and Pro-Slavery Arguments, Comprising the Writings of Hammond, Harper, Christy, Hodge, Bledsoe, and Cartwright, on This Important Subject, with an Essay on Slavery in the Light of International Law by the Editor*, edited by E. N. Elliot, 691–706. 1860. New York: Negro Universities Press, 1969.

The Case of Dred Scott in the United States Supreme Court. New York: Greeley, 1860.

Catron, John. "Biographical Letter from Justice Catron of the Supreme Court of the United States." *United States Monthly Law Magazine* 5, no. 2 (1852): 145–52.

Chase, Salmon P. *An Argument for the Defendant Submitted to the Supreme Court of the United States, at December Term, 1846, in the Case of Warton Jones vs. John Vanzandt*. Cincinnati: Donogh, 1847.

Clark, Rufus W. *Lectures on the Formation of Character, Temptations, and Mission of Young Men*. Boston: Jewett, 1853.

Curtis, George Ticknor. *A Memoir of Benjamin Robbins Curtis, LL.D.: With Some of His Professional and Miscellaneous Writings*. Boston: Little, Brown, 1879.

Cushing, Caleb. "Relation of Indians to Citizenship." In U.S. Department of Justice, *Official Opinions of the Attorney Generals of the United States, Advising the President and Heads of Departments in Relation to Their Official Duties*, 7:746–56. Washington, D.C.: U.S. Government Printing Office, 1852–.

Douglas, Stephen A. *Popular Sovereignty in the Territories: The Dividing Line between Federal and Local Authority*. New York: Harper, 1859.

Douglass, Frederick. "The Dred Scott Decision: Speech, Delivered, in Part, at the Anniversary of the American Abolition Society, Held in New York, May 14, 1857." In *Two Speeches by Frederick Douglass: One on West India Emancipation and the Other on the Dred Scott Decision*. Rochester, N.Y.: Dewey, 1857.

Elliot, E. N., ed. *Cotton Is King and Pro-Slavery Arguments, Comprising the Writings of Hammond, Harper, Christy, Hodge, Bledsoe, and Cartwright, on This Important Subject, with an Essay on Slavery in the Light of International Law by the Editor*. 1860. New York: Negro Universities Press, 1969.

Foot, Samuel A. *An Examination of the Case of Dred Scott against Sandford, in the Supreme Court of the United States, and a Full and Fair Exposition of the Decision of the Court, and of the Opinions of the Majority of the Judges. Prepared at the Request of, and Read before "The Geneva Literary and Scientific Association," on Tuesday Evening, 28th December, 1858.* New York: Bryant, 1858.

Gray, Horace, and John Lowell. *A Legal Review of the Case of Dred Scott, as Decided by the Supreme Court of the United States.* Boston: Crosby, Nichols, 1857.

Huber, Ulrich. *The Jurisprudence of My Time.* Translated by Percival Gane. 5th ed. 2 vols. Durban, S.A.: Butterworth, 1939.

Jackson, Andrew. "Farewell Address." In *A Compilation of Messages and Papers of the Presidents, 1789–1897,* compiled by James D. Richardson, 4:1511–27. New York: U.S. Government Printing Office, 1896–99.

Jensen, Merrill, John P. Kaminski, and Gaspare J. Saladino, eds. *The Documentary History of the Ratification of the Constitution.* 20 vols. to date. Madison: State Historical Society of Wisconsin, 1976–.

Johannsen, Robert, ed. *The Lincoln-Douglas Debates.* New York: Oxford University Press, 1965.

Kent, James. *Commentaries on American Law.* 6th ed. 4 vols. New York: Kent, 1848.

A Kentucky Lawyer. *A Review of the Decision of the Supreme Court of the United States in the Dred Scott Case.* Louisville, Ky.: Morton and Griswold, 1857.

Madison, James. *Notes of the Debates in the Federal Convention of 1787.* Edited by Adrienne Koch. New York: Norton, 1969.

McLean, John. "Has Congress the Power to Institute Slavery?" *National Intelligencer,* December 22, 1847.

Missouri General Assembly. *A Solemn Public Act, Declaring the Assent of This State to the Fundamental Condition Contained in a Resolution, Passed by the Congress of the United States, Providing for the Admission of the State of Missouri into the Union on a Certain Condition.* In *Acts of the First General Assembly of the State of Missouri,* 8–11. St. Charles: McCloud, 1821.

Parker, Joel. *Personal Liberty Laws: (Statutes of Massachusetts) and Slavery in the Territories (Case of Dred Scott).* Boston: Wright and Potter, 1861.

Rawle, William. *A View of the Constitution of the United States of America.* Philadelphia: Carey and Lea, 1825.

Sergeant, Thomas. *Constitutional Law: Being a View of the Practice and Jurisdiction of the Courts of the United States, and of Constitutional Points Decided.* 2nd ed. Philadelphia: Nicklin and Johnson, 1830.

Story, Joseph. *Commentaries on Equity Pleadings, and the Incidents thereto, According to the Practice of the Courts of Equity in England and America.* Boston: Little and Brown, 1838.

———. *Commentaries on the Conflict of Laws, Foreign and Domestic, in Regard to Contracts, Rights, and Remedies, and Especially in Regard to Marriages, Divorces, Wills, Successions, and Judgments.* Boston: Hilliard, Gray, 1834.

———. *Commentaries on the Constitution of the United States: With a Preliminary Review of the Constitutional History of the Colonies and States, before the Adoption of the Constitution.* Boston: Hilliard, Gray, 1833.

Story, William W., ed. *Life and Letters of Joseph Story, Associate Justice of the Supreme Court of the United States and Dane Professor of Law at Harvard University.* 2 vols. Boston: Little and Brown, 1851.

Thoreau, Henry David. "Civil Disobedience." In *Walden and Other Writings*, 85–104. New York: Bantam Classic, 1981.

Thorpe, Francis Newton, ed. *The Federal and State Constitutions, Colonial Charters, and Other Organic Laws of the States, Territories, and Colonies, Now or Heretofore Forming the United States of America.* 7 vols. Grosse Pointe, Mich.: Scholarly Press, 1968.

Tocqueville, Alexis de. *Democracy in America.* Translated by Henry Reeve. 2 vols. 1838–40. Mattituck, N.Y.: Amereon House, n.d.

"Trial by Jury and the Federal Court." *Southern Quarterly Review* 1, no. 2 (1850): 452–80.

U.S. House Committee on Commerce. *Free Colored Seamen—Majority and Minority Reports.* 27th Cong., 3rd sess., 1843. House Report 80 (serial 426).

Van Evrie, John H., ed. *The Dred Scott Decision: Opinion of Chief Justice Taney with an Introduction by Dr. J. H. Van Evrie. Also, an Appendix, Containing an Essay on the Natural History of the Prognathous Race, Originally Written for the New York Day-Book, by Dr. S. A. Cartwright of New Orleans.* New York: Van Evrie, Horton, 1857.

Verplanck, Gulian. *An Essay on the Doctrine of Contract: Being and Inquiry How Contracts Are Affected in Law and Morals.* New York: Carville, 1825.

Wilson, James. "Of Citizens and Aliens." In *The Works of James Wilson*, edited by Robert Green McCloskey, 2:573–84. Cambridge: Harvard University Press, 1967.

SECONDARY SOURCES

Ackerman, Bruce A. *We the People: Foundations.* Cambridge: Belknap Press of Harvard University Press, 1991.

Allen, Austin. "Containing Slavery, Imposing Sovereignty: Federalism, Corporate Law, and the Origins of the *Dred Scott* Case." Ph.D. diss., University of Houston, 2001.

Altschuler, Glenn C., and Stuart M. Blumin. "Limits of Political Engagement in Antebellum America: A New Look at the Golden Age of Participatory Democracy." *Journal of American History* 84, no. 3 (1997): 855–85.

———. *Rude Republic: Americans and Their Politics in the Nineteenth Century.* Princeton: Princeton University Press, 2000.

Appleby, Joyce Oldham. *Capitalism and a New Social Order: The Republican Vision of the 1790s.* New York: New York University Press, 1984.

Ashworth, John. *"Agrarians" and "Aristocrats": Party Political Ideology in the United States, 1837–1846.* London: Royal Historical Society, 1983.

———. *Slavery, Capitalism, and Politics in the Antebellum Republic.* Vol. 1, *Commerce and Compromise, 1820–1850.* New York: Cambridge University Press, 1995.

Atack, Jeremy, and Peter Passell. *A New Economic View of American History from Colonial Times to 1940.* 2nd ed. New York: Norton, 1994.

Ayers, Edward L. *Vengeance and Justice: Crime and Punishment in the Nineteenth-Century American South.* New York: Oxford University Press, 1984.

Bailyn, Bernard. *The Ideological Origins of the American Revolution.* Cambridge: Belknap Press of Harvard University Press, 1967.

Balbus, Isaac. "Commodity Form and Legal Form: An Essay on the 'Relative Autonomy' of the Law." *Law and Society Review* 11, no. 3 (1976–77): 571–88.

Baxter, Maurice G. *Daniel Webster and the Supreme Court.* Amherst: University of Massachusetts Press, 1966.

Berlin, Ira. *Generations of Captivity: A History of African American Slaves.* Cambridge: Belknap Press of Harvard University Press, 2003.

Bestor, Arthur. "State Sovereignty and Slavery: A Reinterpretation of Proslavery Constitutional Doctrine, 1846–1860." *Journal of the Illinois State Historical Society* 54, no. 2 (1961): 117–80.

Bickel, Alexander M. *The Least Dangerous Branch: The Supreme Court at the Bar of Politics.* Indianapolis: Bobbs-Merrill, 1962.

Blumin, Stuart M. *The Emergence of the Middle Class: Social Experience in the American City, 1760–1900.* New York: Cambridge University Press, 1989.

Bodenhorn, Howard. "Capital Mobility and Financial Integration in Antebellum America." *Journal of Economic History* 52, no. 2 (1992): 585–610.

Brandon, Mark E. *Free in the World: American Slavery and Constitutional Failure.* Princeton: Princeton University Press, 1998.

Bridwell, R. Randall. "Theme v. Reality in American Legal History: A Commentary on Horwitz, *The Transformation of American Law, 1780–1860* and the Common Law." *Indiana Law Journal* 53, no. 3 (1978): 473–87.

Burke, Joseph C. "What Did the Prigg Decision Really Decide?" *Pennsylvania Magazine of History and Biography* 93, no. 1 (1969): 73–85.

Butler, Jon. *Becoming America: The Revolution before 1776.* Cambridge: Harvard University Press, 2000.

Carroll, Mark M. *Homesteads Ungovernable: Families, Sex, and the Law in Frontier Texas, 1823–1860.* Austin: University of Texas Press, 2001.

Casto, William. *The Supreme Court in the Early Republic: The Chief Justiceships of John Jay and Oliver Ellsworth.* Columbia: University of South Carolina Press, 1995.

Corwin, Edward S. "The Dred Scott Decision in the Light of Contemporary Legal Doctrines." *American Historical Review* 17, no. 1 (1911): 52–69.

Cottroll, Robert. "Liberalism and Paternalism: Ideology, Economic Interest, and the Business Law of Slavery." *American Journal of Legal History* 31, no. 4 (1987): 359–73.

Cover, Robert M. *Justice Accused: Antislavery and the Judicial Process.* New Haven: Yale University Press, 1975.

Currie, David P. *The Constitution in the Supreme Court: The First Hundred Years, 1789–1888.* Chicago: University of Chicago Press, 1985.

Curtis, Michael Kent. "Historical Linguistics, Inkblots, and Life after Death: The Privileges or Immunities of Citizens of the United States." *North Carolina Law Review* 78, no. 4 (2000): 1071–1151.

Cushman, Barry. *Rethinking the New Deal Court: The Structure of a Constitutional Revolution.* New York: Oxford University Press, 1999.

Davis, David Brion. "The Culmination of Racial Polarities and Prejudice." *Journal of the Early Republic* 19, no. 4 (1999): 757–75.

———. *The Problem of Slavery in the Age of Revolution, 1770–1823.* 2nd ed. New York: Oxford University Press, 1999.

Dean, Eric T., Jr. "Reassessing *Dred Scott*: The Possibilities of Federal Power in the Antebellum Context." *University of Cincinnati Law Review* 60, no. 3 (1992): 713–55.

Degnan, Daniel A. "William Paterson: Small States' Nationalist." In *Seriatim: The Supreme Court before John Marshall,* edited by Scott Douglas Gerber, 231–59. New York: New York University Press, 1998.

Dennison, George M. *The Dorr War: Republicanism on Trial, 1831–1861.* Lexington: University Press of Kentucky, 1976.

Diamond, Raymond T. "No Call to Glory: Thurgood Marshall's Thesis on the Intent of a Proslavery Constitution." *Vanderbilt Law Review* 42, no. 1 (1989): 93–131.

Dickinson, Edwin D. "The Law of Nations as Part of the National Law of the United States [Parts I and II]." *University of Pennsylvania Law Review* 101, nos. 1, 6 (1952–53): 26–56, 792–833.

Earle, Jonathan H. *Jacksonian Antislavery and the Politics of Free Soil, 1824–1854.* Chapel Hill: University of North Carolina Press, 2004.

Ehrlich, Walter. "The Origins of the Dred Scott Case." *Journal of Negro History* 59, no. 2 (1974): 132–42.

———. *They Have No Rights: Dred Scott's Struggle for Freedom.* Westport, Conn.: Greenwood, 1979.

———. "Was the Dred Scott Case Valid?" *Journal of American History* 55, no. 2 (1968): 256–65.

Elkins, Stanley, and Erik McKitrick. *The Age of Federalism: The Early American Republic.* New York: Oxford University Press, 1993.

Ellis, Richard E. *The Jeffersonian Crisis: Courts and Politics in the Young Republic.* New York: Oxford University Press, 1971.

———. *The Union at Risk: Jacksonian Democracy, States' Rights, and the Nullification Crisis.* New York: Oxford University Press, 1987.

Fede, Andrew. "Legal Protection for Slave Buyers: A Caveat on *Caveat Emptor.*" *American Journal of Legal History* 31, no. 4 (1987): 322–58.

Fehrenbacher, Don E. *Constitutions and Constitutionalism in the Slaveholding South.* Athens: University of Georgia Press, 1989.

———. *The Dred Scott Case: Its Significance in American Law and Politics.* New York: Oxford University Press, 1978.

———. *The Slaveholding Republic: An Account of the United States Government's Relations to Slavery.* Edited by Ward M. McAfee. New York: Oxford University Press, 2001.

Feller, Daniel. "A Brother in Arms: Benjamin Tappan and the Antislavery Democracy." *Journal of American History* 88, no. 1 (2001): 48–74.

———. *Jacksonian Promise: America, 1815–1840.* Baltimore: Johns Hopkins University Press, 1995.

Ferguson, Robert A. *Law and Letters in American Culture.* Cambridge: Harvard University Press, 1984.

Finkelman, Paul. "The Dred Scott Case, Slavery, and the Politics of Law." *Hamline Law Review* 20, no. 1 (1996): 1–42.

———. "Evading the Ordinance: The Persistence of Bondage in Indiana and Illinois." *Journal of the Early Republic* 9, no. 1 (1989): 21–52.

———. " 'Hooted Down the Page of History': Reconsidering the Greatness of Chief Justice Taney." *Journal of Supreme Court History* (1994): 83–102.

———. *An Imperfect Union: Slavery, Federalism, and Comity.* Chapel Hill: University of North Carolina Press, 1981.

———. "*Prigg v. Pennsylvania* and the Northern State Courts: Anti-Slavery Use of a Pro-Slavery Decision." *Civil War History* 25, no. 1 (1979): 5–35.

———. *Slavery and the Founders: Race and Liberty in the Age of Jefferson.* Armonk, N.Y.: Sharpe, 1996.

———. "Slaves as Fellow Servants: Ideology, Law, and Industrialization." *American Journal of Legal History* 31, no. 4 (1987): 269–305.

———. "Story Telling on the Supreme Court: *Prigg v. Pennsylvania* and Justice Joseph Story's Judicial Nationalism." *Supreme Court Review* (1994): 247–94.

Foner, Eric. *Free Soil, Free Labor, Free Men: The Ideology of the Republican Party before the Civil War.* New York: Oxford University Press, 1970.

Foucault, Michel. *Discipline and Punish: The Birth of the Prison.* Translated by Alan Sheridan. New York: Pantheon, 1977.

Frank, John P. *Justice Daniel Dissenting: A Biography of Peter V. Daniel, 1784–1860.* Cambridge: Harvard University Press, 1964.

Freehling, William W. *Prelude to Civil War: The Nullification Controversy in South Carolina, 1816–1836.* New York: Oxford University Press, 1965.

Freyer, Tony A. *Forums of Order: The Federal Courts and Business in American History.* Greenwich, Conn.: JAI, 1979.

————. *Harmony and Dissonance: The Swift and Erie Cases in American Federalism.* New York: New York University Press, 1981.

————. *Producers versus Capitalists: Constitutional Conflict in Antebellum America.* Charlottesville: University Press of Virginia, 1994.

Friedman, Barry. "The History of the Countermajoritarian Difficulty, Part One: The Road to Judicial Supremacy." *New York University Law Review* 73, no. 2 (1998): 333–433.

Friedman, Lawrence M. *A History of American Law.* 2nd ed. New York: Simon and Schuster, 1985.

Gable, Peter. "Intention and Structure in Contractual Conditions." *Minnesota Law Review* 61, no. 4 (1977): 601–43.

Genovese, Eugene D. *The Slaveholders' Dilemma: Freedom and Progress in Southern Conservative Thought, 1820–1860.* Columbia: University of South Carolina Press, 1992.

Gerber, Scott Douglas. "Deconstructing William Cushing." In *Seriatim: The Supreme Court before John Marshall,* edited by Scott Douglas Gerber, 97–125. New York: New York University Press, 1998.

————. "Introduction: The Supreme Court before John Marshall." In *Seriatim: The Supreme Court before John Marshall,* edited by Scott Douglas Gerber, 1–25. New York: New York University Press, 1998.

Gettleman, Marvin E. *The Dorr Rebellion: A Study in American Radicalism: 1833–1849.* New York: Random House, 1973.

Gilje, Paul A. *The Road to Mobocracy: Popular Disorder in New York City, 1763–1834.* Chapel Hill: University of North Carolina Press, 1987.

Gjerde, Jon. " 'Here in America There Is Neither King nor Tyrant': European Encounters with Race, 'Freedom,' and Their European Pasts." *Journal of the Early Republic* 19, no. 4 (1999): 673–90.

Goebel, Julius, Jr. *Antecedents and Beginnings to 1801.* Vol. 1 of *The Oliver Wendell Holmes Devise History of the Supreme Court of the United States.* New York: Macmillan, 1971.

Gordon, Robert W. "Legal Thought and Legal Practice in the Age of American Enterprise, 1870–1920." In *Professions and Professional Ideologies in America,* edited by Gerald L. Geison, 70–110. Chapel Hill: University of North Carolina Press, 1983.

Graber, Mark A. "Desperately Ducking Slavery: *Dred Scott* and Contemporary Constitutional Theory." *Constitutional Commentary* 14, no. 2 (1997): 271–318.

————. "The Nonmajoritarian Difficulty: Legislative Deference to the Judiciary." *Studies in American Political Development* 7, no. 2 (1993): 35–73.

Greenberg, Kenneth S. *Honor and Slavery: Lies, Duels, Noses, Masks, Dressing as a Woman, Gifts, Strangers, Humanitarianism, Death, Slave Rebellions, the Proslavery Argument, Baseball, Hunting, and Gambling in the Old South.* Princeton: Princeton University Press, 1996.

Greenblatt, Stephen. *Marvelous Possessions: The Wonder of the New World.* Chicago: University of Chicago Press, 1991.

Grossberg, Michael. *Governing the Hearth: Law and the Family in Nineteenth-Century America.* Chapel Hill: University of North Carolina Press, 1985.

Hall, Kermit. *The Magic Mirror: Law in American History.* New York: Oxford University Press, 1989.

Halttunen, Karen. *Confidence Men and Painted Women: A Study of Middle-Class Culture in America, 1830–1870.* New Haven: Yale University Press, 1982.

Hammond, John Craig. "'They Are Very Much Interested in Obtaining an Unlimited Slavery': Rethinking the Expansion of Slavery in the Louisiana Purchase Territories, 1803–1805." *Journal of the Early Republic* 23, no. 3 (2003): 353–80.

Hartog, Hendrik. *Public Property and Private Power: The Corporation of the City of New York in American Law, 1730–1870.* Ithaca: Cornell University Press, 1983.

Hartz, Louis. *The Liberal Tradition in America: An Interpretation of American Political Thought since the Revolution.* New York: Harcourt Brace, 1955.

Haskins, George Lee, and Herbert A. Johnson. *Foundations of Power: John Marshall, 1801–15.* Vol. 2 of *The Oliver Wendell Holmes Devise History of the Supreme Court of the United States.* New York: Macmillan, 1981.

Hatch, Nathan O. *The Democratization of American Christianity.* New Haven: Yale University Press, 1989.

Higginbotham, A. Leon. *Shades of Freedom: Racial Politics and Presumptions of the American Legal Process.* New York: Oxford University Press, 1996.

Hobson, Charles F. *The Great Chief Justice: John Marshall and the Rule of Law.* Lawrence: University Press of Kansas, 1996.

Hodder, F. H. "Some Phases of the Dred Scott Case." *Mississippi Valley Historical Review* 16, no. 1 (1929): 3–22.

Hofstadter, Richard. *The American Political Tradition and the Men Who Made It.* New York: Knopf, 1948.

Holden-Smith, Barbara. "Lords of the Lash, Loom, and Law: Justice Story, Slavery, and *Prigg v. Pennsylvania.*" *Cornell University Law Review* 78, no. 6 (1993): 1086–1115.

Holt, Thomas. "Marking: Race, Race-Making, and the Writing of History." *American Historical Review* 100, no. 1 (1995): 1–20.

Hopkins, Vincent Charles. *Dred Scott's Case.* 1951. New York: Atheneum, 1971.

Horwitz, Morton J. *The Transformation of American Law, 1780–1860.* Cambridge: Harvard University Press, 1977.

Howe, Daniel Walker. "The Evangelical Movement and Political Culture in the North during the Second Party System." *Journal of American History* 77, no. 4 (1991): 1216–39.

Huebner, Timothy S. *The Southern Judicial Tradition: State Judges and Sectional Distinctiveness, 1790–1890.* Athens: University of Georgia Press, 1999.

Hughes, Charles Evans. *The Supreme Court of the United States: Its Foundations, Methods, and Achievements.* New York: Columbia University Press, 1928.

Hurst, James Willard. *Law and Economic Growth: The Legal History of the Lumber Industry in Wisconsin, 1836–1915.* Madison: University of Wisconsin Press, 1964.

———. *Law and the Conditions of Freedom in the Nineteenth-Century United States.* Madison: University of Wisconsin Press, 1956.

———. *The Legitimacy of the Business Corporation in the Law of the United States, 1780–1970.* Charlottesville: University Press of Virginia, 1970.

Hyman, Harold M., and William M. Wiecek, *Equal Justice under Law: Constitutional Development, 1835–1875.* New York: Harper and Row, 1982.

Ignatiev, Noel. *How the Irish Became White*. New York: Routledge, 1995.

Jaffa, Harry V. *Crisis of the House Divided: An Interpretation of the Issues in the Lincoln-Douglas Debates*. Garden City, N.Y.: Doubleday, 1959.

Johnston, Richard Malcolm, and William Hand Brown. *The Life of Alexander H. Stephens*. Freeport, N.Y.: Books for Libraries Press, 1971.

Karsten, Peter. *Heart versus Head: Judge-Made Law in Nineteenth-Century America*. Chapel Hill: University of North Carolina Press, 1997.

Kaufman, Kenneth C. *Dred Scott's Advocate: A Biography of Roswell M. Field*. Columbia: University of Missouri Press, 1996.

Kerber, Linda K. "Women's Citizenship in the Early Republic: The Case of *Martin v. Massachusetts*, 1805." *American Historical Review* 97, no. 2 (1992): 349–78.

Kettner, James H. *The Development of American Citizenship, 1608–1870*. Chapel Hill: University of North Carolina Press, 1978.

Keyssar, Alexander. *The Right to Vote: The Contested History of Democracy in the United States*. New York: Basic Books, 2000.

Kloppenberg, James T. *The Virtues of Liberalism*. New York: Oxford University Press, 1998.

Kolchin, Peter. "Whiteness Studies: The New History of Race in America." *Journal of American History* 89, no. 1 (2002): 154–73.

Kramer, Larry. "The Lawmaking Power of the Federal Courts." *Pace Law Review* 12, no. 2 (1992): 263–302.

Kutler, Stanley I. *Privilege and Creative Destruction: The Charles River Bridge Case*. Baltimore: Johns Hopkins University Press, 1990.

La Croix, Summer, and Christopher Grandy. "Financial Integration in Antebellum America: Strengthening Bodenhorn's Results." *Journal of Economic History* 53, no. 3 (1993): 653–58.

Lamoreaux, Naomi. "Rethinking the Transition to Capitalism in the Early American Northeast." *Journal of American History* 90, no. 2 (2003): 437–61.

LaPiana, William. "*Swift v. Tyson* and the Brooding Omnipresence in the Sky: An Investigation of the Idea of Law in Antebellum America." *Suffolk University Law Review* 20, no. 4 (1986): 771–832.

Larson, John L. *Internal Improvement: National Public Works and the Promise of Popular Government in the Early United States*. Chapel Hill: University of North Carolina Press, 2001.

Leonard, Gerald. *The Invention of Party Politics: Federalism, Popular Sovereignty, and Constitutional Development in Jacksonian Illinois*. Chapel Hill: University of North Carolina Press, 2002.

Leslie, William R. "The Influence of Joseph Story's Theory of the Conflict of Laws on Constitutional Nationalism." *Mississippi Valley Historical Review* 35, no. 2 (1948): 203–20.

———. "The Pennsylvania Fugitive Slave Act of 1826." *Journal of Southern History* 18, no. 4 (1952): 429–45.

Levinson, Sanford. "Slavery in the Canon of Constitutional Law." *Chicago-Kent Law Review* 68, no. 3 (1993): 1087–1111.

Lynd, Staughton. *Class Conflict, Slavery, and the United States Constitution: Ten Essays*. Indianapolis: Bobbs-Merrill, 1967.

Magrath, C. Peter. *Yazoo: Law and Politics in the New Republic*. Providence: Brown University Press, 1966.

Maizlish, Stephen E. *The Triumph of Sectionalism.* Kent, Ohio: Kent State University Press, 1983.

Malone, Laurence J. *Opening the West: Federal Internal Improvements before 1860.* Westport, Conn.: Greenwood, 1998.

Maltz, Earl M. "The Unlikely Hero of *Dred Scott*: Benjamin R. Curtis and the Constitutional Law of Slavery." *Cardozo Law Review* 17, no. 6 (1996): 1995–2016.

Marshall, Thurgood. "Reflections on the Bicentennial of the United States." *Harvard Law Review* 101, no. 1 (1987): 1–5.

McClellen, James. *Joseph Story and the American Constitution: A Study in Legal and Political Thought with Selected Writings.* Norman: University of Oklahoma Press, 1990.

McCloskey, Robert G. *The American Supreme Court.* 2nd ed. Chicago: University of Chicago Press, 1994.

McCormac, E. I. "Justice Campbell and the Dred Scott Decision." *Mississippi Valley Historical Review* 19, no. 4 (1933): 565–71.

McCoy, Drew R. *The Elusive Republic: Political Economy in Jeffersonian America.* Chapel Hill: University of North Carolina Press, 1980.

———. *The Last of the Fathers: James Madison and the Republican Legacy.* New York: Cambridge University Press, 1989.

McPherson, James M. *Battle Cry of Freedom: The Civil War Era.* New York: Oxford University Press, 1988.

———. "Politics and Judicial Responsibility: *Dred Scott v. Sandford.*" In *Great Cases in Constitutional Law,* edited by Robert P. George, 90–93. Princeton: Princeton University Press, 2000.

Meister, Robert. "The Logic and Legacy of *Dred Scott*: Marshall, Taney, and the Sublimation of Republican Thought." *Studies in American Political Development* 3, no. 1 (1989): 199–260.

Mendelson, Wallace. "Dred Scott's Case—Reconsidered." *Minnesota Law Review* 38, no. 1 (1953): 16–28.

———. "Dred Scott's Case—Revisited." *Louisiana Law Review* 7, no. 2 (1946): 398–405.

Meyers, Marvin. *The Jacksonian Persuasion: Politics and Belief.* Stanford, Calif.: Stanford University Press, 1957.

Miller, Perry. *The Life of the Mind in America, from the Revolution to the Civil War.* New York: Harcourt Brace, 1965.

Milsom, C. F. C. *Historical Foundations of the Common Law.* London: Butterworths, 1969.

———. *The Legal Framework of English Feudalism: The Maitland Lectures Given in 1972.* New York: Cambridge University Press, 1976.

———. "The Nature of Blackstone's Achievement." In *Studies in the History of the Common Law,* 197–208. Ronceverte, W.Va.: Hambledon, 1985.

Mintz, Steven. *Moralists and Modernizers: America's Pre–Civil War Reformers.* Baltimore: Johns Hopkins University Press, 1995.

Montgomery, David. *Citizen Worker: The Experience of Workers in the United States with Democracy and the Free Market during the Nineteenth Century.* New York: Cambridge University Press, 1993.

Moore, Glover. *The Missouri Controversy, 1819–1821.* Louisville: University of Kentucky Press, 1953.

Morgan, Edmund S. *Inventing the People: The Rise of Popular Sovereignty in England and America.* New York: Norton, 1988.

Morris, Thomas D. *Free Men All: The Personal Liberty Laws of the North, 1780–1861.* Baltimore: Johns Hopkins University Press, 1974.

———. *Southern Slavery and the Law, 1619–1860*. Chapel Hill: University of North Carolina Press, 1996.

Morrison, Michael A. *Slavery and the American West: The Eclipse of Manifest Destiny and the Coming of the Civil War*. Chapel Hill: University of North Carolina Press, 1997.

Nelson, William E. *Americanization of the Common Law: The Impact of Legal Change on Massachusetts Society, 1760–1830*. Cambridge: Harvard University Press, 1975.

Nevins, Allan. *The Emergence of Lincoln*. New York: Scribner, 1950.

Newmyer, R. Kent. "Harvard Law School, New England Legal Culture, and the Antebellum Origins of American Jurisprudence." *Journal of American History* 74, no. 3 (1987): 814–35.

———. "John Marshall and the Southern Constitutional Tradition." In *An Uncertain Tradition: Constitutionalism in the History of the South*, edited by Kermit Hall and John Hart Ely, 105–24. Athens: University of Georgia Press, 1989.

———. *Supreme Court Justice Joseph Story: Statesman of the Old Republic*. Chapel Hill: University of North Carolina Press, 1985.

Novak, William J. *The People's Welfare: Law and Regulation in Nineteenth-Century America*. Chapel Hill: University of North Carolina Press, 1996.

Orren, Karren. " 'A War between Officers': The Enforcement of Slavery in the Northern United States, and of the Republic for Which It Stands, before the Civil War." *Studies in American Political Development* 12, no. 2 (1998): 343–82.

Palmer, Robert C. *English Law in the Age of the Black Death, 1348–1381*. Chapel Hill: University of North Carolina Press, 1993.

———. "The Federal Common Law of Crime." *Law and History Review* 4, no. 2 (1986): 267–323.

———. "Liberties as Constitutional Provisions." In *Liberty and Community: Constitution and Rights in the Early American Republic*, edited by William E. Nelson and Robert C. Palmer, 55–145. New York: Oceana, 1987.

———. "Obligations of Contracts: Intent and Distortion." *Case Western Reserve Law Review* 37, no. 4 (1987): 631–73.

———. "The Origins of Property in England." *Law and History Review* 3, no. 1 (1985): 1–50.

———. *The Whilton Dispute, 1264–1380: A Social and Legal Study of Dispute Settlement in Medieval England*. Princeton: Princeton University Press, 1986.

Pessen, Edward. *Jacksonian America: Society, Personality, and Politics*. Homewood, Ill.: Dorsey, 1969.

Potter, David M. *The Impending Crisis, 1848–1861*. Edited by Don E. Fehrenbacher. New York: Harper Torchbooks, 1976.

Pound, Roscoe. *The Formative Era of American Law*. Boston: Little, Brown, 1938.

Preyer, Kathryn. "Jurisdiction to Punish: Federal Authority, Federalism, and the Common Law of Crimes in the Early Republic." *Law and History Review* 4, no. 2 (1986): 223–65.

Publius [Alexander Hamilton]. *Federalist 78*. In *The Federalist Papers*, edited by Isaac Kramnick, 436–42. New York: Penguin, 1987.

———. *Federalist 79*. In *The Federalist Papers*, edited by Isaac Kramnick, 442–45. New York: Penguin, 1987.

———. *Federalist 80*. In *The Federalist Papers*, edited by Isaac Kramnick, 445–50. New York: Penguin, 1987.

Publius [James Madison]. *Federalist 48*. In *The Federalist Papers*, edited by Isaac Kramnick, 308–16. New York: Penguin, 1987.

Purcell, Edward A. *Litigation and Inequality: Federal Diversity Jurisdiction in Industrial America, 1870–1958.* New York: Oxford University Press, 1992.

Redish, Martin. "Federal Common Law, Political Legitimacy, and the Interpretive Process: An 'Institutionalist' Perspective." *Northwestern University Law Review* 83, no. 4 (1989): 761–804.

Richards, Leonard L. *"Gentlemen of Property and Standing": Anti-Abolition Mobs in Jacksonian America.* New York: Oxford University Press, 1970.

———. *The Slave Power: The Free North and Southern Domination, 1780–1860.* Baton Rouge: Louisiana State University Press, 2000.

Rodgers, Daniel T. *Contested Truths: Keywords in American Politics since Independence.* New York: Basic Books, 1987.

Roediger, David R. "The Pursuit of Whiteness: Property, Terror, and Expansion, 1790–1860." *Journal of the Early Republic* 19, no. 4 (1999): 579–600.

Rorabaugh, W. J. *The Alcoholic Republic: An American Tradition.* New York: Oxford University Press, 1979.

Russel, Robert R. "Constitutional Doctrines with Regard to Slavery in Territories." *Journal of Southern History* 32, no. 4 (1966): 468–70.

Russell, Thomas D. "A New Image of the Slave Auction: An Empirical Look at the Role of Law in Slave Sales and a Conceptual Reevaluation of Slave Property." *Cardozo Law Review* 18, no. 2 (1996): 473–523.

Saunders, Robert. *John Archibald Campbell: Southern Moderate, 1811–1889.* Tuscaloosa: University of Alabama Press, 1997.

Schafer, Judith Kelleher. "'Guaranteed against the Vices and Maladies Prescribed by Law': Consumer Protection, the Law of Slave Sales, and the Supreme Court in Antebellum Louisiana." *American Journal of Legal History* 31, no. 4 (1987): 306–21.

———. *Slavery, the Civil Law, and the Supreme Court of Louisiana.* Baton Rouge: Louisiana State University Press, 1994.

Schwartz, Bernard. *From Confederation to Nation: The American Constitution, 1835–1877.* Baltimore: Johns Hopkins University Press, 1973.

Sellers, Charles G. *The Market Revolution: Jacksonian America, 1815–1846.* New York: Oxford University Press, 1991.

Shalhope, Robert E. "Republicanism and Early American Historiography." *William and Mary Quarterly,* 3rd ser., 39, no. 2 (1982): 334–56.

———. "Toward a Republican Synthesis: The Emergence of an Understanding of Republicanism in American Historiography." *William and Mary Quarterly,* 3rd ser., 29, no. 1 (1972): 49–80.

Shirley, John M. *The Dartmouth College Causes and the Supreme Court of the United States.* St. Louis: Jones, 1879.

Skocpol, Theda. *Protecting Soldiers and Mothers: The Political Origins of Social Policy in the United States.* Cambridge: Belknap Press of Harvard University Press, 1992.

———. *States and Social Revolutions: A Comparative Analysis of France, Russia, and China.* New York: Cambridge University Press, 1979.

Skowronek, Stephen. *Building a New American State: The Expansion of National Administrative Capacities, 1877–1920.* New York: Cambridge University Press, 1984.

Smith, Mark M. *Mastered by the Clock: Time, Slavery, and Freedom in the American South.* Chapel Hill: University of North Carolina Press, 1997.

Smith, Rogers M. *Civic Ideals: Conflicting Visions of Citizenship in U.S. History.* New Haven: Yale University Press, 1997.

Stampp, Kenneth M. *America in 1857: A Nation on the Brink.* New York: Oxford University Press, 1990.

Stanley, Amy Dru. *From Bondage to Contract: Wage Labor, Marriage, and the Market in the Age of Slave Emancipation.* New York: Cambridge University Press, 1998.

Stites, Francis N. *Private Interest and Public Gain: The Dartmouth College Case, 1819.* Amherst: University of Massachusetts Press, 1972.

Story, Ronald. *The Forging of an Aristocracy: Harvard and the Boston Upper Class, 1800–1870.* Middletown, Conn.: Wesleyan University Press, 1980.

Stowe, Steven M. *Intimacy and Power in the Old South: Ritual in the Lives of the Planters.* Baltimore: Johns Hopkins University Press, 1987.

Streichler, Stuart A. "Justice Curtis's Dissent in the Dred Scott Case: An Interpretive Study." *Hastings Constitutional Law Quarterly* 24, no. 2 (1997): 509–44.

Sunstein, Cass R. "*Dred Scott v. Sandford* and Its Legacy." In *Great Cases in Constitutional Law*, edited by Robert P. George, 63–89. Princeton: Princeton University Press, 2000.

Swisher, Carl Brent. *The Taney Period, 1836–1864.* Vol. 5 of *The Oliver Wendell Holmes Devise History of the Supreme Court of the United States.* New York: Macmillan, 1974.

Taylor, Alan. *William Cooper's Town: Power and Persuasion on the Frontier of the Early American Republic.* New York: Knopf, 1995.

Temin, Peter. *The Jacksonian Economy.* New York: Norton, 1969.

Tribe, Laurence. *American Constitutional Law.* Mineola, N.Y.: Foundation Press, 1978.

[Tushnet, Mark V.] "*Swift v. Tyson* Exhumed." *Yale Law Journal* 79, no. 4 (1969): 284–310.

VanderVelde, Lea, and Sandhya Subramanian. "Mrs. Dred Scott." *Yale Law Journal* 106, no. 4 (1997): 1033–1117.

von Holst, Hermann Eduard. *The Constitutional and Political History of the United States.* Translated by John Joseph Lalor and Alfred Bishop Mason. 8 vols. Chicago: Callaghan, 1881–92.

Wahl, Jenny Bourne. *The Bondsman's Burden: An Economic Analysis of the Common Law of Southern Slavery.* New York: Cambridge University Press, 1998.

Warren, Charles. "New Light on the History of the Federal Judiciary Act of 1789." *Harvard Law Review* 37, no. 1 (1923): 49–132.

———. *The Supreme Court in United States History.* 3 vols. Boston: Little, Brown, 1922.

Watson, Alan. *Joseph Story and the Comity of Errors: A Case Study in the Conflict of Laws.* Athens: University of Georgia Press, 1992.

Watson, Harry L. *Liberty and Power: The Politics of Jacksonian America.* New York: Hill and Wang, 1990.

Weinberg, Louise. "Federal Common Law." *Northwestern University Law Review* 83, no. 4 (1989): 805–52.

Weisenburger, Francis P. *The Life of John McLean: A Politician on the United States Supreme Court.* Columbus: Ohio State University Press, 1937.

White, G. Edward. *The American Judicial Tradition: Profiles of Leading American Judges.* Expanded ed. New York: Oxford University Press, 1988.

———. *The Marshall Court and Cultural Change, 1815–1835.* Abridged ed. New York: Oxford University Press, 1991.

Wiebe, Robert H. *Self-Rule: A Cultural History of American Democracy.* Chicago: University of Chicago Press, 1995.

Wiecek, William M. *Liberty under Law: The Supreme Court in American Life.* Baltimore: Johns Hopkins University Press, 1988.

———. *The Lost World of Classical Legal Thought: Law and Ideology in America, 1886–1937*. New York: Oxford University Press, 1998.

———. "Slavery and Abolition before the United States Supreme Court, 1820–1860." *Journal of American History* 65, no. 1 (1978): 34–59.

———. *The Sources of Antislavery Constitutionalism in America, 1760–1848*. Ithaca: Cornell University Press, 1977.

Wilentz, Sean. "Many Democracies: On Tocqueville and Jacksonian America." In *Reconsidering Tocqueville's* Democracy in America, edited by Abraham S. Eisenstadt, 207–28. New Brunswick: Rutgers University Press, 1988.

———. "Slavery, Antislavery, and Jacksonian Democracy." In *The Market Revolution in America: Social, Political, and Religious Expressions, 1800–1880*, edited by Melvyn Stokes and Stephen Conway, 202–23. Charlottesville: University Press of Virginia, 1996.

Wood, Gordon S. *The Creation of the American Republic*. New York: Norton, 1969.

———. "The Enemy Is Us: Democratic Capitalism in the Early Republic." In *Wages of Independence: Capitalism in the Early American Republic*, edited by Paul A. Gilje, 137–53. Madison, Wis.: Madison House, 1997.

———. "Equality and Social Conflict in the American Revolution." *William and Mary Quarterly*, 3rd ser., 51, no. 4 (1994): 703–16.

———. "Interests and Disinterestedness in the Making of the Constitution." In *Beyond Confederation: Origins of the Constitution and American National Identity*, edited by Richard Beeman, Stephen Botein, and Edward C. Carter II, 69–109. Chapel Hill: University of North Carolina Press, 1987.

———. *The Radicalism of the American Revolution*. New York: Knopf, 1992.

Wyatt-Brown, Bertram. *Southern Honor: Ethics and Behavior in the Old South*. New York: Oxford University Press, 1982.

Young, Ernest A. "The Last Brooding Omnipresence: *Erie RR. Co. v. Tompkins* and the Unconstitutionality of a Preemptive Federal Maritime Law." *St. Louis University Law Journal* 43, no. 4 (1999): 1349–66.

Index

opinions of, 206; and slavery, 83; in
Swift, 53, 57–59. See also *Conflict of
Laws* (Story)
Story, William W., 82
Strader v. Graham, 92–94; condemned by
Birney, 116; and *Dred Scott*, 134, 182;
and *Emerson*, 147; federal jurisdiction
in, 93; followed by Wells in *Dred Scott*,
148, 154; impact on factionalism, 95;
Nelson's use of, 152; as precedent in
Dred Scott, 139–40, 158, 169; Taney's
revisions of, 206
Streichler, Stuart A., 174
Subramanian, Sandhya, 143
substantive due process, 191
Supreme Court. *See* U.S. Supreme Court
Swift doctrine, 55–56, 60, 61–62, 155–57
Swift v. Tyson, 51–55; academic criticism
of, 56; as affirmation of popular
sovereignty, 57–58; anticipated in
Charles River Bridge, 104; Blair's
use of in *Dred Scott*, 151; case law
in, 55; centrality of in Taney Court
jurisprudence, 56–58, 61; commercial
implications of, 57–58; and *Dred Scott*,
53, 62, 140, 155; McLean's use of in *Dred
Scott*, 157; relation to *Dred Scott*, 136;
timing of, 62, 66–67
Swisher, Carl Brent, 241n35

Taney, Roger B., 1, 3, 10, 15, 134; in
Ableman, 210; agenda in *Dred Scott*, 161;
amoral jurisprudence of, 18; in *Bank of
Augusta*, 16–17; on black citizenship, 77,
121; and Campbell's territorial ruling,
192–93; in *Charles River Bridge*, 103–5;
in *Covington*, 208–9; Daniel's influence
on in *Dred Scott*, 165; in *Debolt*, 112;
in *Dennison*, 211; dispute with Curtis,
41, 203–7; dispute with Wayne, 91;
excess of citizenship ruling, 160; in
Flemming, 184; function of citizenship
ruling, 176–77; in *Groves*, 65–66, 81;
implicated in proslavery conspiracy,
2, 135–36; influence on court, 33–34,
49; and jurisdictional path in *Dred
Scott*, 158; on legislative discretion,
18–19; in *Luther*, 20; on Negro Seamen

Act, 18–19; in *Passenger Cases*, 88–89;
and plea in abatement in *Dred Scott*,
150–51; in *Prigg*, 81–82; on primacy
of state citizenship, 123–24, 125; on
public opinion and judicial duty, 205;
rejection of Calhounism, 186; response
to Curtis in *Dred Scott*, 200; response
to McLean in *Dred Scott*, 197; response
to southern faction, 169; revision of
Dred Scott opinion, 161–62, 165, 167,
171–72, 176, 180, 196, 206–7, 246n16; on
secession, 220; selected to write opinion
in *Dred Scott*, 152; and slavery, 72, 76, 84,
88; in *Strader*, 92–94; territorial ruling
in *Dred Scott*, 186–92; on territories
and jurisdiction, 181; use of history in
Dred Scott, 166–69; use of racism in
Dred Scott, 162–63; vision of expansion,
189–90
Taney Court, 13–15; amorality of, 18–19,
25; antiabolitionism of, 76–80, 91;
antislavery litigants before, 77–79, 191;
appeal of *Swift* for, 53; assumptions
of members on, 224–25; attitude
toward Marshall Court, 10–11;
coalitions and factions on, 34–35;
and common-property doctrine,
183, 190; and compact theory, 23;
conception of judicial authority,
14; constitutional interpretation
on, 14, 21, 30; and contracts, 40;
and corporate citizenship, 126; and
corporations, 98–99, 130; criticized by
Southern Quarterly Review, 13, 24; as
defender of corporations, 110, 113–14;
definition of law on, 12; desire to limit
corporate power, 17; dissent on, 30–31;
distinguished from Marshall Court,
13; distinguishes between law and
judicial decisions, 52; enforcement of
market obligations, 37; expectations of
litigants, 44; as facilitator of popular
will, 15–16; factionalism on, 86, 114;
and federal power, 27; and federal
territories, 178–79; fragmentation of,
after *Dred Scott*, 203; internal dynamics
of, 5, 226–27; judging on, 208; and
jurisdiction, 27–28; and jurisdictional